THE
PARABLES
OF
JESUS

This book is dedicated to the men of the
Chatham Bible Study, Savannah, Georgia,
who for ten years have eagerly studied God's word,
patiently endured the limitations of the teacher,
and in whom the word has taken root
and is bearing fruit.

THE PARABLES OF JESUS

ENTERING, GROWING,
LIVING AND FINISHING
IN GOD'S KINGDOM

TERRY L JOHNSON

CHRISTIAN
FOCUS

Terry Johnson is the Senior Minister of the historic Independent Presbyterian Church in Savannah, Georgia. Amongst other titles he has published *When Grace Comes Home* (ISBN 978-1-85792-539-5) on the doctrines of Grace, *When Grace Transforms* (ISBN 978-1-85792-770-2) looking at the Beatitudes and *When Grace Comes Alive* (ISBN 978-1-85792-882-2) on the Lord's Prayer. He is also author of *The Family Worship Book* (ISBN 978-1-85792-401-5), a resource book for family devotions. He is married to the former Emily Billings and they have five children.

Unless otherwise indicated scripture quotations taken from the *New American Standard Bible*® (NASB), Copyright © 1960, 1962, 1963, 1968, 1971, 1972, 1973, 1975, 1977, 1995 by The Lockman Foundation Used by permission. www.lockman.org

Scripture quotations marked NIV are taken from the *Holy Bible, New International Version*® NIV®. Copyright© 1973, 1978, 1984 by International Bible Society. Used by permission of Zondervan. All rights reserved.

Scripture quotations marked ESV are taken from The *Holy Bible, English Standard Version*, copyright © 2001 by Crossway Bibles, a division of Good News Publishers. Used by permission. All rights reserved.

Scripture quotations marked RSV are taken from the *Revised Standard Version of the Bible*, copyright 1952 [2nd edition, 1971] by the Division of Christian Education of the National Council of the Churches of Christ in the United States of America. Used by permission. All rights reserved.

Scripture quotations marked KJV are taken from the King James Version.

ISBN 1-84550-292-2
ISBN 978-1-84550-292-8

© Terry L Johnson

10 9 8 7 6 5 4 3 2 1

Published in 2007
by
Christian Focus Publications,
Geanies House, Fearn, Ross-shire,
IV20 1TW, Scotland, UK

www.christianfocus.com

Cover design by Moose77.com

Printed and bound by CPD Wales

CONTENTS

V. Finishing in God's Kingdom

PREFACE

Bridging the gap between the outlook and culture of the first century AD Mediterranean world and the twenty-first century modern world is a daunting task by any standard. But it is exactly the task that preachers and Christians of every age must embrace. We are charged to translate the teaching of Jesus, the Apostles, and the prophets from the ancient, pre-industrial, pre-technological environment of antiquity into our own highly complex modern one. Let's not kid ourselves. This is difficult to do. We don't want to lose any permanent principles that Jesus meant for us to know in the process. Nor do we want to retain that which was meant only to be temporary.

Jumping into the comprehension gap between the centuries are the parables. Granted, they have their own difficulties. But the parables are (mostly) simple stories that teach us about God's kingdom. The kingdom of God, as so many commentators have pointed out, is His *rule* more than an identifiable *realm*. His kingdom is found wherever His rule is established, whether in a nation, a family, or in one human heart. The parables of the kingdom teach us how to live under Christ's rule, or as disciples of Christ. They teach us how to live the Christian life. Quite appropriately W. Tullian Tchividjian subtitled his booklet, *The Kingdom of God*, 'A Primer on the Christian Life.'[1]

One day the thought occurred to me: Why not collect the parables together in a single book and offer it as a theology of the Christian life? A book of parables would be a book of stories about life as Jesus would have us live it. Perhaps the

---

[1] W. Tullian Tchividjian, *The Kingdom of God: A Primer on the Christian Life* (Edinburgh: The Banner of Truth Trust, 2005).

story format, so much of Jesus' own pedagogic methodology, would help us more clearly grasp what Jesus has in mind for Christians today.

I have classified the parables in a way unlike anything else I have seen:

> *Entering* God's kingdom: parables of faith, repentance, conversion, decision, and commitment
>
> *Growing* in God's teaching: parables of growth, and the environment of growth for individuals and for the church
>
> *Living* in God's kingdom: parables of the Christian life – word, prayer, love, forgiveness, outreach, discipline, and restoration
>
> *Finishing* in God's kingdom: parables of the end and final judgment.

Stories, being stories, don't fit easily into categories. The lines between my classifications are fluid. Some of those about 'finishing' are equally about 'entering.' Many touch each of the categories: entering, growing, living, and finishing. I have tried to place them into the category which best reflects their emphasis. Part of the genius of the parables is their comprehensiveness – single parables are able to touch every aspect of life in God's kingdom. This is not a source of frustration for the classifier, but thanksgiving.

The opening section ('Introduction to the Parables') deals with Jesus' own explanation of why He used parables. He did not use a parable to make this point, so this section has no parables. Those eager to get right to the stories may wish to jump ahead to Section II.

Most of the quotations I've used are referenced in the text. Some of the authors have written multiple books on multiple gospels. My citations refer to their commentary on the gospel upon which the exposition is based unless otherwise noted. Because there are so many versions of Matthew Henry's Bible Commentary, my references to his work are not accompanied by page numbers, but may be found in his text under the verses discussed. Unless otherwise noted, Bible quotations are from the NASB Lockman Foundation, 1977.

Special thanks are extended to my secretary, Mrs. James Parker (Debbie). Without Debbie's skill and patience, this book would not have been written. Thanks is also extended to the congregation of the Independent Presbyterian Church, without whose understanding and consent these studies could not have been put in readable form, and the men of the Chatham Bible Study, who, like the members of the Independent Presbyterian Church, have more or less heard all of this over the course of many months of teaching.

I

INTRODUCING
THE PARABLES

What are parables? Why did Jesus teach in parables? Why is so great a proportion of His teaching in parabolic form? These are the questions that we will attempt to answer in this opening section. We will turn to Jesus' own words to answer them.

~ 1 ~

WHY PARABLES?

Matthew 13:10-17

Revealing and Veiling the Truth

[10]*And the disciples came and said to Him, 'Why do You speak to them in parables?' *[11]*And He answered and said to them, 'To you it has been granted to know the mysteries of the kingdom of heaven, but to them it has not been granted. *[12]*For whoever has, to him shall more be given, and he shall have an abundance; but whoever does not have, even what he has shall be taken away from him. *[13]*Therefore I speak to them in parables; because while seeing they do not see, and while hearing they do not hear, nor do they understand. *[14]*And in their case the prophecy of Isaiah is being fulfilled, which says, "You will keep on hearing, but will not understand; and you will keep on seeing, but will not perceive; *[15]*for the heart of this people has become dull, and with their ears they scarcely hear, and they have closed their eyes lest they should see with their eyes, and hear with their ears, and understand with their heart and return, and I should heal them." *[16]* But blessed are your eyes, because they see; and your ears, because they hear.*[17]*For truly I say to you, that many prophets and righteous men desired to see what you see, and did not see it; and to hear what you hear, and did not hear it' (cf. Mark 4:10-12; Luke 8:9, 10)*

W hen Jesus began to teach in parables, it represented a new direction in His ministry. We are told that from the point at which they were introduced forward, Jesus typically taught the multitudes in this distinctive form (Matt. 13:34; Mark 4:11; Luke 8:9-10). Mark's parallel to our text in Matthew reads,

> *And He was saying to them, 'To you has been given the mystery of the kingdom of God; but those who are outside get everything in parables'* (Mark 4:11).

He continued to teach his disciples in a plain manner, but the crowds primarily got parables (see ch. 2 for further explanation of 'only' and 'everything').

Definitions
What are parables? Agreed upon definitions and lists of parables are difficult to find. Morris defines them as 'wise sayings of a pictorial kind' (*Matthew,* 354). For J. M. Boice (1938–2000), former minister of Tenth Presbyterian Church in Philadelphia, 'A parable is a story taken from real life (or a real-life situation) from which a moral or spiritual truth is drawn' (14). They are not fables, with talking animals and walking trees. They are not allegories, where every detail conveys hidden meaning. The old Sunday School definition of a parable, 'an earthly story with a heavenly meaning,' can hardly be improved upon. A parable is a figurative saying or simile expounded into a picture or a story. New Testament scholar A. M. Hunter (1906–1991) considers them 'examples of popular story-telling' that are 'meant to evoke a response and to strike for a verdict.'[1] Robert F. Capon defines parabolic more broadly as 'a comparison, a putting of one thing beside another to make a point.'[2] By this definition (one which we will not entirely share), up to one-third of all of Jesus' teaching was in the form of parables. Capon continues:

---

1. *Interpreting the Parables*, pp. 11,12.
2. Robert F. Capon, *The Parables of the Kingdom* (Grand Rapids: Eerdmans, 1985), p. 10.

'Some of his parables are not stories; many are not agreeable; most are complex; and a good percentage of them produce more confusion than understanding.'[3]

We will work with a more narrow definition than Capon, distinguishing parables from illustrations ('no one puts new wine into old wineskins') and proverbs ('a blind man cannot guide a blind man'). This limits our study to the more familiar story-parables, many of which are vividly memorable: The Sower, The Rich Man and Lazarus, The Good Samaritan, The Prodigal Son, and The Rich Fool, among others. For our purposes a parable must be a story about the kingdom of God. Although the story may not mention the word 'parable,' and it may not mention the kingdom of God by name, those two elements must be present. Consequently, we will not deal with either illustrations or proverbs.[4]

The lines separating parable, illustration, and proverb are blurry at best. Some of the foregoing classifications involved 'close calls.' Still, the Parable of the Sower is clearly a parable, 'physician, heal thyself' is a proverb, and the tree and its fruit is an illustration. We will avoid the latter two categories for now.

Why does Jesus make such prominent use of parables? We are not the first to ask. The church has long wrestled with the question. Modern scholars such as Adolf Jülicher

---

3. Capon, p. 1.
4. I have classified the following as illustrations: Bridegroom and guests (Mark 2:19); Patch and wineskins (Mark 2:21, 22); Strong man (Mark 3:27; Luke 11:21-23; Matt. 12:29); Savorless salt (Mark 9:50; Luke 14:34ff; Matt. 5:13); Budding fig tree (Mark 13:28ff; Doorkeeper (Mark 13:34-37); Tree and fruit (Luke 6:43, 44; Matt. 7:16-20); Playing children (Luke 7:31ff; Matt. 11:16ff); Harvest and workers (Luke 10:2; Matt. 9:37); Asking son (Luke 11:11-13; Matt. 7:9-11); Empty house (Luke 11:24-26; Matt. 12:43-45); Lamp and bushel (Mark 4:21; Luke 11:33; Matt. 5:3); Body's lamp (Luke 11:34-36; Matt. 6:22ff); Waiting servants (Luke 12:35-38); Head of house and thief (Luke 12:39; Matt. 24:43ff); Servant in authority (Luke 12:42-46; Matt. 24:45-51); Defendant (Luke 12:57-59; Matt. 5:25ff); City on hill (Matt. 5:14); Tower builder (Luke 14:28-30); Warring king (Luke 14:31ff); Places at the table (Luke 14:7-11); Farmer and his servant (Luke 17:7-10); Going before a judge (Matt. 5:25ff; Luke 12:58ff); Children in the marketplace (Matt. 11:16-19; Luke 7:31-35). I have classified the following as proverbs: Blind leading blind (Luke 6:39; Matt. 15:14); Mote and beam (Luke 6:41; Matt. 7:3-5); Divided realm (Luke 11:17; Mark 3:24-26; Matt. 12:25ff); Physician, heal thyself (Luke 4:23); Fig tree (Matt. 24:32); Physician and the sick (Matt. 9:12; Luke 5:31; Mark 2:17); Weather signs (Luke 12:54-56).

(1857–1938), C. H. Dodd (1884–1973), and Joachim Jeremias (1900–1979), among others, have argued back and forth as to what the parables are intended to do. Are they designed to reveal the truth or veil it? Do they shed light or create a fog? The supposedly self-evident truth that parables make the truth easier to grasp turns out not to be so self-evident. Jesus' disciples ask what we ask,

Why do You speak to them in parables? (13:10b).

Their question is, why teach 'them,' the crowds, in this new form that they are finding difficult to understand? Jesus' parables are often confusing, as Capon points out: *bad* people are commended (as in the Publican, the Prodigal Son, and the Unjust Steward), *good* people are scolded (the praying Pharisee, the dutiful brother), unanticipated people rewarded and punished (e.g. Wedding Feast, Lazarus and Dives).[5] The parables, in fact, without Jesus' explanation, are not so simple. The context of our passage (Matt. 13:10-17) is surrounded by the parable of the Sower, a story which is not easily interpreted on first read (vv. 3-9, 18-23). It is not obvious what is meant by sower (preacher), seed (word), ground (heart), birds (evil one), thorns (worry of world, riches), or fruit. The parables illuminate the truth for those with the key, but obscure and confuse the same truth for those for whom the explanation is not given. The 'multitude' is taught in parables, and is confused by them (13:2, 3, 10, 11). The disciples are dependent upon the explanation, given in private (13:10). We are told again that only when Jesus 'left the multitudes,' then

His disciples came to Him saying, 'Explain to us the parable of the tares of the field' (Matt. 13:36b; cf. 13:10).

The disciples' question in verse 10, 'Why do You speak to them in parables?', may be paraphrased as, 'Why use this cryptic form of teaching rather than plain statement?', says

---

5. Capon, p. 10.

New Testament commentator R. T. France (221). Jesus' answer is that parables are uniquely suited to the central principles of redemption in that they in fact both *reveal* the truth and *veil* it. They are illuminating for some and at the same time obscuring for others. Jesus explains this in Matthew 13:10-17.

Divine Sovereignty

Rarely, if ever, is God doing only one thing on any given occasion. My wife Emily once asked Scottish theologian Sinclair Ferguson why God allowed a certain event to take place. 'What is God doing?' she wanted to know. His answer was, 'He is doing many things, even hundreds and thousands of things, all at the same time.' God's purposes are multiple in every ordained method or event. It is not surprising that parables serve a variety of purposes in the plan of God. Jesus answers the disciples' question:

> To you it has been granted to know the mysteries of the kingdom of heaven, but to them it has not been granted (13:11).

The first of these purposes is to reinforce God's sovereignty. We can see this in two ways:

First, the parables are suited to God's purposes in election
Notice the distinction. Something has been 'granted' or given to the disciples; to others that something 'has not been granted.' The 'something' is knowledge. The disciples are privileged 'to know,' the rest are not. What is the difference between the two? Why is one group made up of disciples who know and other of non-disciples who do not know? 'The doctrine of election lies behind these words,' says New Testament scholar Leon Morris (339). They are disciples because Jesus chose them to be His disciples and God has given them understanding. 'You did not choose me but I chose you,' Jesus said (John 15:16).

The word 'because' does not show up in our English translation of verse 11, but it is there in the Greek (*hoti*) – 'because to you it has been granted ...' American New

Testament scholar D. A. Carson argues that its meaning is 'fully causal' (307). They ask 'why?' and Jesus says, 'Because the secrets of the kingdom have been given to the disciples but not to others.' God chooses some to understand and leaves others in their ignorance.

Parables are used because, as D. A. Carson points out, 'at least one of the functions of parables is to conceal the truth, or at least to *present it in a veiled way*' (307). They not only vividly reveal truth, they also conceal it.

Many, many, many people are highly uncomfortable with the idea that God favors some over others. Yet, how else are we to read these words? Of course we can try and explain them away, but why try? Why not just believe them? If I am a disciple of Christ today, if I understand the gospel, it is because God has 'granted' to me 'to know' the truth. My understanding is His gift, a gift not given to all. If I have faith, it is a 'gift of God' (Eph. 2:8, 9). If I love God, it is because He first loved me (1 John 4:19). If I am united to Christ, it is 'by His doing (I) am *in* Christ Jesus.' (1 Cor. 1:30). If I have knowledge in the things of God, it is because He became to me 'wisdom from God' (1 Cor. 1:30) and gave to me 'a spirit of wisdom and of revelation in the knowledge of Him' and so has 'enlightened' the 'eyes of (my) heart' (Eph. 1:17, 18). I have to say with hymn writer and pastor John Newton (1725–1807),

> Amazing Grace! – how sweet the sound – that saved
> a wretch like me!
> I once was lost, but now am found, was blind but now
> I see.

The people of God have always recognized that they were 'lost' and God 'found' them, they were 'blind,' but God made them to 'see.' They have recognized this with the sense of wonder with which Isaac Watts (1674–1748), father of English hymnody and Presbyterian pastor, wrote,

> While all our hearts and all our songs join to admire the
> feast,

Each of us cries with thankful tongue, 'Lord why was I a
   guest?
Why was I made to hear your voice, and enter while
   there's room,
When thousands make a wretched choice, and rather
   starve than come?'

'Why was I made to hear,' he asks, yet others 'make
a wretched choice?' The truth was revealed to me, he says,
while to others it was not. Parables are used by Jesus because
they are suited to the sovereign purposes of God in election,
in revealing Himself to some, and concealing Himself from
others, according to His own inscrutable will.

*Second, similarly, the parables are suited to God's purposes in
revelation*
Let's look at verse 11 again:

> And He answered and said to them, 'To you it has been granted
> to know the mysteries of the kingdom of heaven, but to them it
> has not been granted.'

The parables are suited to the principle of God's sovereign
initiative in His self-revelation. Jesus identifies what He reveals privately and plainly to his disciples as 'the mysteries of the kingdom of heaven.' The word 'mysteries' means
something more like our word 'secrets.' D. A. Carson defined them as 'divine plans or decrees' (307). These are contrasted with parables. The 'mysteries' are presumably the
things that Jesus continues to teach privately and in plain
speech to His disciples. He speaks publicly to the crowds
in parables, and only privately does He speak plainly of the
mysteries of God's kingdom. For example, Mark's parallel to
Matthew's passage says that the explanation of the meaning
of the Parable of the Sower was given when 'He was alone'
with the twelve (Mark 4:10). The 'mysteries' that He reveals
are truths that were hidden. They cannot be seen unless they
are revealed, cannot be known unless they are explained.
The Greek word *mustçrion* is used in the New Testament 'to

indicate that God's truth comes only by revelation, not by natural insight,' says R. T. France (221). In a general sense, it indicates all the gospel truth revealed in Scripture. The great eighteenth century commentator, Matthew Henry, says,

> Christ's incarnation, satisfaction, intercession, our justification, and sanctification by union with Christ, and indeed the whole work of redemption, from first to last, are *mysteries*, which could never have been discovered but by divine revelation.

More specifically, *mustçrion* may refer to the mystery of the presence of the kingdom in the person of Jesus prior to its apocalyptic or cataclysmic appearance at the end of time. Carson cites Fuller Theological Seminary theologian George Eldon Ladd (1911–1982),

> The new truth, now given to men by revelation in the person and mission of Jesus is that *the Kingdom which is to come finally in apocalyptic power, as foreseen by Daniel, has in fact entered into the world in advance in a hidden form to work secretly within and among men.* (307)

The essential point is that Jesus came to reveal crucial spiritual truths. He is the 'truth' (John 14:6). Yet He does not reveal these truths, or Himself, to all. This second point complements well our first point. What we know about God and the things of God, we know only at God's good pleasure. We are entirely dependent on God's gracious self-revelation. If He doesn't show Himself, we will not see Him. We cannot climb up into heaven to find Him. We cannot demand that He come down from heaven. We cannot compel Him to reveal Himself. He can choose to remain above and apart. If we are to know Him, we must go humbly to Him and plead that He make Himself known. Earlier Jesus said,

> *I praise Thee, O Father, Lord of heaven and earth, that Thou didst hide these things from the wise and intelligent and didst reveal them to babes* (Matt. 11:25).

The Father, says Jesus, 'reveals' the truth to some and 'hides it' from others. This means that potential disciples of Christ cannot rely upon their reason, their wisdom, or their best thoughts if they are to know God. I am not to begin my search for God autonomously, or self-sufficiently, thinking that I can discern the truth on my own. Instead I go submissively, to receive from Him what He has revealed.

Back in my college days, I had many an argument with non-Christian friends who, while rejecting biblical teaching and making up their own doctrines, still called themselves 'Christian.' My argument with them always was, 'it is not for us to decide what the Christian religion is. If it were, we might as well be honest about what we're doing and start a completely new religion. But if we are to claim to be Christians then we must believe and follow what Jesus and the prophets before Him taught.' A true knowledge of God is only to be gained through the self-revelation of God in His word. Parables suit the sovereign purposes of God in that they make it possible for Jesus to divide His ministry – speaking plainly to the disciples while addressing the multitudes in parables.

Human Responsibility
Parables are not only suited to the fact of God's sovereignty in election and self-revelation, but they are also suited to the doctrine of human responsibility. The parables underscore not only that God is sovereign, but also that we are responsible for our actions and the resulting consequences. Parables highlight this principle of culpability and are especially compatible with it. Jesus affirms this in two ways.

First, Jesus affirms human responsibility through the use of a proverb
His next statement is,

> *For whoever has, to him shall more be given, and he shall have an abundance; but whoever does not have, even what he has shall be taken away from him* (13:12).

To those who have much, more is given. To those who have little, even what they have is taken away. The commentators refer to this principle as 'proverbial.' A proverb is a widely agreed upon wisdom principle understood through common observation. This one is found in other places (e.g. Matt. 25:29; cf. Mark 4:25; Luke 8:18). It speaks of a person's responsibility to use and build upon that which he or she has been given. Those who do, get more. Those who don't, lose what they have. Does this seem unfair? Why should the rich get richer? Yet a moment's reflection reminds us that this is a 'wisdom issue,' a principle found in the nature of things. Consequently, it is eminently fair.

We can cite a number of examples. In *athletics*, those who exercise and train become more proficient, while those who do nothing lose whatever athletic ability they had. In *language study*, those who study with persistence acquire increasing aptitude in the use of that language, while those who neglect language study lose whatever knowledge they had. In the *work world*, those who practice industry and frugality accumulate more wealth, while those who are slothful and profligate lose whatever wealth they had. Those who have some proficiency with a *musical instrument* and build upon it gain greater still, while those who have little aptitude and do nothing lose what skill they may have had.

So it is in the spiritual realm. Those who take the little bit of knowledge that God has given them and embrace it, believing and applying what they have, are given more. Those who neglect or despise it, lose what they had. The responsibility is ours. Jesus teaches in parables because it is His intention to veil the truth from those who have had access to it already but have hardened their hearts and refused to receive it, while at the same time multiplying the knowledge of those who have been eager to receive the truth and gain more. Speaking of the former of these two classes of persons, Jesus says,

> *Therefore I speak to them in parables; because while seeing they do not see, and while hearing they do not hear, nor do they understand* (13:13).

Notice the 'because.' 'Therefore I speak in parables – because ...' Why? 'Because while seeing they do not see, and while hearing they do not hear ...' In other words, parables are a form of teaching that both enlighten the believing and judge the unbelieving, who while 'seeing' refuse to 'see' (see Morris, 341). Carson explains,

> Verse 13 recapitulates the reason for speaking in parables but now frames the reason, not in terms of *election*, but in terms of *spiritual dullness*. Matthew has already given Jesus' answer in terms of *divine election* (v.11); now he gives the *human reason*. (309, emphasis mine)

Jesus places the failure to see or hear on us. It is our responsibility. We see yet fail to see, that is, truly see. We hear yet fail to truly hear. Why? Because we fail to pay attention. We fail to listen with openness. We are spiritually dull, insensitive. Jesus' point is that this condition is our fault. We choose not to listen. We choose not to hear. We neglect spiritual means. We despise spiritual disciplines. Jesus places the responsibility for this upon our own shoulders. He will not forever speak plainly to the hard-hearted. He will not forever cast his pearls before swine (Matt. 7:6). He continues to teach all, but does so in a way that hardens the stubborn while enlightening receptive disciples.

How does this harmonize with what we've said about God's sovereignty? Neither Jesus nor the other biblical writers are troubled by this question. Typically, they affirm these seemingly contradictory truths side-by-side. This is exactly what we must do as well.

Second, Jesus affirms human responsibility as taught in the Old Testament

And in their case the prophecy of Isaiah is being fulfilled (13:14a).

Jesus quotes Isaiah 6:9, 10, which originally applied to the unbelieving in Isaiah's own day, and applies it to His use of parables. The 'fulfillment' of which Jesus speaks is not so much predictive as typological. It is not 'predictive' in the sense of intending to tell us of future events but 'typological' in the sense of establishing a pattern that was to be repeated until finally fulfilled in the time of Messiah (for more on this see ch. 2, 'The Fulfillment,' on Matt. 13:34-35). Isaiah's experience of unreceptivity among the people 'formed a typological pattern which is now *fulfilled* as Jesus re-enacts the role of the Old Testament prophet,' says France (223). Jesus continues to cite Isaiah:

> You will keep on hearing, but will not understand; and you will keep on seeing, but will not perceive; (13:14b).

Isaiah's words *addressed* the people. Now his words (as Jesus quotes them) *describe* them:

> For the heart of this people has become dull, and with their ears they scarcely hear, and they have closed their eyes lest they should see with their eyes, and hear with their ears, and understand with their heart and return, and I should heal them (13:15).

The people won't hear His teaching because their minds are made up. They are set in their ways. The 'heart,' or 'the whole of the inner being' of the people has become 'dull' or 'sluggish,' even fat. They 'scarcely hear,' *bareôs* having the root meaning of 'heavily,' of hearing 'ponderously' and so 'with difficulty' (all of the above from Morris, 342-3). They have even 'closed their eyes.' It's one thing for one's ears not to work. That implies one level of responsibility. It's another to deliberately close one's eyes. Why would they behave so defiantly? Jesus continues to quote Isaiah: 'Lest they should see ... hear ... understand ...and turn.' They do not *want* God to 'heal' them. In other words, they love their corruption. They love their darkness (John 3:19). They want to be left alone. They want to be left to pursue their lusts and idols. Sin may be like a disease, but they 'decline to be healed of it' (Carson, 343). The unbelieving are not helpless victims. Parables underscore the redemptive reality that God is sovereign and yet we are all responsible. We cannot shift the blame for our unbelief to someone else.

Gospel Graciousness

Not only do parables suit the principles of God's sovereignty and man's responsibility, but they also underscore the graciousness of the gospel.

> *But blessed are your eyes, because they see; and your ears, because they hear* (13:16).

Verses 16 and 17 overflow with grace. The disciples are distinguished from the crowd not by their own righteousness, but by the blessing of God. He gave to them the eyes that see and ears that hear. They have been 'granted' to know (v. 11). For this they are 'blessed' or 'favored' by God. These are God's gifts. The pronoun is emphatic. *Your* eyes and ears are blessed in that they perceive the mysteries of the kingdom that so many of your contemporaries do not. Indeed, what you see the saints of old longed to see and did not. *You* alone are so privileged.

> *For truly I say to you, that many prophets and righteous men desired to see what you see, and did not see it; and to hear what you hear, and did not hear it* (13:17).

The great prophets who spoke God's word and had such insight into God's ways 'desired' to see these things, as did the 'righteous men' who labored alongside of them without the prophetic gift. Henry explains,

> The Old Testament saints, who had some glimpses, some glimmerings of gospel light, coveted earnestly further discoveries. They had the types, shadows, and prophecies, of those things, but longed to see the Substance.

Jesus' emphasis is upon the high privilege of the disciples. They have been 'granted' to know the 'mysteries.' Their eyes and ears are 'blessed.' They are graced to know what the saints for generations longed to understand. Likewise, how great is our privilege! We must not take for granted the clarity of the gospel in our age. At this point the disciples still don't understand the fullness of what they see and hear. That will come later, after the resurrection and especially after the day of Pentecost. Today we see the whole picture in ways which they did not. We have the benefit of a completed New Testament canon as well as 2,000 years of Christian reflection on the content of that canon. We see the realities of the Trinity, of the dual nature of Christ, of substitutionary atonement, of justification by faith, and the spiritual nature of God's kingdom. No, let us not take for granted the clarity of the gospel in our age.

Why did Jesus teach in parables? Because they suited His multiple purposes at this stage in His ministry. Why? Because parables both reveal and conceal, both uncover and veil. They are compatible with God's purpose to graciously illuminate those who had been responsive to His ministry, while withholding truth from and hardening those who were stubbornly resistant. They place the responsibility for understanding squarely upon our shoulders, without implying autonomy. At the same moment they teach us that we are both culpable *and* dependent upon God's grace.

These are lessons one does well to learn at the outset of one's Christian life. God is absolutely *sovereign*. We should never compromise this solemn truth. We are absolutely *dependent* upon Him. Apart from Christ we can do nothing (John 15:5).

And yet, and yet, and yet ... we are accountable at every point. Never may we wash our hands of our responsibility to seek, know, love, obey, serve, and please God. Keeping sovereignty, dependence, and responsibility in uncompromised tension with each other, we will not stray far from the truth that is in Christ.

STUDY QUESTIONS

1. What is a parable? How would you define it?

2. Do parables reveal or veil the truth? What is the purpose of a parable as described in Matthew 13:10, 11? Compare with Matthew 11:25.

3. What is the purpose of a parable as illustrated by use of the proverb in verse 12? Can the purpose given in verse 12 be harmonized with the purpose given in verse 11?

4. Can the proverb of verse 12 be illustrated in life generally? In the spiritual realm? (v. 13)

5. How does Jesus further emphasize human responsibility in verses 14-15?

6. Relate the use of parables to verses 16 and 17. In what way are parables gifts to us?

~ 2 ~

'THE FULFILLMENT'

Matthew 13:34-35

The Bible is About Jesus

[34]*All these things Jesus spoke to the multitudes in parables, and He did not speak to them without a parable,* [35]*so that what was spoken through the prophet might be fulfilled, saying, 'I will open My mouth in parables; I will utter things hidden since the foundation of the world' (cf. Mark 4:33, 34).*

On the Emmaus Road, following the resurrection, Jesus rebuked the disciples for failing to recognize His identity and mission in the prophecies of the Old Testament. He said,

> *'O foolish men and slow of heart to believe in all that the prophets have spoken!'* (Luke 24:25).

The prophets had predicted the events of the cross. He said,

> *'Was it not necessary for the Christ to suffer these things and to enter into His glory?'* (Luke 24:26).

It was 'necessary,' because Scripture had prophesied that it would be so. The disciples failed to understand this *not* because it wasn't clear, but because they were 'foolish' and 'slow of heart.' The prophets said that the Messiah must 'suffer these things,' then 'enter into His glory.' The extent to which the Scripture prophesied these things is indicated in the next verse.

> *'And beginning with Moses and with all the prophets, He explained to them the things concerning Himself in all the Scriptures'* (Luke 24:27).

One should not think of the Old Testament as prophesying of Christ here and there only. Rather the message of Christ is *everywhere* in the Old Testament. From Genesis ('Moses') to Malachi ('all the prophets') and everything in between ('all the Scriptures'), Jesus says these writings are about Him. The 'things concerning Himself' are found not only occasionally but 'in all the Scriptures.' Later He repeats Himself,

> *'These are My words which I spoke to you while I was still with you, that all things which are written about Me in the Law of Moses and the Prophets and the Psalms must be fulfilled'* (Luke 24:44).

The 'Law of Moses,' the 'Prophets,' and the 'Psalms' are full of Christ. Add the New Testament revelation to the Old Testament and one can clearly see that *the whole Bible is about Jesus Christ.*

We have provided this long introduction to our text because this perspective is reflected in the verses before us. Matthew says,

> *'All these things Jesus spoke to the multitudes in parables, and He did not speak to them without a parable'* (Matt. 13:34).

Whenever Jesus spoke to the multitudes He used parables. As Capon points out,

> Jesus not only spoke in parables; he thought in parables, acted in parables, and regularly insisted that what he was proclaiming could not be set forth in any way other than

in parables. He was practically an ambulatory parable in and of himself; he cursed fig trees, walked on water, planted coins in fishes' mouths, and for his final act, sailed up into a cloud. [1]

Carson and others point out that this means not that He *only* used parables but that He *always* used parables; not *nothing* but parables but never *without* using parables (Carson, 320; Morris, 354). He used other teaching methods, but parables predominated.

The parabolic pedagogy, says Matthew, fulfills the prophecy of Psalm 78:2.

> ...*so that what was spoken through the prophet might be fulfilled, saying, 'I will open My mouth in parables; I will utter things hidden since the foundation of the world'* (Matt. 13:35).

The Psalmist is called a 'prophet' because there is a true sense in which all of the Old Testament is prophetic of Christ. Psalm 78:2 is 'fulfilled' by Jesus' teachings just as all of the Old Testament is fulfilled in Him. The question is, how? In what sense does Jesus fulfill Old Testament prophecy? Psalm 78:2 is not an example of predictive prophecy. It doesn't say, 'When Messiah comes He will speak in parables.' The Psalmist is speaking of himself in Psalm 78. He is identifying his own teaching method. In what sense can it be said that these verses prophesy Christ, or that Jesus fulfills these verses? If we can answer that question we will have traveled a long way down the road of understanding the central message of the Old Testament.

Our thesis is that Christ fulfills the Old Testament primarily *typologically*. Scripture that applied to others (e.g. the Old Testament prophets, David, Israel, etc.) is applied to Christ on the basis of 'a typological principal,' as R. T. France says (228). He argues (rightly, I think) that the experience of the prophets 'formed a typological pattern which is now fulfilled as Jesus re-enacts the role of Old Testament prophet' (228). What is true of the prophets is true of all of the

---

1. Capon, p. 2.

experiences, institutions, and history of the Old Testament. The prophets, priests, kings and nation as a whole *imperfectly* foreshadow, portray, and illustrate what Christ did *perfectly*.

The Psalmist himself spoke in 'parables' or 'wise sayings' (Heb. *hidot* 'enigmas,' 'dark sayings'), as he says in the 78th Psalm, in the sense that when he recounted the history of Israel he did so in a way that explained the 'riddles and enigmas' of history, says Carson (321). 'The pattern of history is not self-evident,' and the Psalmist shows 'what it is really all about' (Carson, 321). By 'comparing various things' (as do parables) he (the Psalmist) brings out the 'deep and hidden' meaning of Israel's history. Jesus' parables do the same thing. They reveal things that have remained 'hidden since the foundation of the world' (Matt. 13:35; Ps. 78:2). This is consistent with what we have seen of parables both revealing and concealing truth (as in Matt. 13:10-17). In both Psalm 78 and Jesus' parables, 'the righteous acts of God in redemption' are being revealed (Linders in Carson, 322).

Therefore we can say that the prophet in Psalm 78 was a 'type' of Christ. His ministry of teaching in parables foreshadowed and anticipated the ministry of Jesus. Jesus came as *the* prophet, the great prophet, who completes and perfects the work of all the prophets. The prophets revealed truth. Jesus supremely does. They spoke in parables. Jesus supremely does. The larger point is that Jesus fulfills the whole Old Testament: its typology, its history, its predictions, and its teaching method. How so? Typologically. Primarily typologically, Jesus fulfills the prophecies of the Old Testament, including its model of teaching by parables.

Institutions
Let us now show how this is consistently the case. The various institutions of Israel are 'types' that provide a pattern for Messiah's work which He fulfills or completes. These are not predictions but roles that prefigure Christ. We can give a number of examples.

First, Jesus fulfills Israel's kingship

Matthew introduced Jesus as 'the son of David' (Matt. 1:1),
the rightful heir to the throne, and maintains this theme
to the end of his gospel. When Jesus enters Jerusalem, He
does so triumphantly, as Israel's King. 'Behold your King is
coming to you,' the prophets predicted, and Matthew applies
their predictions to Jesus (Matt. 21:5; Isa. 62:11; Zech. 9:9).
'Hosanna to the Son of David,' the multitudes cry out, as
the Psalter indicated they would (Matt. 21:9; Ps. 118:26 ff.).
When Jesus is mocked and crucified, it is as Israel's King
(Matt. 27:11, 27-31, 37). Some of the passages applied to Jesus
are predictive, but many of them are typological. The Psalms
in particular are full of descriptions of the Davidic kings
which initially applied to them, but which neither David nor
his descendants could completely fulfill. The Psalmists wrote
of the Davidic kings (e.g. Pss. 21 and 45), yet they described
ideals that flawed and human kings could not fulfill. For
example, Psalm 45 says of Israel's kings:

> *Gird Thy sword on Thy thigh, O Mighty One, in Thy splendor
> and Thy majesty! And in Thy majesty ride on victoriously,
> for the cause of truth and meekness and righteousness; let Thy
> right hand teach Thee awesome things* (Ps. 45:3, 4).

The ascription of 'Mighty One' goes beyond ordinary
mortals. It points to a Messianic Son of David. Yet, this
Psalm also speaks of the king's daughter (Ps. 45:13). Jesus,
of course, had no daughter. When first written, this Psalm
certainly referred to King David and/or his descendants.
Yet, 'O Mighty One' takes us beyond David. Israel's kings
imperfectly foreshadowed a future King who would be *like*
David, *after* David, and *greater* than David (Matt. 12:41, 42).
So also does verse 6 of Psalm 45,

> *Thy throne, O God, is forever and ever; a scepter of uprightness
> is the scepter of Thy kingdom.*

While addressed to David, Psalm 45:6 looks beyond David to a future Son of David who would also be the Son of God, who alone could rightly be addressed, 'Thy Throne, O God.'

We can cite other examples. God said to David,

> *'He shall build a house for My name, and I will establish the throne of his kingdom forever'* (2 Sam. 7:13).

God promised David an eternal kingdom. But an enduring throne could not be realized in the mortal, flawed descendants of David. The promise of an eternal kingdom could be fulfilled only in the eternal Son, the Messiah, the Christ.

The second Psalm sang of David and his immediate descendants,

> *I will surely tell of the decree of the LORD: He said to Me 'Thou art My Son, today I have begotten Thee. Ask of Me, and I will surely give the nations as Thine inheritance, and the very ends of the earth as Thy possession. Thou shalt break them with a rod of iron, Thou shalt shatter them like earthenware'* (Ps. 2:7-9).

But ultimately, only in Christ could these promises and descriptions be fulfilled (compare Heb. 1:5). The Davidic kings were able to subdue local nations (the Canaanites, Philistines, Amalakites, etc.) but not the 'nations' of the world or 'the very ends of the earth' with a metaphorical 'rod of iron.'

The Old Testament prophets recognized that it would require more than an ordinary son of David to establish this eternal and universal throne. Isaiah takes us beyond the merely human David to a divine David in predicting,

> *For a child will be born to us, a son will be given to us; and the government will rest on His shoulders; and His name will be called Wonderful Counselor, Mighty God, Eternal Father, Prince of Peace. There will be no end to the increase of His government or of peace, on the throne of David and over his kingdom, to establish it and to uphold it with justice and righteousness from then on and forevermore. The zeal of the LORD of hosts will accomplish this* (Isa. 9:6, 7).

Psalm 72 describes the kings of Tarshish and of the Islands bringing presents to David (Ps. 72:10, 11). A secondary fulfillment of this type was realized in Solomon (1 Kings 10:22), yet ultimately the Psalm points to the antitype (i.e. the one[s] to whom the type ultimately points), the Magi and their gifts of gold, frankincense, and myrrh for the Lord Jesus (Matt. 2:1-12).

Second, Jesus fulfills Israel's prophetic office
Moses was the first of the great prophets. Yet he announced,

> 'The LORD your God will raise up for you a prophet like me from among you, from your countrymen, you shall listen to him' (Deut. 18:15).

There would be, said Moses, a prophet *like* me, *after* me, and *greater than* me (cf. Matt. 12: 41, 42). The first fulfillment of this promise came in Moses' time, as God raised up prophets to speak to the nation following his death. Then came a line of prophets right up to John the Baptist. They served God. They spoke the word of God. Yet they were flawed men. God's final, decisive word came only in Christ, whose prophetic word his predecessors anticipated. Peter applied this text to Jesus in his second sermon in Acts:

> Moses said, 'The Lord God shall raise up for you a prophet like me from your brethren; to Him you shall give heed in everything He says to you. And it shall be that every soul that does not heed that prophet shall be utterly destroyed from among the people.' And likewise, all the prophets who have spoken, from Samuel and his successors onward, also announced these days (Acts 3:22-24).

Jesus is that Prophet whom Moses announced in Deuteronomy 18:15, says the Apostle Peter. But it wasn't just Moses who anticipated the coming Prophet, but 'all the prophets,' 'from Samuel and his successors onward.' All the prophets, finally and ultimately, were writing in anticipation of the coming Christ, God's final prophetic word.

This understanding of Jesus as the final and consummate prophet can be seen in Hebrews 1:1, 2.

God, after He spoke long ago to the fathers in the prophets in many portions and in many ways, in these last days has spoken to us in His Son, whom He appointed heir of all things, through whom also He made the world.

Jesus is that prophet of whom the early prophets were a type, whose work anticipated and foreshadowed His, and whose ministry was completed and perfected by His.

Third, Jesus fulfills Israel's priestly office
The Psalmist first applied these words to David:

The LORD has sworn and will not change His mind, 'Thou art a priest forever according to the order of Melchizedek' (Ps. 110:4).

He anticipated a day when a superior priesthood, a Melchizedekian priesthood, fulfilled by a Davidic descendant, would supercede that of the Aaronic or Levitical priesthood. The Old Testament priests anticipated the ministry of Christ, our 'great high priest.' Flawed, human priests foreshadowed our perfect high priest (Heb. 5:1-11). The writer to the Hebrews repeatedly applies this Psalm directly to Christ (Heb. 5:6, 5:10, 6:20, 7:11, 17).

Moreover, the whole sacrifice system around which the priest worked was fulfilled in Christ. The blood of bulls and goats of the Old Testament could not put away sin (Heb. 10:4). They were merely types of the Christ, the lamb of God, who would take away the sins of the world (John 1:29, 36). Indeed, Jesus identified Himself as the whole temple in which the priest would work and sacrifices would be offered (John 2:19-22).

It was not so much that these institutions *predicted* that the Messiah would be a prophet, priest, and king as that they were types, foreshadowing, anticipating, and imperfectly portraying that which Christ would perfectly fulfill.

Historical Fulfillment

Not just the institutions of king, prophet, and priest, but the whole history of Israel foreshadows and portrays what Christ would do. Was Israel God's son? Indeed, 'Israel is My son, my first-born,' God said to Pharaoh (Exod. 4:22, 23). Israel's sonship was deeply flawed, corrupted by idolatry, immorality, and injustice. Jesus comes as the true Israel, the true son of God (Matt. 1:22-25). Did Israel sojourn in Egypt? So did Jesus (Matt. 2:13, 14). Was Israel called out of Egypt back to Canaan? Matthew applies Hosea 11:1 to Jesus: 'out of Egypt did I call my Son' (Matt. 2:15-23). Was Israel 'baptized' in the sea? The Apostle Paul says it was (1 Cor. 10:1-3). So was Jesus (Matt. 3:1-17). Did Israel spend forty *years* in the wilderness? Jesus spent forty *days* tempted there (Matt. 4:1-11). Did Israel receive the law of God from Moses on a mount called Sinai? So did Jesus deliver His law in a Sermon on a Mount (Matt. 5–7). Did Israel have its triumphs? So did Jesus have His triumphal entry (Ps. 118:22-29; Matt. 21:1-11). Did Israel suffer as God's servant people? So is Jesus the suffering servant of God (Isa. 53; Acts 8:30-35). The whole history of Israel and all of its institutions anticipate, foreshadow and portray the life and ministry of Christ. We are right to say the Old Testament is about Christ. Jesus said,

> 'For if you believed Moses, you would believe Me; for he wrote of Me' (John 5:46).

'Moses,' He says, 'wrote of Me.' What is the Old Testament about? It is about the Messiah, about Jesus. Again we cite the Apostle Peter,

> 'And likewise, all the prophets who have spoken, from Samuel and his successors onward, also announced these days' (Acts 3:24).

Predictive Fulfillment

Does the typological fulfillment in Israel's institutions and history mean there is no predictive fulfillment? No, not at all. There are a number of predictive passages which also foretell of the work of Christ with specificity. For example, the Old Testament predicts that the Messiah will be of the nation of Israel (Num. 24:17), of the tribe of Judah (Gen. 49:10), of the root of Jesse (Isa. 11:10), of the house of David (2 Sam. 7:13). It predicts that He will be born in Bethlehem (Micah 5:2), of a virgin, and called Emmanuel (Isa. 7:14); that He will emerge from Galilee at the time of His public ministry (Isa. 9:1); that He will be a light to the Gentiles and to those who are in darkness (Isa. 9:1; 42:6, 49:6); that He will work wonders, opening the eyes of the blind, the ears of the deaf, causing the lame to leap, the tongues of the dumb to shout, releasing prisoners, preaching the good news to the afflicted (Isa. 35:5, 6; 42:6, 61:1, 2 cf. Matt. 11:5, 6; Luke 4:18, 19).

All this and more is predicted of His life. It is also predicted of His death that He will ride on the colt of a donkey (Zech. 9:9); that He will be betrayed by a trusted friend (Ps. 41:9), for 30 pieces of silver (Zech. 11:13); that the kings of the earth will counsel against Him (Ps. 2:1, 2, compare Acts 2:25-28); that He will be a 'man of sorrows and acquainted with grief' (Isa. 53:3 KJV); that He will bear our transgressions and iniquities (Isa. 53:4 ff). From the 22nd Psalm it is predicted that He will cry out, 'My God, My God, why hast thou forsaken me?,' that His bones will be pulled out of joint, that His hands and feet will be pierced, that they will cast lots for His clothing and give Him vinegar to drink. It is prophesied that the nation of Israel will look on Him whom they had pierced (Zech. 12:10).

His resurrection was predicted, the Psalmist promising that God would 'not abandon His soul to Sheol, neither allow the holy One to undergo decay' (Ps. 16:10 paraphrase). Indeed, it was predicted that the 'stone' which the builders rejected would become the 'chief corner stone' (Ps. 118:22). Jesus fulfills the Scripture. 'The Scriptures bear witness of Me,' Jesus claimed (John 5:39 parahrase). He is the fulfillment of all of the history, all of the prophecy, all of the poetry, all of the wisdom to be found in the Bible. The Scriptures are about Christ. This is the sense in which Jesus 'fulfilled' what the 'prophet' had spoken of regarding teaching in parables in Psalm 78:2. He is God's promised One. We need look no further. We need look to no other.

There is no more important lesson to learn at the outset of our Christian pilgrimage than this lesson that the whole Bible, the whole Christian religion, and the whole Christian life is all about Jesus. In Him all the promises of God are fulfilled (2 Cor. 1:20). In Him are hidden all the treasures of wisdom and knowledge (Col. 2:3). He is found on every page of Scripture. He is the point of every passage. He is the goal of every lesson. He is the meaning of all that God has to say to us in His word. If we are able to keep the centrality of Christ in focus, it will keep us from turning Christianity into merely a moral system, a lifeless program of 'do's and don'ts.' Christianity, it has been well said, is Christ.

STUDY QUESTIONS

1. What does Matthew mean when he says, 'Jesus ... did not speak to (the multitudes) without a parable' (v. 34)? Compare with Mark 4:10, 11 and Mark 4:33, 34.

2. In the previous lesson we saw that the parables veil the truth. Here the Psalmist claims that the parables reveal or uncover things 'hidden.' In what sense is this true (v. 35)?

3. Verse 35 quotes Psalm 78:2 and applies it to Jesus' ministry. In what sense has Jesus 'fulfilled' this passage?

4. Read Luke 24:25-27, 44, Acts 3:24, and John 5:39, 46. In what sense is the whole Bible about Jesus Christ?

5. Does Jesus also fulfill predictive prophecy?

6. Keeping in focus Christ as the key to the whole Bible helps to guard us from what?

II

ENTERING
GOD'S KINGDOM

The first and most important thing to know about the kingdom of God is how to get in. If I am to live the Christian life, I must first be sure that I am a Christian. *Many* parables are devoted to this theme. We have classified over one-quarter of the parables as entrance parables (8 of 30). *Most* parables touch on the theme of 'entering God's kingdom' in one way or another. Clearly Jesus gave prominent emphasis to this theme. He was exceptionally concerned that we should truly enter His kingdom and be numbered among His disciples. A careful study of all the parables forces us to give focused attention to this first priority of Christian discipleship, and the entrance themes of faith, repentance, regeneration, and conversion.

~ 3 ~

'THE SOWER'

Matthew 13:1-9, 18-23

The Importance of an Open Heart

¹*On that day Jesus went out of the house, and was sitting by the sea.* ²*And great multitudes gathered to Him, so that He got into a boat and sat down, and the whole multitude was standing on the beach.* ³*And He spoke many things to them in parables, saying, 'Behold, the sower went out to sow;* ⁴*and as he sowed, some seeds fell beside the road, and the birds came and ate them up.* ⁵*And others fell upon the rocky places, where they did not have much soil; and immediately they sprang up, because they had no depth of soil.* ⁶*But when the sun had risen, they were scorched; and because they had no root, they withered away.* ⁷*And others fell among the thorns, and the thorns came up and choked them out.* ⁸*And others fell on the good soil, and yielded a crop, some a hundredfold, some sixty, and some thirty.* ⁹*He who has ears, let him hear.'*

¹⁸*'Hear then the parable of the sower.* ¹⁹*When anyone hears the word of the kingdom, and does not understand it, the evil one comes and snatches away what has been sown in his heart. This is the one on whom seed was sown beside the road.* ²⁰*And the one on whom seed was sown on the rocky places, this is the man who hears the word, and immediately receives it with joy;* ²¹*yet he has no firm root in himself, but is only temporary, and when affliction or persecution arises because of the word,*

*immediately he falls away. *[22]*And the one on whom seed was sown among the thorns, this is the man who hears the word, and the worry of the world, and the deceitfulness of riches choke the word, and it becomes unfruitful. *[23]*And the one on whom seed was sown on the good soil, this is the man who hears the word and understands it; who indeed bears fruit, and brings forth, some a hundredfold, some sixty, and some thirty'* (*cf. Mark 4:1-9, 13-20; Luke 8:4-8, 11-15*).

Several years ago the great black preacher from Los Angeles, Reverend E. V. Hill, began to preach to an almost all-white Conference on Biblical Inerrancy. Several minutes into his sermon, he stopped and said, 'You white folks are sure hard to preach to.' He began to plead with them, 'Help me now ... Help me ...'

If you have never preached, you are probably unaware of the impact that the congregation can have on the preacher. Mr. Hill was accustomed to audible, visible responses from his own congregation, which encouraged him as he preached. A quiet, white congregation was tough business for him.

I remember several years ago preaching the same sermon on consecutive Sundays to different congregations. The first responded with enthusiasm throughout. They nodded. They smiled. They got serious and intense. They rejoiced. It was a pleasure to preach to them. I could have preached all night, though they were glad that I did not. The next week, the second congregation just sat. They did not nod. They showed no interest or even comprehension in their faces. All I saw were blank stares, with occasional glances at their watches. I rushed though the second half of the sermon, anxious to get through and get out. The congregation can 'preach the preacher,' it has been said. He sees their faces and responses (or lack thereof), and this can have a great impact on the delivery of the sermon. One sermon, two very different responses.

Even within most congregations, there is a range of responses. There are the hard, 'he won't get to me,' defiant looks. There are the distant, disinterested looks. There are the curious looks. And there are the enthusiastic supporters.

I usually try to find a couple of the latter and focus on them for encouragement.

I believe this sort of preacherly observation may be the setting of this parable. Through 'The Sower,' Jesus is explaining the increasing opposition encountered in chapters 11 and 12 of Matthew's Gospel. The opposition to Jesus raises the question, why do so many reject His message while others receive it? France summarizes the answer put forth by the Parable of the Sower this way:

> The fault lies not in the message, but in those who receive it. (220)

Let us momentarily review what we have said about the parables so far. Parables come in various shapes and sizes. Some can resemble proverbs, others maxims, still others similes, allegories, comparisons, riddles, taunts, or metaphors. A parable, as we've seen, is 'an earthly story with a heavenly meaning.' The Parable of the Sower is not the first parable in the gospels (e.g. 7:24-27), but it is the first 'fully developed parable,' as Morris puts it (333).

Morris also maintains that, 'the parabolic method is Jesus' own' (333). There were others who used them before Jesus, and some after, but none so extensively or effectively, and few other than Jesus' have survived to our day. Indeed, Jesus so perfected the parable that few Christians have been willing to create their own. The particular genius of parables is their capacity to reveal and hide truth at the same time (13:10-17). They enlighten the disciples as they harden outsiders. The first of these, the Parable of the Sower,

> ...makes effectively the point that the one message can produce different results in different hearers (Morris, 335).

Jesus preaches His message of the kingdom of God and observes four basic responses. He can see it on his listeners' faces. Their faces reflect what is happening in their hearts. Some are hard. Some are superficial. Some are distracted.

Some are open and receptive. Only one of the four responses is profitable. The other three prove to be fruitless.

So, this parable is a call to Jesus' hearers to be sure that the saving word of God has taken root, permanent root, in their hearts. Be sure, He is telling them, that you are not one of the faulty hearers, who never truly receive the gospel. As we now look at these four responses, let us also make sure that we are like the good soil, fruitful in our reception of His word.

Hard Heart

> On that day Jesus went out of the house, and was sitting by the sea. And great multitudes gathered to Him, so that He got into a boat and sat down, and the whole multitude was standing on the beach. And He spoke many things to them in parables, saying, 'Behold, the sower went out to sow;' (Matt. 13:1-3).

Jesus leaves the house in which He was teaching and outside of which His family was standing (Matt. 12:46-50), and walks down to the edge of the sea to teach. But the crowds are so great that He gets into a boat so that the people can press up to the edge of the water and hear. At this point, we note, Jesus is still exceedingly popular with the crowds.

As He begins His parable, Jesus utilizes a common agricultural phenomenon, the sower sowing his seed, as a metaphor in the physical world for what happens in the spiritual world. The sower represents the preacher, the seed represents the word of God, the soil represents the human heart, and the fruit, the results of a life transformed by the word as it takes deep root in the soul. As the farmer plants physical seed, so the preacher plants spiritual seed. It may be that a farmer was sowing seed off in the distance even as Jesus talked. 'There,' he points, 'this is what preaching and teaching is like.'

> '...and as he sowed, some seeds fell beside the road, and the birds came and ate them up' (Matt. 13:4).

'When anyone hears the word of the kingdom, and does not understand it, the evil one comes and snatches away what has been sown in his heart. This is the one on whom seed was sown beside the road' (13:19).

He could speak in the first instance of seed that falls not on the field to be plowed and prepared, but 'beside the road,' where the ground has been packed nearly as hard as the road itself. There it will lie. Soon a bird will come and snatch it away. It has no opportunity for growth. Like sowing seed on pavement, it is a hopeless situation.

Jesus is saying that there are hearts like this. They hear 'the word of the kingdom.' But the word does not penetrate at all. There are people who come under the sound of the gospel. Perhaps they come to church irregularly, only when a spouse drags them there or because of a sense of duty or tradition. But they come with their jaw set. They refuse to listen. They resist and fight what they hear. They have a chip on their shoulder and defy the preacher to knock it off. They don't want God to rule their hearts and minds. They resist His claims, His challenges to their lifestyle, their speech, their practices, their customs and traditions. This sort of person doesn't comprehend spiritual realities. Jesus says he 'does not understand it,' (Matt. 13:19). They are oblivious to their spiritual needs, and of the judgment to come.

The great irony of this type of hearer is that they may tend to think of themselves as strong people: self-made; not subject to the weak thinking of others; self-determining; independent, etc. Actually they are victims, even prisoners, of the 'evil one.' Jesus says that 'Satan' (Mark 4:15), the 'devil' (Luke 8:12) 'snatches away' the word. Satan distorts the message, diverts attention and clouds the memory; he 'has blinded the minds of the unbelieving that they might not see the light of the gospel and the glory of Christ,' (2 Cor. 4:4). He 'snatches away' what was sown; the verb here 'conveys the notion of violence' (Morris, 345).

Morris offers another suggestion. He says that given that the seed is sown 'in his heart' (v. 19), the heart being 'a person's innermost being,' it may imply 'something more than mere outward hearing.' In other words, not so much a *hard* heart as a *careless* heart.

> The word points to a certain receptiveness; this person is not hostile to the message. The hearer knows that there is some spiritual truth here intended for profit, but since he does not act on it, he soon finds that what he heard is lost. (346)

He lacks a due sense of urgency. He fails to realize the stakes that are involved. He fails to act, and the moment passes.

Satan makes many 'play the fool,' so that, as it is stated in Luke's parallel, 'they may not believe and be saved' (Luke 8:12).

The day of salvation comes and goes each time the gospel is preached. Our prayer must be that we not respond like the hard soil. May the Lord Himself batter down our resistance, 'break up (our) fallow ground' (Jer. 4:3; Hosea 10:12), and give us tender, pliable hearts, anxious to receive and obey His word.

Shallow Heart

> *'And others fell upon the rocky places, where they did not have much soil; and immediately they sprang up, because they had no depth of soil. But when the sun had risen, they were scorched; and because they had no root, they withered away'* (13:5, 6).

> *'And the one on whom seed was sown on the rocky places, this is the man who hears the word, and immediately receives it with joy; yet he has no firm root in himself, but is only temporary, and when affliction or persecution arises because of the word, immediately he falls away'* (13:20, 21).

The rocky soil of verses 5 and 6 and 20 and 21 is not soil with rocks in it. It refers rather to thin layers of soil that cover great sheets of bedrock. 'Rocky' soil is shallow soil. 'Rocky' ground has 'no depth of soil' (13:5). The seed gets off to a good enough start, quickly springing up. Shallow soil tends to warm quickly, providing an environment for rapid growth. But because the roots do not go deeply enough, the budding plant withers under the sun's growing intensity.

Jesus says this corresponds to the type of listeners who receive the word, but do so in a shallow, superficial way. They may come to church and hear the gospel and receive it. Initially they respond positively, enthusiastically. They receive the word of God 'with joy' (13:20), with 'happy enthusiasm' (Morris, 346). At first they love the gospel, the church and the fellowship. They are overjoyed with their newfound salvation. They may bring others to services with them. They may even witness to unbelievers. They throw themselves into the work of the gospel, giving of their time and treasure. But 'they have no firm root.' The word never really anchors itself in their hearts. It never really establishes its 'roots.' Then, a situation of stress arises and they fall away. The pressure is too much for them and their faith collapses. Why? Because they have no depth. Their level of involvement with the word was superficial and 'temporary' (13:21). They have 'no staying power' (REB). Their response was never genuine. As John says, 'They went out from us, but they were not really of us' (1 John 2:19). They didn't lose their salvation. They never truly had it. They may have seemed to be Christians. A plant did grow. Something was there. It appeared healthy. The signs of authenticity seemed to be present. But in fact there had been no real faith, repentance or conversion.

The mark of this 'almost-faith' is its impermanence. It doesn't last. Jesus mentions two 'temptations' (Luke 8:13) that expose its hypocrisy.

First, Jesus mentions 'afflictions'
This refers to providential mishaps, such as sickness, accidents, natural disasters, deaths. It 'denotes heavy pressure,' says Morris, and is used of treading out grapes, 'when there is pressure to the point of bursting.' The 'pretty bubble' of the 'shallow enthusiast' is burst (346). The shallow heart emerges from these things disillusioned, or even angry with God. One might begin to question, 'Why would God allow this if He were good?' He thinks/believes that God could have

prevented this disaster and did not. God's goodness is called into question. Gradually the faith of the shallow heart is battered, beaten down, and destroyed. The person is left cynical, bitter and unbelieving.

Second, Jesus mentions 'persecutions'
This refers to deliberate attacks by the enemies of the gospel. The shallow heart may be subject to emotional abuse, such as taunts of his peers. He may be ridiculed, rejected, isolated. Or 'persecutions' may refer to physical abuse such as loss of life or limb. Whichever, the pressure becomes too much. 'I didn't bargain for this,' the shallow one says. He tires of the pain and suffering and opts out. He caves in and goes into the mainstream. Enough is enough, he says. 'Immediately' he received the word, and 'immediately' he falls away. He is a fair weather Christian. He 'falls away' or 'takes offense.'

The problem for some is that they come to Christ for good, but ultimately superficial reasons. They were seeking good things, such as friendships, caring people, nice music, activities, and moral teaching for their children. But they were never decisively convicted of their sins and their need of a savior. So when a trial comes along and they make a quick cost/benefit analysis, they decide that the costs outstrip the benefits and they give up.

True faith is perfected by trials (James 1:2ff., 1 Pet. 1:6ff.). True faith endures. We can assess our own faith by answering a few questions. Have I become stronger or weaker as a result of afflictions and persecutions? Have I rejoiced, or have I become embittered? Have I been heartened or lost heart? Have I become more resolute or caved in? Have I increased in faith or lost faith? The word must take deep root in our hearts if it is to last. We must not settle for a superficial, shallow, and ultimately, temporary faith.

Strangled Heart

> *'And others fell among the thorns, and the thorns came up and choked them out'* (Matt. 13:7).

'And the one on whom seed was sown among the thorns, this is the man who hears the word, and the worry of the world, and the deceitfulness of riches choke the word, and it becomes unfruitful' (Matt. 13:22).

Then there is seed sown among the 'thorns' (Matt. 13:22). Thorns are what we would call weeds. This is soil that initially looks good, but actually has been turned over, not weeded, and is full of weeds. The weeds grow up with the seed and choke the life out of the seedling. The thorny heart is a heart which, like the previous heart, receives the word, but preoccupation with other things eventually overwhelms and destroys its budding life. Jesus mentions three different kinds of distractions.

First, Jesus mentions 'worry of the world'
The intention to nurture the word may have been characteristic of the thorny soil at one time. Initially the desire to focus on the eternal, to care for the soul, was present. Perhaps an individual awakened to the things of God at one time. They initially may have had quite high spiritual aspirations. But they returned to the real 'world' (v. 22). That is the meaning of 'world.' It means the present age. It indicates temporal, material concerns. They had to worry about school or exams or the business or the bills or the children. None of these things are evil in themselves, but when they take on undue importance, they crowd the word out of one's life. One may never find the Savior because one is overwhelmed by the cares of this life.

Second, Jesus mentions the 'deceitfulness of riches'
The 'worries of the world' have to do with survival. 'Riches' have to do with luxury. Money doesn't end the worry problem. Those who have always want more. They often engage in the endless pursuit of things bigger and better: the best clothes, best cars, and best homes in the best neighborhoods. They crave all the finer things of life. They also fret and fuss to preserve and protect what they have. If there is a false god in America today, surely this is it. We are a nation awash in

materialism. We are obsessively preoccupied with riches. We worship wealth. Jesus highlights the 'deceitfulness' of this preoccupation with luxury. It has a 'seductive effect' says France (219). And it can be subtle. One 'may not be aware of the choking that is going on' (France, 219). Yet wealth's seductions are constantly warned against in the Bible. Jesus said, 'It's easier for a camel to pass through the eye of a needle than for a rich man to enter the kingdom of God' (Matt. 19:24). He also said,

'No one can serve two masters; for either he will hate the one and love the other, or he will hold to one and despise the other. You cannot serve God and mammon' (Matt. 6:24).

Third, Jesus mentions the 'desires for other things' (Mark 4:19)
Luke adds 'the pleasures of this life' (Luke 8:14). This 'desire' goes along well with riches. The phrases Jesus uses indicate the desire for a comfortable, pleasurable life. They may include all manner of sensual delight, entertainments, recreation, or whatever else one might enjoy in this world. They may include the avoidance of every occasion of pain and trouble and responsibility.

The modern world has, in many ways, become a constant amusement park. We are incessantly being entertained – in our homes (of course), but also in our cars, at the airport, in the elevator, even between plays at football games. The thirty seconds between plays of National Football League games is now filled with pounding music, dancing girls, and flashing images on video screens. Apparently there mustn't be even a moment that passes that is not filled with multiple amusements. The ubiquitous T.V. screen now can be found above checkout lines in grocery stores, in banks, and in our automobiles.

Jesus' parable is designed to provoke questions and self-examination. Could it be that we are so busy with the concerns and pleasures of this life that we have little time for the things of God, and little interest? Even among strong, believing people, these days it is difficult to hold a congregation together because of the distractions that the world offers. Spiritual life is being choked out of us. Christian people are being seduced. Perhaps too much of the love of the world is still in us (1 John 2:15; James 4:4). We need to pull out the weeds. Sadly we are victims of the prosperous times in which we live and the abundance of our resources. We must pull out the weeds and get rid of any and everything that distracts us from the fruitful reception of God's word.

Open Heart

> *'And others fell on the good soil, and yielded a crop, some a hundredfold, some sixty, and some thirty'* (Matt. 13:8).

> *'And the one on whom seed was sown on the good soil, this is the man who hears the word and understands it; who indeed bears fruit, and brings forth, some a hundredfold, some sixty, and some thirty'* (Matt. 13:23).

Jesus speaks of the 'good soil,' which corresponds to the 'honest and good heart,' which 'hold(s) it fast,' (Luke 8:15), which 'hears', 'understands,' and 'accepts' it (Mark 4:20), and 'bears fruit, and brings forth, some a hundred-fold, some sixty, some thirty,' 'with perseverance' (Luke 8:15). Like the previous two, this heart receives the truth. Unlike the others, it perseveres, and most importantly, it bears fruit.

The word takes root in the 'good soil' and bears fruit. The good soil produces holy living and the fruit of the Spirit. It bears the fruit of obedience and love for God and others, and increasing conformity to the image of Christ, resulting in increasing 'fruitfulness' in witness to unbelievers. We can distinguish *qualitative* fruit, what the Apostle Paul calls the 'fruit of the light' which 'consists in all goodness and righteousness and truth' (Eph. 5:9), and *quantitative* fruit, such as the numbers of people being sanctified and converted through one's influence or witness. Both kinds of fruit spring from the heart which has rightly received God's word.

This does not mean that the good heart is a perfect heart. There are variations in gifts, abilities, and opportunities. Some are young, some weak, and some immature. Some will bear fruit 30-fold, some 60, some 100. If I am a young struggling Christian, I am not to despair because I am not all I should be or will be. The question is, am I growing? Has the word taken root? Is the fruit developing? 'There are different responses that are acceptable,' Morris observes (348). There are differing degrees of fruitfulness. The constant for all who are true Christians is that they will bear fruit. This is inevitable. They will 'bear fruit with perseverance' (Luke 8:15). Jesus said we 'prove' ourselves to be His disciples by bearing 'much fruit' (John 15:8). The authentic, genuine, 'rooted' believers can be known 'by their fruits' (Matt. 7:20).

This message is both encouraging and challenging. It is an encouragement for all those involved in Christian ministry to know that the variables in response, from receptive to completely unreceptive, are 'out there' in the listeners and not necessarily with those ministering God's word. The sower and the seed are the same in all four cases. Yet there are four different responses. There are hard, shallow, distracted, and good hearts. One might be the finest sower in the world, and yet there are hard, shallow, distracted and good hearts. Neither the sower nor seed gets the blame or credit. As France puts it, 'the fault lies not in the message, but in those who receive it' (220). When the seed fails to grow, it is not the sower's fault and it's not the seed's fault. When the seed grows, it is not to the sower's credit or the seed's credit. The responsibility lies in the hearer, not the messenger or message, not the church, its members, or the preacher. This is what the disciples were to know then and what we are to know today.

There are people who will never believe. No matter what we do they won't accept it. We are going to lose some. They will never agree. This is inevitable, and it's not necessarily our doing. There are *unreceptive hearts*. Many of our so-called failures, past, present, and future, are not failures at all, but are inevitable responses of unprepared hearts. There are also those who are ready and will receive the word, irrespective of the skill of the sower. Just as we don't get blamed for those who don't receive the gospel, so we don't get credit for those who do. We don't get the credit for this either. We merely water and plant. God causes the growth (1 Cor. 3:6, 7).

The parable is also challenging. It is challenging because none of us can escape the heart-directed implications of this text. I am one of these four types of soil. Am I a hard heart? Do I come ready *not* to hear? Do I refuse to let the word deal with me? This is a dangerous condition to be in. If so, our prayer must be, 'O Lord, soften our hard hearts! Make us pliable and receptive to your word.'

Am I a shallow heart? Do I superficially receive the word and never allow it to sink its roots into my heart? Is my 'faith' ready to collapse at the first sign of trouble? If so, our prayer must be, 'O Lord, dig deeply into my soul and plant your word where it will never be uprooted.'

Am I a distracted heart? Am I too busy? Too preoccupied? Too wrapped up in this world and its concerns? If so, my prayer must be, 'O Lord, pull out my weeds! Tear them out by the roots and replace them with your own good plants.'

Am I good soil? Do I receive and keep His word? If so, I may be known by my good fruit.

Perhaps none of us is all one soil. There are areas in which each of us is hard, or shallow, or distracted, or good. But which am I predominately? Which is characteristically descriptive of me?

The kingdom of God begins in the heart. The question raised by Jesus in this parable is this: how has my heart responded to His gospel? Has the gospel taken root? If so, rejoice. If there is any doubt about this at all, turn immediately to the Lord of the harvest and plead with Him to plow and clear you heart once more. Lord, break up the hard soil and the rocky soil and pull out the weeds and plant Your gospel-word deeply and permanently in my heart (Jer. 4:3). He will do it. The question is, will you pursue it and receive it?

STUDY QUESTIONS

1. Identify the common elements of the parable: sower, seed, soil, fruit.

2. What does the soil 'beside the road' represent? What do the birds represent? (13:4, 19.)

3. What does the 'rocky' soil represent? What is the problem with this heart? What causes its plant to wither? (13:5, 6, 20, 21).

4. What does the soil with 'thorns' represent? What causes its plant to be strangled and die? (13:7, 22).

5. What does the 'good' soil represent? How does it differ from the previous soils? (13:8, 23).

6. Upon whom does Jesus place the responsibility for a fruit-bearing reception of God's word? What does this mean for the church and its ministry? What does this mean for me personally?

~ 4 ~

'THE WEDDING FEAST'

Matthew 22:1-14

Accepting the Invitation

[1]*And Jesus answered and spoke to them again in parables, saying,* [2]*'The kingdom of heaven may be compared to a king, who gave a wedding feast for his son.* [3]*And he sent out his slaves to call those who had been invited to the wedding feast, and they were unwilling to come.* [4]*Again he sent out other slaves saying, "Tell those who have been invited, 'Behold, I have prepared my dinner; my oxen and my fattened livestock are all butchered and everything is ready; come to the wedding feast.'"* [5]*But they paid no attention and went their way, one to his own farm, another to his business,* [6]*and the rest seized his slaves and mistreated them and killed them.* [7]*But the king was enraged and sent his armies, and destroyed those murderers, and set their city on fire.* [8]*Then he said to his slaves, "The wedding is ready, but those who were invited were not worthy.* [9]*Go therefore to the main highways, and as many as you find there, invite to the wedding feast."* [10]*And those slaves went out into the streets, and gathered together all they found, both evil and good; and the wedding hall was filled with dinner guests.* [11]*But when the king came in to look over the dinner guests, he saw there a man not dressed in wedding clothes,* [12]*and he said to him, "Friend, how did you come in here without wedding clothes?" And he was speechless.* [13]*Then the king said to the servants, "Bind him*

hand and foot, and cast him into the outer darkness; in that place there shall be weeping and gnashing of teeth." [14]For many are called, but few are chosen' (cf. Luke 14:15-24).

What is life like in God's kingdom? What is it like under God's rule? Is it pleasant or harsh? Is it exciting or dull? Is it liberating or suffocating? As we have argued, the parables of the kingdom are meant to answer these kinds of questions. The Parable of the Wedding Feast is similar to the seven parables in Matthew 13 and to that of Matthew 20:1-15 (Laborers in the Vineyard). They all begin with a simile – 'the kingdom of God is like,' or 'the kingdom of God may be compared ...' Jesus is teaching His disciples what His realm is like. We need not be ignorant of the manner of the kingdom's development in this world or of its completed state in eternity. What will heaven be like? Jesus tells us a great deal about it in these parables of the kingdom.

This parable also has similarities with the parables that immediately preceded it in Matthew. The Parable of the Two Sons (Matt. 21:28-32), the Parable of the Wicked Vine-growers (21:33-41), and the Parable of the Wedding Feast (22:1-14) all carry the same message – the failure of Israel to meet God's requirements. This parable, then, is also a warning to Israel and to us, that for God's gifts to be received, His word must be believed and obeyed, and we must bear His fruit.

We must make one more note about this parable's relation to other parables. The Parable of the Wedding Feast closely resembles a parable told by Jesus recorded in Luke 14:15-24 but in a different setting and with a number of variations. Indeed it is different enough to be considered 'another parable,' says Morris, 'embodying features Jesus had used before' rather than 'a second form of the same parable' (547). For our purposes, however, we will make reference to those differences and treat them both as one.

This is a parable of the kingdom, describing both the history and nature of the kingdom. Would you be pleased to know about the workings of God's kingdom? Then stay tuned. Here is what the kingdom is like.

Banquet

And Jesus answered and spoke to them again in parables, saying
(Matt. 22:1).

In delivering this parable Jesus 'answered' no questions in
particular, but the hostility of the chief priests and Pharisees
generally (Matt. 21:45).

*'The kingdom of heaven may be compared to a king, who gave
a wedding feast for his son'* (Matt. 22:2).

The kingdom of God, says Jesus, may be 'compared' or
likened to a rich, sumptuous feast. It is not just a feast, but
a *wedding feast*. It is a wedding feast thrown not by a pauper
but by a *king*. It is a wedding feast thrown by a king not for
a friend but for a *son*, which means that it is an 'especially
significant' royal occasion, says Morris (547). The eating and
drinking, the celebrating and rejoicing, the laughter, the
singing and dancing would go on for days. The King would
likely provide a 'magnificent banquet,' continues Morris
(547). The people would covet invitations and would be
honored to be there. The kingdom of God is likened not to
a *desert*, not to a *fast* (as though His kingdom were all about
self-deprivation), but a *feast*. It is a place of abundance, of
richness, of satisfied and satiated spiritual appetites. The
banquet 'symbolizes the blessings of God's salvation,' says
France (312). 'There is in the Gospel,' says Ryle, 'a complete
provision for all the wants of man's soul: there is a supply of
everything that can be required to relieve spiritual hunger
and spiritual thirst' (280). A feast is an apt metaphor for
what believers enjoy now as well as what they will enjoy in
eternity. Present feasting anticipates the great feast to come,
the 'marriage supper of the lamb' (Rev. 19:7-9). Heaven will
be a place of feasting.

This representation of the kingdom of God would come
as a surprise to many of our contemporaries. Often in the
popular mind God and His rule (kingdom) is associated with
deprivation. This is why the young in particular often flee

from the gospel. All they can see is a long list of 'thou shalt nots' and frustrated human appetites. Serious Christianity, for them, means movies they can't see (that all their peers get to see), music they can't listen to, concerts they can't attend, places they can't go, things they can't do. In what sense is it a feast? The answer is, the gospel is a feast *for the soul*. It is a feast that satisfies the deepest needs and longings and desires of the human heart, now in part, and in its fullness in eternity.

Let's ask the question this way: What do we long for? Love, joy, peace, rest, fulfillment, community, and order. The gospel delivers on all of these. Because Christ's atonement provides for the forgiveness of sin, reconciliation with God, life eternal, love, joy and peace fill our hearts. Our souls find rest. We are united with other believers in the Christian community. Order is brought to our disorder. We repeat, the fundamental desires of the human heart are fulfilled in Christ. Those who 'hunger and thirst after righteousness' find satisfaction (Matt. 5:6). The world *pretends* to offer a feast, but it is an illusion. The world spreads a banquet, but borrowing from the subtitle of Ed Welch's book *Addiction*, it is a 'banquet in the grave.' It looks good, smells good, even tastes good, but like food poisoning, causes sickness and even death. Granted, this can be difficult to see. Among the devil's schemes is dressing up sin in pleasant clothes. He makes evil appear desirable. The devil disguises himself as an angel of light (2 Cor. 11:14). Where the world promises light, it delivers darkness; where it promises riches, it delivers bankruptcy of the soul; where it promises abundance, it delivers a desert; where it promises life, it delivers death. The world's pleasures are counterfeits. They are temporary, superficial, and soul destroying. Let me repeat the words of the author Jack Higgins, who at the peak of his career, having written a best-selling book which became a Hollywood movie, said, 'I wish someone had told me that when one gets to the top that there is nothing there.' 'Solid joys and lasting treasures none but Zion's children know,' wrote John Newton. Likewise, the great English hymn writer Isaac Watts wrote,

While all our hearts and all our songs
Join to admire the feast,
Each of us cry, with thankful tongues,
'Lord, why was I a guest?'

'Why was I made to hear thy voice,
And enter while there's room,
When thousands make a wretched choice,
And rather starve than come?'

'Twas the same love that spread the feast
That sweetly drew us in;
Else we had still refused to taste,
And perished in our sin.

The world's choice is a 'wretched choice' that starves, says Watts. For us, Christ spreads a 'feast.' 'Blessed is everyone who shall eat bread in the kingdom of God,' Jesus said (Luke 14:15).

Unlimited Invitations
Initially the invitations to the feast were sent to a select few.

And he sent out his slaves to call those who had been invited to the wedding feast, and they were unwilling to come (Matt. 22:3).

Verse 3 actually depicts a second invitation to the select invitees. The slaves are sent to those 'who had been invited.' This phrasing 'presupposes a previous invitation that had been accepted,' says Morris (548). That slaves (plural) are sent indicates there were a large number of people to contact, informing them that the dinner was now ready. A second invitation was customary, because this was a time before watches and when banquets took a long time to prepare. But Jesus tells us that 'they were unwilling to come.' Morris says that their refusal was 'completely unnatural' (548). Normally one would be thrilled to have made the invitation list. Normally one would be excited to come. The point Jesus is making is that it is strange, unnatural, perhaps even bizarre that the leadership of Israel had not responded to God's summons to honor His Son. There had to be some mistake. So more slaves are sent, and the details of the banquet are elaborated.

> *'Again he sent out other slaves saying, "Tell those who have been invited, 'Behold, I have prepared my dinner; my oxen and my fattened livestock are all butchered and everything is ready; come to the wedding feast'"'* (Matt. 22:4).

This time the slaves are instructed by the king to highlight the bounty of the banquet – the feast was 'prepared,' 'fattened livestock' had been 'butchered' and 'everything is ready.' Still they would not come:

> *'But they paid no attention and went their way, one to his own farm, another to his business'* (Matt. 22:5).

One group of invitees is *indifferent*. They 'paid no attention,' Jesus says. They 'did not care,' as Morris renders *ameleō* (549). They are reneging on their previous promise, similar to the case of the disobedient son in Matthew 21:30 and the tenants in Matthew 21:35ff. None of the guests seems to have compelling conflicts in their schedule which require immediate attention. One goes to his 'farm.' Another goes to his 'business.' Nothing urgent detains them. Luke's parallel parable details their excuses:

> *'But they all alike began to make excuses. The first one said to him, "I have bought a piece of land and I need to go out and look at it; please consider me excused." And another one said, "I have bought five yoke of oxen, and I am going to try them out; please consider me excused." And another one said, "I have married a wife, and for that reason I cannot come"'* (Luke 14:18-20).

None of the invitees face a crisis. The land could be looked at later, the oxen could be tried out later, the presence of a new wife does not conflict with participation in the feast. They simply don't care. In Matthew's version, they don't even bother to make excuses. Note as well that none of these endeavors are harmful in themselves. Morris calls this 'an incredible attitude to take up in the face of a royal command and the almost sacred duty of complying with an accepted invitation' (549). Instead, Morris continues, 'They just go off to pursue their own concerns' (549). There is no evil in attending to one's farm or business or wife. The pursuits of this world only become harmful when they supersede the pursuit of God. Note further that the parable is aimed at the 'already religious,' as France points out (312). The rebuke is of those who have made an idol of their worldly pursuits. They are seeking to serve both God and mammon (Matt. 6:24). They mean to compartmentalize religion, to give it a place, but a safe, limited place. When it comes time to decide between the demands of money or pleasure or business and the demands of God, God loses. They are indifferent, or busy, or distracted. The concerns of the world and the deceitfulness of riches are choking out the word (Matt. 13:22).

> '…and the rest seized his slaves and mistreated them and killed them' (Matt. 22:6).

The 'rest' are *hostile*. They 'mistreated' some of the slaves, a word (*hubrizō*) meaning to 'insult, treat insolently,' says Morris (549, n.12). The others they killed. They do not respect the king, or fear him.

These invitees represent those who, while still religious, are hostile to the truth. They are still in church. They still tithe. They still observe the Sabbath. But they find the gospel offensive and resist it violently.

> 'But the king was enraged and sent his armies, and destroyed those murderers, and set their city on fire' (Matt. 22:7).

The snubbing of the king and killing of the slaves were acts of disloyalty and rebellion. The king was 'enraged' and sent 'armies' (*strateuma*), a word which can also mean 'a body of soldiers,' says Morris (550, n.14). Carson takes it as an idiom similar to the English phrase, 'sending in the police.'

The burning of their city recalls Old Testament judgments (Isa. 5:24-25). In real life it would have taken time for all of this to take place. In the parable Jesus is showing us ultimately what became of those who refused the king's invitation. There are two responses from the religious community – indifference and hostility. Both bring the judgment of God.

Because the few would not come, the invitation to the wedding feast is extended to 'whosoever will.'

'Then he said to his slaves, "The wedding is ready, but those who were invited were not worthy"' (Matt. 22:8).

They were considered 'not worthy' because they refused the invitation. 'A considerable understatement,' says Morris (550).

'Go therefore to the main highways, and as many as you find there, invite to the wedding feast' (Matt. 22:9).

The 'rejection' of Israel means 'the reconciliation of the world' (Rom. 11:15; cf 11:11, 12). All are now invited. The 'main highways' is an expression which seems to mean 'places where the main highways go out from the city to the country, evidently places where poor people tended to congregate,' says Morris (550). In other words, go find ordinary folks who would not normally be invited to a royal banquet. Carson understands it as 'street corners' (as in NIV), or as 'forks in the road, where they would find many people' (457). In Luke's parallel parable, more emphasis is given to the search for participants. The host instructs his servants,

'Go out at once into the streets and lanes of the city and bring in here the poor and crippled and blind and lame' (Luke 14:21b).

Not just the common people, but the outcasts, the 'crippled and blind and lame' are to be invited. No one, and no class of person, is to be excluded.

When once the slave returns from inviting one and all and finds 'still there is room,' the master sends him back out again:

> *'And the master said to the slave, "Go out into the highways and along the hedges, and compel them to come in, that my house may be filled'* (Luke 14:23).

'Compel' is a strong word, indicating the strength with which potential guests are to be urged to come. The point is that they are to seek out people to invite aggressively, and that they are to invite everyone they encounter.

> *'And those slaves went out into the streets, and gathered together all they found, both evil and good; and the wedding hall was filled with dinner guests'* (Matt. 22:10).

The slaves retrieve all they can find, 'both evil and good.' In other words, they gather many whom the Jewish leaders would have found totally unacceptable for ceremonial, moral, or ethnic reasons. Verses 8-10 correspond to the conclusions of the preceding two parables in Matthew (Matt. 21:31-32, 41-43). The gospel goes to the tax gatherers and harlots, to Gentiles and sinners (Rom. 11:11, 12; Eph. 3:8). God invites all who will come to His feast of love, forgiveness, peace, joy, purpose, and eternal life. No one is excluded. However wicked, evil, morally degraded, twisted, perverse, or violent, it matters not. The invitation is 'full, broad, and unlimited,' says Ryle (280).

Would you like to be invited to God's feast for His Son? You are! No one can claim that he is not. Once the invitation to the feast was limited to the nation of Israel. But no more. Today the rule is 'whoever will call upon the name of the Lord will be saved' (Rom. 10:13). No excuses remain. We are all invited. However far we may have plunged into evil, however degraded by sin we may have become, however distant from God we may have strayed, still we are invited. Come, He says. Enjoy my banquet, He urges. If we miss the opportunity, it is no fault but our own. 'God will be found clear of the blood of all lost souls,' says Ryle (281).

Honor the Son
Yet there is one qualification: that you honor the Son. Matthew records the addendum to the parable in verses 11-14, not found in Luke.

> *But when the king came in to look over the dinner guests, he saw there a man not dressed in wedding clothes* (Matt. 22:11).

'Wedding clothes' refers not to a special kind of garment but to 'clean clothes,' says France (313). It matters what you wear. To come in dirty clothes would be an insult to the host. It was true then and remains true today because our apparel is a form of communication. We commonly speak of one's 'body language,' indicating that one's posture and gestures send messages as surely as do words. Perhaps we also ought to speak of 'garment language.' Body and garment language are not as accurate as words; they are subject to misunderstanding, but still they communicate. What we wear to a given event says something about how we value it. Think of the young man meeting the family of a young lady whom he wants to marry. How he dresses says something about how much he values her and them. Or consider an invitation to dinner at the White House. How would it be perceived if one arrived in a t-shirt, cut-offs and flip-flops? How do we dress for proms, weddings, and funerals? Show up in jeans, sandals, and a golf shirt and you dishonor the occasion and those associated with it. The point of the underdressed guest is that he dishonors the king and the son. He didn't bother to make the effort to clothe himself properly. He failed to honor the hosts. One could ask, why was he there? Answer? He was there for the party! He was after the food and drink. He was interested only in the benefits, and was unwilling to bear the cost, or fulfill the requirements of the feast, however slight.

Perhaps you can see where this is going.

> *'…and he said to him, "Friend, how did you come in here without wedding clothes?" And he was speechless'* (Matt. 22:12).

He was speechless because he was defenseless. He knew he was wrong not to have worn appropriate clothing. He was 'convicted and condemned by his own conscience,' says Matthew Henry. The lesson is that 'though entry to God's salvation is free for all, it is not therefore without standards or to be taken lightly,' says France (313). In the language of previous parables, guests must produce fruit (Matt. 21:41, 43). 'The wedding garment is a frame of heart, and a course of life agreeable to the gospel and our profession of it,' Matthew Henry adds. The man without the wedding clothes was attempting to partake of the feast 'without an appropriate change of life,' says France. It was this, says France, 'which characterized the old Israel and brought about its rejection; the new people of God must not fall into the same error' (313). France adds that the garments represent 'simply a life appropriate to one of God's new people' (313). Yes, all are invited, but not without repentance, not without faith, not without the intention to honor the King and His Son. The underdressed man is using the gospel as 'fire insurance.' He wants to stay out of hell and go to heaven, but without honoring the Son. It can't be done.

> 'Then the king said to the servants, "Bind him hand and foot, and cast him into the outer darkness; in that place there shall be weeping and gnashing of teeth"' (Matt. 22:13).

Jesus shifts from the real life situation to a description of final judgment. Hell is a place of bondage, of 'darkness' and continuous 'weeping and gnashing of teeth.' In addition to those who refused to come to the feast, there are those who came but without any intention of honoring Christ. Destruction awaits both. 'Some refuse to come, and others who do come refuse to submit to the norms of the kingdom and are therefore rejected,' says Carson (457). In the meantime, only the King can distinguish between guests; we cannot. The wheat and the tares grow up together (Matt. 13:30). Only the final judgment reveals the true guests.

Finally, Jesus concludes with a summarizing principle.

> 'For many are called, but few are chosen' (Matt. 22:14).

'Many are called.' The invitation goes out to many. All the guests are there because of the generosity of the King. Yet, 'few are chosen' – not all those called are chosen. Not all who hear believe. 'Few' does not mean few in an absolute sense, but comparatively. 'Fewer' are chosen than are called.

There is that bothersome word again, 'chosen' (see ch. 2). The subject of the verb is God. God chooses. The Bible, always carefully nuanced on these questions, balances human responsibility and divine sovereignty. We are responsible. But finally God chooses. God is in control. Never is He taken by surprise. He knows who are His. Yet He invites us all. He requires of us all that we come intending to honor the Son. All who will do so are guaranteed a place at the table, a feast beyond compare.

STUDY QUESTIONS

1. It is noteworthy that the kingdom of God may be likened not to a desert or a fast, but what? What does this indicate about life with God? Is this a surprising metaphor?

2. The king sends second (v. 3) and third (v. 4) invitations to his invited guests, emphasizing the bounty of his banquet. What two responses do his pleas elicit (vv. 5, 6)? What do these responses represent in relation to God?

3. The king's response to the rejection of his invitations to his banquet is two-fold (vv. 7-10). What is it? What does his response represent in the history of redemption? (cf. Rom. 11:15)

4. While the invitation to the banquet is extended to all, there is a qualification. What is it (vv. 11, 12)? What do such represent?

5. Why would one show up to a wedding underdressed? Why was the underdressed one 'speechless' (v. 12)?

6. The parable shifts from the scene on earth to a description of final judgment in verse 13. How is it described?

7. How are we to understand the final verse (v. 14)?

~ 5 ~

'THE TWO SONS'

Matthew 21:28-32

Receiving Jesus

[28]*'But what do you think? A man had two sons, and he came to the first and said, "Son, go work today in the vineyard."* [29]*And he answered and said, "I will, sir;" and he did not go.* [30]*And he came to the second and said the same thing. But he answered and said, "I will not;" yet he afterward regretted it and went.* [31]*Which of the two did the will of his father?' They said, 'The latter.' Jesus said to them, 'Truly I say to you that the tax-gatherers and harlots will get into the kingdom of God before you.* [32]*For John came to you in the way of righteousness and you did not believe him; but the tax-gatherers and harlots did believe him; and you, seeing this, did not even feel remorse afterward so as to believe him.'*

What parent has not had a rude and sullen teenager respond to a parental directive with loud complaining and refusals, only to find later that the child reconsidered and did what he or she was told? Alternately, what parent hasn't had a sweet and compliant teenager immediately agree to a parental directive, respectfully saying, 'Yes, Sir,' or 'Yes, Ma'am,' only to fail to follow through? This common human experience provides the background for this 'homely' parable, as Morris calls it

(536). Commonplace though the setting of this parable is, it has teeth. It is the first parable aimed directly at the religious leadership of the nation, and flows out of the conflict between Jesus and those authorities that immediately preceded it in Matthew 21:23-27. The 'you' of verse 28 to whom Jesus is speaking are the 'chief priests and the elders of the people' of Matthew 21:23.

Jesus interprets this parable unambiguously. It has to do with who 'will get into the kingdom of God' (v. 31), exactly the concern in this first section of our study. The common people, often despised by the religious leadership because of their carnality and irreligion, received both John and Jesus and will get in. However, the chief priests and elders, those who ought to be most eager to know the truth, who ought to know better, who feign religiosity and spirituality, rejected them and will not. The point would seem to be that religious observance, *per se*, cannot save us. Only Christ can save us, and He saves those who are committed to knowing, believing, and serving Him.

The Parable

> 'But what do you think? A man had two sons, and he came to the first and said, "Son, go work today in the vineyard." And he answered and said, "I will, sir;" and he did not go. And he came to the second and said the same thing. But he answered and said, "I will not;" yet he afterward regretted it and went' (Matt. 21:28-30).

At first glance everything about these boys appears to conflict. One says he will work for his father and doesn't, the other says he won't work for his father and does. Yet we should first note a number of *similarities* between the two sons.

1. They have the *same father*. 'A man,' that is, one man, 'had two sons.' These boys have been reared in the same household, the same family, the same environment. The first son should probably be understood as the elder, the second the younger (Carson, 449). The older would have had

certain privileges as the firstborn. Still, the similarities would probably have outweighed the differences. We often see our children as very different from each other. Outside observers tend to see the similarities. This is why we can see family characteristics run through the generations, sometimes embracing all the children and grandchildren. This is why common sayings such as 'like father, like son,' or 'the acorn doesn't fall far from the tree,' ring true. The training and upbringing of these boys would have been very similar.

2. They were given the *same command*, 'Go work today in the vineyard.' No more was being expected of the older than of the younger. This would seem to be a point of the parable. Same father, same household, same requirements, same expectations, same upbringing, same command. The broader lesson of this parable would be that God the Father is the Father of us all and expects the same of us all. He has one law, one truth, and one standard of judgment. He calls us all to faith, to repentance, and to serious discipleship. We are called as His disciples to offer Him public worship, to serve His gospel-people, to spread His gospel-kingdom. He asks this of the best of us and the worst of us; of the religious and the irreligious; the rich and the poor; black and white, young and old, good and bad, we all have the same fundamental duty. *Believe* what He commands, *do* what He says, *go* where He sends.

Second, we should now note the *differences* between the two boys.

1. The elder son *agrees* to work but *doesn't*.

'And he answered and said, "I will, sir;" and he did not go' (Matt. 21:29).

At this juncture we need to point out that our various translations reflect some textual variations. The KJV and the NIV both show the elder son not agreeing to work, but later changing his mind and going. The NASB shows the opposite, with the younger son not agreeing and later changing his mind and going. We'll not solve the textual problems but, thankfully, whichever reading is correct, the essential situation is unaltered. One son agrees to work and doesn't, the other refuses and then does. Following the NASB, the elder son is respectful. He says, 'I will, *sir.'* He is a good, well-mannered, even well-intended, boy. But then he doesn't go. He 'said better than he did, promised better than he proved,' said Matthew Henry. What happened? We're not told. But we can assume the normal distractions. Perhaps he forgot. Maybe he flipped on the first century equivalent of the TV and got lost in a good program. Maybe he found the work to be too hard, too costly, requiring too much sacrifice. He meant well. He intended to obey his father. But as Matthew Henry points out, 'Buds and blossoms are not fruit.'

The older son is meant to represent the church-going, religious community. Religious people talk a good game. They know what's been called 'the language of Zion.' Bunyan's 'Talkative' comes to mind. They say the right things. But then they don't do what they say. They pretend to be righteous, but they are not. They speak of loyalty and obedience, but they don't practice it. Religion turns out to be a matter of image, not of the heart. Their religion is a facade.

2. The younger son *refuses* to work, but *does*.

'And he came to the second and said the same thing. But he answered and said, "I will not;" yet he afterward regretted it and went' (Matt. 21:30).

'I will not,' the younger son says, an answer scarcely imaginable in a Middle Eastern context. He is rude. He is disobedient and rebellious. He dishonors his father.

The younger son represents the non-religious community. The tax-gatherers and harlots of verse 31 clearly come to mind. They have no intention of obeying God. They have another agenda altogether.

But 'afterwards,' we read, after the passage of some time, he 'regretted it.' Time had to pass. Whatever had prompted his rebellion had to pass on. The parable envisions a short period of time. But there is no reason to restrict the time frame in this way. I have often lamented that it is very difficult to reach people with the gospel between roughly their 14th and 24th birthdays. Decadent pop culture is a corrupting and overwhelming influence upon our young people. The gospel can hardly be heard above the shouts of hedonism. Tragically, time has to pass. Many get dragged down into the party environment of drugs and promiscuity. It enslaves and degrades them. Ten years after their initiation into pop culture they finally burn out, or, we might say, their wounds scar over and they become open again to the truth they may have heard and owned as a child. 'Afterward' they 'come to their senses,' as Jesus says in another of His parables (Luke 15:17). Finally, their consciences begin to bother them. They grow to regret their contempt for God's law. They experience a change of heart. After saying no, the younger son then 'regretted it' (*metamelomai*, Matt. 21:30). He 'changed his mind' (NIV). Literally, this means, 'change what one has at heart.' The nuance of 'repent' may be intended here (Morris, 537). He thought it over. His outlook changed. He repented. He regretted what he said. He realized that what he said to his father was wrong. So he 'went.' He changed course and got to work.

We have seen this pattern repeatedly. After years of corrupt and wasteful behavior, many wayward ones come to regret it. They look back over the wasted time, the shameful behavior, the ruined lives, and are overcome with bitter remorse. What are they to do? Submit to the Father's will. Comply with the Father's commands. Their consciences awaken to the wrongfulness of life as they have lived it. They realize the void that is there and begin to look to God for answers and relief.

This then prompts Jesus' question:

'Which of the two did the will of his father?' (Matt. 21:31a).

Common sense takes over.

They said, 'The latter' (Matt. 21:31a).

The religious leaders give the right answer. Most people 'would rather deal with one who will be *better* than his word, than with one who will be *false* to his word,' says Matthew Henry. But as was the case in Matthew 21:23-27 and the questions raised by Jesus' exercise of authority, the religious leaders are trapped by their own words. The point of the story is 'obvious,' says France. Its point is 'that what counts is not promise but performance' (306). 'This homely parable,' continues Morris, 'brings out the importance of doing what is right and not merely talking about it' (536). Again, 'It is not enough to say 'I will;' we must put our good intentions into effect,' Morris adds (536). Faith (as mere assent) without works is dead, as the Apostles teach (James 2:26).

The Application

> *Jesus said to them, 'Truly I say to you that the tax-gatherers and harlots will get into the kingdom of God before you'* (Matt. 21:31b).

'Truly I say to you,' indicates a solemn saying. Here is something about which you can be absolutely certain. The 'tax-gatherers and harlots' are 'the scum of society,' says Carson (450). They are identified by France as 'those whom they most despised and regarded as furthest from pleasing God' (306), and 'almost proverbial for wicked people outside the number of true servants of God,' adds Morris (507). They 'will get into the kingdom before you.' The verb translated 'will get into ... before' is *proagō*. A few verses later, Matthew 21:43ff., Jesus threatens to remove the kingdom of God from Israel, saying,

> *'Therefore I say to you, the kingdom of God will be taken away from you, and be given to a nation producing the fruit of it'* (Matt. 21:43).

This threat suggests to France that the use of *proagō* in Matthew 21:31 indicates 'displacement and not only precedence' (307). Carson concurs, stating that 'and you will not' is how *proagō* must be understood here (450). The sense of Jesus' words is *not* that the harlots and tax-collectors will get into the kingdom first and the religious leaders will be second, *but that the former will get in and the latter will not at all*. In other words, the religious establishment is the elder son. Like the elder brother, they are all talk, and form, and appearance. They look and sound correct. But they fail to do what God asks. Yet the outcasts, the younger sons, who initially refuse to obey the will of God, will get in!

> 'For John came to you in the way of righteousness and you did not believe him; but the tax-gatherers and harlots did believe him; and you, seeing this, did not even feel remorse afterward so as to believe him' (Matt. 21:32).

Jesus provides two 'proofs' of the religious leaders' identity as the elder son, drawn from their response to John's ministry. Remember (as Jesus does) that the ministries of John and Jesus were bound together. Jesus submitted to John's baptism and John identified Jesus as the 'lamb of God who takes away the sin of the world' (John 1:29). The leaders' response to John is predictive of their response to Jesus.

1. *You rejected John's message of righteousness*

> 'For John came to you in the way of righteousness and you did not believe him;' (Matt. 21:32a).

The 'way of righteousness' means 'God's will about what is right,' says Carson (450). 'It is a Semitic expression meaning "the right way,"' says France (307). John preached righteousness and truth. That was his message. Yet you rejected it! France also says, 'The leaders could not recognize for themselves *the way of righteousness* ... which he both preached and exemplified' (307). Perhaps a given pastor may not be your favorite. Maybe you have a personality conflict with him. But can you hear the sound of truth in what he says and how he lives?

2. You ignored John's success or fruitfulness

'...but the tax-gatherers and harlots did believe him; and you, seeing this, did not even feel remorse afterward so as to believe him' (Matt. 21:32b).

The outcasts 'did believe him,' repented, and in massive numbers were baptized. Jesus reminds the leaders that they had seen all the good that was being done. The most hardened sinners were being won. Jesus repeats the words of 'remorse' and 'afterward' used of the younger son in verse 30. The consciences of the outcasts 'worked.' Those of the religious leaders did not. They did not ponder their hardness of heart and repent. Instead, they remained unbelieving, even with the evidence of good all around them. 'Even the evidence of what a true response to John's preaching could do in people's lives did not produce a change in the conventionally religious,' Morris observes (538). They didn't believe John 'even after seeing society's vilest sinners repenting and believing him and his message,' says Carson (450). Success is not conclusive proof of the validity of a ministry, but it is a factor. Jesus said, 'You will know them by their fruit' (Matt. 7:16ff.). John produced fruit. The lost were being won. Lives were being transformed. Again, not every ministry may be our favorite. But is the truth being preached? Are lives being transformed? If so, personal grievances ought to be put aside, and the ministry ought to be supported (cf. Phil. 1:15ff.).

Apply this now to today. Along the spectrum, moving from the elder to the younger brother, where do we fall? Since this parable is about 'getting in,' no more crucial question could be asked. Who gets into heaven? Ultimately it's not the religious or the immoral , but those who 'receive' Jesus after the manner of the tax-gatherers' and harlots' reception of Jesus. Heaven's door swings open to those who submit to the will of the Father, and receive Jesus' message of righteousness. It opens to those who experience 'remorse' for their rebellion against God, and acknowledge and repent of their sin. Prior to this, one may have been a liar, a cheat, or a whore. On the other hand, one may have been a Pharisee, a highly religious and strictly observant individual. But neither condition either saves or excludes one from salvation. What saves is receiving Jesus, repenting of sin, sitting at His feet, and surrendering to His will.

Which are you then? The younger or the older brother? Let me say, especially to our younger people, there is no reason to be either of these sons. Best of all is to *say* 'yes' to the Father, and to *do* your 'yes.' Best of all is to have believed and obeyed from the day of your birth and to have spared yourself the wounds and scars of rebellion against God. Any repentant rebel will tell you, you don't break the law of God, it breaks you. There is no joy, no peace, apart from walking with Christ.

Are you the younger son who has been saying no? Up to this point have you been saying 'no' and doing your 'no?' Now is the time to say 'yes.' It's not too late. Let the spirit of remorse fill your heart, turn away from rebellion, and turn to God. He will greet you with mercy and grace and the blood of Christ which atones for all our sin.

Or have you been the elder son, playing at 'yes,' projecting 'yes,' while living 'no'? Has your life been one of religious hypocrisy? If so, then now is the time to turn from your religious facade, believe, and be reconciled to God. For all of us, the time to decide is now. Determine in your heart: do I believe I am a sinner? do I want God's pardon? do I believe in the gospel of the cross and forgiveness through Christ's sacrifice? Then by the grace of God, I will follow through and act on what I say I believe. The God who saves the harlots and tax-gatherers and religious hypocrites will save me as well.

STUDY QUESTIONS

1. Who are the 'you' of verse 28? To whom is the parable addressed?

2. How are the two sons similar? How would their similarities apply to Jesus' listeners and to us?

3. How are the sons different? Who does each of them represent?

4. What would you say is the point of the parable?

5. What is the full implication of Jesus' statement that the harlots and tax-gatherers will get into the kingdom of God 'before' the chief priests and elders of Israel?

6. What does Jesus cite as proof of the identities of the religious leaders as the elder brother, as those who *talk* but do not *do*? (21:32)

7. As we apply the parable to ourselves, where do we fall along the spectrum from the elder to the younger brother?

~ 6 ~

'THE RICH FOOL'

Luke 12:13-21

Living for Eternity

¹³*And someone in the crowd said to Him, 'Teacher, tell my brother to divide the family inheritance with me.'* ¹⁴*But He said to him, 'Man, who appointed Me a judge or arbiter over you?'* ¹⁵*And He said to them, 'Beware, and be on your guard against every form of greed; for not even when one has an abundance does his life consist of his possessions.'* ¹⁶*And He told them a parable, saying, 'The land of a certain rich man was very productive.* ¹⁷*And he began reasoning to himself, saying, "What shall I do, since I have no place to store my crops?"* ¹⁸*And he said, "This is what I will do: I will tear down my barns and build larger ones, and there I will store all my grain and my goods.* ¹⁹*And I will say to my soul, 'Soul, you have many goods laid up for many years to come; take your ease, eat, drink and be merry.'"* ²⁰*But God said to him, "You fool! This very night your soul is required of you; and now who will own what you have prepared?"* ²¹*So is the man who lays up treasure for himself, and is not rich toward God.'*

If the Middle Ages, the age of monks, cathedrals, and Crusades, was an age of *faith*, ours is an age of *unbelief*. If theirs was a time of concern for the *next world*, ours is an age of concern for *this world*. If they were focused on the *soul,* we are focused on the *body.* If they were focused on the *spiritual,* we are focused on the *material.* Rarely has any era of history, if any, been as temporally minded and materialistic as ours.

We need to be aware of our materialism as we begin to look at the Parable of the Rich Fool. The warnings that Jesus gives about the dangers of wealth are particularly important for us today, a time of material abundance and physical well-being for many in the United States. The Bible in general and Jesus in particular do not condemn wealth as inherently evil. Abraham, Isaac, Jacob, Joseph, Job, and Joseph of Aramathea were all rich. But Scripture does warn us about the dangers of wealth in the strongest terms. Wealth is spiritually dangerous for both those who have it, and those who aspire to have it. For example, the Apostle Paul warns,

> *But those who want to get rich fall into temptation and a snare and many foolish and harmful desires which plunge men into ruin and destruction. For the love of money is a root of all sorts of evil, and some by longing for it have wandered away from the faith, and pierced themselves with many a pang. But flee from these things, you man of God;* (1 Tim. 6:9-11a).

The target of the parable is the 'greed' mentioned in verse 15 of our passage. No one is exempt from the temptation of greed, neither 'those who want to get rich' and are 'longing for it,' nor those who already have it.

The Context
Yet in every age there will be both those who are other-worldly and this-worldly in their outlook. We see this is the context of this parable. We read in verse 13,

> *And someone in the crowd said to Him, 'Teacher, tell my brother to divide the family inheritance with me.'*

Jesus has been teaching about deeply spiritual and eternal matters. Imagine you are there. The crowds are pressing in upon Jesus. Very few are able to get close to Him. You are one of the blessed ones who is. Jesus looks up. You've been dying to ask Him a question. He pauses ever so briefly between sentences. His eyes seem to encourage a question. This is probably your only shot. What do you ask the Great Teacher? How to invest your money? What might be the best materials of which to construct a house? Jesus was a carpenter. He would know, wouldn't He? The question of verse 13 is about that foolish. If you happened to be granted an audience with Jesus, wouldn't you be sure to ask Him about something of eternal consequence? You wouldn't waste His time and your opportunity on something merely temporal. 'Yet someone in the crowd,' some unidentified person who is obsessed with the affairs of this world, asks, 'Teacher, tell my brother to divide the family inheritance with me.' The request is abrupt. It doesn't fit the context. We might even say it is rude. The one asking ignores Jesus' teaching about God numbering the hairs on his head, and a coming day of judgment, and the ministry of the Holy Spirit (Luke 12:1-12). He changes the subject from the eternal to the mundane. The matter on his heart is his wealth. 'How many are incessantly planning and scheming about the things of time, even under the very sound of the things of eternity?' asks J. C. Ryle (I, 71). 'Tell my brother to divide the family inheritance with me,' he says. 'Christ saw this man ignoring his teaching and interested only in his personal welfare,' says Calvin, a 'too common disease,' he says, even among those who confess the gospel (II, 91). The problem, says Boice, is 'an attitude that would be so preoccupied with material possessions it would exclude spiritual concerns' (104).

There are other problems with the man's request. He doesn't ask for Jesus to evaluate his and his brother's rival claims to the inheritance. We cannot be sure if the man is making an unjust claim on his brother, or if his brother has unjustly kept him from what is his due. Marshall suggests that the younger brother wanted 'to separate off his own share of the inheritance and be independent' (522). Often heirs would live together in order to keep the inherited property intact. He may want to sell his assets and go out on his own. Either way, he is asking for a unilateral decision on his behalf. 'He does not ask Jesus to arbitrate between him and his brother, but to give a decision against his brother,' Plummer observes (322). This Jesus refuses to do:

> But He said to him, 'Man, who appointed Me a judge or arbiter over you?' (Luke 12:14).

'Man' is a 'far from cordial' form of address, Morris notes (212). Plummer calls it 'severe' (322). 'Who appointed Me a judge or arbiter?' He asks. While rabbis would often be called upon to arbitrate those sorts of disputes, Jesus is saying that this is outside the sphere of His calling. That the man from the crowd would make this request at this time shows that he is completely out of touch with Jesus' ministry and mission. He doesn't understand who Jesus is and what He has come to do. There was no shortage of judges and magistrates who could settle legal disputes. Jesus refuses to intervene, not because He is *unqualified* to do so, but because he is *not called* to do so. Moreover, 'He is opposed to the covetous desire which underlies the request for his arbitration,' says Marshall (521). Geldenhuys calls the one asking a 'materialistically-minded man' (354). His materialism warps his perspective. Jesus has a far more important mission to fulfill (Marshall, 522). He did not come to resolve disputes about matters of this world, but to open for us the door to wealth in the next world.

> And He said to them, 'Beware, and be on your guard against every form of greed;' (Luke 12:15a).

What is the man's problem? Greed. 'Beware,' Jesus says. 'Be on your guard,' He underscores. What is the dangerous 'form' of which he warns? It is *pasin*, 'all' or 'every kind' or 'every form' of *plenexia*, 'greed' or 'covetousness.' Zerwick renders it 'ruthless greed' (230). It is the consuming desire to have more and more material things. It is living as though life consists in an abundance of possessions, and therefore living as though the accumulation and enjoyment of those possessions were the meaning and purpose of life. Morris says that 'be on guard' indicates 'the taking of positive action to ward off a foe' (212). Greed will destroy the soul. It is an enemy which must be beaten back. Why? Because it diverts attention from that of which life truly consists to that which is of temporal and secondary importance. Questions of inheritance are of little consequence. But greed, when it takes root, will blow such issues out of all reasonable proportion.

We are not accustomed to this perspective. We tend to view wealth as benign at worst, and normally as positively desirable. We pursue it. We yearn for it. Jesus says it is an enemy. He explains:

> '...for not even when one has an abundance does his life consist of his possessions' (Luke 12:15b).

Zerwick renders this statement: 'Not even when it abounds to a man is his life made up of his possessions' (230). Jesus says this because it directly contradicts the outlook of most of the human race. What is the life worth living? What is the good life, the desirable life, the life longed for by countless millions? It is a life of boundless material wealth. It is the life portrayed on commercials, on TV shows, and in the movies. People love to envy the rich and famous, even while their wealth is coveted. We fantasize about their homes, furnishings, cars, clothes, and vacations. We dream of living their lives and having their things. Theirs is the life worth living. This is what we long for. Oh that I might enjoy that lifestyle! Who doesn't dream and scheme to make it so? Students pick their courses of study based on greed – how can I make the most money?! Employment decisions are driven by the bottom line. Massive debts are incurred in order to finance the dream. Why? Because the life of wealth is *the* life, the life worth living, the life that we must have.

> Jesus says, 'Life,' real life, true life, 'does not consist in the abundance of his possessions' (esv).

But if Jesus' words mean anything, they mean this – the acquisitive philosophy of life is a lie. If it were true that life consists 'in the abundance of (one's) possessions,' then greed would make sense. Get all you can. Then when you have enough, go get more. But if life does not truly consist of possessions, if this world is passing away (1 John 2:17), the philosophy that says life is about things will drive you in the wrong *direction*. It will send you down the wrong *road*. Greed is dangerous because it aims one's life in a direction contrary to the things that really matter. Wealth cannot bring happiness. It cannot extend life. Man cannot live by bread alone (Matt. 4:4). The 'fullness of joy' is known only in God's presence (Ps. 16:11). Only those who 'hunger and thirst for righteousness' are satisfied (Matt. 5:6). Jesus alone is the bread of life that can fulfill the hunger of the human soul (John 6:35). He alone is the living water that can quench our heart's thirst (John 7:37).

This is the context within which Jesus teaches the Parable of the Rich Fool. It is meant to illustrate the dangers of greed, of living as though life consisted of an 'abundance' of 'possessions.' Too many lived this way then. Even more do so now. The parable is given to explain the foolishness of this.

The Parable

> *And He told them a parable, saying, 'The land of a certain rich man was very productive. And he began reasoning to himself, saying, "What shall I do, since I have no place to store my crops?"'* (Luke 12:16, 17).

Jesus speaks of 'a certain rich man' whose land is so 'productive' that he has insufficient room to store his wealth. Jesus tells us of his presumption that he has 'many years to live' and his determination to spend those years eating, drinking, and being merry (v. 19). What can we say about this man?

First, this is a man who lives as though there is no God
He is not called an atheist. But he may as well be. I doubt that many professed *atheists* and agnostics actually are what they claim. Their numbers are relatively few. But there are many, many even professed *theists* who, like this man, may as well

be atheists. God is not a factor in their perception of life's meaning or any of life's decisions. They live as though He did not exist. So it is with the subject of the parable.

1. *He is unaware of the source of his wealth.* The 'rich man' faces a dilemma that few of us face. He is in the enviable position of having land so productive that he is unable to store all the wealth that he has obtained. This is wonderful. This is a great blessing. The question is, how did he become rich? Why is his land so productive? The Proverbs teach that it is the blessing of God that makes one rich (Prov. 10:22). The Apostle Paul asks, 'What do you have that you did not receive?' (1 Cor. 4:7). He is oblivious to the Source of his riches. *He is unaware of God's hand in his wealth.* 'What shall I do?' he asks. He could be thanking God. He could endeavor to serve God by giving some away, by doing good for others. Instead he sees it as entirely his own. His primary concern is how to hang onto it. Like so many who have wealth, his focus is on how to keep it, and his worry is that he might lose it.

Matthew Henry makes the keen observation that,

> 'The poorest beggar in the country, that did not know where to get a meal's meat, could not have said a more anxious word. Disquieting care is the common fruit of an abundance of this world, and the common fault of those that have abundance.'

2. *The 'rich fool' is unaware of any higher use of his wealth than personal consumption.* As he ponders what to do, he doesn't pray about it or seek godly counsel. He reasons 'to himself.' Instead of giving the glory to God or giving away his wealth, he determines to first hoard it, and then consume it. He betrays his self-centered outlook with his overuse of personal pronouns.

> 'And he said, "This is what **I** will do: **I** will tear down **my** barns and build larger ones, and there **I** will store all **my** grain and **my** goods"' (Luke 12:18 my emphasis).

Notice the repetition of the word 'my' – 'my crops' (v. 17), 'my barns,' 'my grain,' 'my goods,' 'my soul' (v. 18). This points to 'an ingrained selfishness,' says Morris (212). 'He is not trying to help other people. He is not even concerned to have a richer and fuller life for himself. He is concerned only with self-indulgence' (Morris, 212). He fails to see that his wealth is a gift of God, a gift of which he is a steward. The rich man presumes that his wealth is his own, and that it is at his disposal and at his beckoning.

'And I will say to my soul, "Soul, you have many goods laid up for many years to come; take your ease, eat, drink and be merry"' (Luke 12:19).

What is he to do with his wealth? Consume it. Finance his 'ease.' 'Eat, drink and be merry.'

3. *He is unaware of his mortality.* He assumes he has 'many years to come' (v. 19). 'With everything safely stored in barns he can 'relax and enjoy his wealth.' He looks forward to years of pleasure,' says Morris (212). He plans to live out his years 'reveling in worldly and material pleasures,' says Geldenhuys (355).

This is how most people live. They assume that they have time. They assume that their wealth is theirs to enjoy. They assume that their time is their own. They accumulate material things so that they might enjoy a secular version of heaven the last years of their lives. I know a couple in Miami who saved and planned for years for their retirement. The time came, and within a matter of days the husband died suddenly and unexpectedly. They assumed what they could not know.

This is not a problem just for the elderly. Youth, in particular, live as though they are immortal. During World War II, the armed services found that eighteen-year-olds made the best fighter pilots. They were markedly even better than the twenty-two-year-olds. Why? Because by twenty-two years old, young people are beginning to be aware of their mortality, whereas eighteen-year-olds are sure they will live forever. But the fact is, we don't know if we have another day, and so it is unwise to live as if we do. We could die at any instant. This brings us to our next major point.

Second, the man without God meets Reality
Jesus says,

> 'But God said to him, "You fool! This very night your soul
> is required of you; and now who will own what you have
> prepared?"' (Luke 12:20).

'You fool!' God says to the rich man. What is a fool? A fool is someone who lives contrary to reality. A builder who ignores the laws of gravity, or a farmer who ignores the seasons, or anyone who ignores the nature of things, as in the discerning of what is appropriate in a given circumstance, time or place is a fool. The greatest fool is one who ignores the greatest Reality, God. This fool has ignored two brute facts.

1. *You are mortal.* 'This very night,' is 'emphatically placed' in the text, says Marshall (524). 'Your soul is required of you.' Your life is over. Tonight. Now. There will be no second chance. There will be no more opportunities. You will stand before God and you are utterly unprepared. Why have you been wasting your time? Jesus says,

> 'Do not work for the food which perishes, but for the food which
> endures to eternal life, which the Son of Man shall give to you,
> for on Him the Father, even God, has set His seal' (John 6:27).

The man in this parable has been laboring for the 'food which perishes' while neglecting his soul and eternity. He has lived like one unaware of his mortality, and so unprepared for death. He was utterly unprepared to stand before his Maker.

2. *You are accountable.* 'This very night your soul is *required*.' This term 'may convey the idea of life as a loan which must be returned to God,' says Marshall (524). We have borrowed our lives from God. They are not ours. God loaned them to

us. Now He wants to know what we did with the lives He granted. This provides us with a window into the judgment day. How did we use what God loaned? Did we waste it? Did we consume it on ourselves? Did we live for the present? Did we put it to good use? Did we address the needs of our soul? Did we prepare for eternity?

The Rich Fool is appropriately considered foolish. 'Thou fool' is God's own verdict. Notice again the present tense, '*is* required.' Plummer finds its use 'very impressive' (325). It is required *right now*. 'The really stupid thing was the rich man's easy assurance that the future was in his control,' says Morris (213). Life is uncertain. It hangs by a thread. At any moment we might be called upon to give an account of ourselves. To live for material things and to rely on them is foolish; it is to ignore reality; it is to live contrary to the true nature of things.

> '*This very night your soul is required of you; and now who will own what you have prepared?*' (Luke 12:20b).

Jesus describes a tragedy of epic proportions. You wasted your life accumulating things, 'and now who will own what you have prepared?' You can't take it with you, as a bit of folk wisdom puts it. Since you can't, a life spent accumulating things is wasted. As Jesus asks elsewhere,

> '*For what will a man be profited, if he gains the whole world, and forfeits his soul? Or what will a man give in exchange for his soul?*' (Matt. 16:26).

The Conclusion

> '*So is the man who lays up treasure for himself, and is not rich toward God*' (Luke 12:21).

To 'lay up treasure for (one)self' is both a terrible sin, and an act of consummate folly. To 'lay up treasure' for oneself means to use wealth for the sake of indulging one's flesh, 'as if the body were the man,' says Matthew Henry. It is to accumulate wealth for the sake of now, for the present, for this world's pleasure, prestige, and power. Why is this foolish? Because we are mortal. Because one day we will give an accounting of ourselves. Because life, real life, is more than an abundance of things. Instead, Jesus says (further along in Luke 12),

'Sell your possessions and give to charity; make yourselves purses which do not wear out, an unfailing treasure in heaven, where no thief comes near, nor moth destroys. For where your treasure is, there will your heart be also' (Luke 12:33, 34).

Beware of the dangers of having wealth and pursuing wealth. The potential of worldly wealth to close heaven's doors to us is enormous. Take the threat that it poses seriously. Do not lay up treasures upon earth. Do not make the mistake of thinking that one can serve God and mammon (Matt. 6:19-24). To be 'rich toward God,' on the other hand, 'means being rich in those things which are pleasing to Him,' says Plummer (325). It is to lay up treasures in heaven. 'Rich' means 'rich through living in close communion with Him and faithfully serving Him,' says Geldenhuys (355).

We can elaborate briefly on what it means to be 'rich toward God' in two well-recognized directions.

1. *Love God* – This is the first and greatest commandment. Devote yourself to seeking God. Seek His grace and mercy and forgiveness in Christ. Pursue the worship of God, the study of God, the service of God, and live for the glory of God, all in Christ Jesus.

2. *Love your neighbor* – Live to please God by loving your neighbor. Give to your needy neighbors, care for your sick neighbors, strengthen your weak neighbors, befriend your lonely neighbors, likewise, all in Christ Jesus.

Difficult? Of course it is. But this is where the Christian life begins. To have treasure in heaven we need Christ in our hearts. We cannot do this in our own strength. I need to know that I am weak and foolish, repent of my sin, worldliness, love of things and pleasure, and look to Christ alone to save me. I need for God the Holy Spirit to dwell within my heart and transform me so that I can begin to live not for me, but to love God and my neighbor and have true riches. The Apostle Paul put it this way –

> For the love of Christ controls us, having concluded this, that one died for all, therefore all died; and He died for all, that they who live should no longer live for themselves, but for Him who died and rose again on their behalf (2 Cor. 5:14, 15).

Let us then live, 'no longer for (our)selves,' but as those controlled and enabled by the love and grace of Christ. Let us live 'for Him who died and rose again on (our) behalf.' This is what it means to be a Christian. This is how we enter the kingdom of God.

STUDY QUESTIONS

1. Historians have long characterized the Middle Ages as an era of faith, of concern for eternity and the soul. How would you characterize the present era, particularly in its outlook on the family, work, recreation, politics, and education? How does this effect the way we read the biblical text?

2. What is surprising, even abrupt, even unseemly about the question of verse 13? What is Jesus' response in verse 14?

3. What is the root problem that the parable of the Rich Fool is designed to address (v. 15)?

4. What spiritual problems do the pronouns of verse 18 reveal? His proposed use of wealth in verse 19?

5. What does the Rich Fool presume in verse 19? Can you think of instances in which you or others have made this error?

6. What is a fool? Why does God say that the Rich Fool is a fool? (v. 20)

7. What is the difference, in practical terms, between laying up 'treasure for oneself,' and being 'rich toward God?' (v. 21)

8. What do I need if I am to be rich toward God?

~ 7 ~

'THE RICH MAN AND LAZARUS'

Luke 16:19-31

Believing God's Word

[19]*'Now there was a certain rich man, and he habitually dressed in purple and fine linen, gaily living in splendor every day.* [20]*And a certain poor man named Lazarus was laid at his gate, covered with sores,* [21]*and longing to be fed with the crumbs which were falling from the rich man's table; besides, even the dogs were coming and licking his sores.* [22]*Now it came about that the poor man died and he was carried away by the angels to Abraham's bosom; and the rich man also died and was buried.* [23]*And in Hades he lifted up his eyes, being in torment, and saw Abraham far away, and Lazarus in his bosom.* [24]*And he cried out and said, "Father Abraham, have mercy on me, and send Lazarus, that he may dip the tip of his finger in water and cool off my tongue; for I am in agony in this flame."* [25]*But Abraham said, "Child, remember that during your life you received your good things, and likewise Lazarus bad things; but now he is being comforted here, and you are in agony.* [26]*And besides all this, between us and you there is a great chasm fixed, in order that those who wish to come over from here to you may not be able, and that none may cross over from there to us."* [27]*And he said, "Then I beg you, Father, that you send him to my father's house —* [28]*for I have five brothers — that he may warn them, lest they also come to this place of torment."* [29]*But Abraham said,*

"They have Moses and the Prophets; let them hear them." [30]*But he said, "No, Father Abraham, but if someone goes to them from the dead, they will repent!"* [31]*But he said to him, "If they do not listen to Moses and the Prophets, neither will they be persuaded if someone rises from the dead."'*

Have you ever wondered what happens to our conscious selves when we die? Do we cease to exist or do we live on? Do we all go to the same place or are we separated according to some standard? Is the next life pleasant for all or only for some, while for others it is unceasingly unpleasant? Before I was forty years of age, rarely did I think of death. Now I admit to thinking about it often. No passage in the Bible gives us more answers to the eternal questions than the one which is before us.

The Parable of the Rich Man and Lazarus is peculiar to Luke's gospel. It is addressed to the Pharisees to whom Jesus has been speaking since verse 15 of Luke 16. It is unique, as Ryle points out, in that 'It is the only passage of Scripture which describes the feelings of the unconverted after death' (212). Jesus takes us into the hereafter in order to give us a glimpse of the irreversible plight of the damned, as well as the blessedness of the saved. Jesus powerfully reminds us that 'our destiny in that world depends on what we do with the "here and now"' (Wilcock, 163).

It is another parable among the many lessons that Jesus taught emphasizing the dangers of wealth (e.g. 'The Rich Fool;' the 'thorny' soil in 'The Sower;' the 'Sermon on the Mount,' etc.). Jesus is not teaching that wealth must be renounced. But He does insist that it cannot be regarded as our highest good. The rich man in this parable indulged himself with fine things while he ignored any higher calling, any God-honoring use of his wealth. He should have used the treasures of this world as a means of laying up treasures in heaven. 'His riches were "his good things,"' says Plummer, 'the only good things that he knew; and when he lost them he lost everything' (390).

Jesus teaches us the certainty of judgment in the next world by contrasting 'a bad rich man and a virtuous poor man,' first in this life, then in the world to come (Morris, 252). He then underscores the sufficiency of Scripture to prepare and warn us of that judgment in the hereafter.

Certain Judgment
Our eternal condition will not be determined by our wealth or status in this world. Rather, we will be judged then by our deeds now. Jesus outlines this by contrasting the differing circumstances of a rich man and a poor man.

First, Jesus contrasts their circumstances in this world

> *'Now there was a certain rich man, and he habitually dressed in purple and fine linen, gaily living in splendor every day'* (Luke 16:19).

'Purple' was the color of royalty and of the rich in the ancient world. Only one drop of purple dye could be extracted from each shellfish murex, making collecting sufficient dye a very expensive process. The rich man's outer garment was purple and his inner garment 'fine linen,' then as now, a costly commodity. Together they stand for 'the ultimate in luxury,' says Morris (252). Jesus characterized the rich man as 'gaily living' (*euphrainomenos*) or 'living cheerfully,' or even 'feasting' (cf 12:19; 15:23, 32), 'in splendor' (*lamprōs*) or 'sumptuously' (Zerwick, 247). This was the character of his life 'every day.' Did he take time off for religion? for service of his neighbor? for charity? Apparently not. He pursued pleasure and comfort and luxury 'every day.' Is there a problem with this? Yes. The rich man, in one sense, is a very up-to-date fellow. Today we are so inundated with hedonism (the philosophy that life consists of the pursuit of pleasure) that the rich man's life sounds not just normal to us, but desirable. Many of our contemporaries advertise no higher aim. They pursue not the saving of souls, building of churches, feeding of the hungry or curing of cancer. They just want to have fun – constantly.

Yet the Bible teaches that life was given to us for higher ends than this. We were created first to know, love, and serve God. In addition, we were created to love and serve our neighbor. Instead of pursuing these higher ends, the rich man is living for pleasure. Morris notes that 'he is not said to have committed any grave sin, but he lived only for himself. In that lay his condemnation' (252). Barclay calls the rich man as described by Jesus a picture of 'indolent self-indulgence,' of 'wealthy luxury' (222). He wasn't cruel to Lazarus, lying at his gates (v. 20). He just never noticed him. He was too busy having fun. Ryle calls him 'a thoughtless, selfish worldling, dead in trespasses and sins' (I, 212). Jesus' words indicate, says Calvin, 'a very pampered life, full of luxury and display' (II, 116). Purple and linen! Life for him was fun and ostentation. He lived to be noticed, admired, and coveted by others. Geldenhuys summarizes: 'He strove after no higher purpose in life than to use his riches in selfishness and ostentation for worldly pleasure' (425).

> *'And a certain poor man named Lazarus was laid at his gate, covered with sores,'* (Luke 16:20).

On the other hand, there was Lazarus. The name 'Lazarus,' the Latinized form of Eleazor, means 'God has helped,' or 'He (whom) God helps.' His name may be significant, contrasting God's help with the absence of help from his fellow man, or perhaps it 'hints at the piety of the poor man,' as Marshall suggests (635). This is the only name given to any character in a parable of Jesus. The rich man is sometimes called 'Dives,' but that is merely the Latin for 'rich man.'

Lazarus is said to lie, perhaps even live, at the gate of the rich man's palatial home. He was 'covered with sores,' probably ulcers, indicating that he lived in both poverty and misery, and may have been unpleasant even to look at. The house has a 'gate,' which 'indicates the grandeur of the house,' says Plummer (391). It would have been 'a high ornamental gate, indicating the luxury of the rich man's dwelling,' Geldenhuys concurs (428).

'...and longing to be fed with the crumbs which were falling from the rich man's table; besides, even the dogs were coming and licking his sores' (Luke 16:21).

Further, he was constantly hungry, 'longing to be fed with the crumbs which were falling from the man's table.' Apparently those crumbs, normally eaten by the dogs, were not made available to him, his longing remaining unfulfilled.

Finally, even the wild dogs of the city aggravated his sores by licking them. Dogs were filthy, mean, and despised animals among the Jews. Think not of a cute little puppy, but a junk yard dog, a dog barely more civil than a wolf. 'Lazarus,' says Barclay, 'is the picture of helpless and abject poverty' (222).

The contrast is established. The rich man had all he wanted and lived for himself. Lazarus, living at his gates and longing for his crumbs, was ignored by the rich man, and had nothing.

Second, Jesus contrasts their circumstances in the next world

'Now it came about that the poor man died and he was carried away by the angels to Abraham's bosom;' (Luke 16:22a).

The scene now shifts abruptly to the next world. While we are told nothing directly about Lazarus' religious commitment, we are meant to understand that he was a faithful servant of God. Consequently, when he died 'he was carried away by the angels to Abraham's bosom.' Jesus paints a beautiful picture of what happens upon the death of believers. They are greeted by angels who then gently escort them, even carry them, to a blessed place. You may recall that children's game where you close your eyes and fall backward into the arms of one promising to catch you. One is fearful as one falls but immediately relieved when caught. Death is like this. We fear its approach. When we close our eyes in death we embark on a frightening journey. But God immediately comforts His children by providing an angelic escort to heaven. Jesus calls heaven 'Abraham's bosom,' an uncommon expression. Plummer says it 'is not a synonym for paradise; but to repose on Abraham's bosom is to be in paradise, for Abraham is there' (393). Participants in Middle Eastern meals would lean on their left elbows, legs outstretched away from the table, each leaning 'on the bosom of (his) neighbor, signifying being in his intimate company,' says Zerwick (248). Consequently, 'Abraham's bosom' indicates a banquet with Abraham and the whole people of God in heaven. The one whose head rested on Abraham's bosom occupied the place of greatest intimacy and of highest honor. Jesus describes Lazarus as enjoying no less. Lazarus' life in the hereafter contrasts sharply with his life on earth. He suffered dishonor and want in this world, he enjoys the highest honors and feasting among the people of God in the next.

> '...and the rich man also died and was buried. And in Hades he lifted up his eyes, being in torment, and saw Abraham far away, and Lazarus in his bosom' (Luke 16:22b-23).

No mention was made of Lazarus' burial. But the rich man was 'buried.' We are probably meant to imagine a beautiful, well-attended funeral service and an ostentatious burial site. This is the last advantage that he will hold over Lazarus. Unlike Lazarus, when he dies, he awakens in 'Hades.' Hades signifies the abode of the departed in Greek literature, but in the New Testament it is never the place of the saved. It is the equivalent of Gehenna, the place of punishment. Jesus mentions no supernatural escorts corresponding to those experienced by Lazarus. But on the basis of the parallel between the two, Jonathan Edwards and others surmised that the rich man, and all of the damned, are pounced upon by horrid demons and dragged off to hell. The rich man 'lifted up his eyes being in torment.' These are haunting words. We can imagine his shock and horror at his sudden reversal of circumstances.

Surprisingly, Jesus indicates that the saved and the damned are able to see each other and communicate (cf 13:28). He 'saw Abraham far away,' and worse yet, 'and Lazarus in his bosom.' Compounding his torment, he sees the once pitiful

Lazarus in the place of honor and bounty. How can they see each other, since they are disembodied spirits, their bodies not yet having been raised from the dead? Marshall says that 'the dead are visualized in bodily terms, since there is no other way in which they can be visualized.' However, continues Marshall, 'the story has no bearing on the question of the resurrection of the body' (637). That is a lesson for another day.

> 'And he cried out and said, "Father Abraham, have mercy on me, and send Lazarus, that he may dip the tip of his finger in water and cool off my tongue; for I am in agony in this flame"' (Luke 16:24).

The rich man apparently was a religious man. He immediately recognizes Abraham and is deferential, calling him 'Father Abraham.' He is a child of the covenant. Abraham is his father in the faith, though he despised and ignored that faith. He begs for mercy, even the smallest mercy. He not only sees but recognizes Lazarus. Lazarus had not gone unnoticed at his gates, only unhelped. 'Send Lazarus,' he says. He assumes that Lazarus is available even in eternity to do his bidding, though he had ignored Lazarus' needs in this world. 'He remains totally blind and unrepentant,' concludes Marshall (637).

Every word of the rich man underscores his pain. He longs for the slightest alleviation of his suffering. He asks merely for Lazarus to 'dip the tip of his finger in water' and let a drop of it fall on his tongue, providing some coolness, 'for I am in agony in this flame,' he says. It is hard to say what is meant to be figurative and symbolic in this parable and what is meant to be literal, since spirits do not have tongues or fingers. What is unmistakably clear is that hell is a terrible, terrible place from which its inhabitants long for the *slightest* relief for even the *briefest* moment. He doesn't ask for access to a swimming pool or a pitcher of ice water. He doesn't even ask for a cup of water. He pleads for just a drop of water on his tongue. The picture Jesus is painting is horrible in the extreme. From the gospels to the Book of

Revelation, from the 'fire (that) is not quenched' to the 'lake of fire,' hell's torments are represented by fire (Mark 9:48; Revelation 19:20; 20:10-15). As Plummer says of the rich man, 'On earth no enjoyment was too extravagant: now the most trifling is worth imploring' (394). Now he who suffered no need in this world is a tormented beggar, while the beggar in this world has no need.

Relief is not to be granted:

> 'But Abraham said, "Child, remember that during your life you received your good things, and likewise Lazarus bad things; but now he is being comforted here, and you are in agony"' (Luke 16:25).

Abraham is tender in answering the rich man, addressing him as 'child,' but firm. Yes, you are one of my physical descendants, 'my child.' Yes, you practiced a form of religion. But your superficial faith will do you no good now. He speaks of his reversal as just. In your life you had *your* 'good things' and Lazarus had 'bad things,' and you were 'comforted' then and Lazarus now. The implication is that this is as it should and must be. Morris explains:

> 'The adjective *your* is significant. He had had what he chose. He could have spent time with the things of God and delighted in the word of God. He could have engaged in almsgiving ... For him *good things* had been purple and fine linen, daily merriment and feasting ... now he must abide by his choice' (253).

Geldenhuys agrees that the implication of verse 25 is that the rich man 'had striven exclusively after worldly things and amassed nothing for heaven. So he has received all he strove after, all that he chose' (430). 'But now,' Jesus says through Abraham, things have changed. 'The balance is redressed. Justice is done,' says Morris (254). 'The judgment is thus irrevocable,' adds Marshall (638).

> 'And besides all this, between us and you there is a great chasm fixed, in order that those who wish to come over from here to

you may not be able, and that none may cross over from there to us' (Luke 16:26).

'Besides all this,' Jesus says, 'there is a great chasm fixed.' There is not just a 'chasm,' but a *'great* chasm.' And that chasm is 'fixed.' And what is that great, fixed chasm designed to do? It makes the separation between the righteous and the wicked permanent. In other words, in the next life there is no possibility of moving from one place to the other. One's eternity is fixed. The gap between Paradise and torment cannot be bridged. The separation between the blessed and the damned is permanent. The gulf between them cannot be crossed. This fact alone must compound the misery of the damned as they see the comforts of heaven, which might have been theirs, but they have foolishly forfeited them. Beyond the flames and the physical agonies of the damned, the torments of conscience will be horrible in the extreme. Every missed opportunity, every foolish decision will be relived and lamented over and over again forever. If only, if only, if only, they will say. *Eternity hinges on choices made in this life, choices that fix an irreversible destiny on the next.*

Let us now pause to summarize what we have learned from Jesus up to this point.

1. *There is a hereafter*
You will not be obliterated at death. Annihilation is not our destiny. John Gerstner used to call non-being the pagans' heaven. The pagan is happy to be annihilated upon death because it means that he can go on sinning in this world with impunity. Non-being *then* is fine with the unbelieving if it guarantees safe self-indulgence *now*. No, Jesus teaches, we will live on, passing immediately from this world to the next. As the Apostle Paul says of Christ's disciples, 'to be absent from the body' is to be 'at home with the Lord' (2 Cor. 5:8). Lazarus was escorted by angels to Abraham's banquet. The rich man 'lifted up his eyes' in the next world, 'being in torment.'

2. *There is a judgment*

What we do in this life counts forever. We will be held accountable then for what we do now. Great wealth may not be regarded as proof of God's favor, a 'sign either that God loves them *in* giving them so much, or that they love God *for* giving them so much,' says Matthew Henry. J. C. Ryle adds, 'A man's worldly condition is no test of his state in the sight of God' (212). There will be a judgment in the next world based on what we believe and do, and not on what we have. Our belief and behavior now determines how we will spend eternity, not our economic status. Jesus said elsewhere,

> 'Do not marvel at this; for an hour is coming, in which all who are in the tombs shall hear His voice, and shall come forth; those who did the good deeds to a resurrection of life, those who committed the evil deeds to a resurrection of judgment' (John 5:28, 29; cf. Matt. 16:27).

Deeds, good and evil, determine our final destiny, says Jesus. The Apostle Paul says the same thing:

> For we must all appear before the judgment seat of Christ, that each one may be recompensed for his deeds in the body, according to what he has done, whether good or bad (2 Cor. 5:10).

We are judged on the basis of 'deeds,' 'according to what (we have) done.' What separates Lazarus from the rich man? We can conclude on the basis of verses 29-31 that Lazarus believed Moses and the Prophets, repented of his sins, and so was saved. The rich man and his wealthy family members did not believe and were unrepentant. The issue of the parable, we should say again, is not wealth itself. Wealth provides an especially sharp contrast for teaching the lesson that there isn't anything in this world that may be relied upon for safe passage into the next. Do we have wealth or social status or power or intellect or charm or athletic prowess or some other gift of God? What then do we do with it? Do we see them as Scripture teaches us to see them, as gifts of God which humble us, remind us of our unworthiness of being given them, and lead us to repentance, to reliance upon a Deliverer, a Savior, a Reconciler to pardon our sin and make us right with God? And do we then use our gifts to serve and please God? The Apostle Paul says that the kindness of God is meant to lead us to repentance (Rom. 2:4).

Or, regrettably, God's gifts can fill us with pride, with contempt for lesser mortals, leading to self-indulgence and neglect of our neighbors and their needs. This is what happened in the case of the rich man. He indulged his wealth and trusted in it as a sign of divine approval. The rich man's use of his riches mattered to God. Because he trusted in his wealth, he was unbelieving and unrepentant towards God. Our lifestyle decisions and choices in this world are weighted with eternal significance. What we do now counts forever.

Similarly, there is no virtue or vice in poverty per se. Lazarus responded to his poverty not with anger, as some do, not with shaking his fist at God, but with humility and trust. He believed the Scripture. His poverty led him to repentance. His material poverty provided a metaphor for his spiritual poverty, illustrating for him his need of a Savior through whom his sins could be forgiven, through whom his spiritual poverty could be made rich, his spiritual weakness could be made strong (2 Cor. 8:9; 13:9).

Our circumstances, riches or poverty, are essentially irrelevant. After all, 'the pauper Lazarus is carried into the bosom of wealthy Abraham,' as Calvin points out (II, 119). What matters is how we respond. Does the goodness of God lead us to repentance (Rom. 2:4; Acts 14:17)? If so, that repentance will issue forth love for God and care for the poor. Do physical poverty and affliction lead to dependence upon Christ alone? How we respond counts forever. *There will be no second chances.* The parable reveals a fearsome finality. A 'chasm' is set. Change is impossible. Excuses are not even attempted. Mercy, not justice, is sought. *In the hereafter, the truth will finally be understood by all.* The unconverted in hell will finally realize their error. 'Hell is nothing more than truth known too late,' says Ryle (215). Too late! The skeptics will be skeptics no more.

Now is the time to get right with God. Shall there be a judgment according to deeds? Then we're doomed. A moment's sober reflection will show this. Our 'good deeds' are too few and not good. Like Lazarus, we will be saved only by faith and repentance. May I suggest that our inadequacy to stand before a judgment of deeds is the whole reason behind the incarnation, the life, death, and resurrection of Christ? If we could pass the final test on the basis of our own deeds, Christ need not have come. Rather, the fact that we cannot stand before that judgment is the explanation for Jesus' mission. The life and death of Jesus calls us to acknowledge our sin and our inability to save ourselves. Now is the time to repent and turn to Christ, the only Savior of the world. He saves those who cannot save themselves. Do you wish to escape the awful judgment of the rich man? Do you wish to enter the blessed eternity of Lazarus? Then recognize the poverty of your soul. Our only way of salvation is in Jesus. He is the way. He is the truth. He is the life. He is the way to the Father (John 14:6).

Way of Escape

Jesus has warned of a terrible contrast in eternity. On the one hand, there is Paradise. Upon death Lazarus is escorted by angels to 'Abraham's bosom,' that is, the place of the saved, the faithful, where banqueting and honor are enjoyed. On the other hand, there is Hades, hell. Lazarus is being 'carried away by angels' to heaven, while the rich man, we may perhaps surmise, is pounced upon and dragged into hell by horrid fiends and devils. Jesus describes the rich man as awakening in 'torment,' of describing himself as being 'in agony in this flame,' and as suffering in a place from which there is no return and no escape. If you believe what Jesus describes, you now know the most important question you have to answer in life: How does one stay out of such a horrible place, and ensure that one ends up with Lazarus at the heavenly banquet? We can focus now on verses 27-31, which tell us how: repent and believe on the basis of what God says in the Bible. The rich man ended up in hell because he did not believe God's word and repent. He lived as though it were not true. Lazarus, on the other hand, through all his suffering, and all that might discourage faith, believed.

False Claims

The complaint of inadequate warning is raised by the rich man. Seeing that there is no escape for him, the rich man (for the first time) expresses concern for others.

> *'And he said, "Then I beg you, Father, that you send him to my father's house –* (Luke 16:27).

If the 'chasm' can't be bridged, the rich man 'begs' that Abraham should send Lazarus to his 'father's house.'

> *'...for I have five brothers – that he may warn them, lest they also come to this place of torment"'* (Luke 16:28).

Notice that the rich man once again thinks that Lazarus may be dispatched on his errands. More important, he 'implies that he had not been treated fairly. If he had really been given all the information he needed, he would have acted differently,' says Morris (254). 'I am here,' he says, 'because I was not adequately warned. If I had known ...! If someone had told me! If Lazarus were to go to my brothers from the grave, they would believe and avoid this terrible judgment.' He thinks, says Plummer, that 'If God had warned him sufficiently he would have escaped this place of torment' (396). He had not had a fair chance.

Blame-shifting is the last refuge of scoundrels. When things go badly, it is easy to blame someone else. Abraham will have none of it.

> *'But Abraham said, "They have Moses and the Prophets; let them hear them"'* (Luke 16:29).

'Moses and the Prophets,' that is, the Hebrew Scriptures, were enough witness to the hereafter for the rich man and his five brothers. 'Let them hear them,' he says, as they are read in the Synagogue week by week. That is sufficient witness.

It is a myth to think that the real need of the unbelieving, or even the nominally believing, is for more information. It isn't so. They don't need stronger arguments or more convincing proof. The problem of unbelief is a problem of disposition and will. People do not believe because they will not. They choose not to believe. They refuse to believe. They don't want to believe. Moses and the Prophets were witness enough.

The rich man can't believe this:

'He said, "No, Father Abraham, but if someone goes to them from the dead, they will repent!"' (Luke 16:30).

No, the rich man insists, the problem is a lack of proof. He recognizes what he and they have failed to do and need to do: 'repent!' Why have they not? Because of insufficient witness to the truth. He knows his family doesn't take Scripture seriously. It is not authoritative for them. They've never let the Bible affect their beliefs and practices. They don't listen to its warnings. But if one were raised from the dead, then his brothers would believe, he thinks. Again, the assumption is that they would believe if there were convincing proof. The problem of unbelief is a lack of information, he insists. Abraham is firm: the Bible is all the proof they need.

The real problem for the rich man was not his riches, but his failure to believe and heed the teaching of Scripture. 'Only incidentally, we realize, does this parable deal with wealth,' says Wilcock (161-62). It could just as well have dealt with a politician and his power, or an academic with his intellect, or a preacher with his eloquence. We all have gifts and resources and exposure to the truth and opportunities for repentance and service.

But the rich man still cannot see it. He is convinced of the inadequacy of Scripture. What Scripture cannot do (convince the living of the nature of things in the hereafter), he insists someone who went to them 'from the dead' could. An eyewitness returning from the grave could convince them and lead them to 'repent.' No, he could not, Abraham insists:

'But he said to him, "If they do not listen to Moses and the Prophets, neither will they be persuaded if someone rises from the dead"' (Luke 16:31).

Don't kid yourself, Abraham tells the rich man. Moses and the Prophets provide sufficient evidence for faith and basis for repentance. Plummer points out, 'If a man (says Jesus) cannot be humane with the Old Testament in his hand and Lazarus on his doorstep, nothing – neither a visitant from the other world nor a revelation of the horrors of hell – will teach him otherwise' (254-55).

'If there were a miracle of some sort,' a skeptic thinks, 'then I'd believe.' They have in mind a voice from heaven, or a mighty work of power, a healing, or a resurrection. 'Then I'd have proof, then I'd believe,' they claim. Jesus, through the voice of Abraham, says it isn't so. It's never been so. Did Israel believe when God visited the plagues on Egypt? How about when He parted the Red Sea? No, that whole generation had to die in the wilderness. Did Israel believe when God sent fire down on Mt. Carmel (1 King 18)? How about when Elijah was taken up into heaven in a chariot of fire (2 Kings 2)? Closer to home, how about when Jesus walked on water? or fed the 5,000? or raised the dead? Were any of these mighty acts convincing? Not to those who determined not to believe. The human mind is remarkably adept at finding excuses for unbelief. Answer one objection and the ground will shift elsewhere. As Marshall says, 'Miracles will not convince those whose hearts are morally blind and unrepentant' (639). Answer the historic objections, those to the virgin birth, Noah's Ark, Jonah and the 'whale,' the resurrection, and the ground will shift to the moral. What about the problem of evil? Why would a good God allow so much suffering? Answer those objections, and the ground may shift to the religious: Why are there so many denominations? How can you say that other religions are wrong? Answer those, then the question of why the church is full of hypocrites is raised. On and on it goes. Ryle noted the same reasons for unbelief back in the nineteenth century: 'It is not more evidence that is wanted in order to make men repent, but more heart and will to make use of what they already know' (215).

Scripture is a sufficient witness to the truth of God and final reality. It is all the witness that we need. How do we know that it is true? Scripture is its own witness. It bears the stamp of divinity and truth. Those whose ears are open can hear it, those whose eyes are open can see it. It needs no external verification. Jesus put it this way: the sheep know the shepherd's voice (John 10:4). Scripture's descriptions of God, of the origins of the universe, human nature and dignity, the problem of evil, redemption, and the meaning of life, *ring true*. One Chinese convert said, 'The One who wrote that book made my heart.' Those whose hearts are open see that what it describes corresponds with reality. Moreover, they see in Jesus' words and works verification of His claims of divinity and His role as Redeemer and final judge. The Scriptures provide all the verification, all the proof that we need to avoid hell and arrive in heaven.

We cannot but see in Jesus' final words a reference to Himself. Jesus says,

'But he said to him, "If they do not listen to Moses and the Prophets, neither will they be persuaded if someone rises from the dead"' (Luke 16:31).

The rich man was no doubt thinking of Lazarus being sent from the dead. We cannot help but think of Jesus' resurrection. Those who refused to see Him as the Messiah of the Scriptures also refused to believe even when He was raised from the dead. Even His enemies, who conceded that Jesus' body was gone, refused to follow through with the implication and made up the story that it had been stolen (Matt. 28:11-13). *There can be no proof for those who are determined not to believe.*

Back to our original question – how does one ensure that one ends up on the right side of eternity? It is quite simple: believe what Scripture teaches and repent. Jesus describes the rich man still making excuses in hell for his unbelieving and unrepentant living. He wants supernatural visitations from beyond the grave to warn others. This is unnecessary, then and now. What is necessary is that we listen to the Scriptures and believe. Believe what it says when it teaches that God, the good and kind and loving God of heaven, is also a righteous God who will judge us all according to our deeds (Rom. 2:5-10). Believe what it says when it teaches that we are poisoned by evil and unfit for heaven and unwelcome in God's eternal realm. Believe what it says when it teaches that hell and flames and agony and torment await us. Believe what it says when it teaches that we must repent of our pride, selfishness, lust, hatred, cruelty, idolatry, judgmentalism, and self-righteousness. Believe what it says when it teaches that Jesus Christ is the Savior of the world. Believe what it says when it teaches that His once-for-all atoning sacrifice, forgiveness, and eternal life may be found if we will repent and believe.

Need more proof? You have Moses, the Prophets, and now the gospels and epistles as well. J. C. Ryle points out, 'If the Old Testament alone was better than a dead man's testimony, how much better must the whole Bible be' (219). Jesus says we have proof enough in the writings of Scripture. Make no mistake. You have been fairly warned. Jesus has given us a preview of life in the hereafter. He has described the terrible plight of the damned and the wonderful blessing of the saved. He has told us the key to salvation: believe God's gospel and repent. Now we have no excuses. We know all that we need to know to escape the wrath that is to come, if we but will.

STUDY QUESTIONS

1. Jesus is targeting the rich in yet another of His parables. Is he picking on the wealthy? What should we learn by Jesus' return to this theme?

2. How do verses 19-21 contrast the rich man and Lazarus?

3. As the scene shifts to the hereafter in verses 22-25, the contrasts continue. Two sharp contrasts are described. What are they and why does Jesus highlight them?

4. How does Jesus emphasize the permanence of one's eternal abode?

5. Summarize what we learn through verse 26.

6. What do the rich man's pleas in verses 27-30 teach us about his outlook, even in hell?

7. Abraham identifies the real reason for Lazarus' damnation in verses 29 and 31. What is it? What does this teach us about unbelief in every age? What happened when One was raised from the dead?

~ 8 ~

'THE PHARISEE AND THE PUBLICAN'

Luke 18:9-14

True Repentance

[9]And He also told this parable to certain ones who trusted in themselves that they were righteous, and viewed others with contempt: [10]'Two men went up into the temple to pray, one a Pharisee, and the other a tax-gatherer. [11]The Pharisee stood and was praying thus to himself, "God, I thank Thee that I am not like other people: swindlers, unjust, adulterers, or even like this tax-gatherer. [12]I fast twice a week; I pay tithes of all that I get." [13]But the tax-gatherer, standing some distance away, was even unwilling to lift up his eyes to heaven, but was beating his breast, saying, "God, be merciful to me, the sinner!" [14]I tell you, this man went down to his house justified rather than the other; for everyone who exalts himself shall be humbled, but he who humbles himself shall be exalted.'

Robert Murray McCheyne, the saintly nineteenth century Scottish Presbyterian pastor, once said,

'What a man is alone on his knees before God, that he is – and no more.'

What McCheyne meant was that the content and manner of our prayers reveal our true convictions about God, life, and eternity. Our prayers reveal our theology *lex orandi, lex credendi.* According to this ancient principle, the 'law' of faith is the 'law' of prayer. What we (truly) believe is revealed in how we pray. Moreover, our approach to prayer reveals our approach to life. We live as we pray. Our manner of addressing God reveals the theology through which we address the whole of faith and life. We may put it this way: nothing so reveals our true convictions about life and eternity as our prayer life. Am I weak? foolish? guilty? needy? dependent? grateful? eager to serve? If so, my prayer life will reflect these convictions. What I am as a Christian, I prove on my knees. We can say, for example, that those who do not pray live life as practical atheists. Non-praying folks may *say* that they believe, but their prayerlessness proves otherwise. Those who pray seldom live life as practical agnostics. Those who pray flippantly live life flippantly and worship a flippant God. Those who pray earnestly live life earnestly and believe in a serious God. We live as we pray. We pray as we believe. Why did McCheyne devote hours to prayer? Because he believed that he was weak, and foolish, and corrupt, and condemned, so he needed God's strength, wisdom, mercy, and pardon.

This connection between one's true beliefs and prayer is the unstated assumption behind the Parable of the Pharisee and the Publican. The publican is 'justified' because behind his humble prayer lies the spirit of true repentance.

The Issue

But let's first set the context. The section in Luke that stretches from 18:9–19:10 is concerned with 'the qualifications required for entry to the kingdom,' says Marshall, and 'demonstrates that entry is on the basis of divine grace and human faith, all claims of legal righteousness being rejected' (677). The immediate issue addressed by the parable is found in verse 9:

> *And He also told this parable to certain ones who trusted in themselves that they were righteous, and viewed others with contempt:* (Luke 18:9)

'This parable' contrasting two approaches to prayer attacks the cancer of self-righteousness within the religious community. He is addressing 'certain ones' who 'trusted in themselves,' says Luke, 'that they were righteous.' That is, they were putting their faith in their moral and religious accomplishments to qualify themselves for God's kingdom, or heaven. They were sure that they were able to do the things that make one acceptable to God. Their prayers reflected their spiritual pride.

So did their lives. A person who thinks that he is *that* righteous, *righteous enough for God*, will also see himself as *too righteous for others*. The traveling companion of self-righteousness is disdain for others. These self-righteous ones 'treated others with contempt,' says Luke. Why? Because those 'others' didn't, couldn't, or wouldn't measure up to their standards. Others were seen by them as weak, or fleshly minded, or self-indulgent, or undisciplined. So they were viewed with 'contempt.'

An inflated view of self is always accompanied by a deflated view of others. 'The one springs from the other,' says Calvin (II, 127). If I think I am particularly smart, then I'll tend to view others as dumb. If I think I am particularly athletic, then I'll tend to view others as uncoordinated. If I think I am particularly cool, then I'll tend to view others as uncool. If I think I am particularly rich, then I'll tend to view others as paupers. This is the propensity of human nature. In each case we'll tend to view the 'have nots' as lesser mortals, and regard them with contempt. The zealously religious and the rigorously righteous are tempted to view the irreligious and unrighteous with disdain and contempt. By the way, the reverse is the same in all the examples cited above. The non-academic, non-athletic, uncool, and unwealthy all tend to show contempt for their opposites as well. The contempt of reverse-snobbery can be as damaging as the contempt of conventional snobbery, religious and otherwise. Our beliefs directly shape both our prayers and our life. We live as we pray. We pray as we believe.

The Parable

So, Jesus attacks the problem of self-righteousness by describing in this parable the prayers of two very different men. Their prayers reveal the heart attitudes which lie behind their behaviors. He contrasts two approaches to prayer with surprising results.

> 'Two men went up into the temple to pray, one a Pharisee, and the other a tax-gatherer' (Luke 18:10).

Two men 'went up,' up to Jerusalem, up to the temple, 'to pray.' They are probably participating in the official daily prayers of the temple, which took place twice daily, in the morning and in the evening (or mid to late afternoon). One was a Pharisee, whom we would expect to see at prayer. Pharisees were famous for their religious zeal, devoting themselves to prayer, fasting, Sabbath observance, and detailed obedience to the law of God. We are not surprised to see a Pharisee at prayer. The other was a publican, a tax-collector, whom we *are* surprised to see in this setting. He is 'an unlikely candidate for religious exercises, being normally both dishonest and a betrayer of his own countrymen,' explains Morris (264).

The Pharisee

> 'The Pharisee stood and was praying thus to himself' (Luke 18:11a).

The Pharisee, Jesus said, 'stood,' and prayed. 'Standing was the normal posture for prayer,' notes Marshall (679; cf Morris, 264; etc.). But standing may also indicate a pompous attitude. He prayed 'to himself,' Jesus says, meaning privately, though it was common Jewish practice even in private to pray aloud, though quietly (cf. 1 Samuel 1:13).

First, the Pharisee's prayer highlights his moral superiority

> 'God, I thank Thee that I am not like other people: swindlers, unjust, adulterers, or even like this tax-gatherer' (Luke 18:11b).

The Pharisee gives thanks that he is not 'like other people.'
He is superior to all others, he means. 'He is in a class by
himself,' says Plummer (417). He highlights his upright
moral behavior, mentioning 'swindlers,' or 'robbers': those
who are 'unjust' or 'cheaters,' and 'adulterers.' He then
seems to look over at the 'tax gatherer,' called a 'publican'
in the King James Version, and is thankful that he is not like
him. 'The tax-collector is not worse than those just listed, but
is simply contemptible,' notes Marshall (679). The Pharisee
is a moral man. He is ethically upright. He leads a virtuous
life. He is aware of no deficiency in himself. He is certain of
God's acceptance of him. He is perhaps even confident of
a place in heaven.

Second, the Pharisee's prayer highlights his religious superiority

'I fast twice a week; I pay tithes of all that I get' (Luke 18:12).

The Pharisee commends to God not only his morality, but
his religion. He is righteous not only in what he *does not do
ethically*, but also in *what he does religiously*. He lists 'vices
from which he abstains' as well as 'pious practices in which
he engages,' explains Morris (265). He fasts twice a week,
as was the custom of good Pharisees. He tithed from all his
income. No doubt he kept a strict Sabbath as well. And of
course his presence in the temple indicates a disciplined
prayer life. Plummer says,

> 'He is superior not only in what he avoids, but in what he
> performs.' (417)

In each case the Pharisee goes beyond what the law of God
required. The law required only an annual fast, on the day of
atonement (Lev. 16:29). He fasts not weekly, but twice weekly.
Tithing was required only of some income, not of all. Yet he
tithed 'all,' as did many Pharisees (Deut. 14:22; Luke 11:42).

This all sounds good, doesn't it? The Pharisee is a very
devout man. If he were in our church he would be among
our strongest members. We would all admire his devotion

to God. No doubt someone would say of him, 'If anyone is going to get into heaven, he will.'

Before we show too much contempt for him (ironically, one of his problems) note that he does say, 'God, I thank thee that ...,' and so on (v. 11). He is thanking God, implicitly giving God the credit for his superior moral and religious life. He is not far from a legitimate prayer of thanksgiving in which he praises God for delivering him from a life of immorality and irreligion. But his prayer is deeply flawed. Matthew Henry will scarcely allow it to be classified as a prayer. He went up to pray, Henry observes, 'but forgot his errand.' The 'prayer' is more self-congratulation than prayer. What he is really doing is 'giving himself a testimonial before God,' says Barclay (232).

'The Pharisee's prayer is so laden with self-congratulations that it can hardly get off the ground, let alone wing its way to the listening ear of God' (Wilcock, 165).

Why does he pray like this? Because, as Henry describes, he 'was so full of himself and his own goodness that he thought he had need of nothing, no, not of the favor and grace of God, which, it would seem he did not think worth asking.' Morris points out that his prayer expresses 'no sense of sin nor of need nor of humble dependence on God' (265). 'I am not like other people ... or even like this tax gatherer.' 'He glances at God,' says Plummer, 'but contemplates himself' (417). His prayer is but 'a proud vainglorious ostentation of himself,' adds Henry.

He expresses no sense of sin, the commentators agree. Should we be concerned? He expresses no sense of need. Is this a problem? Indeed it is. He fails to confess his sin, or to petition for pardon, or to supplicate for grace to sustain him in his walk with God and empower him in his pursuit of holiness. What his prayer omits betrays a profound blindness to his true spiritual condition. Jesus tells us his basic sin in verse 9, and then again in verse 14. He trusts in his own righteousness (v. 9), he shows contempt for others, and he exalts himself (v. 14). The root sin is pride. His flawed prayer arises from a flawed theology. He makes what we might call the classic mistake in all of man's religion, of thinking he can rise to heaven by his own power, that he, through religion and morality, can make himself good enough for God. This, the Bible teaches, is impossible. It cannot be done. Further, because he is convinced of his own righteousness, a righteousness achieved by his own efforts, he 1) hardly prays at all, and 2) he looks with disdain on those who do not live up to his standards. Ironically, he misses the whole point of biblical religion. The religion of the Bible teaches us from cover to cover that we are lost sinners needing the mercy of God. This we must understand if we are to be forgiven. The Pharisee really does not know God or himself. Ironically, what he, the religious man, misses, the publican grasps.

The Publican

Surprisingly, the publican, not the Pharisee, demonstrates the right approach to prayer and the right outlook on life.

> 'But the tax-gatherer, standing some distance away, was even unwilling to lift up his eyes to heaven, but was beating his breast, saying, "God, be merciful to me, the sinner!"' (Luke 18:13).

By way of contrast, there is another man at prayer, a tax-collector. As noted, he would not be a respected member of the community. He was viewed as a traitor for his collaboration with the Romans, in collecting their taxes, and as corrupt, or unclean, for his associations with Gentiles and neglect of the ceremonial law. We would not expect him to pray acceptably or have a right relationship with God. But remarkably, he does.

First, the publican's prayer highlights his sense of unworthiness
Jesus describes him as 'standing some distance away,' perhaps in the outer court of the temple, says Marshall (680). This positioning of himself implies that he felt unworthy to approach any closer, humbly avoiding more worthy religious people and what Geldenhuys calls 'the holier parts of the temple' (451). Jesus says he was 'even unwilling to lift up his eyes to heaven.' 'Even unwilling' is rendered 'dare not'

117

by Marshall (680; cf. Zerwick, I, 254). He 'dare not lift up his eyes to heaven.' To 'lift up' one's eyes was a common posture in prayer: head tilted up, eyes open. This he 'dare' not do, so overcome was he by a sense of his unworthiness. He was 'beating his breast,' the heart being regarded as the 'seat of sin,' says Marshall. This act is 'one of grief or contrition,' Marshall adds (680), a 'sign of sorrow,' says Morris (265).

Second, the publican's prayer highlights his need of mercy
'God be merciful to me,' he cries. What this literally says is God be 'propitiated' (*hiláskomai*) (cf. Hebrews 2:17). God be merciful by forgiving my sin. 'Let thine anger be removed,' Morris renders it (265). He calls himself 'the sinner' (as in the original Greek), not merely 'a sinner' (as in the KJV). 'He is in a class of his own,' says Morris, even as the Pharisee saw himself to be (265). He is the sinner 'par excellence,' as Barclay understands his meaning, *the* worst sinner, worse than all the rest (233).

This humble, broken, contrite plea is commended by Jesus. The publican's prayer is not a sign of poor self-esteem on his part, or a weak self image. Today's church might be tempted to send a person with his outlook to a counselor. We'd want to beef-up his self-worth. Jesus, on the other hand, regards his outlook not merely as healthy, but accurate. The publican has correctly assessed his condition and shown appropriate, even necessary, shame and remorse. He is a sinner. He does need mercy. His prayer has it right. He knows exactly what he is and what his need is.

The key to the difference between the Pharisee and the Publican is this: the Pharisee compares himself with others, the Publican measures himself in relation to God. When we mortals evaluate ourselves relative to each other, we may look pretty good. We may seem to be moral, unlike the swindlers and adulterers. We may seem to be religious, unlike tax-collectors and others. The problem is that the human average is not the standard. God Himself is the standard. The publican grasps this. We need to grasp this today. God does not grade on the curve. His standard is absolute, and that is why we are doomed. That is why we need mercy. We are sinners needing a Savior. Knowing this, knowing God's standard and our need of mercy, is our only hope for eternal life, as Jesus goes on to show.

> 'I tell you, this man went down to his house justified rather than the other;' (Luke 18:14a).

Jesus draws a sharp contrast between the outcome of the two prayers. The tax-collector went home 'justified,' meaning according to Marshall, 'declared to be acquitted by God' (680), or 'declared as righteous,' says Morris (265), 'accounted as righteous,' says Plummer (419). This is the only place in the gospels where the concepts of propitiating (*hilaskomai*) and justifying (*dikaioō*) are brought together, as more often happens in the epistles (e.g. Rom. 3:24ff; cf Ps. 51:19). Notice the contrast: this (*outos*) man, i.e. this man despised by the Pharisee in verse 11 (*outos*), is justified. He is justified 'rather than the other' or 'contrary to the other,' or even 'and not the other' (Zerwick, I, 254). How are we to be 'justified' or made righteous, or made right with God? By recognizing our unworthiness, by surrendering all claims of righteousness and humbly crying out for mercy.

The Conclusion

> '...for everyone who exalts himself shall be humbled, but he who humbles himself shall be exalted' (Luke 18:14b).

Jesus' last clause may be considered a concluding summarizing principle. The Pharisee exalted himself and as a result was 'humbled,' rejected by God. The publican humbled himself and as a result was 'exalted,' accepted and approved by God. The difference between the two men is the difference between the humble and needy and the proud and disdainful; between the self-righteous and the self-loathing; between those who claim to be without sin and those who know their sin and can plead only for mercy. Underlying the two different approaches to prayer are two different relationships with God.

Religion and morality are good things. We should be moral. God wants us to be moral. God wants us to be religious. He commands us to pray, fast, tithe, observe the Sabbath, attend services of worship, and so on. But we are never to make the performance of these religious or moral acts the ground of our hope of heaven. When we have done all that we have been commanded, we are still 'unworthy slaves' in that 'we have done only that which we ought to have done,' says Jesus (Luke 17:10). When we truly understand ourselves and God, we will approach Him with an overwhelming sense of our unworthiness, and cry out not for what we deserve or have earned. That would bring only condemnation and death. Instead, we will cry only for mercy.

Will God hear our cry? Oh yes. The parable assures us that He will hear us. Even more so, the cross guarantees us that He will. There He 'demonstrates' His love in providing a propitiating sacrifice for lost sinners (Rom. 5:8ff.). All that He requires of us is that we acknowledge our sin, hate and forsake it, and cry out for mercy in Jesus' name. Those who so humble themselves cannot but be accepted, and cannot but be gracious in turn toward others. Why? Because they will live as they believe. How have you approached life and prayer? Has it been self-righteously and pridefully, with contempt for others? Not if you understand the gospel. A true grasp of the gospel produces the opposite: humility, poverty of spirit, and the gracious acceptance of other poor sinners, who need mercy, like we do. By true repentance, humbly prayed and humbly lived out in relationships with others, we enter the kingdom of God

STUDY QUESTIONS

1. Interact with the statement of Robert Murray McCheyne that 'What a man is alone on his knees before God, that he is – and no more.' What did he mean? Do you agree?

2. What immediate concern does the parable address (v. 9)? What does this mean?

3. What is the 'traveling companion' (as we might call it) of self-righteousness that Luke identifies (v. 9)?

4. Who are the two men at prayer? What contrast is being established (v. 14)?

5. What self-concept does the prayer of the Pharisee reveal? (vv. 11, 12)

6. What self concept does the prayer of the tax-gatherer reveal? (v. 13)

7. Why was the Publican 'justified' and the Pharisee not? What does this mean? (v. 14) How can I be justified?

> *[1]Therefore having been justified by faith, we have peace with God through our Lord Jesus Christ. [8] But God demonstrates His own love toward us, in that while we were yet sinners, Christ died for us. [9] Much more then, having now been justified by His blood, we shall be saved from the wrath of God through Him* (Rom. 5:1, 8, 9).

> *[8] For by grace you have been saved through faith; and that not of yourselves, it is the gift of God; [9] not as a result of works, that no one should boast* (Eph. 2:8, 9).

8. Back to the first question: do we pray as we believe? Do we live as we pray?

~ 9 ~

'THE HIDDEN TREASURE AND THE PEARL OF GREAT PRICE'

Matthew 13:44-46

Single-Minded Commitment

[44]'The kingdom of heaven is like a treasure hidden in the field, which a man found and hid; and from joy over it he goes and sells all that he has, and buys that field. [45]Again, the kingdom of heaven is like a merchant seeking fine pearls,[46]and upon finding one pearl of great value, he went and sold all that he had, and bought it.'

Church attendance continues to decline nearly everywhere in the Western world, as it has for the last 100 years. Nations that were once church-going, such as Great Britain, Germany, and Holland, no longer are. Even in the U.S., attendance has been down over the last decade or two. Ordinary people, it seems, have ceased to see the relevance of religion. They fail to see any value in organized Christianity. Its services and programs don't appear to be worth their time.

Setting aside for the moment the question of what institutional Christianity may have become, what can we say about the worth of the religion of Jesus? In the next two parables, Jesus likens it to objects of the greatest value, of the sort which elicit total sacrifice and commitment in order to obtain them. The message of the parables of the 'Hidden Treasure' and the 'Pearl of Great Price' (as in the language of the KJV) is the same. The two 'are a pair,' says Carson, and 'make the same general point,' though he adds, not without 'significant individual emphasis' (327, 328). They 'convey one and the same lesson,' agrees J. C. Ryle (150). That lesson is the 'superlative worth of the kingdom of heaven,' in Carson's words, (328) and the necessity of a 'whole-hearted response,' adds France (229). The kingdom of God, Jesus teaches, is *worth* all and it *requires* all.

The kingdom of God, we remind ourselves, is the rule of God. It is that place where He reigns, where His commands are obeyed, where His people are safe and secure in His protection and care for them, both in time and eternity. It is the place of salvation. One enters the kingdom through faith, whereby one is immediately justified and adopted into the family of God, and becomes a beneficiary of God's fatherly provision and protection. What is it worth to possess such privileges?

We may simplify our discussion by substituting 'salvation' for 'kingdom.' What is it worth to know that I am saved, that God is my Father, that my sins are forgiven, and that I am eternally secure? Sometimes we have to step back and ask questions like that. For a number of years now the U.S. has been developing a missile defense system. What might such a system cost? One way to answer that is to add up the numbers. It would cost 'X' hundreds of billions of dollars. Another way to answer is to add up the costs of a rogue missile actually detonating a nuclear device in one of our major cities with incalculable loss of life and property. What is it worth to avoid that catastrophe? What is the value of avoiding another terrorist attack? The answer is obvious: whatever it takes!

Likewise, what is it worth to stay out of hell? From the preceding parables, we have seen that for us to enter God's kingdom we must receive the seed of God's word into our hearts, repent of our sin, forsake our worldly wealth, and submit to the will of God. Is this difficult? Costly? Yes, it is. Is it worth it? Absolutely. Securing a place in heaven is worth everything that we have. It is worth whatever sacrifice is necessary for possession of that kingdom/salvation to be realized.

Hidden Treasure

'The kingdom of heaven is like a treasure hidden in the field, which a man found and hid; and from joy over it he goes and sells all that he has, and buys that field' (13:44).

We should remember that in the ancient world banks were uncommon. The average person did not place his valuables in a safety deposit box. Most people buried their treasures for safekeeping. In Steinbeck's *The Pearl*, the pearl diver does that very thing when he discovers a giant, magnificent pearl. This is what people have done since time immemorial. Mark Twain in *Tom Sawyer* says that all little boys dream of the possibility of finding buried treasure. Rarely does this ever happen. Tom and Huck did. But the likelihood of doing so for most people is minuscule. This underscores the exceptional joy in finding the unexpected. What has happened in this parable is rare, unusual, almost impossible. The man does what most anyone would do. He liquidates all his assets in order to buy the field and acquire the treasure. He gladly does whatever it takes.

This is the case respecting salvation. Salvation is a treasure and finding it is an exceptional blessing. To obtain it we must understand the following.

First, I must understand the exceptional value of salvation
Is the kingdom of God a treasure? Salvation depends upon my understanding that it is, otherwise I'll not buy the field. Otherwise I'll not pursue the treasure.

There would be no question of acquiring the field if gold coins, or diamonds, or oil were buried there. Worldly treasure would mean worldly wealth, luxury, and power. These are treasures for which great sacrifice is easy to understand. They result in temporal, real, space-time, this-world benefit. But for me to buy the field in which the treasure chest is 'filled' with the kingdom of God means that I must come to place supreme value on spiritual things. Do I understand the worth of my eternal soul? Do I understand the value of knowing that my sins are forgiven, that I have peace with God, that I have eternal life, that when I die I will go to heaven and not hell? Do I see the value of this? Do I understand as well the worth of a new heart, of freedom from sin, of a new life, of the indwelling of the Holy Spirit, of laws and commands that guide us through life, of a church fellowship that encourages and sustains me?

So far I have described the benefits that are ours in Christ in eternity and in time. But let me take it a step further. Beyond these external benefits there is also the fulfillment, satisfaction, and joy in knowing God *in Himself*. There is deep satisfaction in knowing and loving another human being. We get a glimpse of this in marriage. The other day my wife Emily joined me unexpectedly at a friend's house. As she walked through the door, my heart leapt. After nineteen years of marriage I can still say that I love her with a school boy's crush. Her presence is my joy. Similarly, when my children come around the corner early in the morning it is a joy to see them, to hug and hold and kiss them. There is joy and satisfaction in knowing and loving other special people. But there is no joy like that found in knowing God.

He fulfills the desires of our hearts (Ps. 37:4). He puts 'gladness' in our hearts (Ps. 4:7). He 'satisfies' us with His likeness (Ps. 17:15). His 'lovingkindness' is better than life itself (Ps. 63:3). His 'nearness' is our good (Ps. 73:25-28). The Apostle Paul speaks of the 'surpassing value' of knowing Christ (Phil. 3:8). We were made to know God. We were made to have fellowship with God. Our hearts have a 'God-shaped void,' in Pascal's famous phrasing, that God alone can fill. Our hearts are hungry, and Jesus says, 'I am the bread of life; he who comes to Me shall not hunger, and he who believes in Me shall never thirst' (John 6:35). We are thirsty and Jesus says, 'If any man is thirsty, let him come to Me and drink. He who believes in Me, as the Scripture said, "From his innermost being shall flow rivers of living water"' (John 7:37, 38). We are restless. Augustine said in his

Confessions, 'Our hearts are restless until we find our rest in Thee, O Lord.' Jesus says, 'Come unto Me all who are weary and heavy-laden, and I will give you rest' (Matt. 11:28).

Money is a treasure, we say. Things are a treasure, pleasure is a treasure, travel is, too. But entering the kingdom of God? Only when we can see the supreme worth of knowing God will we find it, and finding it will we pursue it.

Second, I must understand the exceptional opportunity for salvation

The opportunity to find treasure or to be saved is rare. It is not in any way ordinary or common. It is an exceptional event occasioned by God's special grace. It is an unexpected and unanticipated opportunity. As the man was not hunting treasure but merely happened upon it, so salvation surprises us. Look at what I have found! I have found a gracious God, and a sin-bearing Savior, and an invitation to repent, believe, and be saved. Who would have thought that I could ever have had such an opportunity? Could I, who am so unworthy? So blind? So oblivious? So corrupt? So ungifted? So ordinary? How can it be? Why should I come to have this opportunity?

We should never tire of reminding ourselves that this is the perspective of the saints in Scripture, throughout the history of the church, and in our great devotional hymns and literature. 'Who am I ... and what is my house, that Thou has brought me this far?' David asks (2 Sam. 7:18). Why would 'amazing grace' save a 'wretch like me?' John Newton asks. This is extraordinary. This 'amazing love, how can it be?' asks Charles Wesley, 'that Thou my God shouldst die for me?' 'Alas and did my Savior bleed, and did my Sovereign die? Would He devote that sacred head for such a worm as I?' inquires Isaac Watts. They are all astonished that this great treasure of salvation should be made available to them.

Third, I must understand the exceptional cost of salvation

He 'sells all that he has' and buys the field and acquires the treasure. It costs him everything. Yet he sacrifices all with 'joy.' Why? Because he understands its value. It is a treasure.

It is a rare offer to an unworthy subject. 'From joy over it,' he sells all to obtain it. He is not reluctant. He is not burdened by the cost. He is not wringing his hands. He joyfully pursues it at whatever price is necessary.

Some have raised objections to the morality of concealing the fact of the hidden treasure while buying the field. A brief review of the legal situation might be helpful. In Israel, the rule was *what is found belongs to the finder*. Find a treasure, even in the field of another, and it is yours. However, if the finder were an employee of another person, the employer could claim that the finder was acting as his agent at the time of the discovery. If the claim could be established, then the treasure belonged to the employer. This was especially the case if the employer owned the land on which the discovery was made. Consequently, it was legally safer for the finder to buy the land on which the treasure was found and thereby eliminate any ambiguity. If the finder also owned the land, 'he removed all possibility of dispute,' says Morris (359). Morris continues, 'the legal position was that the find belonged to him, but buying the field was the surest way of making his possession absolutely secure' (Morris, 359; cf. Barclay).

But beyond this, it must be kept in mind that the point of the parable is not the legality or morality of the purchase but the value of the treasure. Because Jesus comes as a 'thief in the night' doesn't mean that he endorses thievery (Matt. 24:43). Jesus uses metaphors and parables to teach truth without endorsing every point in them. The point here is that salvation is the greatest of treasures and worthy of acquisition at whatever price is necessary. It is *worth* all, and it *requires* all.

Pearl of Great Price

> *'Again, the kingdom of heaven is like a merchant seeking fine pearls,'* (13:45).

'Again' ties the parable to the preceding. The 'merchant' is a traveling merchant, a wholesaler, and so 'a substantial trader,' says France (229). A wealthy man is envisioned.

As was true of the hidden treasure, the emphasis is on the exceptional worth of what was found. It is a pearl of 'great value,' says Jesus. Unlike the previous parable, here the discoverer is actively pursuing the pearl prior to finding it. He knows its value and wants it. As in the previous parable, the emphasis is also upon the magnitude of the sacrifice that the merchant makes to obtain it. The merchant demonstrates that 'no cost is too great when it is a matter of gaining the kingdom' (Morris, 360). He is seeking 'fine pearls,' says Jesus.

> *'and upon finding one pearl of great value, he went and sold all that he had, and bought it'* (13:46).

What does he do to obtain the 'one' pearl of salvation? He sells 'all that he (has),' though he is a wealthy man and has much to lose. In other words, he too will do whatever he must do. No cost is too great. No burden is too heavy. It is *worth* all he has. It *requires* all he has. Ryle says that, 'men really convinced of the importance of salvation will give up everything to win Christ, and eternal life' (151). Carson says that the kingdom of God is 'worthy of every sacrifice,' it is 'worth much more than the price paid,' and 'worth infinitely more than the cost of discipleship.' Those who understand this 'joyfully abandon everything else to secure it' (328).

To understand this, one must comprehend that the kingdom of God is worthy in itself, as we have seen. One must also come to understand that it is good compared with other things, even other good things. This is true, whatever costs are involved.

Some time ago our little Jack Russell terrier (named 'Jack,' of course) died suddenly. We were swimming at a friend's pool when he started to act strange, and then keeled over. We hurried him home, not sure what was wrong, suspecting overheating or dehydration. Instead, the opposite was the case. His lungs had filled up with water and he had suffocated, or drowned. He died before we could get him to the vet. The Johnson household grieved for months, even years. Jack was not just a pet. He was a member of the family.

Well, his death has been the occasion of much discussion. Naturally we asked and tried to answer the question, what should we learn from this? We said a number of things –

1. God is sovereign – He has a plan.
2. God is good – His plan is a good plan.
3. God is to be trusted in everything – even when the goodness of His plan cannot be perceived.

But the main point was this – nothing in this life lasts. We must not set our affections, our dreams, our hopes on anything in this world. Everything in this world will decay and return to dust. We must not lay up treasures upon earth where moth and rust destroy and thieves break in and steal (Matt. 6:19 ff.). This world is passing away (1 John 2:17). This is why we can put the question in such absolute and categorical terms – what have you gained if you have managed to obtain *the whole world*, this whole world that is passing away, and lose your own soul, the one thing that is eternal (Matt. 16:26)? The only thing that lasts, that endures, is the knowledge of God. Only His kingdom is eternal. Therefore, if I am thinking sensibly, I will do whatever is required, and lose whatever I must to know God. When the Apostle Paul speaks of the 'surpassing value' of knowing Christ Jesus as Lord, he admits that for this privilege he had indeed 'suffered the loss of all things' but counted these things as 'rubbish' (Phil. 3:8). In other words, there was no comparison between what he got and what it cost him. He may have had to forego worldly reputation and recognition. He may no longer have been a bigshot in leadership circles in Jerusalem. He surely had to renounce the sinful pleasures of the flesh in which others seemed to indulge with impunity. He also had to suffer persecution and loss. But he says, it is as nothing. Elsewhere he says,

'For I consider that the sufferings of this present time are not worthy to be compared with the glory that is to be revealed to us' (Rom. 8:18).

These losses are as nothing. There is no comparison. They are barely worth mentioning.

What is the key? Placing supreme value on the spiritual and eternal. This is what I must perceive. God's kingdom is a treasure. Salvation is a 'pearl of great price.' For it I would gladly and joyfully relinquish everything if I might gain Christ. If I will not do that, then whether I be 4 or 40 or 84 years of age, I have failed to grasp what life is about.

There is a great irony at the center of the Christian life. Salvation is a 'gift of God' (Eph. 2:8, 9; Rom. 6:23). On the one hand, it costs us nothing. There is no prior religious or moral work that we must perform in order to receive it. There is no price that we must pay in order to secure it. We receive salvation by faith alone and apart from works. On the other hand, salvation costs us everything. We relinquish all, forsake all, commit all, believe all. We hold back nothing. We pursue salvation without regard for cost. The kingdom of God is free. But it costs us everything.

Will our contemporaries ever come to understand this? Will we? Can a world so in love with the present, so addicted to the flesh, so habituated to temporal things, ever grasp the worth of God's eternal kingdom? May God give us the grace to understand what life is about, what we are here to do and what our aim in life ought to be.

STUDY QUESTIONS

1. Why has church attendance declined in the western world over the last 100 years, and in the U.S. over the last twenty years? What have you noticed about church attendance in your own community or in your extended network of family and friends?

2. What is the kingdom of God? How does one get in?

3. What is it worth to be a part of that kingdom (i.e. to know that I am saved, that God is my Father, that my sins are forgiven, that I will enjoy unending life in heaven after death)? What is it worth to avoid hell?

4. To what does Jesus liken His kingdom in verse 44? What must one understand to obtain it?

5. What does the 'pearl of great price' (vv. 45, 46) have in common with the preceding parable? What is the main point of this parable?

~ 10 ~

'THE LABORERS IN THE VINEYARD'

Matthew 20:1-16

Receiving Free Grace

[1]'For the kingdom of heaven is like a landowner who went out early in the morning to hire laborers for his vineyard. [2]And when he had agreed with the laborers for a denarius for the day, he sent them into his vineyard. [3]And he went out about the third hour and saw others standing idle in the market place; [4]and to those he said, "You too go into the vineyard, and whatever is right I will give you." And so they went. [5]Again he went out about the sixth and the ninth hour, and did the same thing. [6]And about the eleventh hour he went out, and found others standing; and he said to them, "Why have you been standing here idle all day long?" [7]They said to him, "Because no one hired us." He said to them, "You too go into the vineyard." [8]And when evening had come, the owner of the vineyard said to his foreman, "Call the laborers and pay them their wages, beginning with the last group to the first." [9]And when those hired about the eleventh hour came, each one received a denarius. [10]And when those hired first came, they thought that they would receive more; and they also received each one a denarius. [11]And when they received it, they grumbled at the landowner, [12]saying, "These last men have worked only one hour, and you have made them equal to us who have borne the burden and the scorching heat of the day." [13]But he answered and said to one of them, "Friend, I am doing you no wrong; did you not agree

with me for a denarius? [14]Take what is yours and go your way, but I wish to give to this last man the same as to you. [15]Is it not lawful for me to do what I wish with what is my own? Or is your eye envious because I am generous?" [16]Thus the last shall be first, and the first last.'

A number of years ago a soon-to-be executed mass-murderer, guilty of particularly gruesome and abhorrent crimes, made a last-minute, jailhouse conversion to Christ. He understood that Christ died for even the worst sinners and rejoiced, along with his preacher, in the forgiveness of sins and the promise of eternal life.

More than a few Christians grumbled, 'He doesn't deserve to go to heaven.' They even said, 'He ought to fry in hell for what he did.' If we are honest, we may have to admit some sympathy for this sentiment. Perhaps most of us feel some discomfort that the mass-murderer might get off free and not suffer for his evil. Insofar as we do feel this way, we have failed to understand grace. That may be a harsh thing to say, but it is a conclusion that is hard to avoid if you take seriously the words of Jesus in our text.

The parable of the laborers in the vineyard, found only in Matthew, is bracketed by the same expression found in 19:30 and 20:16.

'But many who are first will be last; and the last, first' (Matt. 19:30).

It is likely that the parable is so bracketed because it should be understood as an explanation of the principle of reversal found in the parable. Heaven will be full of surprises. As will hell. Many whom we would expect to be numbered among the first of God's people will be last. Likewise, many whom we would expect to be numbered among the last of God's people will be first. Some whom we 'knew' would be in will be out. Others whom we 'knew' would be out will be in. 'Matthew intends this parable to underline the point he has just made,' says Morris (498). From it, says Carson, we learn *how* the last can be first and the first last – 'by free grace' (427).

The context out of which this parable arises is a question of Peter's about rewards (19:27). Jesus spoke of a future in which the disciples would rule over the twelve tribes of Israel, when losses of homes and family members would be restored a hundred-fold, and when eternal life would be inherited (Matt. 19:28-30; Mark 10:29, 30). How can this be? How can this happen, particularly when worldly appearances are so utterly contrary to expectation? The disciples are outcasts, having nothing in this world. How is it possible that they could come to have such prominence in the next world, that those who are last could come to be first? It is by God's free grace, Jesus answers. The parable teaches this.

Moreover, the parable anticipates the question, 'How can the Gentiles be received into the kingdom of God on equal terms with the Jews, who have been God's people for two thousand years?' Further, it anticipates more personal questions. How can someone converted late in life receive the same reward as one who has been serving Christ from his youth? How can the mass-murderer be treated the same as the obedient 'cradle' Christian? The answer of the parable is, 'God acts in grace toward us all' (Morris, 504). At least since Matthew Henry, commentators have noted the similarity between this parable and the Parable of the Prodigal Son (Luke 15). France says that similarity can be seen in that it is 'structured around the contrast between the one who receives (and deserves) fair treatment and the one who deserves nothing but is given everything, and the jealousy which results' (289). For both parables the answer to the question of how God distributes His gifts is to be found in His grace. None of God's gifts are earned, none are merited, none are deserved.

The Call

'For the kingdom of heaven is like a landowner who went out early in the morning to hire laborers for his vineyard' (Matt. 20:1).

Typically a farmer would go to the marketplace located in a village's central square to find workers, leaving 'early in the morning,' perhaps at 6:00 a.m., in order to get a full day's labor out of his men.

> *'And when he had agreed with the laborers for a denarius for the day, he sent them into his vineyard'* (Matt. 20:2).

A denarius was the expected pay for a day's labor. It was 'normal pay for normal work,' says Morris (500).

Apparently the landowner was eager to get his work done. Perhaps it was harvest time and he feared his crop might rot in the vineyard. So he went 'early.' At regular intervals he went back to hire additional workers, who, for whatever reason, were unavailable earlier.

> *'And he went out about the third hour and saw others standing idle in the market place; and to those he said, 'You too go into the vineyard, and whatever is right I will give you.' And so they went'* (Matt. 20:3, 4).

The 'third hour' would be at 9:00 a.m. This second batch of workers was promised to be paid 'whatever is right,' which they would have 'assumed to be the appropriate fraction of a denarius,' says France (290).

This pattern repeats itself, thereafter without the promise of remuneration. At the 'sixth hour'(noon) and the ninth hour (3:00 p.m.), he collects more workers.

> *'Again he went out about the sixth and the ninth hour, and did the same thing'* (Matt. 20:5).

At 5:00 p.m., the eleventh hour, the last hour of the working day, the landowner hires his last set of workers.

> *'And about the eleventh hour he went out, and found others standing; and he said to them, "Why have you been standing here idle all day long?" They said to him, "Because no one hired us." He said to them, "You too go into the vineyard"'* (Matt. 20:6, 7).

The kingdom of heaven is like this, Jesus says. The landowner is God. He calls workers into His vineyard to serve Him. Looking at redemptive-historical categories, the Jews came early. They began work at 6:00 a.m. The Gentiles came late. The Jews bore the burden of kingdom work alone for 2,000 years. The Gentiles joined in God's work at the 'last hour.'

Similarly, within any given era, there are those who served God early in life, and those whose call came late. John the Baptist was filled with the Holy Spirit from the womb (Luke 1:15). Timothy knew the sacred Scriptures from childhood (2 Tim. 3:15). Obadiah 'feared the Lord from (his) youth' (1 King 18:12). Then there are others for whom the pattern is different. The Apostle Paul was converted as an adult. He squandered many years as a self-righteous Pharisee (Phil. 3:5). The thief of the cross was a criminal who only came to faith in the moments before his death (Luke 23:39-43). Over the centuries there have been many who ignored the call of God in childhood, youth, as young adults, at middle-age, and only came to Christ as life was drawing to a close. The call of God comes to each of His servants at different stages in the history of redemption and at different stages in their personal lives. Jonathan Edwards grew up in a Christian home and was converted as a child. Malcolm Muggeridge was reared in an unbelieving home and was converted as an elderly adult. What is there for them? Are they to share equally in the rewards of God's kingdom?

Rewards

'And when evening had come, the owner of the vineyard said to his foreman, "Call the laborers and pay them their wages, beginning with the last group to the first"' (Matt. 20:8).

It was required in Israel that workers be paid at the end of the day (Lev. 19:13; Deut. 24:15). The landowner called his 'foreman' or 'manager' (NIV) to distribute wages, beginning with those who joined the work crew last.

'And when those hired about the eleventh hour came, each one received a denarius' (Matt. 20:9).

Surprisingly, he gives them not a fraction of a denarius, but a whole one! The landowner was generous. But this gave rise to the expectation that those who had worked the longest would receive proportionally more. They had worked perhaps twelve times as long. Might they receive twelve times as much? That might be unrealistic, but at least they would get paid more than the eleventh-hour workers! Yet this was not to be.

> *'And when those hired first came, they thought that they would receive more; and they also received each one a denarius. And when they received it, they grumbled at the landowner'* (Matt. 20:10, 11).

They are upset and they express their disappointment. They 'grumbled at the landowner,' Jesus says.

> *'These last men have worked only one hour, and you have made them equal to us who have borne the burden and the scorching heat of the day'* (Matt. 20:12).

They had worked twelve times as long, and in worse conditions. They had endured the 'burden' of the work and the 'heat of the day.' Our natural sympathy is with them. It seems to us not to be fair. This is why this parable is so important. Its genius is in its capacity to uncover our confusion about grace (to put it generously) and our self-righteousness (to put it bluntly).

The landowner states his principles,

> *'But he answered and said to one of them, "Friend, I am doing you no wrong; did you not agree with me for a denarius?"'* (Matt. 20:13).

'Friend,' he says, addressing one of them (their spokesman) with warmth. 'I am doing you no wrong' – there has been no injustice. They had a legal agreement and he kept his side of the bargain. They got exactly what they had agreed upon. Morris says, 'The fact that he chose to be generous to other people gave these men no new rights. Their discontent was due to envy, not to the overlooking of any of their rights' (503). The landowner continues,

> *'Take what is yours and go your way, but I wish to give to this last man the same as to you'* (Matt. 20:14).

Notice he says, 'I wish to *give*' – not merely to pay. You should have no objection. If you do object, consider why this might be:

> *'Is it not lawful for me to do what I wish with what is my own? Or is your eye envious because I am generous?'* (Matt. 20:15).

Is it not 'lawful,' do I not have the right to do what I wish with what is mine? If he does do what he wishes with his own wealth, and others don't like it, the problem is not with the landowner, but with the grumblers. 'Is your eye envious,' or literally 'evil,' because 'I am generous?' Bottom line: 'They were objecting to an act of sheer generosity that he had displayed toward other people,' says Morris (504). France summarizes the point in this way: God's 'generosity transcends human ideas of fairness. No one receives less than they deserve, but some far more' (289).

Still, we may find this parable unsettling. It doesn't sit right. It doesn't seem quite fair. It disturbs us. It seems to me that there are two barriers to appreciating the meaning of this parable.

First, our egalitarian bias undermines our ability to appreciate this parable. This is not a parable about wise management of labor. We may (correctly) think that it would be prudent for a manager to handle his workers differently. The parable aims instead at our understanding of God and His gifts. We assume justice requires that all gifts be distributed equally and that labor be rewarded proportionally. For us that ideal often trumps other values, such as the rights of property owners, business owners, and entrepreneurs to sell, buy, give and otherwise dispose of goods and services at agreed-upon rates. The bias against this is so strong that it is difficult for us to transcend our egalitarian philosophy and think outside of our cultural box. But the fact remains, I can sell my bag of candy or give it away as I please. If you are excluded from the circle of recipients, you should not begrudge my generosity because you were not a beneficiary. This is to be guilty of an 'evil eye.'

I have the right to give what is mine to whom I please. This is an important fact in human relations. No one owes me any part of what is his. It might be nice if he'd share it with me. But he's not obligated to do so. Politicians may wish to mandate that he do so and use the powers of the state to confiscate his wealth, and even use high-sounding words such as 'justice' and 'equality' while they do so. But the parable assumes the rightness of the principle that one has the right to dispose of what one has how one wishes. In a very real sense, it is mine to give or not give. It is mine and not yours.

This is an even more important principle in relation to God. God is not obligated to bless all, give to all, or share with all. Indeed, God is not obligated to bless, give, and share with any! If He blesses and gives to one and not another, it is His right. He 'has mercy on whom He has mercy and compassion on whom He has compassion' (Rom. 9:15). God makes distinctions. He distributes His gifts as He pleases. He owes no one anything.

> So then He has mercy on whom He desires, and He hardens whom He desires (Rom. 9:18).

God has the right to deal with us as He chooses.

> Or does not the potter have a right over the clay, to make from the same lump one vessel for honorable use, and another for common use? (Rom. 9:21).

Do you see how the Apostle refuses to allow God to be placed under obligation? Even as the potter has the right to assign honorable and less honorable uses for clay, so God has the right to dispose of us as He wishes. If he distributes gifts to one and not another, it is His right to do so.

Second, our self-righteousness undermines our ability to appreciate this parable. The same resentment that we feel against the laborers who worked only one hour carries over into our resentment of eleventh hour conversions. Imagine a very evil Ebenezer Scrooge of a man who has robbed widows and starved orphans all of his life. On his deathbed his spiritual eyes open, he sees his sin, weeps and mourns over his wickedness, cries out to God for mercy, hears of the gospel of Jesus Christ, repents, seeks forgiveness through the cross, is flooded with a sense of the grace of God in Christ, receives the assurance of reconciliation with God and eternal life, and then dies.

Do we have just the slightest sense that there is something not quite fair about this? If so, it is because we continue to think of salvation in terms of merit and reward. Even evangelical Christians, who ought to know better, fall into the trap of thinking that they somehow deserve salvation while others don't. Analyze the outlook – the eleventh hour convert who is saved –

'He doesn't deserve to go to heaven!'
Oh, and we do?

'But he was so evil.'
And we aren't?

'But he never righted his wrongs. He never made up for his evils.'
Isn't that what the cross is about? Doesn't Christ pay a debt that we owe?

'He should be punished.'
Shouldn't we?

'He deserves to pay for his evil.'
Don't we?

'His evils were so much worse.'
Does Christ suffer only for 'good' sinners?

Do you see the problem that the parable is exposing? We've begun, slowly and subtlely, to think of ourselves as deserving a place in God's kingdom which others don't. We've earned or deserve a spot which others haven't. The point of the parable is that participation in the kingdom of heaven is *all of grace*. This is true regardless of *when* one was called by Christ or from *where* one was called, whether from morally upright paganism or the depths of hedonistic depravity. All who are saved into God's kingdom, whether they are first or last, are there by God's grace. Have you believed in Christ all your life, and been in church since an infant? Or perhaps today you first walked through the door into God's kingdom? Either way, and on every point along the spectrum, we are what we are by God's grace (1 Cor. 15:10). 'By grace you have been saved through faith' (Eph. 2:8, 9). No one is superior to any one else. Many who are first will be last, the last, first.

When the mass-murderers or the Ebenezer Scrooges experience genuine death-bed conversions – if I'm thinking about this right – I will rejoice. I will know that I am no better than they. Their gross and public sins are paralleled by my hidden, but in many ways more lethal, sins of the heart. And I will give thanks for the same grace of God which saved them, has also saved me. If any of the previous parables left any ambiguity in our minds about the graciousness of the gospel, this one should resolve it. Yes, a saving response to the gospel requires total commitment, a forsaking of the world, and true repentance. But these responses of ours, and the kingdom itself, are all gifts of God's free grace.

STUDY QUESTIONS

1. A soon to be executed mass-murderer makes a last-minute jailhouse conversion to Christ. He repents of his sins and rejoices in the promise of forgiveness and eternal life. How do you respond to this?

2. Notice the verses that bracket the parable in 19:30 and 20:16. What do they indicate?

3. Laborers are hired at 6:00 a.m. (perhaps), 9:00 a.m., 12:00 noon, 3:00 p.m., and 5:00 p.m. What is the point? What do these various laborers represent? (vv. 1-7).

4. Granted that this is not a parable about wise labor management, explain the logic of the disgruntled laborers of 20:9-12. Where do our natural sympathies lie?

5. Where does the logic of the disgruntled laborers break down? What do they fail to understand? (vv. 13, 14).

6. What does Jesus, through the landowner, identify as the problem of disgruntled laborers? (v. 15).

7. What are the spiritual lessons of the parable? What obstructs our ability to grasp these lessons?

8. Back to our original question – what should be our response to a genuine deathbed conversion?

III

GROWING IN
GOD'S KINGDOM

When the seed of the gospel is planted, it grows. This is true whether considered from the perspective of the church, as a collective manifestation of the kingdom of God, or an individual human heart. The following parables describe how disciples and churches grow.

Together these six parables give particular attention to the power of the word of God in guaranteeing growth, and the certainty of the ultimate triumph of grace in the hearts of disciples and in the church collectively. But they also feature prominently the theme of ambiguity in this world. The *progress* of grace is hidden, slow, gradual. The *results* are mixed: wheat and tares, good and bad fish. But the *triumph* of grace is certain. In the end the kingdom of God is preeminent and universal. The implications of these parables for life and ministry are profound.

~ 11 ~

'THE GROWING SEED'

Mark 4:26-29

Growth through God's Word

> [26]*And He was saying, 'The kingdom of God is like a man who casts seed upon the soil;* [27]*and goes to bed at night and gets up by day, and the seed sprouts up and grows – how, he himself does not know.* [28]*The soil produces crops by itself; first the blade, then the head, then the mature grain in the head.* [29]*But when the crop permits, he immediately puts in the sickle, because the harvest has come.'*

The second half of the twentieth century saw an unprecedented interest in the principles by which the church grows. When Donald A. McGavran founded the Institute of Church Growth in Eugene, Oregon in 1959, which in 1965 became Fuller Seminary's School of Church Growth, a movement was born. The 'Church Growth Movement' has spawned thousands of articles and books, and has been exceptionally influential. Focusing on measurable results, it has constantly asked the question, what causes the church to grow? What practical steps can be taken to produce growth? What methods and techniques, what strategies and programs are most conducive to the growth of the church?

These are important questions, and answering them can be fruitful. Every church should constantly be evaluating its ministry and asking if it can't be doing things more effectively than they are currently being done. But one of the unintended consequences of this movement has been the gradual secularization of church-building. Increasingly the business of growing the church has been understood in increasingly secular ways. The same methods by which businesses and institutions grow have been applied to the church. Management and marketing principles have taken on greater and greater importance. Demographic surveys and focus groups have been used to fine-tune the method by which the gospel is presented, and even the message itself. Sometimes in the name of relating to the culture, sometimes in the name of removing what might offend, revolutionary changes have been made in the public ministry of the church, all in the name of growth. The *motives* have been noble, but many of these changes have been ill-considered. Most important, the line separating what God does and what we do, between God's sovereignty and man's responsibility, has been blurred. At times, it has seemed that the progress of the kingdom has been reduced to a natural process that can be engineered by human agents. The supernatural and spiritual character of the church has been diminished in the process.

Is the growth of the church fundamentally a work of man or a work of God? If things have gotten seriously confused, we should not be surprised. Most, if not all, of the error in the history of the church, from the ancient Arians and Pelagians, to the modern-day Schleiermacher-inspired liberals, to New England's Unitarians, has been perpetrated in the name of evangelism. Positive motives do not guarantee biblical results.

Background

The balance that we have lost today can be found in Jesus' Parable of the Growing Seed. The parable is unique to Mark's Gospel. Its theme is the growth of the kingdom of God. 'The kingdom of God is like a man who casts seed,' Jesus says. 'This is how God works out his purposes,' R. T. France paraphrases

Jesus' meaning (*Mark*, Doubleday, 38). The parable's original design was to equate Jesus' ministry with the sower, and the temporary hiddenness of the kingdom of God with the seed that lies hidden in the ground (i.e. the gospel was largely rejected in Jesus' own day) This same hidden seed offers the certainty of a fruitful harvest at the end.

The expectation then, it seems, was much like it is today. It was widely believed that when Messiah came He would establish His kingdom instantly, cataclysmically, and universally. Immediately He would vanquish the Romans, claim His throne, and rule the nations with a rod of iron (Ps. 2). In other words, quick, immediate, and extraordinary growth was expected. For many observers it seemed as though nothing were happening. If Messiah has come, where is the kingdom, they wondered? We understand their expectation. We want this kind of growth in God's kingdom today, and the leaders who can produce it. We admire those who are able to 'make things happen.' We want results, and we want them instantly.

Jesus provides the parable to explain that this is not the way it will be in the kingdom of God. New Testament scholar William Lane says,

> The parable clarifies the relationship between what was then seen of Jesus within the context of his mission and what may still be expected of him. His work was sowing; *only after a certain lapse of time will there be the gathering of the harvest* (169, my emphasis).

The kingdom is sown. Then there is a lapse of time. At the end, it is harvested. In the meantime, the time between the advents, the kingdom grows. How does it grow? In hidden ways. In mysterious ways. It grows even without human agency. It grows quietly. 'There is a hidden energy at work below the surface,' says Donald English (102). It grows by 'the sovereign initiative of God,' says Lane (170). We have our part. 'I planted, Apollo watered, *but God caused the growth*,' as the Apostle Paul says (1 Cor. 3:6). Christ builds His church (Matt. 16:18).

The Human

What is the human side of the growth of the kingdom of God? Jesus explains:

> And He was saying, 'The kingdom of God is like a man who casts seed upon the soil;' (Mark 4:26).

First, we are to sow the seed of God's word

The 'man' of verse 26 can be understood as either Jesus in His lifetime, or Jesus through His servants, after the ascension and before His return. We are to sow the seed. A few verses above in Mark's account of the Parable of the Sower, the seed is identified as God's word (4:14). That word is received through hearing (vv. 15, 16, 20).

Our responsibility, then, is to ensure that others hear the word. We are to be faithful in our public ministry to read God's word, preach God's word, echo God's word in our prayers, and sing songs that are filled with God's word. 'Faith comes by *hearing* ... the word of Christ' (Rom. 10:17). People are sanctified by the truth of God's word, Jesus said (John 17:17). Clearly evangelism, outreach, and mission are our responsibility. Consequently, our public services are to be filled with God's word. Beyond this, we are to go out into the highways and byways with the gospel (Matt. 22:9), proclaiming Christ from the street corners, in the taverns, and across our kitchen tables.

Second, we are to gather the fruit of God's kingdom

We skip to the last verse:

> 'But when the crop permits, he immediately puts in the sickle, because the harvest has come' (Mark 4:29).

When the crop is ripe, it is harvested. The 'he' of verse 29 is the same 'man' in verse 26, and 'he' of verse 27. Ultimately this person represents Jesus sowing His word, and then at the end of time using His 'sickle' to gather His people (cf. Joel 3:13; Rev. 14:15). It is also, in the meantime, His servants acting as His agents in sowing the seed and harvesting the converted into churches. We are to sow the word. Those in whom the word takes root (cf. 4:20) and bears fruit (4:28) are then to be gathered into the church. We are responsible to build biblical churches with biblical polity, biblical worship, and biblical doctrine into which believers may be baptized (Matt. 28:18ff). We are to gather saints into the churches where they can be nurtured until the day when they are finally and completely harvested (at death) or when Christ returns. The church is responsible for more than just increasing church attendance. We have not fulfilled the Great Commission until believers have been baptized into the church and been taught all that Christ commands (Matt. 28:19, 20).

It is readily apparent that the church does not play a secondary role in God's program. It is God's preliminary gathering place for His people. He has no other. Christians should not allow the church to develop a secondary role in their programs either. We keep hearing of people who claim to be disciples of Christ, and yet feel no obligation to be involved in a church. They're busy. Rarely do they come. They show no love for Christ's church, which itself is problematic. If Christ loves His church, whom He calls His bride, whom He nourishes and cherishes, and for whom He shed His blood, those who love Christ will necessarily love His bride as well. God's plan for believers does not end with the word planted in their hearts. It aims at their being harvested first into the church, and then finally on judgment day into the consummated kingdom of Christ.

The Divine

We speak imprecisely when we speak of God's part and our part, of human and divine responsibilities. There is a true sense in which everything is God's doing. Jesus said, 'I will build my church' (Matt. 16:18). There are aspects of the church's growth for which we, as enabled by the Holy Spirit, are responsible, as we've just seen. Yet there are also some aspects in which *we play no part at all*. In particular, this has to do with the growth itself. It is not our responsibility to make the seed of God's word grow, whether in individuals, or in the church as a whole. Jesus said that the man 'casts seed upon the ground,'

> 'and goes to bed at night and gets up by day, and the seed sprouts up and grows – how, he himself does not know' (Mark 4:27).

Look at what Jesus is emphasizing. Realize as we examine Jesus' words that what He emphasizes we must incorporate in our methods of growing the church.

First, Jesus emphasizes human passivity
What does the sower do after he sows the seed? He 'goes to bed.' He is responsible to sow. The seed is responsible to grow. The sower is not responsible to make the seed grow. While he sleeps, the kingdom of God grows. The sower doesn't assist it. He doesn't even understand it. How it grows, 'he himself does not know.' He can't help the process, or assist it, or encourage it, or manipulate it because he doesn't even understand it! Jesus detaches him completely from the growth of the seed itself. This is not a lesson on farming, we should note. Jesus might have said something about watering and fertilizing and weeding, that is, He might have described those things that one might do to enhance the environment for growth. He omits all that in order to focus attention on the mystery of growth. When I fly to the west coast I have one job: get on the plane. I cannot help the plane or pilot. I don't understand how it works. I just get myself on board and take a seat. Our role in growing the kingdom is to sow the word and gather the fruit. Growth is not our responsibility. 'A higher power than (man's) must do the real work,' says T. M. Lindsey (110). The sower 'goes to bed,' says Jesus, clearly emphasizing human passivity with respect to the growth of the kingdom of God.

Second, Jesus emphasizes divine sovereignty

> 'The soil produces crops by itself; first the blade, then the head, then the mature grain in the head' (Mark 4:28).

How does the earth produce its crop? 'By itself,' Jesus says. Jesus uses the word *automatē*, from which we get our word 'automatic.' It is used in Acts 12:10 of a gate opening by itself. The seed grows 'spontaneously,' Lane renders it (169). That is, God has constituted His word with inherent properties, so that of its own accord it converts the unbelieving and sanctifies the saints. 'It possesses its own power to germinate and bear fruit,' says Sinclair Ferguson (57). 'The ultimate effect is wholly independent of man's industry and care, however necessary these may be,' says Alexander (103). We sow the seed. We do so by preaching the gospel. Then God takes over and empowers that proclaimed word. That gospel itself is the 'power of God for salvation' (Rom. 1:16). The word is 'able to build' (Acts 20:32). It 'performs its work' (1 Thess. 2:13). It causes spiritual rebirth (1 Pet. 1:23-25). It is 'living and active and sharper than any two-edged sword' (Heb. 4:12). It is not a dead word. It is living and has its own dynamic. Through Jeremiah, God says,

> 'Is not My word like fire?' declares the Lord, 'and like a hammer which shatters a rock?' (Jer. 23:29).

God's word is like a fire that burns and a hammer that shatters. It does not 'return void' but accomplishes all that God has for it (Isa. 55:11 KJV). The Scriptures 'equip' us for 'every good work' (2 Tim. 3:16, 17; cf. 1 Thess. 1:5; Col. 3:6; 1 Pet. 2:2; Eph. 6:1ff). The word goes right on doing its work until the last day, when Christ harvests the fruit of His kingdom.

> 'But when the crop permits, he immediately puts in the sickle, because the harvest has come' (Mark 4:29).

Ministry Today

The emphasis that Jesus is giving to human passivity on the one side, and divine sovereignty (through the word's inherent power) on the other, has to mean something for the ministry of the church. The great German Reformer Martin Luther (1483–1546) said of his extraordinary work, 'I simply taught, preached, and wrote God's word; otherwise I did

THE PARABLES OF JESUS

nothing.' Indeed, it was 'while I slept,' he said, obviously alluding to this parable, that God reformed His church. 'I did nothing. The word did it all.'[1] This old biblical and Reformational perspective, if true, has to affect how we go about 'doing' church. We have a finite amount of time, energy, and resources. Upon what are we going to focus or concentrate? Let me elaborate.

First, the truth of the parable will lead us to concentrate on proclamation

It could hardly be more ironic that the biblical content of worship services in the last hundred years, and especially in the last twenty-five, has been drastically reduced. The word-content of public services has been reduced by those whose motive is to grow the church. This is the equivalent of removing gasoline from the gas tank of cars by those whose motive is to empower automobiles. The unchurched and various seekers are put off by Bible reading and exposition, they say. The answer to this problem for many has been to eliminate them. Sermons are no longer expositions of Scripture, but psychological, financial, career, and familial counseling. Felt needs for improved circumstances in this world are addressed. Little or no Bible is read. Seekers don't like to sing, they say, so the music ministry has been transformed into performances by professionals which the audience watches. However, the mythical seeker *does* like the rock/pop genre, so praise bands are 'in.' The biblical content of the songs has been reduced because 'unchurched Charlie' can't understand the language of Zion. Seekers are turned off by prayer, so prayer has been largely eliminated. The net biblical content of the church's public services today has been fatally reduced. What do we call services in which the Bible is not being read, preached, sung, or prayed? What can we hope will be the effect of such services in the long run? If we are born again, sanctified, and made wise by God's word, what will remain of such ministries once their gush

---

1. As quoted in Herman Hanko, *Portrait of Faithful Saints* (Reformed Free Publishing Association, n.d.). Also found in *Luther's Works*, American Edition, vol. 51, p. 77.

of popularity subsides? Despite the fact that Evangelicalism is America's largest religion (*Business Week*, May 23, 2005), having a larger share of the U.S. population (26%) than Roman Catholicism (22%) or mainline Protestantism (16%), it is far too shallow to sustain itself for long. The decline of *interest* in the Bible, *knowledge* of the Bible, and *public use* of the Bible spells catastrophe for the church's future. No, if Jesus' words mean anything, then know that we must remain faithful to our task to sow God's word.

One senses a kind of frenetic panic about growth out there in churchland. This panic betrays a lack of confidence in the word as God's appointed means of growing His church. Again (for the third time), we remind ourselves of Jesus' words: '*I will build my church*' (Matt. 16:18). Will He? How? By His word. If we believe that Jesus builds the church through His word, we will sow the word and leave the results of our sowing and harvesting up to God.

Instead, we see today widespread vulnerability to every trick and gimmick that comes down the pike promising a growth that it cannot deliver. I've been around long enough to see program after program come across my desk promising 'success' in ministry. Most of these novelties transform ministers of the word into managers of people and movements. Shortly after I arrived in Savannah I received a large packet promising eye-popping growth through a field-tested telemarketing program. Mobilize your people to telemarket the neighborhood, they urged. One silver bullet after another has followed suit, promising spiritual or numerical growth. Small groups were once the key, then discipleship groups, then a Scripture memory program, then praise choruses (74% of all U.S. churches now use 'praise and worship' songs), then the 'prayer of Jabez.' More recently we've had 'Forty Days of Purpose,' then 'the Passion of Christ.' The latter was touted by one evangelical leader as the greatest evangelistic opportunity in the history of the church. Our response should have been that faith comes by *hearing* the *word* of Christ not by *seeing* the *wounds* of Christ. We've been told that what we really need is a praise band. The praise team, in one sense, is just the bus ministry of thirty five years ago. Then it was, send out your fleet of yellow buses. This was thought to be the key to the growth so many American churches were desperate to experience. Now it's the worship team. It's the latest silver bullet. According to a recent article by Sally Morgenthaler in Fuller Seminary's *Theology, News and Notes* (Spring 2005), video clip usage has increased 625% from 1999 to 2004, with 29% of all U.S. churches using video clips at least once per month, and 21% using them once per week (vs. 4% in 1999). At the same time, actual church attendance for any given week in 2003 stood at 18% nationally, and is dropping among evangelicals (from 9.2% to 9%), mainline Protestants (from 3.9% to 3.4%), and Roman Catholics (from 7.2% to 6.2%). Still, hope springs eternal that finally, at last, *video clips* will grow the church. Or maybe not. The *Business Week* article cited above describes mega-churches offering food courts, coffee shops, athletic programs, even banking services and auto repair. They've taken a page from Wal-Mart's playbook – put it all under one roof.

Any one of the above-named items considered in isolation and in the right context might not be a concern. But taken together they represent a tendency to grasp at fads, to turn to gimmicks, to jump on the latest growth bandwagon, rather than to trust in God and His gospel.

No, God's word will build the church. How? We don't know how (v. 27). It is a mystery. It grows 'by itself' (v. 28). We don't need to manipulate the process, or distort it.

And we certainly don't need to change our message because of what a focus group says. This just in: the unchurched don't like to hear about sin, declarations about right and wrong, warnings about hell, or calls to surrender to Christ. A news flash this isn't. We are not surprised by this. Again, the *Business Week* article cited above also points out that the impact of the new methods on attendance has been negligible or negative: 'despite the megachurch surge, overall church attendance has remained fairly flat.' It then adds, 'And if anything, popular culture has become more vulgar in recent years.' In other words, for all the gimmicks and fanfare, we are not reaching more people, and those we are reaching are being influenced only superficially. A compromised gospel cannot produce change.

Second, the truth of this parable will lead us to concentrate on gathering and perfecting the church

The expansion of the mission of the church (into Day Care, athletics, fast-food, auto repair, banking) inevitably involves the corruption of the mission of the church. The church is not called or qualified to do these other things. They are distractions. They deflect our time and energy from our calling, which, put simply, is worship and witness. They consume our resources on tasks for which we are neither called nor capable. Let the church be the church. The church has a simple assignment: offer to God the public worship that He requires and desires, and bear witness to the world of His grace in Christ Jesus.

A church that believes the gospel will be content to preach and pray, and 'let the chips fall where they will,' as the saying goes. We have our responsibility – to faithfully proclaim God's word – and through the word to gather and perfect the saints. God's part is to cause the growth. When we sow, we can be sure that God's efficacious word will grow God's kingdom, and the harvest will be rich.

When I began my ministry at the Independent Presbyterian Church of Savannah on the first Sunday of 1987, I was asked, 'What are you going to do to make this church grow?' The question had in mind a description of the various programs that might be implemented to attract attention and bring in the crowds. Attendance was quite low and funds were drying up. Something, anything, needed to be done, quickly, if the church was to survive. Having thoroughly experienced and been convinced of the inherent power of the word by the ministries of John MacArthur in Southern California, and William Still of Aberdeen, Scotland (whose *Work of the Pastor* is priceless), my answer was, we will preach and we will pray. Of course we also renovated the nursery, replaced the organist, and added another minister. We are not blind to practical concerns. But we must never lose sight of that which is central and crucial. We must never lose our sense of perspective and proportion, or allow ourselves to dissipate our energies on lesser endeavors.

Let's gather the saints. Let's nurture and perfect the saints. Let's offer to God the public worship He requires and deserves. And let's leave it at that. Don't manipulate the process. Don't force results. Be patient. Trust God. He has given us more than enough to do.

Third, the truth of this parable will lead us to pray
We will ask God to do that hidden work of grace that *only He can do*. We will sow the word and then call upon God to do the supernatural work of regenerating and sanctifying sinners. Let's put it this way: if we think that we can change human hearts and grow the kingdom, then let's go ahead and do whatever it takes to produce results. Let's rework the message and make it winsome to unbelievers. Let's redesign our services to make them attractive to seekers. Let's take what is 'foolishness' to the unbeliever and make it to him seem wise (1 Cor. 1:18-25). But if it is God's work to convert and transform, then we better be less ambitious. Let's concentrate on sowing, gathering, and praying for God to make His simple, ordinary means effectual. This, after all, is exactly how the Apostles prayed. They did their work and then prayed that God would enlighten the heart, that love, knowledge, and discernment would grow, that worthy walking and fruit bearing would result (Eph. 1:16-23; Phil. 1:9-11; Col. 1:9-12).

J. C. Ryle (1816–1900), that wise old saint, once Bishop of Liverpool, summarizes the lesson of this parable admirably. It 'supplies an admirable antidote to overcarefulness and despondency,' he says. 'Our principle work is to sow the seed. That done, we may wait with faith and patience for the result' (75).

STUDY QUESTIONS

1. The 'Parable of the Growing Seed' is a parable of growth. If the church were just another secular organization (business, academic, political, etc.), on what might we focus in order to grow the church?

2. If secular models of growth are adopted by the church, what might change?

3. If the church were to significantly compromise its ministry in order to grow, what positive motives might it have for doing so?

4. What immediate problem did Jesus address through teaching this parable?

5. What is the *human* side of the growth of God's kingdom? (vv. 26, 29) What does this mean about the church?

6. What is the *divine* side of the growth of God's kingdom? (v. 27) What does this mean for the church?

7. If we have correctly understood this parable, upon what will the church concentrate?

~ 12 ~

'THE WHEAT AND THE TARES'

Matthew 13:24-30; 36-43

Mixed Growth and Opposition

[24][Jesus] presented another parable to them, saying, 'The kingdom of heaven may be compared to a man who sowed good seed in his field. [25]But while men were sleeping, his enemy came and sowed tares also among the wheat, and went away. [26]But when the wheat sprang up and bore grain, then the tares became evident also. [27]And the slaves of the landowner came and said to him, "Sir, did you not sow good seed in your field? How then does it have tares?" [28]And he said to them, "An enemy has done this!" And the slaves said to him, "Do you want us, then, to go and gather them up?" [29]But he said, "No; lest while you are gathering up the tares, you may root up the wheat with them. [30]Allow both to grow together until the harvest; and in the time of the harvest I will say to the reapers, "First gather up the tares and bind them in bundles to burn them up; but gather the wheat into my barn."'

[36]Then He left the multitudes, and went into the house. And His disciples came to Him, saying, 'Explain to us the parable of the tares of the field.' [37]And He answered and said, 'The one who sows the good seed is the Son of Man, [38]and the field is the world; and as for the good seed, these are the sons of the kingdom; and the tares are the sons of the evil one; [39]and the enemy who sowed them is the devil, and the harvest is the end

of the age; and the reapers are angels. [40]Therefore just as the tares are gathered up and burned with fire, so shall it be at the end of the age. [41]The Son of Man will send forth His angels, and they will gather out of His kingdom all stumbling blocks, and those who commit lawlessness, [42]and will cast them into the furnace of fire; in that place there shall be weeping and gnashing of teeth. [43]Then the righteous will shine forth as the sun in the kingdom of their Father. He who has ears, let him hear.'

According to popular Jewish conception, the Messiah would usher in the kingdom of God, which would establish righteousness and destroy wickedness. Evil and the enemies of Israel would be destroyed. Justice and peace would prevail.

Jesus claims to be the Messiah. He claims to usher in the kingdom of God. Yet evil continues in the world. Indeed even in the church, that place where Christ's kingdom or 'rule' has been established most comprehensively, unrighteousness continues. Just look at the scandals in the headlines. Recall your own experience of cruelty and hypocrisy from professing Christians, and perhaps even your own failing in these areas. How can these things be? The incongruity between the claims and the reality of the kingdom was as troubling to the disciples then as it is to us now.

The seven parables of Matthew 13 were designed to answer these kinds of questions. Each parable begins with the formula, 'the kingdom of heaven is like...,' which is followed with a description of the true nature of God's kingdom. The first four are primarily concerned with the theme of growth, the gradual growth of God's kingdom.

Like the others, the Parable of the Wheat and Tares tells us why the presence of the kingdom did not result in a 'cataclysmic disruption of society' and with it, 'an immediate and absolute division between the *sons of light* and the *sons of darkness*' says France (225). Jesus' audiences were eager for this separation. They wanted to see their pagan oppressors, the Romans, defeated. They were losing patience. France says,

It was to this impatience that the parable was primarily directed (225).

The parable itself is presented to the multitude. 'He presented another parable to them,' we read, the 'to them' meaning the crowd (v. 24). Hence in verse 36 we read,

> *Then He left the multitudes, and went into the house* (13:36a).

The parable was presented in public. But the explanation is reserved for the disciples in private.

> *And His disciples came to Him, saying, 'Explain to us the parable of the tares of the field'* (13:36b).

This is consistent with what we have seen in Matthew 13:10ff (the Parable of the Sower) and Matthew 13:34 (discussed in ch. 2). The parables veil the truth to the unbelieving crowds even as they reveal it to the disciples. Parables are a judgment upon the multitudes. Only the disciples are privileged to hear their expositions. The disciples differ from the multitudes chiefly in this, that they want to understand. They are not unlike people who after a great catastrophe sincerely ask, 'why does God allow all this to go on? Why doesn't He terminate all evil *right* now?' The answer of the parables is, *God's kingdom is established through gradual growth.*
  What is the kingdom of God like?

Growing
First, the kingdom of God is growing

> *He presented another parable to them, saying, 'The kingdom of heaven may be compared to a man who sowed good seed in his field'* (13:24).

This agricultural metaphor is a growth metaphor. Seed is being sown. It takes root and grows. The Sower is the 'Son of Man,' the Lord Jesus Christ. Verse 26 tells us of that point at which 'the wheat sprang up.' Eventually it is harvested.

THE PARABLES OF JESUS

Whereas the seed in the Parable of the Sower was the word of God, this time it is the 'sons of the kingdom.'

> *And He answered and said, 'The one who sows the good seed is the Son of Man, and the field is the world; and as for the good seed, these are the sons of the kingdom;'* (13:37-38a).

The theme of the growth of the kingdom is less prominent in the previous parable in Matthew (The Sower), and more prominent in the two that follow (Mustard Seed and Leaven). Still, growth is an important theme. The kingdom of heaven is compared to 'a man who sowed good seed in his field.' Sowing seed is what Jesus' mission is about. He is a sower of seed. He is growing sons of the kingdom. His 'field' is the 'world' (v. 38). Jesus is growing His kingdom all throughout the world. He is establishing His 'kingdom' or rule by sowing and growing disciples. Likewise this is what the ministry of the church is about. We are sowing and growing sons of the kingdom. We are about the business of saving sinners and sanctifying saints. Our essential tasks are witness (to the unbelieving) and worship (as the gathered people of God). Keeping these things in the forefront of our minds, we shall not stray far from our task.

Second, the kingdom of God is growing though opposed

> *'But while men were sleeping, his enemy came and sowed tares also among the wheat, and went away'* (13:25).

An 'enemy' attacks the kingdom of heaven by sowing 'tares' or weeds among the wheat. That the workers were 'sleeping' is meant to underscore not their negligence, says Carson, 'but that the enemy was stealthy and malicious' (316). 'What is referred to is not culpable napping on the job,' says Capon, but 'the normal nocturnal habits of even the most dedicated farmers' (*Kingdom*, 100). So potentially destructive was this crime of sowing tares in a neighbor's field that it was punishable by Roman law. Jesus identifies this enemy as 'the devil' (13:39). Standing behind the enemies of the church is the Enemy, the devil, Satan. He is a 'roaring lion' seeking those whom he might 'devour' (1 Pet. 5:8). He 'schemes' our destruction (2 Cor. 2:11). He hurls flaming darts in our direction (Eph. 6:16). As the Apostle Paul explains:

> Put on the full armor of God, that you may be able to stand firm against the schemes of the devil. For our struggle is not against flesh and blood, but against the rulers, against the powers, against the world forces of this darkness, against the spiritual forces of wickedness in the heavenly places (Eph. 6:11-12).

He and his dominions are opposed to the kingdom of God. His 'tares' are identified as 'the sons of the evil one' (13:38). While the devil dwells in the invisible world, he has his followers in the visible.

> '...and the field is the world; and as for the good seed, these are the sons of the kingdom; and the tares are the sons of the evil one; and the enemy who sowed them is the devil' (13:38-39a).

There is a true sense in which the 'tolerance' advocated by many of the ungodly is a façade. Supposedly the motto today is, 'live and let live.' Various religions and lifestyles are all to have 'a place at the table,' as they say. We make much of 'acceptance' these days. It is one of the prime virtues of a pluralistic society. Yet we see here that there is no tolerance for the kingdom of God. The kingdom of God faces a hostile power. That God's kingdom is opposed is not necessarily the fault of the sower, or of his workers, or of his disciples. The church can do everything right. The people of God can be perfectly kind, tactful, and gracious. Still they will be opposed. There is hostile, personal, supernatural evil that opposes and seeks to defeat and destroy the growth of Christ's kingdom.

The kingdom of God is characterized by growth and opposition. But that is not all.

Third, the kingdom of heaven is growing though it is an imperfect mixture of wheat and tares, of sons of the kingdom and sons of the evil one

> *'But when the wheat sprang up and bore grain, then the tares became evident also'* (13:26).

We note the following:

1. Initially *the wheat and tares cannot be distinguished.* Most of the commentators identify the tares with the weed darnel. Botanically close to wheat and difficult to distinguish from the tares when young, the difference between them does not become obvious until they mature. Not until the wheat 'sprang up and bore grain' could the tares be identified. 'Then (they) became evident' (v. 26). There are those who are in God's kingdom who appear to be genuine but are counterfeits. The Apostle Paul says that the devil masquerades as an 'angel of light' and his followers disguise themselves as 'servants of righteousness' (2 Cor. 11:14, 15). They appear to be the real thing. They cannot be distinguished from authentic disciples. Their evil is hidden. They are like the seed upon the rocky soil that springs up receiving the word 'with joy' (Matt. 13:20). Or they are like the seed among the thorns. In both cases the word is received and a plant grows. Yet the former is destroyed by 'affliction or persecution,' the latter is choked out by 'the worry of the world, and the deceitfulness of riches' (13:21, 22). At one stage they both were indistinguishable from the authentic. The shallow roots and the thorns were initially hidden.

The church will always have both the true and false believer in its ranks. Counterfeits will appear genuine at the beginning. They will give credible professions of faith. They may even manage to conform to the external requirements of Christian living. Their 'tarishness' will only become evident with time. Only as people bear fruit or fail to do so can they be distinguished as wheat or tares.

2. *Even when finally distinguished, the wheat and tares cannot be separated.*

> 'And the slaves of the landowner came and said to him, "Sir, did you not sow good seed in your field? How then does it have tares?" And he said to them, "An enemy has done this!" And the slaves said to him, "Do you want us, then, to go and gather them up?" But he said, "No; lest while you are gathering up the tares, you may root up the wheat with them"' (13:27-29).

If one were to attempt to separate the tares and the wheat, while 'gathering up the tares' one would 'root up the wheat with them,' Jesus explains through the landowner. The kingdom cannot be purged of its tares. The church will never be pure and cannot be made pure. The cure would kill the patient. The roots of the tares become entwined with the wheat. One cannot extract the one without destroying the other. This is not a denial of all occasions of church discipline. Jesus identifies in Matthew 18 circumstances where separation must be made. Most observers regard these as occasions of public, defiant sins. If there is no repentance, there must be excommunication (Matt. 18:15-17). But these are sins of a notorious nature whose destructive power, if left unaddressed, would be even more destructive for the church, as in 1 Corinthians 5. The Apostle Paul says there, 'remove the wicked man from among yourselves' (v. 13). Neither is it a denial that there can come a point when the church ceases to be the church, when it becomes a field of tares in which no wheat remains. What is affirmed is that the church, even at its best, will be infiltrated by the ungodly. Further, even when identifiable by their fruitlessness, these ungodly ones cannot be removed without damaging the godly. In such cases, the preference goes to preserving the godly. As Matthew Henry points out, Christ would rather permit tares than endanger wheat.

This also helps us to understand much of the evil that is done in the name of Christ. There are many tares among the wheat. They go about doing 'tarish' things. Yet the world thinks they are wheat. They appear to be so. They are in

God's field. They stand beside the wheat. Over time their tarishness becomes more evident. They have cruel tongues. They have uncrucified lusts and tempers. They are ruled by worldly ambition. They are dishonest. They are cheats. They are unfaithful. They flirt with idols. In all this they bring dishonor and disrepute to the name of Christ. Yet they cannot be weeded out. No doubt, real Christians do significant harm to the name of Christ themselves. We should not blame it all on the counterfeits. Still, this helps us to understand many of the church's problems. We do not have the capacity to separate the wheat from the tares, and as a consequence, the church, even at its best, consists of both.

Only God can see hearts. Only He can distinguish between the two. Consequently, we should not get discouraged about the ambiguous workings of God's kingdom, whether as an outside observer or an internal participant. The outsider looks at the church and its history and sees armed crusades and inquisitions and persecutions of fellow Christians and unbelievers, and discredits the whole movement. He needs to know there are tares among the wheat. The sons of the evil one flourish within the kingdom.

Similarly, the internal participant should not become disillusioned by the hypocrisy within the church, for all the same reasons. Of course there are cruel, even vicious people in the church. So many times one hears of Christian people who refuse 'to darken the door of a church' because of 'all the hypocrites' there.

Well yes, we would say, of course the church is plagued by hypocrites. The sons of the evil one are growing up with the sons of the kingdom. The wheat and tares are together. You may be sitting next to a tare. You even may be married to one! But that is not the whole story.

Progressing
Will the presence of tares prevent the church from accomplishing its mission? Certainly the tares damage the mission of the church, dissipating its energies and damaging its reputation. Yet, despite its impure condition, the kingdom is progressing. The wheat goes on growing.

> *'Allow both to grow together until the harvest; and in the time of the harvest I will say to the reapers, "First gather up the tares and bind them in bundles to burn them up; but gather the wheat into my barn"'* (13:30).

Note that though God has His enemies, He is pleased not to deal with them until later. 'Allow both to grow,' Jesus says. The church moves forward even in an imperfect state. Whenever I have studied church history, I've always come away thinking, 'How did the church survive?' Given all its travails, it's amazing that it's still here! Yet it is. And it's not just here, it's growing! The church's imperfections are disappointing to us. But ever thus it shall be. There can be no perfect church in this world. As Spurgeon said, 'If you find the perfect church, don't join it. You'll ruin it.' The church, at its best, is made up of sinners, both converted and unconverted. Yet the imperfect church continues to grow and spread and accomplish Christ's Great Commission. In spite of its imperfections, it conquers.

The church is progressing and will reach its goal. There is a 'harvest' at the end (*sunteleō*) of the age. '*Telos*' is the Greek word for 'end' or 'goal.' The kingdom is headed somewhere, and that somewhere is the 'harvest.' 'Allow them to grow,' Jesus said,

> *'until the harvest; and in the time of the harvest I will say to the reapers, "First gather up the tares and bind them in bundles to burn them up; but gather the wheat into my barn"'* (13:30b).

> *'...and the harvest is the end of the age; and the reapers are angels.'* (13:39b)

The 'harvest,' at 'the end of the age' is the consummation of all things. Jesus describes the process:

> *'Therefore just as the tares are gathered up and burned with fire, so shall it be at the end of the age. The Son of Man will send forth His angels, and they will gather out of His kingdom all stumbling blocks, and those who commit lawlessness'* (13:40-41).

'Out of His kingdom,' Jesus says, will come 'stumbling blocks and those who commit lawlessness' (*anomia*). This is a citation of Zephaniah 1:3. Notice Jesus places Himself in the role of judge.

> 'and will cast them into the furnace of fire; in that place there shall be weeping and gnashing of teeth' (13:42).

Fire is a common figure of judgment (e.g. Matt. 25:41; Rev. 20:15). We can scarcely imagine suffering more terrible than that which fire inflicts. This is not just a fire, but a 'furnace of fire,' hotter yet. The result: 'weeping and gnashing of teeth.' The terrible reality that lies behind these words is almost too horrible to contemplate. At the end of the age, separation, final separation, occurs.

The plight of the righteous is as wonderful as that of the wicked is terrible.

> 'Then the righteous will shine forth as the sun in the kingdom of their Father. He who has ears, let him hear' (13:43).

If now Christ's disciples are hidden and obscure, then they shall 'shine forth as the sun,' an allusion perhaps to Daniel 12:3.

> 'And those who have insight will shine brightly like the brightness of the expanse of heaven, and those who lead the many to righteousness, like the stars forever and ever' (Dan. 12:3).

God shall be our Father. We shall be His sons. Our bodies shall be glorified (1 Cor. 15:52-54). Indeed, He 'will transform the body of our humble state into conformity with the body of His glory, by the exertion of the power that He has even to subject all things to Himself' (Phil. 3:21). When we see Christ we shall be made like Him (1 John 3:2). Even as we were the light of the world in the present age (Matt. 5:14-16), then we shall be as the sun itself, the greatest of all the lights.

Finally, this parable is ultimately all about Jesus. He is really the point. Be warned, Jesus says. 'He who has ears, let him hear.' This is where history is moving. Do not be misled by the current hiddenness of God's kingdom. Do not be misled by the current weakness and corruption in God's kingdom. God's rule is present and growing in Christ and His church. It is headed toward the harvest. He is the Messiah. He is exactly who He says He is. You say you can't see it? Well, it takes faith. Things are not as they appear. Faith, after all, is the conviction of things that we do not see (Heb. 11:1). Your eternal destiny rests on what you decide about Him. What shall it be? Are you wheat or its counterfeit? Are you a son of the kingdom or a son of the evil one? These are the only options Jesus leaves to us. Do you recognize this? Which are you?

STUDY QUESTIONS

1. What is the primary complaint against the church voiced by those who are outside the church and unbelieving? How might those within the church address this complaint?

2. What question is this parable (and many others) designed to answer? (13:24)

3. According to this parable, what is the kingdom of God like? Find at least three characteristics.

4. What does the wheat represent? What do the tares?

5. Why cannot the wheat and tares be separated? What are the implications of their inseparability for church discipline?

6. Since the wheat and tares remain together until the end, what should we better understand and explain about the church in this age?

~ 13 ~

'THE DRAGNET'

Matthew 13:47-50

Mixed Growth and Opposition (cont.)

⁴⁷'Again, the kingdom of heaven is like a dragnet cast into the sea, and gathering fish of every kind; ⁴⁸and when it was filled, they drew it up on the beach; and they sat down, and gathered the good fish into containers, but the bad they threw away. ⁴⁹So it will be at the end of the age; the angels shall come forth, and take out the wicked from among the righteous, ⁵⁰ and will cast them into the furnace of fire; there shall be weeping and gnashing of teeth.'

Jesus tended to teach His parables in pairs. The mustard seed and leaven were paired as parables of the kingdom's growth. The hidden treasure and 'pearl of great price' were paired as parables of the kingdom's worth. The dragnet is paired with the parable of the wheat and tares (13:24-30, 36-43) as parables of the kingdom's composition. Who are the citizens of the kingdom and why? In answering this, Jesus tells us a great deal about the church's mission and experience in the present era.

Christian Mission

'Again, the kingdom of heaven is like a dragnet cast into the sea, and gathering fish of every kind;' (13:47).

173

Remember, the parables teach us about the nature of the kingdom. What is it like? We have seen parables of growth. But how does it *gather* its members?

Gathering kingdom members is like fishing with a net. It is like a 'dragnet,' Jesus says. The fishermen of the ancient world used two kinds of nets, circular hand-nets that were cast from shore, and square dragnets that were pulled between two boats or by ropes from shore. The ends of the dragnet would be brought around to form a great cone in which fish and all manner of things were caught. Jesus is providing a picture of Christian mission. What are we doing? We are dragging the net into which all manner of people are caught. 'Fish of every kind' are caught, Jesus says. This includes both the 'good' and the 'bad'. We'll look at the mixed nature of the catch in a moment, but for now we should focus on our task – to drag the net. The 'sea' is the 'world.' The fishermen are Christian witnesses. The net is the kingdom of God, especially the church. The dragging of the net and the catching of fish is Christian mission. Jesus calls us to be 'fishers of men' (Matt. 4:19). How do we do this? We can list several ways.

First, we fish through personal witness
My personal witness is based upon two factors: profession of faith in Christ (my words) and conduct (my deeds). We are surrounded by people who are as lost as they can be. I am reminded of God's description of the people of Nineveh to the reluctant and resentful Jonah – '120,000 persons who do not know the difference between their right and left hand' (Jonah 4:11). God's point – 'should I not have compassion,' i.e. should I not send a prophet (that is, you) to warn them? This parable does us the extra favor of describing the destiny of the wicked as a 'furnace of fire' where 'there shall be weeping and gnashing of teeth' (13:50). Should we not have compassion on those who don't know Christ? What about our neighbors? What about those folks at work? What about those children on the playground? Remember the truism – we are the only Bible that most people will read. We are the only gospel that most people will hear. Our words and deeds

must add up to gospel truth. 'Well I can't preach a sermon, can I?' Maybe not, but you can care about lost souls, pray for their salvation, and 'give an account of the hope that is in you' (1 Pet. 3:15). We all need to be able to tell others the irreducible minimum - I know that in Christ my sins are forgiven, and I have peace with God and peace in my heart. Christ died to take away my guilt and condemnation. I need to be able to extend the basic invitation as well – 'pray and ask God to show you the truth, pray to receive Jesus as Savior and Lord, acknowledge your sin and repent,' even, 'come to church with me.' We need to cast the net far and wide.

Second, we fish through our public services

Our regular public services are evangelistic. The gospel is preached here twice each Sunday. We have grown so accustomed to thinking of evangelism as either special evangelistic meetings ('crusades') or as personal evangelism, that we have forgotten that most people who have converted to Christ in the last 2,000 years have done so at the regular services of the church. How do I know that? Because essentially that's all there was for the first 1,700 years of the church. Even since then one could put all the converts to Christianity who have come to Christ at special evangelistic meetings in a thimble as compared to the oceans that have done so through the church, its regular ministry, and its church plants at home and abroad. Most people who have an interest in Christianity whet their appetite by going to church and seeing what's up. There they hear the praises of God sung. There they hear the Bible read and preached and hear prayers of praise, confession, thanks, and intercession which model interaction with God. Many will respond as the Apostle Paul expected an unbelieving visitor would respond to the Corinthian church nearly 2,000 years ago:

> ...he is convicted by all, he is called to account by all; the secrets of his heart are disclosed; and so he will fall on his face and worship God, declaring that God is certainly among you (1 Cor. 14:24-25).

Bring people to church. Drag the net. Invite friends. Be aggressive. Be bold. Be positive. Pray and then make things happen.

Third, we fish through Christian institutions and Christianized institutions

We remind ourselves again that the kingdom of God is bigger than the church. There is more to the kingdom than the church, though we might say with Barclay that the church is 'the instrument of God's kingdom upon earth' (II, 99). We also draw people to Christ (or catch them in our nets) by starting Christian institutions such as schools, libraries, orphanages, hospitals, soup-kitchens, crisis pregnancy centers, homes for unwed mothers, and so on. These educational and social institutions can have a magnetic effect on unbelievers. Indeed, many of these (e.g. universities, hospitals, orphanages) have not existed apart from the influence of the Christian religion. When the world sees institutions created to care for the young, for the sick, and for the downcast, some will be drawn to the religion that stands behind it.

I also mentioned Christianized institutions. There are institutions that are not Christian per se, but are run in a Christian way. If I am a businessman, a lawyer, a doctor, a salesman, a delivery man, or teacher, and I conduct my practice, business, trade, or classroom with integrity, treating people humanely, and undergirding my vocation with Christian views of law, medicine, education and so on, this too is light to the world. These institutions can be more, rather than less, conformed to the will of Christ. They too may manifest the rule of Christ in the world and draw others to Christ.

We drag the net in all these ways: personal witness, public services, Christian and Christianized institutions. We drag the net as we live consistent lives at home, in the workplace, and among our neighbors.

Kingdom Composition
This brings us to the second issue raised by the parable, that of results.

Like a net, the kingdom is filled with both good and bad. What happens when the net is dragged throughout the world and in every sphere of the world? As we saw in our previous study, that of the Wheat and the Tares, both the true and false believer will profess faith in Christ. The net catches both. 'Fish of every kind' are gathered. Verse 48 identifies 'good' fish, fish that are edible or marketable, and 'bad' fish, fish that are neither. Verse 49 equates the 'good' fish with the 'righteous,' the 'bad' fish with the 'wicked.' Both the good and bad remain in the net, the provisional or temporary manifestation of the kingdom of God, until the end. Separation does not take place until then. Carson notes,

> The kingdom embraces 'good' fish and 'bad' fish, and only the final sweep of the nets sorts them out (330).

As we saw in the 'Parable of the Wheat and the Tares,' this means that the church, Christian institutions, and Christianized institutions are a 'mixed bag' until the end of the world. There will be many who we caught up in the nets, who for one reason or another have professed faith in Christ, joined the church, put stickers on their car bumpers or business cards, who because known publicly as Christians turn out to be an embarrassment to the Christian community. They may have professed commitment to Christ as an adult and very publicly, or they may have been brought up in the church. Either way, there are those who are in the net, who have been drawn out of the sea (world), but who are hypocrites. They are not real Christians. They treat people badly. They cheat in their marriages. They are dishonest in business. They have a bad reputation all over town. And they seem to get away with it. They never get caught publicly or legally. What can be done? Nothing. Not in this era. There is garbage in the nets. There are bad fish among the good. They stink. They are rotten. They are unclean. But the church is stuck with them. Only God can sort this out, and He does not do so until the end. Again, as we saw in the Parable of the Wheat and Tares, this is not an excuse for neglecting church discipline. Jesus is not nullifying His own words in

Matthew 18. Overt, public, known evil is to be removed from the church through its discipline (e.g. 1 Cor. 5). But church discipline will never completely purify the church. Much will remain intractable.

In the meantime, the church pays a price. Untold damage is done to the cause of Christ. The reputation of the Christian religion is soiled by its hypocrites. This happens in two ways.

1. *Unbelievers are provided with excuses for not believing.* The old, 'they are all hypocrites' excuse is indulged. Christianity is discredited.

2. *Some believers are disillusioned.* They may have utopian expectations for the church. The church is supposed to be x, y, z, they say. It's not. They leave the church, disillusioned and disheartened. This parable is designed, at least in part, to prevent naïve expectations. The church is made up of wheat and tares, of good and bad fish that get caught in our nets. This means that we will encounter people in the church halls who are gossips and unkind. As we travel around town someone may come to one of us and ask, 'Isn't so and so an officer in your church?' They ask because they are amazed or appalled by the way Mr. So and So runs his business, or leaves bills unpaid, or neglects his children, or breaks his marriage vows. Mr. So and So, his personal witness, his Christianized business, and the various Christian institutions in which he is involved are all discredited by his conduct. Unbelievers scoff. Believers leave. Jesus says, 'I warned you.' There are bad apples in the barrel, rotten eggs in the basket.

Final Reckoning

Among the things that are most annoying for some Christians is the idea that some people are getting away with these sorts of things. They aren't caught. They aren't punished. They seem to enjoy the fruit of their hypocrisy. This is where the second half of the parable comes in.

'Again, the kingdom of heaven is like a dragnet cast into the sea, and gathering fish of every kind; and when it was filled,

they drew it up on the beach; and they sat down, and gathered the good fish into containers, but the bad they threw away' (13:47, 48).

When the net is dragged to shore, the fish are separated, the good from the bad. The meaning?

'So it will be at the end of the age; the angels shall come forth, and take out the wicked from among the righteous, and will cast them into the furnace of fire; there shall be weeping and gnashing of teeth' (13:49, 50).

In the end, the wicked are separated from the righteous by God's angels. These verses are nearly identical to verses 41-42, proving that the essential message of the parables of the Dragnet and the Wheat and the Tares is the same. Apparently, our understanding that the church is a mixed multitude is so important that Jesus taught it in two parables, so that we would never be surprised or become disillusioned. He assures us that it is so, and that He will certainly sort it out in the end. So, be relieved, be assured, be aware. Morris defined the wicked as those who, 'lived evil lives and have not repented and sought divine forgiveness' (361). The righteous he defines as 'those who are accepted by God, those who are adjudged as in the right when they are judged before the divine tribunal' (361). Morris is careful to refute the notion that the righteous are deemed such on the basis of their own ethical virtues and efforts. Those blessed of God are 'poor in spirit' and 'mourn' their sins (Matt. 5:3 ff.). They 'realize their own shortcomings and rely on God's mercy,' says Morris (362).

In the end, it all gets sorted out. The wicked are taken out from among the righteous and cast into a terrible place, a 'furnace of fire,' a place of 'weeping and gnashing of teeth.' Conversely, the righteous are blessed. All this is to say that one can fool people, but not God. He knows the truth about us. Since we can be self-deceived, we can say that He knows us better than we know ourselves. One can be in the kingdom, the field, and yet be a tare. One can be in the kingdom, the net, and yet be a bad fish. Here's what we can count on – our church is full of both! But what is imperfect and corrupt now will be perfected by that final separation and the fires of judgment.

Seeing these things are so, what sort of people ought we to be? We ought to be urgent, diligent about ensuring that we are among the righteous and not among the wicked. How can we be sure? Only by receiving the righteousness of Christ by faith. The gospel promises Christ's righteousness by faith to those who believe (Rom. 1:17; 3:21ff; 9:30; 10:5). Our only hope is to be 'found in Him,' as the Apostle Paul puts it,

> not having a righteousness of my own derived from the Law, but that which is through faith in Christ, the righteousness which comes from God on the basis of faith (Phil. 3:9).

So then, let us cast the net. Let us work the fields. Let us grow the kingdom. Let us build the church. The result will be a 'mixed bag.' But this is how the kingdom grows in this era.

Study Questions

1. Some of the parables seem to come in pairs. Which can you remember? With which might one pair the Dragnet?

2. According to the Parable of the Dragnet, to what may the gathering of the members of God's Kingdom be likened?

3. Define each element in the Parable:

   a. Sea –

   b. Net –

   c. Fisherman –

   d. Dragnet fishing –

   e. Separating good fish from bad fish –

4. Apply the parable: how do we cast the net in each of these realms? Be specific.

   a. Personal witness –

   b. Public Services of worship –

    c. Christian institutions –

    d. 'Christianized' institutions (institutions which are not Christian per se but can be run in a Christian way) –

5. The second issue raised by the parable is that of kingdom composition. What is gathered when the gospel net is dragged throughout the world?

6. When does the final separation of the wicked and righteous take place? Apply this to the following:

    a. Church discipline (cf. Matt. 18:15-18; 1 Cor. 5) –

    b. Imperfect churches –

    c. Christians who disappoint us –

7. Why does Jesus use such strong language to describe the end of the wicked (13:50)?

8. How can we know that we are among the righteous who will not be cast 'into the furnace of fire'? (v. 50).

~ 14 ~

'THE MUSTARD SEED AND LEAVEN'

Matthew 13:31-33

Small Beginnings, Irrepressible Growth

[31]*He presented another parable to them, saying, 'The kingdom of heaven is like a mustard seed, which a man took and sowed in his field;* [32]*and this is smaller than all other seeds; but when it is full grown, it is larger than the garden plants, and becomes a tree, so that the birds of the air come and nest in its branches.'* [33]*He spoke another parable to them, 'The kingdom of heaven is like leaven, which a woman took, and hid in three pecks of meal, until it was all leavened' (cf. Mark 4:30-32; Luke 13:18-21).*

We have noted that throughout the gospels the 'kingdom' of God means the 'rule' of God. His kingdom is present wherever His rule is established, whether in one human heart, in a family, in a nation, or, as it will be one day, throughout the world!

As we have seen, Jesus claims to be the Messiah. He announces the presence of the kingdom of God (Matt. 4:17). But this raises the simple questions – Where is His kingdom? Is He the Son of God? Does He have all power in heaven and earth? Then where is His rule? Where is His dominion over the nations? Over families? Where is His victory over evil in even *one* human heart, much less the whole world?

Perhaps I can illustrate from my own experience what a problem this can be. When I was in college I was discouraged mainly by two struggles, which I thought surely were incongruous with what the Bible would lead us to believe.

One was a struggle with *personal* holiness. I was an enthusiastic, hungry Christian. But I wrestled with sin. I was surrounded by energetic, bold, outgoing Christians whose strong qualities left me with feelings of inferiority. I did not read my Bible as I should, or pray as I should. Worse yet I was plagued by sinful attitudes that I couldn't shake. I felt like a total failure and couldn't understand why there wasn't an easier cure. I was not what I wanted to be and I couldn't understand why God couldn't or wouldn't help me more.

The second struggle was the fact that the Christian movement on campus was not what I thought it should be. We had a strong Christian fellowship of 90-120, but on a campus of 13,000! In dorms, on athletic teams, in fraternities, in classrooms, and wherever we went, we were a tiny minority. Why were we so few? If we had the truth, why were the vast majority unpersuaded?

These are the kinds of questions that Jesus answers through the parables of the kingdom. 'The kingdom of God is like,' He says, as He introduces the parables of the Mustard Seed, Leaven, Hidden Treasure, Pearl of Great Price, and Dragnet (Matt. 13:31-52). The kingdom is present in Jesus' ministry. But it did not resemble at all what the disciples were anticipating. They were expecting the Messiah to come in power, subdue Israel's enemies, and establish in Jerusalem a kingdom that would encompass the whole world. They anticipated an immediate and perfected kingdom. Instead they remained on the fringes of society; small, despised, poor, weak. So Jesus is answering questions that arise from what Lane calls the 'enigmatic present manifestation of the kingdom,' (*Mark*, 171). How are we to understand the weakness and smallness of Christ's rule at the present in our hearts and in our world in light of its promised future prominence? These parables of growth are answering this for us.

The Growth of God's Kingdom

To understand the discrepancy between the kingdom's present condition and future greatness, we must understand the nature of its growth.

First, the kingdom of God begins small

> *He presented another parable to them, saying, 'The kingdom of heaven is like mustard seed, which a man took and sowed in his field; and this is smaller than all other seeds; but when it is full grown, it is larger than the garden plants, and becomes a tree, so that the birds of the air come and nest in its branches'* (13:31, 32).

Jesus tells us two things about the mustard seed in this parable. First, the mustard seed 'is smaller than all other seeds.' Second, when 'full grown' it is 'larger than the garden plants.' The point, says France,

> 'lies in the contrast between this insignificant beginning and the *greatest of shrubs* which results' (227).

The mustard seed itself was not literally the smallest seed. There were and are smaller ones. But it was 'proverbially small,' as all the commentators point out. The seeds represent 'unimpressive beginnings' (France, 227), or the 'smallest beginnings' (Barclay, *Matthew*, 85). They are 'a metaphor emphasizing the kingdom's tiny beginning,' says Carson (318).

The same point is emphasized in the parable of the leaven.

> *He spoke another parable to them, 'The kingdom of heaven is like leaven, which a woman took, and hid in three pecks of meal, until it was all leavened'* (13:33).

France reckons that the 'three pecks' equals forty liters, enough to feed 100 people. He points out that 'the theme is again of contrast between the tiny quantity of yeast and the size of the effect' (227). 'The general thrust,' says Carson, 'is the same' (310). Matthew Henry concurs: 'the scope of this is much the same with that of the foregoing parable.'

Closely connected with the theme of smallness is the theme of *hiddenness*. Because the kingdom of God is small at its beginning, it also remains hidden. The woman 'took, and hid' the leaven, Jesus says. 'Hid' (NIV = 'mixed') is not the natural verb to use here. It underscores the smallness of the leaven against the vastness of the dough. It is *enveloped* by the 'meal' and hidden as a result. France concludes that the use of the word 'hid' by Jesus 'must be designed to emphasize the secret, inconspicuous way the kingdom of heaven begins to take effect' (228). This is both historically and typically the case. The kingdom of heaven begins small, hidden, and inconspicuously.

God's work is typically unimpressive initially. This is how God confounds the world. Worldlings are impressed with strength and power and pomp and show. God begins with quiet, hidden works. This is not to deny that sometimes God's works are spectacularly visible. But perhaps we have been tempted to make visible impressiveness the norm. How are individuals transformed by the gospel? Typically it begins with a seed of faith. God gives us new hearts at the moment that we are born again (John 3:1ff.). But change begins in small, hidden ways. We love the stories of drug-addicts or criminals who are instantly transformed. But usually a person is regenerated in such a way that initially he may not even be aware it has occurred. It is a hidden work. Typically, works of grace progress slowly. Quietly, lusts are crucified and victory is won. Likewise, most of the great works done in the history of the church have begun in a small, inconspicuous manner. One Augustinian monk serving in a small town within the Holy Roman Empire in the sixteenth century tacks ninety-five Theses on the door of the parish church and quietly, inconspicuously, the Reformation is launched. An obscure member of Parliament introduces anti-slavery legislation which is scorned by all, and thirty years later the British Empire abolishes slavery. We must not despise the day of 'small things' (Zech. 4:10). Carson says, 'The kingdom of heaven operates, not apocalyptically, but quietly and from small beginnings,' (319).

Second, the kingdom of God grows gradually
This point is closely connected with the preceding one. The transition from seed to tree is gradual. Jesus speaks of 'when it (the mustard seed) is full grown,' but this takes time. The transformation from unleavened to leavened loaf takes time. *Rome* was not built in a day. *Saints* are not made in a day. Growth doesn't happen all at once. Like growth in the physical realm, it is a 'natural' process. Sanctification takes a lifetime. Movements gradually pick up steam. Growth isn't instantaneous. The kingdom grows gradually, steadily.

Third, the kingdom of God grows to dominance
The mustard seed grows up and 'becomes larger than the garden plants' (13:32). From the position of insignificance as the smallest of seeds, it grows into the position of dominance in the garden. Of course a garden would have other plants. But the plant that grows from the mustard seed dominates the garden. It 'becomes a tree.' Even the 'birds of the air' find shelter in its branches. France finds in the ascription 'tree' an 'exaggeration' for what is really a large bush. But Jesus calls it a tree, not to alert us that 'something is wrong in the parable,' as Boice argues, as he attempts to mute the theme of growth so as to fit a premillennial eschatology (126). Rather, Jesus calls the mustard plant a tree in order to underscore the contrast between small beginning and massive ending. The tree is 'an image for a great empire,' France notes (227). It is used of Egypt, Assyria, and Babylon (Ezek. 17:23; 31:3-9; Dan. 4:10-12). The birds, he continues, represent not the devil (as in verse 19), but the 'nations gathered under the protection of the empire' (Ezek. 31:6; Dan. 4:20-22), and may represent 'the coming of the Gentiles into the kingdom of heaven,' (227). Together the tree and birds represent the worldwide dominance of the kingdom of God.

Some (like Boice and other premillenialists) have been confused by Jesus' use of leaven as a positive metaphor. They will note that leaven normally is a metaphor of evil (e.g. Matt. 16:6; 1 Cor. 5:6). This is true, but it is not always the case (e.g. Lev. 7:13; 23:17, 18). As Carson points out, 'metaphors may have diverse uses' (319). The leaven can serve as a symbol of both good and evil. The point of the leaven metaphor in this parable is not metaphysical but functional. The kingdom of God will permeate and transform *like leaven does*. Even as leaven alters and transforms the whole loaf, so will the kingdom of God alter and transform the whole world. God's kingdom begins small, gradually grows, and one day achieves dominion over the kingdoms of this world. Through a mysterious divine working, it grows into dominion.

Implications for Spiritual Growth

The implications of these two parables for personal spiritual growth as well as church growth are as encouraging as anything in Scripture. Think of the struggling, young Christian, or the struggling church. They are discouraged by their failures and inadequacies. They see strong Christians or large churches and compare themselves unfavorably with them. What do we say to them? Take heart! You are not what you should be – you are right! But neither are you what you *were* nor what you *will* be! These truths can be applied in several ways.

First, gradual growth is the norm

Why? Because that's the way it is in the kingdom of God. God is at work. Slowly but surely He will cause us to grow until His rule (kingdom) is firmly established in our hearts and in this world. 'I am confident of this very thing,' says the Apostle Paul, 'that He who began a good work in you will perfect it unto the day of Christ Jesus' (Phil. 1:6).

We would all like to have dramatic, instantaneous growth and transformation. 'O Lord,' we might pray, 'make a miracle of my mess – now!' And there is no shortage of people who will promise a quick fix. They will claim to have found the secret, the formula, they may even say, the *hidden knowledge* that will transform individuals or churches overnight! Then others will enjoy the victorious life, the higher life, the abundant life (it has various names – this is only a sample) free from the trials and stress of struggle. Some promise that if we pray this, trust that, implement the other, and then all will fall into place, the church will explode with growth, and all will be fair and bright. The fact is, God has not promised this. God could completely sanctify us or grow His church instantly if He so chose. But for His own reasons, He chooses not to. This is not the way things work in God's kingdom. For most of us God's rule begins with a toehold in our hearts. It begins in a small, mustard seed-like way. Slowly but surely we shed our sins and become more like our Master. Gradually we are transformed, like leaven leavening a loaf. Gradually we become less selfish, less prideful, less worldly. We are never perfected. We can never say that we have arrived (Phil. 3:12, 13). It may be that we progress three steps forward and then fall two back. We may fall. In fact, falling is inevitable. But so is getting up and getting better. In due time, we will grow. Like the Apostle, we 'press on' (Phil. 3:14). What is true for us personally is true of the church collectively as well.

Maybe you have tried the Christian life and failed. There is perhaps a sinful habit you cannot master. Your tongue is always getting you into trouble. Your temper periodically explodes. You have tried to have daily devotions and failed. Your family life is empty. Or perhaps your church has sought to grow. You have prayed. You have revised and improved the program of the church. You have faithfully proclaimed God's word. Yet, growth has been meager to non-existent. So now what? Quit? No, keep trying, knowing that slow growth is the norm. Persistence will pay off in the end.

We can take this a step further.

Second, progress is gradual because it is difficult
We have much to overcome. Our foes (the flesh, the world, and the devil) are shrewd and powerful. Consequently the Christian life is a marathon, not a sprint. It is a fight, not a dance. We put on the 'full armor of God' (Eph. 6:11). We 'crucify the flesh with its passions and desires' (Gal. 5:24). We put to death the deeds of the body (Rom. 8:13). Daily we 'die to sin and live to righteousness' (1 Pet. 2:24). We're at war. We 'fight the good fight' (1 Tim. 1:18). We are the 'good soldiers of Christ Jesus' who put our enemy, sin, to death

(2 Tim. 2:3; Col. 3:5). Progress is difficult for us personally and for the church's ministry. God has not ordained that we should be sanctified in a day. Progress is not achieved in a fortnight. We may at times wish He had ordained instant growth. But He hasn't. Our path is growth through lifelong, difficult struggle.

Third, victory is inevitable

One drop of red dye in a swimming pool makes no impact on the color of the water. Right? No, it makes an imperceptible impact, but nonetheless – an impact. As the drops keep dripping, eventually the pool water will become visibly red.

This is the way God works. Slowly but surely, He will have His way with us. Sin and the old nature will be put to death. The fruit of the Spirit will become increasingly manifest. Patience will defeat our temper. Moderation will defeat our excesses. Self-control will defeat our self-indulgence. Kindness and gentleness will defeat our sour tongues. This is inevitable. God's kingdom is irrepressible. It is a long process. But it will come to pass. In Christ we are 'more than conquerors' (Rom. 8:37). We are to be 'steadfast, immovable, always abounding in the work of the Lord, knowing that our toil is not in vain in the Lord' (1 Cor. 15:58). Why? Because Christ 'gives us the victory' (1 Cor. 15:57). We will grow and God will have dominion over us. He will master us slowly but surely. Likewise will He build His church.

I find this to be a liberating teaching. Why? Because it is *true to life*. It is *realistic*. Think again of the young, struggling Christians or the faithful but struggling churches who are comparing themselves unfavorably with others. Everywhere they look, what do they see? They see happy, smiling, trouble-free lives, and successful dynamic mega-churches. Everyone at church is doing marvelously. All the other churches are booming. Only they struggle. What is reality? Behind every single smile, there are problems. Half of the apparently 'troublefree' lives were disrupted by a major family fight between waking up and arriving at church. Some lost their tempers. Some were unkind. Some were disrespectful. Some arrived and immediately gossiped about so and so. Others deliberately avoided this one and are not on speaking terms with that one. And the churches? Despite appearances, the tares infect them all, and *real* growth (as opposed to shallow or carnal growth) comes only with difficulty, over time.

We are all in process; none of us has arrived. I know of a teacher at seminary who said that he hadn't sinned for thirty years. Of course, he was deluded. We are all failing, falling, struggling Christians and churches who are slowly but surely gaining victory through our Lord Jesus Christ. 'PBPGINFWMY,' it is said. 'Please Be Patient God Is Not Finished With Me Yet!' We must be realistic about what we can expect of others, ourselves, and our churches.

This is a good cause for *humility*. If I have experienced spiritual growth; if I find myself now alive and awake to the things of Christ where once I was blind and deaf, who gets the credit? If my church is bursting at the seams, who gets the glory? God has done it. He is building His kingdom. 'By His doing you are in Christ Jesus,' Paul tells us (1 Cor. 1:30), and so I can never look down my nose at another. Do I observe poor judgment or insensitivity or hypocrisy or selfishness or promiscuity in another? Do I see small, remnant churches struggling with pettiness and barely surviving? Insofar as we are beyond petty attitudes or carnal behavior or serious problems, it is only by the grace of God. So, who can boast? 'Who regards you as superior? And what do you have that you did not receive?' (1 Cor. 4:7) 'By the grace of God, I am what I am' (1 Cor. 15:10). God causes the growth. He gets the glory.

Implications for Christian mission

Though we have already given much attention to the individual and local church application of this parable, I do not believe that is the primary point. Remember again our context. The disciples were expecting of the Messiah's kingdom a subjugation of Israel's enemies and worldwide rule. What they observed instead, and would continue to observe, was a poor little band of followers, a drop of dye in an ocean of humanity. This was the kingdom's 'enigmatic present manifestation.'

The garden and the loaf represent the world. At first, the presence of the seed and leaven is hidden and invisible. But one day the mustard seed becomes the dominant feature of the garden, of the world. Ultimately the leaven alters and transforms the *whole world*. 'Christ shall have dominion!' 'Jesus shall reign!' as the hymns say. His kingdom will be universal. 'The kingdom of the world (will) become the kingdom of our Lord and of His Christ' (Rev. 11:15). 'Every knee shall bow ... and every tongue confess that Jesus Christ is Lord' (Phil. 2:10, 11). Jesus 'must reign until He has put all His enemies under His feet' (1 Cor. 15:25).

This surely helps explain the amazing triumph of the early church. Consider the obstacles. Their leader was born in a stable. His followers were largely uneducated fishermen and tax collectors. One betrays Him. The leader is crucified. Eleven men remain. One more is added. They are opposed by Jewish and Roman authorities. They are despised, persecuted, and powerless. Eleven of twelve apostles are executed. For 300 years their numbers grow through steady, severe persecutions. All the while, the 'blood of the martyrs' becomes 'the seeds of the church.'

The Christian church conquers the Roman empire. Why? How? They had a vision. These parables taught them that they would start small, grow gradually, and yet ultimately end victoriously. Jesus commanded them to 'go' into all the nations, and though they were ever so weak and few, they went. They began like a mustard seed, the smallest of seeds, and believed that they would grow into the largest of trees. They believed that they were the leaven that would transform the whole loaf. They were told to wait for the Holy Spirit who would give them the power to be witnesses 'even to the remotest part of the earth' (Acts 1:8). Did Jesus not have all authority in heaven and earth? Did He not say that He would be with them always, even to the end of the age (Matt. 28:18, 19)? Against overwhelming odds and brutal opposition they went, 'conquering and to conquer ,' knowing that the kingdom of God would start small, grow gradually, and finally prevail.

Among the greatest needs in our day is that God would baptize us afresh with the early believers' vision for mission. What are we supposed to do as a church? We are supposed to go out and conquer this generation for Christ. We may face overwhelming odds. We may face cruel opposition. But in all these things (as well as our personal satisfaction) we 'overwhelmingly *conquer*' (Rom. 8:37). 'Thanks be to God who gives us the *victory*' (1 Cor. 15:57).

Let me suggest that the kingdom of God always grows in this manner. Again, we tend to glamorize instant success and eschew plodders. We admire the churches and ministries that spring up overnight, from zero to 10,000 in five years. We have little patience for the slow, painful, careful work of the kingdom. This is our bias these days. We want quick, measurable results. But this is not the norm. God does sometimes build a church overnight. I am not suggesting that He doesn't. But it is not His ordinary way of doing things. This conviction, that true kingdom work starts small, builds upon solid foundations, grows slowly, but one day achieves dominion, ought to shape everything about how we do ministry.

There is a sense in which it is not difficult to build a ministry today. Wall Street and Madison Avenue can supply us with all of the necessary tools. If one is willing to compromise principles, one can draw a crowd. Many churches are shamelessly up front about their tactics. They alter the content of the message, saying what people want to hear, and they wrap it up in pleasant packaging, entertaining the people as they hear it. They get results. But is it kingdom work? Are they building up the kingdom? What more biblically faithful ministries do, by way of comparison, is boring. They read so much Bible in the old, traditional services. They preach so long! They sing those long and dreary hymns and Psalms! They pray so much! Their services are not user friendly, seeker friendly, or designed to 'win friends and influence people.' But a biblically faithful ministry is laying a foundation upon the 'apostles and prophets' which will endure (Eph. 2:20). This must be done by faith. It won't see the results that others see. It may be overwhelmed by the noses, nickels, and noise of more trendy ministries. But it can trust that it is planting mustard seeds and leavening loaves, small, contemptible, hidden, imperceptible work, but growing and enduring work.

I have given a significant portion of my time and energy as a pastor to building churches beyond our own. I've written books such as *Leading in Worship, Reformed Worship, The Pastor's Public Ministry, The Family Worship Book, The Case for Traditional Protestantism,* and even *When Grace Comes Home* (on the subject of personal spiritual growth) because I've wanted to urge the broader church in a certain direction. An observer might argue that this has been a huge waste of time, and in a worldly sense, it has. Frankly, few people read these things. But I am convinced that the truth has its own power (Rom. 1:16), and we mustn't despise the day of small things. Some do read them, and are convinced and build their churches along 'classical' or faithful lines as a result. *Trinity Psalter,* another project with which I have been involved, has sold over 30,000 copies and is now in its fifth printing. These are all mustard seeds that are growing, leaven that is transforming. How do we know this? Faith is the assurance of things *not seen* (Heb. 11:1). These things we see are temporal. The unseen is eternal. (2 Cor. 4:18).

For the same reasons, our congregation has planted new churches, four out of town, and two in-town. We'd like to see a dozen more. Impossible, you say? Don't despise the mustard seed. One denomination has over fifty churches in our county. There are over 250,000 people in Chatham County. Why not? Shall we leaven our whole loaf or not?

These kingdom principles apply to institution building as well! Our congregation wants to reach college students. So we've been involved in starting Reformed Union Fellowship chapters at the University of Georgia, Georgia Southern, and the Savannah College of Art and Design. The latter two are not huge ministries. They are currently relatively small. There are other campus works that are larger. Some are more visible. Some are huge! Some make a bigger splash. But we are planting seeds. We are hiding leaven. We may not see visible results now, but we will. Consequently we are not afraid of pouring resources, time, and energy into college ministry. We believe that we will see it grow and that its influence will ripple out across time and space.

We also want to properly educate our children. Most of us are attached to our educational choices and defensive about other options. Many factors go into our decisions. I would not want to be heard judging those decisions. There are good reasons for parents to send their children to *this* school rather than *that* or to no school at all. Whether we ourselves ever make use of a Presbyterian day school, we should be able to see that our churches must build educational institutions. The current Christian community cannot leave the education of its young children to others. Others will not do the job that must be done. Just as it may be said that if Muslim parents want to transmit their worldview to their children, they had better put them into Muslim school, so also we Presbyterians must have Presbyterian schools in which to teach our children a Reformed world and life view. We have been involved in Westminster School, Providence Christian School, and now Veritas Academy because of this conviction. At any point, one could say of these institutions that other schools have better facilities, more enrichment programs (athletics, music, computers, etc.), and a more stable staff. Still I would say, in the language of Zechariah, do not despise the day of 'small things.' (Zech. 4:10). Do not despise the mustard seed. Do not despise hidden leaven.

Back in the 1730s, William Tennent was eager to provide a theological education for his four sons and other young men who had experienced the call of God into the ministry. So he founded a Christian academy, which its detractors called the 'Log College,' after the humble building within which it met. That 'Log College' grew up to be what we today call 'Princeton University,' one of the great universities of the world, which for nearly 200 years faithfully served the kingdom of God. Archibald Alexander, who himself was the founding faculty member of Princeton Seminary (1811), in his book about Tennant's academy entitled *The Log College*, commented 'it is good policy for Presbyterian ministers to establish schools in their charges' (22). Why? Because we must educate our own. Sure there are safer, easier choices.

But we cannot leave this vital task to others. Training up the next generation is a crucial part of our church's mission to our whole city. We have not made an enormous amount of progress thus far. But we have planted a seed and we will see a tree!

I had a frank conversation with a Presbyterian minister and radio preacher before I left Miami. He asked me 'what motivates you to serve Christ?' My answer was and is the vision of the majesty and glory of God and the desire that His glory be known in the entire world. I was muddling along as a young college student with an impotent and sentimental faith until someone showed me something of the greatness of God's glory: that captured my imagination. Finally there was Someone and Something big enough to give my whole life to, and engage every faculty, all my energy, heart, mind, soul, and strength. Does our work seem to be to no effect? One day we will see the successful fruit of our labors. There will be a mustard-tree-dominated garden. There will be a leaven-permeated loaf.

The parable leads us to this question: To whom are we giving ourselves? So many of us are giving ourselves to serving self, or work. The best of us give ourselves to our spouses or our country or to humanity. Still, our vision is too small!

The gospel is the ultimate cause and the ultimate winning cause. Everything else by comparison is insignificant. It is behind this cause that the parable invites us to throw ourselves. We must begin to work and pray with all our hearts and strength to see Christ made known, and exalted and glorified. We must lose ourselves in the vision of the majesty of Christ's rule as every knee bows and every tongue confesses that Jesus is Lord (Phil. 2:11).

As a church, as the people of God, as subjects of Christ's kingdom, should we not be optimistic about our future? Whatever our current circumstances, shouldn't we believe God for the future? As we continue to faithfully cast seeds, should we not plan and pray for a ripening harvest? When it comes to church growth, sometimes we worry too much about too much. We worry about church finances. We worry about numbers of attendees and dollars. We are like Peter looking at the waves. God's kingdom is going to grow! It may start small. The effects may be hidden for a good long time. But inevitably, irrepressibly, His seeds will ripen into a full harvest.

STUDY QUESTIONS

1. Review: What does Jesus mean by 'kingdom?'

2. Review: Why does the announcement of the kingdom, as in Matthew 4:17, raise a credibility problem?

3. What is the contrast being emphasized by Jesus in Matthew 13:31, 32? Again in 13:33?

4. What do the garden and the loaf represent?

5. What kind of growth can be anticipated?

6. What kind of outlook do these parables imply for us today?

    a. Regarding personal spiritual progress?

    b. Regarding Christian mission?

~ 15 ~

'THE HOUSEHOLDER'

Matthew 13:51-53

Understanding God's Treasures

[51]*'Have you understood all these things?' They said to Him, 'Yes.'* [52]*And He said to them, 'Therefore every scribe who has become a disciple of the kingdom of heaven is like a head of a household, who brings forth out of his treasure things new and old.'* [53]*And it came about that when Jesus had finished these parables, He departed from there.*

The thirteenth chapter of Matthew, a chapter filled with parables, concludes with the 'Parable of the Householder.' Not every commentator has considered this a parable. But it follows the 'is like' formula of the others and the theme of the 'kingdom of heaven.' Moreover, the final verse of this section seems to lump it in with the rest.

And it came about that when Jesus had finished these parables, He departed from there (Matt. 13:53).

Having used the parables to instruct us in the nature of God's kingdom, Jesus now reminds us of the keys to profiting by His teaching.

Aim

> *'Have you understood all these things?' They said to Him, 'Yes'* (Matt. 13:51).

Jesus highlights the importance of understanding. His aim in teaching is comprehension. It was not enough merely to hear Jesus, or to be with Jesus. Spiritual benefit would come only through understanding. Remember their request:

> *'Explain to us the parable of the tares of the field'* (Matt. 13:36b).

Jesus complied with their request and provided explanations leading to understanding. Then He asks, 'Have you understood?' This is the key to their spiritual progress. The mind must grasp the truth if the conscience is to be affected, the heart changed, and behavior altered. J. C. Ryle rightly points out,

> The heart is unquestionably the main point: but we must never forget that the Holy Ghost generally reaches the heart through the mind (Ryle, *Matthew*, 155).

This is a good question to ask oneself – Do I understand? The question is not: Have I gone to church? Did I attend the youth meetings? Did I go to the Bible study? The real question is: Have I understood what God is saying through His word? This is the key.

It is true that understanding alone is not enough. One can have merely an intellectual grasp of truth, such as fails to lead to changes in thought or life. More than mental comprehension is needed. James says this to his readers: 'You believe that God is one. You do well; the demons also believe, and shudder' (James 2:19). The demons' orthodox belief was merely intellectual. But while understanding alone is not enough, it is vital. The Puritans argued that 'grace is mediated through the understanding.' Undoubtedly they were right. Grace is not mystically dispensed through irrational means. Rather God speaks to us through His word, calling us to believe and obey all that He says.

The Apostle Paul underscored the importance of this in 1 Corinthians 14. Elements of the irrational and incomprehensible had crept into the Corinthian worship. So he asked them,

> *But now, brethren, if I come to you speaking in tongues, what shall I profit you, unless I speak to you either by way of revelation or of knowledge or of prophecy or of teaching?* (1 Cor. 14:6).

The terms 'revelation,' 'knowledge,' 'prophecy,' and 'teaching' emphasize verbal content. There must be doctrinal content and there must be comprehension.

> *Yet even lifeless things, either flute or harp, in producing a sound, if they do not produce a distinction in the tones, how will it be known what is played on the flute or on the harp? For if the bugle produces an indistinct sound, who will prepare himself for battle? So also you, unless you utter by the tongue speech that is clear, how will it be known what is spoken? For you will be speaking into the air* (1 Cor. 14:7-9).

Indistinct sounds and unknown tongues (languages) are worthless, are 'speaking into the air.' He argues that the 'spirit' and the 'mind' must not be divided.

> *What is the outcome then? I shall pray with the spirit and I shall pray with the mind also; I shall sing with the spirit and I shall sing with the mind also* (1 Cor. 14:15).

His conclusion:

> *...in the church I desire to speak five words with my mind, that I may instruct others also, rather than ten thousand words in a tongue* (1 Cor. 14:19).

Note the weight he assigns to comprehension. Five words that are understood are preferred to 10,000 that are not!

Why? Because words that are understood may instruct, and instruction is the key to edification, spiritual profit, fruitfulness, and blessing (vv. 6, 12, 14, 16, 17).

If these things are so, if we have got this right, the central role of understanding has everything to say about how we conduct our ministries and what goes on in our public worship services.

1. *Christian ministry must be word-centered.* Jesus is concerned about understanding. We must address the understanding. It is the key. This is obvious from how the Apostles describe the ministry of the word.

> *All Scripture is inspired by God and profitable for teaching, for reproof, for correction, for training in righteousness; that the man of God may be adequate, equipped for every good work* (2 Tim. 3:16, 17).

Through Scripture we are 'equipped for every good work.' Do you see his vocabulary? The Scripture is 'profitable for teaching, for reproof, for correction, for training in righteousness.' When properly handled Scripture teaches, reproves, corrects, and trains. Consequently, it is to be read:

> *Until I come, give attention to the public reading of Scripture, to exhortation and teaching* (1 Tim. 4:13).

and preached:

> *...preach the word; be ready in season and out of season; reprove, rebuke, exhort, with great patience and instruction* (2 Tim. 4:2).

The Scripture read is to be accompanied by 'exhortation and teaching.' Proper preaching *reproves* and *rebukes* wrong behavior and belief, and *exhorts* the right. Do you see the vocabulary again? 'Reprove,' 'rebuke,' 'exhort.' Biblical preaching aims at change. There are many, many other places to which we can turn to see the importance of the word understood. Let's try just one more:

> For the word of God is living and active and sharper than any
> two-edged sword, and piercing as far as the division of soul and
> spirit, of both joints and marrow, and able to judge the thoughts
> and intentions of the heart (Heb. 4:12).

The word of God is 'living,' 'active,' and 'piercing.' It is no
dead letter. What is it able to judge? Our 'thoughts' and
'intentions.' It asks questions. It makes distinctions. It causes
us to evaluate our thinking and motives. The word is the key
to our sanctification. Jesus said,

> 'Sanctify them in the truth; Thy word is truth' (John 17:17).

One of the virtues of 'traditional' worship that we are losing
amid the stampede to 'contemporary' forms is its word-
centeredness. This can be seen in the traditional liturgies
(e.g. *Book of Common Prayer*, Calvin's *Form of Church Prayers*,
Westminster's *Directory*), as well as in the non-liturgical
worship of the 'free' churches of a generation ago. From
start to finish, the worship of our ancestors was saturated
with the word: the call to worship was a verse or two of
Scripture, the hymns were theologically and biblically rich,
metrical Psalms were sung, extended passages of the Old
Testament and New Testament were read, sermons were
expository, prayers were rich with scriptural language and
allusions, and the benediction was scriptural. The 'blood' of
the older worship, Spurgeon might say, was 'bibline.'[1] Today
little Bible is read, sermons are topical, songs are simple,
repetitious, and devoid of content, and prayers are token at
best, disappearing altogether in some quarters. If one were
to graph the biblical content of evangelical worship over the
last fifty years (even the last 100 years), the trajectory would
show a steep decline. Since the gospel is the power of God
(Rom. 1:16), we are born again by the word (1 Pet. 1:23-25),
faith comes by hearing the word (Rom. 10:17), and we grow
by the pure milk of the word (1 Pet. 2:2), this development is
ominous for the future of gospel ministry.

---

1. C. H. Spurgeon, *Autobiography* (Pasadena, TX: Pilgrim Publications, 1992),
4:268.

There are many today who would appear to believe that grace is meditated to us through the emotions or the will. If we held this conviction, our services would and should look quite different than they do. If the *emotions* were the key to the progress of the kingdom, our primary aim might be to move them. Our services might be dominated by mood-altering techniques and especially singing. If the *will* were the key, our services might aim at producing decisions. A stronger coercive element would be present in our services. Instead, we aim at conviction. I am reminded of what Martyn Lloyd-Jones said a number of years ago. Singing, he said, has gotten entirely out of hand. Congregations gather and sing 10, 20, even 30 minutes without stopping. The twenty-minute song set, so much a part of the contemporary form of worship, is not a new thing. He says,

> I am no opponent of singing, we are to sing God's praises in psalms and hymns and spiritual songs. Yes, but again there is a sense of proportion even here. Have you not noticed how singing is becoming more and more prominent? People, Christian people, meet together to sing only. 'Oh,' they say, 'we do get a word in.' But the singing is the big thing. At a time like this, at an appalling time like this, with crime and violence, and sin, and perversions, God's name desecrated and the sanctities being spat upon, the whole state of the world surely says that this is not a time for singing, this is a time for preaching. I am reminded of the words of Wordsworth about Milton, 'Plain living, and high thinking are no more.' It is almost true of us to say plain speaking and high thinking are no more. We are just singing. We are wafting ourselves into some happy atmosphere. We sing together. My dear friends, this is no time for singing. 'How shall we sing the Lord's song in a strange land?' (Ps. 137:4). How can we take down our harps when Zion is as she is?
>
> This is no time for singing, it is a time for thinking, for preaching, for conviction. It is a time for proclaiming the message of God and his wrath upon evil, and all our foolish aberrations. The time for singing will come later. Let the great revival come, let the windows of heaven

be opened, let us see men and women by the thousands brought into the Kingdom of God, and then it will be time to sing (*Revival*, 63).

Christian ministry must be word-centered if it is to bear true and lasting fruit for God's kingdom. Our public gatherings for worship should be times when we simply read, preach, sing, and pray God's word, and administer the 'visible word,' the sacraments.

2. *We must be good listeners.* Communication is a two-way street. There is speaking and there is listening. Jesus wants to know if you've understood. Have you? To understand you must listen. Many of us, I'm afraid, are guilty of lazy listening. We fail to pay attention. We've grown accustomed to turning off our minds when we come to church. This is fatal. Far from it being the case that the church's spiritual concerns require less of your mind, rather, they require more. 'Come let us reason together,' God says to us (Isa. 1:18). Love God with all your *mind*, the greatest commandment says. The gospel aims at the renewed mind (Rom. 12:1, 2). Interestingly, the *Larger Catechism* (Question 160) takes up this question. It asks,

What is required of those that hear the word preached?

And it answers,

It is required of those that hear the word preached, that they attend upon it with diligence, preparation, and prayer; examine what they hear by the Scriptures; receive the truth with faith, love, meekness, and readiness of mind, as the word of God; meditate, and confer of it; hide it in their hearts, and bring forth the fruit of it in their lives.

This wisely places a great deal of responsibility upon us as we listen. 'I didn't get anything out of the sermon,' one might say. Well, what did you put into it? Did you pray for the preacher, that he would preach well? Did you pray beforehand that God would give you understanding? Did you listen with eager anticipation expecting that God would speak to you? 'Sleepy, idle, inattentive hearers are never likely to be converted,' adds Ryle (*Matthew*, 155).

If we are to grow in grace, we must all be students of God's word.

Task

Jesus goes on to describe the role of the teacher in spreading the message of the kingdom. What is his task? To dispense treasures 'new and old.'

> And He said to them, 'Therefore every scribe who has become a disciple of the kingdom of heaven is like a head of a household, who brings forth out of his treasure things new and old' (Matt. 13:52).

Of whom is Jesus speaking here? Who is this 'scribe?' France points out that normally the term would refer to a 'professional teacher of the Jewish law,' as in 5:20, 7:29, and 8:19 (230). But here, he argues, 'Jesus is designating his disciples as the 'scribes' of the kingdom of heaven' (231). In other words, the disciples are the 'scribes' or teachers of the kingdom that Jesus establishes. He also calls them 'disciple(s).' A disciple is one who is trained and instructed by another. Carson renders the phrase, 'every discipled scribe of the kingdom of heaven' (333). Jesus is using the labels 'scribe' and 'disciple' to describe the leaders of His church, the 'skillful, faithful minister of the gospel,' as Matthew Henry puts it. Now that they have been taught or discipled by Jesus, now that they understand, what can be expected of them?

First, they are to dispense treasure

They are like the 'head' or 'owner' (NIV) of the house who possesses a 'treasure' (same word as in 13:44) or a 'storehouse' (NIV). The gospel is a thing of great value. The gospel is a treasure. It provides for us the answers to all of the questions of life – who am I? How did I get here? Where am I going? It teaches us that we are made by God to know God and that we can know Him through Jesus Christ. This we have discussed at some length already in the Parables of the Hidden Treasure and the Pearl of Great Price (Matt. 13:44-46). The main point here is that they are not to hide or horde these things. The message of Christ's atonement, of the forgiveness of sin, of reconciliation and peace with God, of life eternal and everlasting, is a great treasure. It is to be freely dispensed.

Second, the treasure they dispense includes things both new and old The gospel, the message of the kingdom of Christ, is a message consisting of both new and old in beautiful harmony with each other. The gospel reveals mysteries long hidden (Eph. 3:3-13; cf. 1:19; Col. 1:25-28; Rom. 16:25-27; 1 Pet. 1:10-12), particularly respecting the inclusion of the Gentiles as full partners in the covenant of grace. Yet, in another sense, Jesus taught nothing new. He merely clarified and elaborated what the law and prophets already taught (Matt. 5:17ff.). His teaching was new, yet it went back to the 'foundation of the world' (v. 35). 'It is new and revolutionary,' says R. T. France, 'but its validity lies in that it is grounded in God's eternal truths, now at last brought to light' (231). The good householder, the Christian leader, 'despises neither the new nor the old as such,' adds Morris (363).

It remains for us briefly to discuss newness and oldness and properly distinguish them, both in the ministry of Jesus and for us today.

1. *The old truths remain valid.* Jesus did not abolish the law and the prophets (Matt. 5:17ff).

2. *The new truths amplify, clarify, and build upon the old, while remaining consistent with them.* The 'mystery' of Gentile inclusion, for example, was long anticipated in the Old Testament (e.g. Pss. 22:25ff.; 47; 67; 72; 96; 100; Isa. 2:1-5; etc.)

3. *The new truths are new primarily in the freshness with which they are stated.* Then and now we are constantly repeating 'new' old truths. But it is necessary that we restate them for each succeeding generation. Every generation must restate the old truths in such a way as to not alter their truth, but

so as to be understood in the new context created by the passage of time. One example – I cannot read to you John Owen's or John Bunyan's sermons in place of my own. Wonderful as they are and wonderfully blessed as they were when originally written and delivered, they are in archaic language and must be restated for today. This is the task of each generation. The truth must be restated with fresh insight and contemporary application. We don't preach *new* truths. The moment you hear something new from us, head for the doors, or the pulpit. Neither do we preach *old* truths. We cannot allow ourselves to get stuck in the 1st or 16th or 20th centuries stating the old truths in the old ways. We'll not be understood if we do this. Our task is to bring forth the old truths in fresh ways so as to reach our generation. We bring forth both the new and the old, primarily the old stated anew.

Notice again the 'therefore' in verse 52. Since understanding is so important, and since they say 'yes' they do understand, *therefore* Christian ministry is to aim at comprehension as it dispenses the treasures of the gospel. It is a ministry of scribes, explaining both the old and the new, and the relation between the two. Why? Because that is how the kingdom of God grows. It grows through the ministry of the word, addressed to the understanding, resulting in conviction and change. This is the seed that we plant (Matt. 13:1-9, 18-23), that mysteriously grows (Mark 4:26-29), that competes with the tares (Matt. 13:24-30; 36-43), but finally prevails (Matt. 13:31-33). It is this ministry that Jesus commends to us once more.

STUDY QUESTIONS

1. Should this be considered a parable? (cf. v. 53) Why or why not?

2. At what does Jesus aim in His teaching (v. 51)? What does this mean?

3. What does the importance of the 'understanding' imply for Christian ministry and worship?

'All Scripture is inspired by God and profitable for teaching, for reproof, for correction, for training in righteousness; that the man of God may be adequate, equipped for every good work' (2 Tim. 3:16, 17).

'Preach the word; be ready in season and out of season; reprove, rebuke, exhort, with great patience and instruction' (2 Tim. 4:2).

'For the word of God is living and active and sharper than any two-edged sword, and piercing as far as the division of soul and spirit, of both joints and marrow, and able to judge the thoughts and intentions of the heart' (Heb. 4:12).

'This I command you, that you love one another' (John 15:17).

4. Discuss Martyn Lloyd-Jones' comments on the relative importance of preaching and singing.

'I am no opponent of singing, we are to sing God's praises in psalms and hymns and spiritual songs. Yes, but again there is a sense of proportion even here. Have you not noticed how singing is becoming more and more prominent? People, Christian people, meet together to sing only. "Oh," they say, "we do get a word in.' But the singing is the big thing. At a time like this, at an appalling time like this, with crime and violence, and sin, and perversions, God's name desecrated and the sanctities being spat upon, the whole state of the world surely says that this is not a time for singing, this is a time for preaching. I am reminded of the words of Wordsworth about Milton, "Plain living, and high thinking are no more." It is almost true of us to say plain speaking and high thinking are no more. We are just singing. We are wafting ourselves into some happy atmosphere. We sing together. My dear friends, this is no time for singing. "How shall we sing the LORD's song in a strange land?" (Ps. 137:4). How can we take down our harps when Zion is as she is?

'This is no time for singing, it is a time for thinking, for preaching, for conviction. It is a time for proclaiming the message of God and his wrath upon evil, and all our foolish aberrations. The time for singing will come later. Let the great revival come, let the windows of heaven be opened, let us see men and women by the thousands brought into the Kingdom of God, and then it will be time to sing' (Martyn Lloyd-Jones, *Revival*, 63).

5. Whose role is Jesus describing in verse 52?

6. What does the 'discipled scribe' do? How does Jesus describe his job?

7. In what sense are the new things of the gospel new, and in what relation do they stand to the truth of the Old Testament? Does the following summary help?

    i. The old truths remain valid (Matt. 5:17ff.).

    ii The new truths amplify, clarify, and build upon the old, while remaining consistent with them.

    iii The new truths are new primarily in the freshness with which they are stated.

IV

LIVING IN GOD'S KINGDOM

How is the Christian life to be lived? We've seen that Christians are to grow. We have looked at the parables that describe the *means* of growth (the word), the *progress* of growth (hidden, gradual, but inevitable), and the *context* of growth (mixed results until the end). Now we will examine the parables that describe how the Christian life is actually lived. What are its *priorities*? What are the *attitudes* of Christ's disciples? What are its *disciplines*? The parables introduce us to all of these themes. They provide us with a vision of what the life of a disciple of Christ looks like. More parables are devoted to the question of how life is to be lived in God's kingdom (12 of 30) than to any other category.

~ 16 ~

'THE TWO FOUNDATIONS'

Matthew 7:24-27

Christ: The True Foundation for Life

[24]*'Therefore everyone who hears these words of Mine, and acts upon them, may be compared to a wise man, who built his house upon the rock.* [25]*And the rain descended, and the floods came, and the winds blew, and burst against that house; and yet it did not fall, for it had been founded upon the rock.* [26]*And everyone who hears these words of Mine, and does not act upon them, will be like a foolish man, who built his house upon the sand.* [27]*And the rain descended, and the floods came, and the winds blew, and burst against that house; and it fell, and great was its fall' (cf Luke 6:47-49).*

The present 'little parable,' as Morris calls it (181), comes to us at the end of the Sermon on the Mount, concluding the greatest of all sermons with a fifth and final warning to carefully hear and follow all Jesus' teaching. Jesus is pressing His audience to listen carefully to Him and obey His voice. He has already done so with the following paired contrasts:

Two *ways*, the narrow and the broad (vv. 13,14)
Two *teachers*, the true and the false (vv. 15-20)
Two *claims*, the credible and the spurious (vv. 21-23)

213

Throughout, He urges His disciples: be *careful*, be *vigilant*, be *discerning*.

We come now to the final paired contrast:

Two *foundations*, the enduring and the crumbling (vv 24-27).

Observations

It may be helpful to make several general observations as we proceed.

First, everyone is building a structure
The metaphor behind the parable is that of life as a building under construction. All of us are 'making a life' or 'building a career,' as we sometimes say. Our 'building' is unique to us. There is not another quite like it. But the sum of our character, decisions, experiences, actions, and choices construct an entity that we might liken to an edifice. Pause for a moment and think about it. Of what does yours consist? What does it look like? What are you building?

Second, everyone is building upon some foundation
There is an organizing principle or philosophy that forms the foundation for each person's life, that determines the fabric, the direction, the tone, the character of that life. Some are molded and directed by a religion. Some are molded and directed by a humanistic philosophy. Others go and do and decide based on nothing more than their own personal pleasures. Whether we are conscious of this philosophical foundation or not is irrelevant. We have one. We all live out a 'world and life view,' as it is called. It determines where we choose to live, our preferred line of work, whom we may marry, and so on. We all have a foundation. On that foundation we are all building a structure.

Third, the quality of the foundation is often not apparent until tested by storms
'Each house looks secure in good weather,' notes Carson (194). One foundation seems as good as another when

untested. Sand seems as viable as rock. Godless foundations, selfish foundations, cultic or hedonistic or nominal Christian foundations can all seem sufficient for a good life. The structures erected upon unstable foundations look as good as those anchored in rock. The difference between a good and a flawed foundation is not initially apparent. Its corruption is hidden, as was the case with the false way, the false prophet, the rotten tree, and the false claim (Matt. 7:13-23). It looks deceptively good.

We would do well to pause again and ask, upon what foundation am I building? And, what kind of life am I building? This is a very biblical question, one which requires self-examination, and one which Scripture urges upon us. The Apostle Paul, identifying the basis upon which churches are built, establishes a principle that applies to all of life. He says,

> For no man can lay a foundation other than the one which is laid, which is Jesus Christ (1 Cor. 3:11).

There is but one foundation, he says, and that is Christ. What then are we building upon it?

> Now if any man builds upon the foundation with gold, silver, precious stones, wood, hay, straw, each man's work will become evident; for the day will show it, because it is to be revealed with fire; and the fire itself will test the quality of each man's work (1 Cor. 3:12, 13).

Are we building our lives out of enduring materials? Or are our lives nothing but unworthy choices, decisions, and endeavors, doomed to vanish without a trace when tested by the fires of judgment day? This is the Apostle's question and an excellent one for all of us to consider. We may take stock of our lives right now. Are our decisions and subsequent endeavors based on no more than our personal pleasure? material wealth? power and position? reputation and fame? Come judgment day we will watch the whole edifice of our lives go up in smoke, with nothing of value (as God defines value) remaining at all. Nothing! Completely wasted lives! Some people may be able to look back and see a whole life of nothing but selfish and self-serving endeavors. Not one thing of eternal value was ever done. Not one thing will endure!

Malcolm Muggeridge, the great English satirist, entitled the two volume autobiography of his life before becoming a Christian *The Chronicles of Wasted Time*. His whole life, he said, was a self-centered waste. Young people, right now you are making decisions about the eternal significance of your life. Are you wasting your time? You may be calculating almost daily how you can have the most money and the most fun, and plan on making every decision based on what will maximize your fame, fortune and pleasure. This is 'wood, hay, stubble' (KJV). It will not last. It will not endure. It may seem to endure. You may know a Mr. Worldly-Wise who has all the good things that the world has to offer. His life may appear to be a fine edifice. But it will not stand before the storms, especially the blazing storm of final judgment. Only 'gold, silver, precious stones' will last, only those things that are of eternal worth will survive.

Fourth, in this parable the two builders are both professing Christians
The contrast here, as with the two ways, two teachers, two trees, and two claims that precede it in Matthew 7, is not between the world and believers. It is between true believers and the counterfeits. Each 'hears these words of mine,' says Jesus. John Stott says 'both are members of the visible Christian community. Both read the Bible, go to church, listen to sermons and buy Christian literature' (*The Message of the Sermon on the Mount*, 209). Because their foundations are hidden, it is difficult to tell them apart. Because 'the deep foundations of their lives are hidden from view,' Stott continues, 'you cannot tell the difference between them' (209).

How then are we to discern the difference between the true and false builder, and avoid the errors of the latter?

The Wise Builder

> 'Therefore everyone who hears these words of Mine, and acts upon them, may be compared to a wise man, who built his house upon the rock. And the rain descended, and the floods came, and the winds blew, and burst against that house; and yet it did not fall, for it had been founded upon the rock' (Matt 7:24, 25).

The 'wise' man is the one who both 'hears' and 'acts upon' 'these words of mine,' says Jesus. This is comparable to the man who carefully builds a house on a solid foundation, on a rock. The solid foundation for life urged by Jesus is established by putting into practice His words. The contrast just preceding these verses was between *saying* and doing:

> 'Not everyone who says to Me, 'Lord, Lord,' will enter the kingdom of heaven; but he who does the will of My Father who is in heaven' (Matt. 7:21).

In our parable the contrast is between *hearing* and doing. The wise don't merely listen. They do. They apply His words. They obey. They alter their lives to bring them into conformity with the teaching of Jesus. 'It is one thing to hear what he said and even approve of it,' says Morris, 'it is quite another to obey' (181).

Normally one doesn't speak of 'doing' someone's words. It is an odd expression, as Morris points out. Yet its meaning is clear enough. Morris continues, 'The person in view is not content with admiring some outstanding teaching; he makes it his guide and models his life on it' (182).

More than a few times in recent years we've heard the claim that God is interested in what we *are* not in what we *do*; He cares about our *being* not our *doing*. This is another of the many platitudes today that is a half-truth and dangerous if not qualified. Certainly God cares most about *who* we are, not *what* we do. The heart is primary. Nothing could be clearer from the Sermon on the Mount, where character (5:1-16), heart obedience (5:17-48), pure religious motives (6:1-18), singleness of heart (6:19-24), trust (6:25-34), and wisdom

(7:1-7) are paramount. But it simply is not true that God does not care about what we are doing. There is no reason to set up this sort of false dichotomy. *Doing* is absolutely critical because it reveals *being*. What we *do* says a great deal about who and what we are. When my children ignore what I say, it reveals a great deal about the condition of their hearts. What we *do* and *how* we do it expresses what we *are*. The wise man 'acts upon' Jesus' words. The one who enters the kingdom of heaven 'does the will of My Father' (Matt. 7:21).

Jesus regularly emphasized the importance of doing.

> *'For whoever **does** the will of My Father who is in heaven, he is My brother and sister and mother'* (Matt. 12:50).

> *'Blessed are those who hear the word of God, and **observe** it'* (Luke 11:28).

> *'If you know these things, you are blessed if you **do** them'* (John 13:17).

Notice that Jesus commends the one who 'does the will of My Father.' The blessed ones hear God's word and 'observe it.' They 'do them.' Similarly James, whose writing often seems to be an exposition or application of Christ's Sermon on the Mount, says,

> *'But prove yourselves doers of the word, and not merely hearers who delude themselves'* (James 1:22).

The wise builder puts Jesus' words into practice. He is a 'doer of the word.' Those who only hear 'delude themselves.' The wise builder doesn't just admire the Beatitudes, he lives them. He hears Jesus say that the 'poor in spirit,' 'those who mourn,' the 'meek,' and so on, are 'blessed,' and he seeks to become those things (5:3-12). He hears Jesus say that we're to rid our hearts of hate or lust, that we're even to cut off the offending hand and pluck out the offending eye, and he sets out to do it (5:21-37). He turns the other cheek, gives the coat off his back, and walks the extra mile (5:38-48). He prays in closets rather than on street corners, and gives in secret rather than sounding the trumpet (6:1-18). He makes deliberate attempts not to serve God and mammon. He endeavors to trust God, to not be anxious about life, and to seek first the kingdom of God (6:19-34). Jesus says 'don't judge,' and he deals with the log in his own eye before concerning himself with the speck in the eye of his neighbor. Jesus says 'don't cast pearls before swine' and he guards God's pearls (7:1-6). Jesus says 'ask, seek, knock,' so he prays (7:7-12). He accepts that to be a disciple of Jesus is to pass through the narrow gate and walk with the few on the narrow path (Matt. 7:13-14).

This zeal to apply Jesus' words affects everything he does. He is a different kind of husband and father be-cause of Jesus' words. He has different priorities. He has a different perspective. He is a new man. Everyone can see it. The people he works with notice it. The people in his neighborhood notice it. Jesus makes him a tower of strength, a bulwark of the faith.

Then when trials and temptations come, he remains unshaken. When the 'rain,' which in this context 'clearly denotes heavy rain, torrential rain,' and 'floods,' which 'are to be understood as the mountain torrents or winter torrents which arrive in ravines after heavy rain and carry everything before them' (*BAGD*, 1, quoted in Morris 182), he withstands them. The rain, the flood waters, and the winds may 'burst against' or 'beat against' his house, but the house does not fall. Why? Because it has been 'founded upon the rock.' He may experience persecution or affliction. He may suffer financial reversals or loss of health. Disease or death may strike his family. Discord and division may rip through his church. Racial conflict may come to his community. War or depression may come to his nation. In the face of such trials many are undone. You've seen it. They collapse. They lose faith or lose heart. But in all of this he is not shaken. Why? Because he built his life 'upon the rock.' His life is based upon the words of our Lord Jesus Christ. His life is founded upon the eternal. Christ is the rock upon whom he has built. He has received a kingdom 'which cannot be shaken' (Heb. 12:28).

Foolish Builder

'And everyone who hears these words of Mine, and does not act upon them, will be like a foolish man, who built his house upon the sand. And the rain descended, and the floods came, and the winds blew, and burst against that house; and it fell, and great was its fall' (Matt. 7:26, 27).

The 'foolish man' is one who also 'hears' Jesus' words, but 'does not act upon them.' He is comparable to the man who carelessly built his house upon sand. Unlike the wise, he merely listens. He has a foundation. It just isn't Jesus' words. He fails to apply, to obey or to live by Jesus' words. Nothing Jesus says alters his life. He takes no steps to bring it into conformity with Jesus' teaching. He is like the deluded one of whom James warned who 'merely hears' the word but doesn't do it (James 1:22). Morris says we shouldn't think of the foolish man as deliberately choosing to build upon sand (182, 183). The problem is, rather, that he is not taking seriously the necessity of a solid foundation. He's being careless. He sees a nice area in which to build his house, it has a beautiful scenic view, so he builds. He pays no attention to the foundation upon which he is building. He settles for the superficial amenities of a given place. Up goes the structure, but no attention is paid to the foundation. Foundation laying would have been too time consuming for him. He was in a hurry. Or he thought it would be too difficult to dig deeply and carefully, and root or anchor his life in the rock. He never applied Jesus' words to his life. He never did what Jesus commanded. He never made concrete changes in his priorities or perspective. He never changed how he conducted himself as a husband or father or in the work place. The expected responses to Jesus' words would have been too difficult or cost too much. He may have been a considerable connoisseur of sermons, he liked to hear them, he appreciated good preaching. He may have been like the multitudes who were 'amazed at his teaching' (Matt. 7:28). They were amazed but they didn't follow Him. They didn't obey Him. They didn't believe Him. Neither does the fool.

Jesus says this is a foolish person. Do note that he will not appear to be foolish at first. He may be like the one dressed up in 'sheep's clothing' (7:15). He may be saying 'Lord, Lord,' in such a way as to be indistinguishable from others (7:21). His house is rising and it has the appearance of being built well and strong. Everything is fine and goes well *until the storm comes*. Then come the trials and tribulations of life. Then come the floods of sickness, sorrow, poverty, disappointments, and bereavements that beat upon him. Because his life has no firm foundation, the house falls. It collapses. His life crumbles and he falls away from the faith. And Jesus says, 'great was its fall.' Someone might say, well I know so and so who was never truly committed to Christ and lived quite a successful and affluent life and died in peace. What are we to say about that? What we're to say is this: the flood that came with its winds and rain did not come until after his death. His storm came only on judgment day. With the troubled Psalmist, we must perceive their 'end' (Ps. 73:17). His house will utterly collapse when faced with the storm of God's judgment.

Whether God's judgments fall in this life or the next, any life built on a foundation other than Christ Jesus is doomed to destruction. We return now to the point that these two builders are both *professing* Christians. They both hear the words that Jesus speaks. One 'acts upon them,' the other does not. Which one are you? Is your outlook one that says 'Whatever Jesus commands I will *do*? Wherever He sends me I will *go*? Whatever He teaches I will *believe*?' Or is your outlook one that instead says 'I enjoy hearing the word of God explained, but don't try to tell me how to live?' In other words, are you one that allows no concrete application of the word of God at all? Tragically, there are some folks who never allow Scripture to change their thinking, their behavior, their choices, or their lifestyle. Indeed, they become embittered, even angry, if it is suggested that actual changes are necessary. They are fine with generalities, but when the Scripture begins to get specific (as inevitably it does) they begin to look for excuses. They like the Christian faith until it begins to require of them things specifically in this life and this world that they must do or stop doing.

I'll never forget one of my important mentors, the Rev. William Still of Aberdeen, saying that his trouble began at the Gilcomston South Church when he quit preaching to the unconverted and began to apply Scripture to allegedly converted church members. He said they nearly went 'mad with rage.' They are willing to hear a good sermon. But they didn't want anyone implying that they had sins from which they needed to repent. This is the great rub. This is the crux. This is perhaps the biggest problem in the church. We have too many connoisseurs of sermons who fail to ever apply the teaching of Scripture to their lives. They have no guilt. They never change. They are unteachable. Tragically, unless we act upon Jesus' words, unless we actually put them into action, unless we believe and obey them, then certain destruction awaits us. Matthew Henry says,

> To *do* Christ's *sayings* is conscientiously to abstain from the sins that he forbids, and to perform the duties that he requires. Our thoughts and affections, our words and actions, the temper of our minds, and the tenor of our lives, must be conformable to the gospel of Christ; that is the doing he requires. All the *sayings* of Christ, not only the laws he has enacted, but the truths he has revealed, must be done by us. *They are a light,* not only *to our eyes,* but *to our feet,* and are designed not only to *in*form our judgments, but to *re*form our hearts and lives: nor do we indeed believe them, if we do not live up to them.

Jesus is making an extraordinary claim in this 'foundations' parable. He is saying no less than that our whole lives will be judged on how we respond to His words. It will not be enough to have merely heard them. A 'hearing only' kind of discipleship is counterfeit and leads to ruin. As R. T. France says, 'The result of spurious or superficial discipleship will be total collapse' (149). His words must be not only heard but believed and put into practice if we are to benefit by them.

Yet the parable contains a promise as well. If we do build our lives on His words, what we do in this world will last forever. Our building will endure. What we do that is founded upon Christ will continue forever. Our labor will not be lost.

Our efforts to build Christian homes and Christian churches and to live as Christians in the marketplace and in the community will not be in vain. Right now counts forever in Christ. Therefore be encouraged! Be energized! Be diligent! Build! As the Apostle Paul puts it, *HOW FIRM A FOUNDATION*

Therefore, my beloved brethren, be steadfast, immovable, always abounding in the work of the Lord, knowing that your toil is not in vain in the Lord (1 Cor. 15:58).

STUDY QUESTIONS

1. What metaphor lies behind the parable?

2. What is the key element in the parable?

3. When or in what context is the quality of the foundation revealed?

4. Read 1 Corinthians 3:11-13. Out of what is your life being built?

5. The two builders have what in common?

6. What distinguishes the wise from the foolish builder? Granted, we are more than what we do; still, what does our 'doing' reveal about who we are?

   'For whoever does the will of My Father who is in heaven, he is My brother and sister and mother' (Matt. 12:50).

   But He said, 'On the contrary, blessed are those who hear the word of God, and observe it' (Luke 11:28).

   'If you know these things, you are blessed if you do them.' (John 13:17)

   'But prove yourselves doers of the word, and not merely hearers who delude themselves' (James 1:22).

7. What does it mean to build upon Jesus' words? What does it mean *not* to build upon Jesus' words?

8. What are the rains, flood waters, and winds meant to represent? Can you think of some examples from your own life when these storms have come?

9. Why would one build upon sand?

10. Of what can we be sure if we build our lives on the Rock?

~ 17 ~

'THE UNRIGHTEOUS STEWARD'

Luke 16:1-13

Focus & Faithfulness

¹*Now He was also saying to the disciples, 'There was a certain rich man who had a steward, and this steward was reported to him as squandering his possessions. ²And he called him and said to him, "What is this I hear about you? Give an account of your stewardship, for you can no longer be steward." ³And the steward said to himself, "What shall I do, since my master is taking the stewardship away from me? I am not strong enough to dig; I am ashamed to beg.*

⁴*I know what I shall do, so that when I am removed from the stewardship, they will receive me into their homes." ⁵And he summoned each one of his master's debtors, and he began saying to the first, "How much do you owe my master?"*

⁶*And he said, "A hundred measures of oil." And he said to him, "Take your bill, and sit down quickly and write fifty." ⁷Then he said to another, "And how much do you owe?" And he said, "A hundred measures of wheat." He said to him, "Take your bill, and write eighty." ⁸And his master praised the unrighteous steward because he had acted shrewdly; for the sons of this age are more shrewd in relation to their own kind than the sons of light. ⁹And I say to you, make friends for yourselves by means of the mammon of unrighteousness; that when it fails, they may receive you into the eternal dwellings.*

¹⁰*He who is faithful in a very little thing is faithful also in much;
and he who is unrighteous in a very little thing is unrighteous
also in much.* ¹¹*If therefore you have not been faithful in the
use of unrighteous mammon, who will entrust the true riches
to you?* ¹²*And if you have not been faithful in the use of that
which is another's, who will give you that which is your own?*
¹³*No servant can serve two masters; for either he will hate the
one, and love the other, or else he will hold to one, and despise
the other. You cannot serve God and mammon.'*

Our present parable has for generations caused fits
for interpreters. It is 'notoriously one of the most
difficult of all the parables to interpret,' concedes
Morris (245). 'There are knots in it which perhaps will never
be untied until the Lord comes again,' admits J. C. Ryle
(196). Little consensus has been reached. Marshall points
out that, 'Few passages in the Gospel can have given rise
to so many different interpretations as the parable of the
prudent steward' (614). Its difficulties are 'well-known,' adds
Plummer (380). The present interpreter will be pardoned, he
trusts, if he stumbles about in his attempts to explain it.

Background

The parable should be understood in 'light of the commercial
practices of the day,' in which 'Jews were forbidden to take
interest from fellow-Jews when they lent them money
(Exod. 22:25; Lev. 25:36; Deut. 23:19),' explains Morris
(245-6). Those wishing to evade interest laws would distance
themselves from the practice of usury by having stewards
write bills in such a way as would incorporate interest in the
total without showing it. A loan of 80 measures of wheat at
25% interest would be written up as 100 measures of wheat.
A legal fiction was perpetrated, by stewards, supposedly
without the knowledge of the owners, allowing them to
collect interest while evading the anti-usury laws.

What we will see as we proceed through the parable is
a desperate steward rewriting his master's bills to omit
the interest, thereby securing the gratitude of the master's
debtors while remaining beyond the legal reach of his

master. Because of the clever maneuvering of the steward, the master 'could not repudiate the steward's action without convicting himself of taking usury,' and 'in the process ... convict himself of acting impiously,' says Morris, as he summarizes the setting (246).

The Parable

> Now He was also saying to the disciples, 'There was a certain rich man who had a steward, and this steward was reported to him as squandering his possessions' (Luke 16:1).

This parable, unlike those of the preceding chapter in Luke (Lost Sheep, Lost Coin, Lost Son), is directed to Jesus' disciples, though the Pharisees are still listening (Luke 16:14). 'He was also saying to the disciples,' Luke tells us. Marshall claims that the 'certain rich man' of verse 1 'is to be regarded as the absentee landlord of a latifundium, such as were common in Galilee at the time' (617). The 'steward' is his 'estate-manager,' entrusted with the owner's enterprises and possessing 'considerable legal powers' (Marshall, 617). He is hired to 'relieve the owner of routine management,' says Morris (247).

However, it was 'reported' (*diaballō*), or he was 'accused,' the word meaning 'to bring charges against with hostile intent' (Marshall, 617). Of what was he accused? Of 'squandering' (*diaskorpizō*), a word used of the prodigal son (Luke 15:13), which can mean anything from wastefulness and carelessness, to 'neglect of duty,' to 'misappropriation of funds,' says Marshall (617).

> 'And he called him and said to him, "What is this I hear about you? Give an account of your stewardship, for you can no longer be steward"' (Luke 16:2).

The steward is being fired. 'You can no longer be steward,' the owner says. And 'an account of [his] stewardship,' is demanded, that is, an updating of the books so that they may be turned over to his successor. Geldenhuys calls this account 'an exact statement of the actual condition of the property with the management of which he was entrusted' (415). He is to account for the disposition of all of the owner's holdings, and leave.

The steward begins to scramble. He weighs his alternatives.

> 'And the steward said to himself, "What shall I do, since my master is taking the stewardship away from me? I am not strong enough to dig; I am ashamed to beg"' (Luke 16:3).

Digging was thought to be particularly strenuous and had become a proverbial expression for hard work. The steward can't do that. He's had what we'd call a 'desk job,' keeping books and managing others who carried out the 'dirty work.' And he's too proud to beg. Then an idea suddenly came to him:

> 'I know what I shall do, so that when I am removed from the stewardship, they will receive me into their homes' (Luke 16:4).

'I've got it,' he says to himself. 'I know what I shall do.' 'When I am removed,' that is, when I lose my job, 'they will receive me.' The 'they' in verse 4b refers to the debtors of verses 5 and following, to whom his thoughts have already 'leapt ahead,' as Marshall puts it (618).

> 'And he summoned each one of his master's debtors, and he began saying to the first, "How much do you owe my master?"' (Luke 16:5).

These debtors are likely to be 'merchants who had received goods on credit,' from the master's estate, says Marshall (618). The steward asks each debtor, 'How much do you owe?'

> 'And he said, "A hundred measures of oil." And he said to him, "Take your bill, and sit down quickly and write fifty"' (Luke 16:6).

A 'measure' is literally a 'bath,' or between eight and nine gallons. He owes 800-900 gallons of olive oil. The commentators, as noted, speculate that the amounts are expressed 'in kind' in order to avoid usury laws. They also speculate that the interest may have been at 100% for the oil and 20% for the wheat, that this would have been understood by Jesus' and Luke's audiences, and that this provides the reason for the amounts being reduced (Marshall, 618-19). The debt for 100 measures of oil would have been 1,000 denarii (a denarius = a laborer's daily wage), a 'considerable debt,' says Morris (247). The reduction was about 500 denarii. In other words, the original bill was for 50 measures of oil, which was doubled because of interest to 100, which the steward reduced back to 50, the amount actually borrowed. The steward won't touch the principal because then he could be legally challenged. He simply eliminates the interest due, to the joy of the debtors.

'Then he said to another, "And how much do you owe?" And he said, "A hundred measures of wheat." He said to him, "Take your bill, and write eighty"' (Luke 16:7).

The 'measures' of verse 7 are literally *kors*, a dry measure equivalent to the Old Testament *homer*, and equaling about forty-eight gallons. The total bill would be about 4,800 gallons, the reduction about 960 gallons, or 20%. In other words, the original loan was eighty measures, plus twenty measures interest. Once again, the principle is retained and the interest eliminated. The rates of discount varied between the oil and wheat because the rates of interest were different for different commodities. Because oil was easy to adulterate, the interest was higher. This pattern was probably repeated over and over again, debtors gratefully receiving reduced bills, and the steward gaining thankful clients while remaining safely beyond the reach of the law. These clients 'owe him one,' as we would say. They 'will receive me into their homes,' as he puts it, perhaps employing him or in some way providing for him (v. 4).

In fact, this quick action by the steward is so clever that even the master responds with commendation:

'And his master praised the unrighteous steward because he had acted shrewdly; for the sons of this age are more shrewd in relation to their own kind than the sons of light' (Luke 16:8).

There is considerable discussion among the scholars as to whether the 'master' (*kurios,* lord) of verse 8, who commends the unrighteous steward, is Jesus or the 'rich man' of the parable, and whether the voice is Luke's about Jesus or Jesus' about the master. The latter seems the more likely and is agreed upon in most of the commentaries (e.g. Marshall, Morris, Geldenhuys, Wilcock, Plummer, Barclay, Calvin, Ryle). The owner is trapped. He cannot expose the steward without revealing his own impiety. So he 'praised the unrighteous steward.' He expressed appreciation for a 'smart rogue' who had outwitted him. The steward is 'unrighteous,' meaning that he is 'simply a worldly man who acts in worldly fashion' (Marshall, 620). The master may be referring to his whole career, his final dealings, or his deeper character. What he did was dishonest. Still, he pays 'tribute to the wisdom, though not the morality, of the act,' says Morris. 'He did not say that he was pleased. He simply admired the astuteness of the steward' (248).

The steward is 'praised' for acting 'shrewdly' (*phronimōs*), which could be translated 'prudently,' or 'intelligently.' 'The steward had seen the urgency of the situation and reached sensibly towards it,' Marshall points out (620).

Lessons
Beginning with the second half of verse 8, Jesus begins to explain the lessons of the parable. What are we to learn from this most unusual parable?

First, Jesus teaches us about prudence
The first of many lessons to be drawn from this parable is an unfavorable comparison between the relative wisdom, energy and focus of the believing and unbelieving in their respective realms.

'...for the sons of this age are more shrewd in relation to their own kind than the sons of light' (Luke 16:8b).

'The sons of this age' are the unbelieving and irreligious. Yet they are more 'shrewd' in their dealings with their 'kind' or 'generation' (*genea*), with their contemporaries, than the 'sons of light' are in dealing with theirs. In other words, the unbelieving are more clever, more energetic in taking care of their temporal, this-worldly wellbeing than the believing are in taking care of their eternal wellbeing.

Look at the steward! He was in a bad spot. He took quick and decisive steps to ensure his future wellbeing. He thought hard about what to do. He ran down all of his master's debtors and struck deals with them. Oh that believers showed such focus, energy, and drive to ensure the wellbeing of their souls! Jesus' point is that His disciples are 'less alert to eschatological situations ... than worldly people are in their own generation, i.e. in their dealings with each other,' says Marshall (621). Think of the energy that worldly people put into the pursuit of money. They work long hours. They study the stock market, the commodities market, the NASDAQ, the interest rates on bonds. They carefully nurture their assets, and grow their portfolios. They work long hours to rise to the top of their professions, or to build businesses from the ground floor. They do all this for what? For temporal, temporary, material, this-worldly gain! No more than that. They are shrewd, energetic, and decisive on behalf of stuff you can't take with you, that passes away, that won't endure. As Plummer points out, 'Worldly people are very farsighted and ready in their transactions with one another for temporal objects' (384). And the point? 'So too, it is implied, should men react to the impending judgment of God,' concludes Marshall (620). If the sons of this age will do all that they do for merely temporary ends, then how much more ought we to show energy, focus, zeal, wisdom, and decisiveness for eternal and everlasting ends? If others show so much energy for their comfort, luxury and names, how much more ought we for our souls and the glory of God?

Sadly, Jesus is saying that seldom is this the way it turns out. The sons of this age outdo the sons of light. Calvin summarizes:

Heathen and worldly men are more industrious and clever in taking care of the ways and means of this fleeting world than God's children are in caring for the heavenly and eternal life ... He reproves our worse than spineless laziness that we do not have the same eye to the future that heathen men have to feathering their nests in this world (II, 112).

How can it be that the irreligious show more energy to build earthly treasures than believers do to build heavenly treasures? J. C. Ryle laments,

The diligence of worldly men about the things of time should put to shame the coldness of professing Christians about the things of eternity (198).

Jesus' implicit exhortation is that we should show this sort of energy, focus, zeal, decisiveness with respect to our souls. We must devote ourselves to the public ministry of the word, sacrament, and prayer. We must devote ourselves to closet prayer and Bible study. We must devote ourselves to family devotions, and zealously pursue sanctification, holiness, and love. The steward is commended, says Plummer, because he 'showed great prudence in the use which he made of present opportunities as a means of providing for the future' (380). Let us do the same. I'm reminded of a man who, as he lay dying of cancer, said to me with the regret of one sensing lost opportunities, 'There's a lot of money to be made out there.' He expressed admirable, if misplaced, zeal! Believers ought to show similar zeal in preparing for eternity. On *our* death beds we ought to be pondering ways that we could accumulate more *heavenly* treasure.

Second, Jesus teaches us about stewardship
Jesus urges shrewdness, zeal, energy, focus and decisiveness similar to that of unbelievers in their realm on believers in the use of our money for eternal ends. In the same way that unbelievers pursue *worldly* wealth through their existing wealth, believers are to pursue *eternal* wealth through their existing wealth.

*'And I say to you, make friends for yourselves by means of
the mammon of unrighteousness; that when it fails, they may
receive you into the eternal dwellings'* (Luke 16:9).

'Make friends,' He says, by the 'mammon' or 'riches'
(*mamōnas*) of 'unrighteousness' (*adikias*). Marshall says that
this 'mammon of unrighteousness' should be understood as
'worldly wealth' as opposed to 'heavenly treasure.' It refers
not only to money, 'but to all the goods of this world, and
indeed to everything that we have here but shall not be able
to take with us into the next life,' says Wilcock (160).

Calvin notes that the mammon is called 'unrighteous' not
because it is evil of itself, but because riches 'are rarely ac-
quired without fraud or violence or other illegal methods,
and rarely, too, possessed without pride or luxury or some
other depraved attitude' (II, 113). Though mammon is unrighteous in this sense, Jesus shows immediately that it can
be properly used.

We are to 'make friends,' that is, eternal friends, with our
mammon. Create 'a fellowship of friends which will survive beyond death,' says Wilcock (160). Use your money
for 'spiritual purposes just as wisely as the children of this
world do for their material aims,' says Morris (249). Marshal
your resources to support the spread of the gospel: outreach,
evangelism, church-planting, mercy ministry, world missions.
We are to do this so that 'when it fails,' that is, when material
wealth comes to an end, when none of it is left, 'when we
die and money is of no more use,' as Morris explains (249), it
will have been consumed serving eternal ends. By the phrase
'when it fails,' 'He means the hour of death,' says Calvin
(II, 113). The 'they' who receive the heaven-bound into the
'eternal dwellings' probably means the angels, or may reflect
a Hebrew plural meaning God. Either way, the faithful will
be received into the 'eternal dwellings,' the place where God
dwells, heaven, the place that Jesus has gone to prepare for us
(John 14:1-6). Jesus' point is not salvation by works, but 'that
the giving of alms is a testimony to the reality of discipleship
and self-denial,' Marshall explains (622). Plummer adds,
'The steward secured a home for a time; but a wise use of

opportunities may secure a home for eternity' (386). Godly stewardship is a sign of authentic commitment, of a credible profession of faith in Christ. We are to take advantage of every opportunity that life affords to use what we have for the spreading of the gospel. 'Seek first His Kingdom and His righteousness,' Jesus said (Matt. 6:33).

Repeatedly, Jesus warned about the dangers of wealth.

> 'Do not lay up for yourselves treasures upon earth, where moth and rust destroy, and where thieves break in and steal. But lay up for yourselves treasures in heaven, where neither moth nor rust destroys, and where thieves do not break in or steal;' (Matt. 6:19, 20).

Let us summarize the point: If an unrighteous steward using fraudulent means for temporal ends was commended by his master for his shrewd preparation for the future, how much more will a righteous steward of God using honest means to prepare for eternity receive his Master's commendation!

Third, Jesus teaches us about character
In verses 10-13, the parable teaches us not only about prudence and stewardship, but also about character as it relates to our use of money. Jesus cites a common proverb:

> 'He who is faithful in a very little thing is faithful also in much; and he who is unrighteous in a very little thing is unrighteous also in much' (Luke 16:10).

We may draw out three principles from this proverb.

1. *Character is proven by faithfulness in the small and ordinary things of life*
One who is 'faithful,' meaning honest and trustworthy, in a 'very little thing' will prove faithful 'in much.' One who is 'unrighteous' in 'a very little thing,' meaning dishonest or untrustworthy, will prove 'unrighteous ... in much.' 'Faithfulness is no accident,' says Morris, 'it arises out of what a man is through and through' (249). How one deals with

small things is an accurate gauge of how one will handle large things. If one is ethically loose, cutting corners, pocketing change, bending the truth, this manifestation of flawed character in small things will reappear when the stakes are higher. We tend to think that small things are 'no big deal,' and if more were at stake we'd behave differently. Jesus is saying small things are a big deal, because the patterns that we establish in small things will be repeated when the big things come around.

How do I treat ordinary people, people who can do nothing for me, not even entertain me? That is the true test of my character, not how I treat people who might enhance my reputation, or my image, or who are part of an 'in-crowd' or 'cool-crowd' from whose goodwill I might derive some benefit.

How scrupulous and precise am I in handling small change, in paying back petty loans from friends, in returning borrowed property?

How accurate am I in my use of words, in making promised contacts, in meeting at a specified time, in honoring a verbal commitment? Words are small things. Granted, we can be over-scrupulous and fail to recognize legitimate hyperbole and imprecision in language. But still, our faithfulness in honoring our promises (whether they are formal promises or not), declared intentions, and verbal commitments are true tests of character. There are no such things as 'little white lies' because when we bend, warp, or shade the truth, we corrupt our souls in the process.

The practice of faithfulness in small things is also how we train our consciences and form our character. Young people, begin now to practice integrity: always speak the truth, always practice honesty, and never cheat. What we do in small things when no one is looking reveals our true character and shapes it. Tithe every dime that we make now and we'll probably tithe with integrity and be less covetous when we are adults. Hallow the whole Sabbath by refraining from work and devoting ourselves to worship and service, and we'll be less likely to cheat God in other areas later. Befriend the awkward new boy in Sunday School now and we'll be less selfish, self-centered, and self-absorbed people later. Avoid immoral images and language now (on the internet, in movies, on TV, in recorded music) and we'll be less likely to indulge in immorality later. Dress modestly and discreetly now, in 5th, 6th, and 7th grades, and we'll be less likely to yearn to put our bodies on sensual display in our teens and 20s. The unrighteous steward knew what to do in a crisis because he had been unrighteously shrewd in worldly matters all his life. Similarly, we must be righteously shrewd in the ordinary and insignificant so that we'll be ready when much is at stake. Faithfulness in small things leads to faithfulness in large things. Unrighteousness in small things leads to unrighteousness in large things. Character is proven in the small and ordinary occasions of life.

2. *Character is proven in our handling of secular things*
Not only is character tested in the ordinary and small things, but our handling of 'secular' matters demonstrates our suitability for handling spiritual matters. Jesus says,

> *'If therefore you have not been faithful in the use of unrighteous mammon, who will entrust the true riches to you?'* (Luke 16:11).

As in verse 9, 'unrighteous mammon' means worldly wealth. As we have seen, it is called 'unrighteous' because wealth 'is commonly a snare and tends to promote unrighteousness,' Plummer reminds us (386). It is contrasted with 'true riches' and so may have the nuance of 'false' or 'temporary.' 'True riches' means real, genuine, or lasting wealth. Only if we have been faithful in the use of 'worldly wealth' will God entrust 'true riches' or 'real riches' to us, that is, spiritual riches. Only then will we receive heavenly and eternal treasure. 'The man who uses his money in the wrong way shows himself unfitted to handle more important things,' says Morris, and 'he must not be surprised if God keeps them from him' (249). Note that this time the lesson drawn from the unrighteous steward is not by way of commendation but by way of contrast. He was fired because he was unfaithful in his handling of his master's funds. Consequently, more was not entrusted to him, and he even lost what he had.

Notice that from Jesus' perspective, worldly wealth is a 'very little thing' (cf. v. 10). To us, it is a very big thing. But to Jesus even the vast amount of worldly wealth is a small thing, and therefore a testing ground which qualifies or disqualifies us for 'true riches,' that is, spiritual and eternal responsibilities or resources. We are to be 'faithful' in our use of worldly wealth. It too is God-given. It too demands our wise stewardship. This is why qualifications for officers in the church include the handling of wealth (1 Tim. 3:3, 4, 8, 12; Titus 1:7). We are *stewards* of our wealth, not its *owners*, and we are required to use it wisely. Dishonesty or foolishness or wastefulness in our handling of worldly wealth disqualifies us for spiritual service. If we cheat to get it, or waste it all on ourselves, or otherwise foolishly squander it, why would God trust us with 'true riches?' Only as we prove ourselves in our stewardship of the small things of worldly wealth will God trust us with spiritual wealth and responsibilities. Even if we were able to make a zillion dollars, God would not trust us with true riches if we wasted it all on ourselves.

Essentially the same thing is said from a different perspective in verse 12:

> 'And if you have not been faithful in the use of that which is another's, who will give you that which is your own?'

Jesus refers to the 'unrighteous mammon' (cf. vv. 9-11), our 'worldly wealth,' as 'that which is another's.' The failure of the unrighteous steward was that he did not faithfully use that which was another's. This point, as with the preceding, is by way of contrast. Worldly wealth is not only a small thing, it is not even ours. 'Earthly wealth is not only trivial and unreal; it does not belong to us,' says Plummer. 'It is ours only as a loan and a trust, which may be withdrawn at any moment,' he continues (386). 'Worldly wealth does not really belong to the disciples,' explains Marshall, 'they hold it on trust from God' (623). 'The money we think we own is not really ours ... we are no more than stewards of it,' adds Morris (250). Typically our perspective is, 'I made that money. I built my business. I was successful in my profession. I invested my money wisely.' The true perspective is, for all that, our wealth ultimately was a gift of God to us, and we hold it in trust.

So the question is, what have we done with the stewardship that God has entrusted to us? Only if we have been faithful in handling the wealth He has given us, which is not really ours but is held in trust, will He give us 'that which is (our) own.' Faithfulness now leads to possession of that which we can never lose. 'The treasure of heaven will be their own inalienable possession,' says Marshall (624). In other words, we are to be 'faithful *now* so that (we) may possess *then*,' Marshall adds (624). Conversely, 'they will be bad custodians of spiritual gifts who administer earthly goods badly,' says Calvin (II, 114).

Do you want to be useful to God? Periodically people will ask me how they can serve God. My usual answer is, serve right where you are in the small, ordinary, and even secular realms of life. Be faithful as a parent, a spouse, a worker, an employer. Serve God by helping to wait at tables, by volunteering in the nursery, by working in the garden. These things are not spiritual, one might object. Exactly, and that's the point. The secular realm is a testing ground for the spiritual, the small for the large, the relatively obscure and unimportant for the public and important.

3. *Character is proven in loyalty*

> 'No servant can serve two masters; for either he will hate the one, and love the other, or else he will hold to one, and despise the other. You cannot serve God and mammon' (Luke 16:13).

Here again, Jesus' lesson is by way of contrast. The steward tried to serve two masters, the owner and himself. As a result, he failed the owner and lost his job. Similarly, God demands exclusive loyalty. 'We either belong to God totally and altogether, or not at all,' as Barclay puts it (218). An *oiketçs* is a household slave. To 'serve' means 'serve as a slave,' says

Morris (250). No one can serve as a slave two masters at the same time. One or the other will get his wholehearted devotion. One cannot be at the 'absolute disposal' of both, explains Plummer (387). The language of 'love' and 'hate,' of 'hold to' and 'despise' is hyperbole, and meant in a 'comparative sense,' as R. T. France notes (*Matthew*, 139). Jesus' point is that the servant will come to prefer one master over the other, to choose sides. Circumstances will eventually force a decision revealing where the slave's true loyalties have been all along. This was probably a common proverb in the ancient world. 'No one can serve two masters.' But the point is spiritual:

'You cannot serve God and mammon' (cf. Matt. 6:24b).

'Cannot,' says Morris, 'signifies a sheer impossibility' (155). What is generally true of slaves and masters is especially true of God and us. We 'cannot' serve both God and 'mammon,' that is, wealth. It cannot be done. We will come to serve one or the other. Geldenhuys speaks of 'the servility accompanying avarice and attachment to material possessions' (417). Moreover, God will not accept divided loyalties. He will accept nothing less than wholehearted obedience. We cannot give half of our hearts to God and half to something else. We cannot serve God and serve our lusts. This is one of our self-deceptions. We want to have it both ways. We want to save our souls and enjoy the world. It is one thing to gain wealth incidentally. It is one thing if 'all these things' are added to us while we are seeking first the kingdom of God (Matt. 6:33). It is another thing to slavishly pursue mammon. This is deception – that one can pursue God and wealth at the same time – that we can lay up treasures in heaven and on earth (Matt. 6:20). It can't be done, Jesus says. Why? Because where our treasure is, there will our hearts be also (Matt. 6:21). 'Follow the money,' as we say today. Our first love may be found where we are most heavily invested.

Jesus deals with us in absolute categories. Jesus promised His disciples the hatred and persecution of the world (John 15:18-23). But He also promised His disciples eternal life (John 3:16). His offer is: persecution and hatred of the world and eternal life, or the love of the world and eternal death. At this point we try to negotiate. Can't we be popular with the world and be disciples? Can't we enjoy the world and still be His followers? Can't we fit in and get along and still be Christians? The answer is no. It cannot be done. Give the world and its treasures a place in your heart, and they will take over. The Apostle John writes,

> *If anyone loves the world, the love of the Father is not in him* (1 John 2:15b).

Similarly James writes,

> *You adulteresses, do you not know that friendship with the world is hostility toward God? Therefore whoever wishes to be a friend of the world makes himself an enemy of God* (James 4:4).

I don't want to make this decision, and neither do you. I want to enjoy the earth's treasures. It rewards its own richly with material things, with 'passing pleasures' (Heb. 11:25), with name, reputation, status, place. There is an important part of me, a huge part of me, that longs for these things, and I *can* have them. I just can't have them and God. God will not allow us to have two loyalties, two treasures, two Lords. It simply 'cannot' be done. The attempt to have both is not merely folly, it is idolatry. You *will* serve one or the other. You cannot serve both.

The sum of it is, Jesus asks of us *complete faithfulness*: like the steward, focused attention and decisiveness and the stewardship of all our resources toward eternal ends; and unlike the steward, faithfulness in the smallest things and in secular things, and undivided service and loyalty to God. There can be no half-measures. No lukewarm commitments (Rev. 3:16). He wants us in or out. He wants our total abandonment, without qualification or negotiation, to Him. As we enter the Christian life (see ch. 9 and the Parables of the Hidden Treasure and the Pearl of Great Price) so we are to continue. Of course this is not an easy commitment or an easy course, but Jesus Himself draws decisiveness out of us. He is worthy of our sacrifices (such as they are) and promises that as we lose our lives, we gain life forever (Matt. 16:25).

STUDY QUESTIONS

1. What background information helps us to understand this parable?

2. The steward is fired (v. 2). How does he respond? (v. 3-7)

3. For what did the owner praise the steward? (v. 8)

4. The lessons of the parable begin in the second half of verse 8. What unfavorable comparison does Jesus make in verse 8b?

5. What does Jesus mean by 'mammon of unrighteousness?' (v. 9) What does He mean for us to do?

6. Jesus grounds His lessons in shrewdness and stewardship in what (vv. 10-12)?

7. In what realms do we prove our fitness for Christian service?

8. Faithful service as God's steward requires what? (v. 13)

~ 18 ~

'THE TWO DEBTORS'

Luke 7:36-50

Loving Gratitude, Grateful Service

36 Now one of the Pharisees was requesting Him to dine with him. And He entered the Pharisee's house, and reclined at the table. 37And behold, there was a woman in the city who was a sinner; and when she learned that He was reclining at the table in the Pharisee's house, she brought an alabaster vial of perfume, 38and standing behind Him at His feet, weeping, she began to wet His feet with her tears, and kept wiping them with the hair of her head, and kissing His feet, and anointing them with the perfume. 39Now when the Pharisee who had invited Him saw this, he said to himself, 'If this man were a prophet He would know who and what sort of person this woman is who is touching Him, that she is a sinner.' 40And Jesus answered and said to him, 'Simon, I have something to say to you.' And he replied, 'Say it, Teacher.' 41'A certain moneylender had two debtors: one owed five hundred denarii, and the other fifty. 42When they were unable to repay, he graciously forgave them both. Which of them therefore will love him more?' 43Simon answered and said, 'I suppose the one whom he forgave more.' And He said to him, 'You have judged correctly.' 44And turning toward the woman, He said to Simon, 'Do you see this woman? I entered your house; you gave Me no water for My feet, but she has wet My feet with her tears, and wiped them with her hair.

⁴⁵You gave Me no kiss; but she, since the time I came in, has not ceased to kiss My feet. ⁴⁶You did not anoint My head with oil, but she anointed My feet with perfume. ⁴⁷For this reason I say to you, her sins, which are many, have been forgiven, for she loved much; but he who is forgiven little, loves little.' ⁴⁸And He said to her, 'Your sins have been forgiven.' ⁴⁹And those who were reclining at the table with Him began to say to themselves, 'Who is this man who even forgives sins?' ⁵⁰And He said to the woman, 'Your faith has saved you; go in peace.'

Jesus! what a Friend for sinners!
Jesus! lover of my soul;
Friends may fail me, foes assail me,
He my Savior, makes me whole.
Hallelujah! what a Savior!
Hallelujah! what a Friend!
Saving, helping, keeping, loving,
He is with me to the end.

The above lyrics are those of the hymn writer J. Wilbur Chapman, Presbyterian minister, former pastor of the First Presbyterian Church of New York City, and Moderator of the General Assembly, PCUSA, in 1910.

Is Jesus a friend of tax-gatherers and sinners (Luke 7:34)? This is the accusation leveled at Him by His enemies. What they meant is similar to what we mean when we accuse a person of 'hanging around' with drug pushers or elements of organized crime. He is mingling with a bad crowd, and He ought to know better. They said He attended social functions with sinners and even 'carried on with them,' as we might say, earning the further accusation that He was Himself 'a gluttonous man, and a drunkard' (Luke 7:34).

Is Jesus the sinners' friend? He is not in the sense that His enemies mean. He does not condone or participate in their evil. He doesn't merely non-judgmentally 'accept' them, as some might say, and leave them unchallenged and unchanged. Yet, because Jesus brings pardon and transformation, He *is* the best friend that sinners ever had. He rescues sinners from their sin and bondage, and gives them liberty and a new life. The incident at the home of Simon the Pharisee (Luke 7:36-39), the explanatory parable that follows (7:40-42a), and the lessons that Jesus draws for us (Luke 7:42b-50), demonstrate how profoundly true this it.

The context

> *Now one of the Pharisees was requesting Him to dine with him. And He entered the Pharisee's house, and reclined at the table* (Luke 7:36).

Jesus was invited to a meal by a Pharisee named Simon (v. 40). Some have speculated that the setting is likely to be a meal after a synagogue service on the Sabbath. Jesus ate both with publicans (i.e. tax collectors, Luke 5:29) and Pharisees (cf. 11:37; 14:1), the bottom and the top of Judean social life. Jesus was willing to minister to the whole social spectrum. Marshall points out that 'the fact that he was especially interested in despised people did not mean that he was uninterested in the more respectable members of society; they too needed the gospel' (308). Geldenhuys concurs: 'We must not forget that He had come to save Pharisees as well, for he loved them too, and longed for a change in their lives ... His was no one-sided ministry' (235-6). Jesus was not a snob. Neither did He indulge the reverse-snobbery that sometimes characterizes social outcasts.

> *And behold, there was a woman in the city who was a sinner; and when she learned that He was reclining at the table in the Pharisee's house, she brought an alabaster vial of perfume* (Luke 7:37).

Each of the gospels has a story of a woman anointing Jesus (Matt. 26:6-13; Mark 14:3-9; John 12:1-8). The other three appear to be describing a different *incident* (one which occurred during the last week of Jesus' life), with different *details* (e.g. they do not speak of her wetting Jesus' feet with her tears), and a different lesson (love and forgiveness versus giving to the poor). The woman is not identified except to be called a 'sinner' from the city. Some have tried to identify her as Mary Magdalene, but as Morris tells us, this is 'sheer speculation' (146). That the woman is identified as a 'sinner' from the city probably means that she is a prostitute, or at least an adulteress (Morris, 146; Marshall, 308; Geldenhuys, 236, Barclay, 94). A sinner was 'a person of notoriously bad character,' says Plummer (26).

The meal would not have been private but something like the 'drop-in' affairs that we sometimes have at holiday time. 'People could come in and watch what went on,' says Morris (146). Barclay argues that when a Rabbi was at a meal, people from all around felt free to come in and listen to 'the pearls of wisdom which fell from his lips' (I, 93). Yet because she was a prostitute, she would *not* have been welcome at the home of a Pharisee. 'It took courage to come,' notes Morris (146; Plummer, 210; Geldenhuys, 236). Luke says they 'reclined at the table,' which means that they did not sit in chairs as we do, but 'reclined on low couches, leaning on the left arm with the head towards the table and the body stretched away from it,' as Morris describes it (147). Sandals were removed before coming to the table.

Luke says that the woman 'brought an alabaster vial of perfume.' The word 'alabaster' 'denoted a globular container for perfumes,' Morris specifies (140). It was long-necked, without handles, sometimes worn around the neck, and ironically, not always made of alabaster. It may have been glass. Its neck was broken when the perfume was removed. The contents would have been expensive, liquid not solid, perfume not ointment.

> ...*and standing behind Him at His feet, weeping, she began to wet His feet with her tears, and kept wiping them with the hair of her head, and kissing His feet, and anointing them with the perfume* (Luke 7:38).

She would have been able to approach Jesus' feet without difficulty, and did so intending to anoint them. Normally the head was anointed (cf. v. 46), but perhaps out of a sense of unworthiness, she only dares to attempt to anoint Jesus' feet.

But as she did, her emotions overcame her. She began to weep, and her tears began to fall, wetting Jesus' feet. She then unbound her hair, 'a significant action,' says Morris, because women did not normally unbind their hair in public, and dried His feet with her hair (147). Barclay calls the unbinding of her hair an act of 'the gravest immodesty' (I, 94). Normally this was something that a woman would not do. But she was overcome by emotion. 'In her anxiety to make up for this mishap, and forgetful of social proprieties, she let down her hair,' says Marshall (328).

'Clearly,' says Morris, 'she was completely oblivious of public opinion in the grip of her deep emotion' (147).

Kissing the feet would have been unusual, though there are examples in Jewish literature of the kissing of the feet of particularly honored rabbis, much as it is when the feet of the Pope or a Cardinal in the Roman Catholic Church are kissed today. Here, says Marshall, this action 'denotes a sign of deep reverence' or even 'an expression of gratitude' (309; cf Plummer, 211; Geldenhuys, 276).

Finally, she anointed His feet with perfume. This too is somewhat unusual, as we've noted. Normally the head was anointed, not the feet. Morris says it is 'probably a sign of humility' (147). Care of the feet was a menial task, normally assigned to a servant.

How are we to interpret the woman's behavior? Why does she wish to anoint Jesus' feet and why is she overcome by emotion? Verse 47 tells us. She has been forgiven much and so she loves much. Morris says, 'It is a fair conjecture that Jesus had turned this woman from her sinful ways and that all this was the expression of her love and gratitude' (147). Marshall summarizes: 'The whole account makes sense when we assume that the woman's original intention was interrupted by her overwhelming emotions' (309). In other words, what we see in her tears is a picture of true repentance. We may elaborate.

First, she sheds tears of sorrow
Her actions as well as her tears are those of grateful love. But the tears are tears. She grieves over her past behavior; she

mourns the loss of innocence and purity, the wasted time and lost years; she cries over the offense that she has committed against God. She understands that her sins are 'many' (v. 47). She needed 'much' forgiveness.

True repentance always involves true recognition of the seriousness of the offense and grief for the damage that has occurred. Perhaps this is most easily seen in human relationships. There are times when we become blind or deaf to our behavior or words. We say things more harshly or do things more hurtfully than we realize. Then comes a moment of illumination. For husbands, this is sometimes at the moment when a wife's tears begin to fall. Then they see what they previously could not see and respond in grief and shame, eager to compensate for the wrong committed against their wives.

This kind of response characterizes true repentance towards God. 'Her eyes had been inlets and outlets of sin, and now she makes them fountains of tears,' says Matthew Henry. Regrettably, sorrow for sin often gets overlooked today. The Apostle Paul speaks of the 'sorrow that is according to the will of God,' that 'produces a repentance without regret (i.e. without regret for what is being given up, for the sin being forsaken), leading to salvation' (2 Cor. 7:10). That sorrow, as in this case, results in action:

> For behold what earnestness this very thing, this godly sorrow, has produced in you: what vindication of yourselves, what indignation, what fear, what longing, what zeal, what avenging of wrong! In everything you demonstrated yourselves to be innocent in the matter (2 Cor. 7:11).

'Earnestness,' 'vindication,' 'indignation,' 'fear,' 'longing,' and 'avenging of wrong' all flow from godly sorrow.

How did the woman come to have this sorrow for sin? We're not told. She may have been exposed to Jesus' teaching. Or her sorrow may have been the effect of merely being in the presence of so holy a One, as in Peter's case when he said,

> 'Depart from me, for I am a sinful man, O Lord!' (Luke 5:8).

Jesus said, 'Blessed are those who mourn' (Matt. 5:4). Sorrow for sin is not a thing to be avoided, a sign of mental instability or spiritual immaturity, but a 'blessed' condition. James says,

> *Cleanse your hands, you sinners; and purify your hearts, you double-minded. Be miserable and mourn and weep; let your laughter be turned into mourning, and your joy to gloom* (James 4:8b-9).

Misery, mourning and weeping are appropriate responses to offenses committed against a holy and loving God. This woman is a picture of one who understands the magnitude of her offense against God and is sorry for the damage that she has done. It is vital that we, like she, arrive at the place where we are able to admit that we are wrong and, beyond that, to even grieve over our misconduct.

Second, she sheds tears of gratitude

The woman is grateful for the promise of forgiveness (v. 47). Her tears, her wiping of Jesus' feet with her hair, her anointing of His feet with perfume, and her kissing of His feet are all the acts of grateful love. She presents us with a picture of the way in which love motivates service. Love prompted the idea of anointing Jesus' feet. But the tears and the wiping of the feet with her hair, and the kissing of His feet, would all appear to be spontaneous expressions of her soul's love for Jesus. Why does she love Jesus? Because she had received the forgiveness of sin through Him. Foul, corrupt, morally degraded though she was, yet Jesus still forgave her sin. He bridged the gap between her and the Holy God of heaven. She, as a result, overflows with gratitude. She has *received*, she wants to *give*. She didn't have to read a book on service, or be brow-beaten into giving. Her heart abounds with gratitude. She is eager to give. She has been forgiven much, and so she loves much. Great grief for sin and great gratitude for forgiveness go together, hand in glove.

If all this is true of the woman-sinner, how are we to understand Simon's response? None of this, we find, sits well with him.

> *Now when the Pharisee who had invited Him saw this, he said to himself, 'If this man were a prophet He would know who and what sort of person this woman is who is touching Him, that she is a sinner'* (Luke 7:39).

Simon responds with incomprehension. 'When he saw this,' he did what? He rejoiced? He perceived the extraordinary nature of the event? He praised God and shouted hallelujah? No. Simon sees all this and disapproves. More than that, Jesus' behavior raises questions for Simon about His piety. Because Jesus allows this sinful woman to do what she does, Simon *doubts who Jesus is.* He says to himself that a true prophet would realize what sort of woman this was and not allow her to touch him. In other words, Jesus must not be a prophet because He did not realize the kind of woman she was. Simon assumes both that a true prophet would not allow himself to be touched and that a true prophet would have the perception or clairvoyance to perceive the woman's character.

Beyond this, he makes no room for change. He speaks of 'what sort of person this woman is.' Well, what sort of person is she? The truth is, she is a transformed sinner. Through Jesus she has become a new person. For Simon, she is still 'a sinner.' Jesus sees that she is a *forgiven* sinner. Pitiful Simon can't see it. He only sees the woman for what she *was*, not for what she had *become.* A supernatural event has taken place before his eyes, and he is unable to see it. In other words, he understands neither Jesus nor His gospel. Jesus came to 'save His people from their sin' (Matt. 1:21). He 'came into the world to save sinners,' says the Apostle Paul, even the foremost of all (1 Tim. 1:15). Simon needs instruction.

The Parable

> *And Jesus answered and said to him, 'Simon, I have something to say to you.' And he replied, 'Say it, Teacher'* (Luke 7:40).

Jesus perceived what Simon was thinking. How? He was speaking only to himself (v. 39). Perhaps Jesus could follow

Simon's eyes and read the expression on his face, much as we do. Still, we note the contrast – Jesus not only knows what kind of woman she is, but is able to perceive Simon's thoughts as well. So Jesus tells a story, a parable, in order to explain the woman's behavior and why Jesus was willing to condone and even commend it.

> 'A certain moneylender had two debtors: one owed five hundred denarii, and the other fifty' (Luke 7:41).

The parable is about a lender who had two debtors. As we learned in the previous chapter, a denarius was a day's wage for a laborer. One laborer owes fifty denarii, the other ten times that amount, five hundred denarii.

> 'When they were unable to repay, he graciously forgave them both' (Luke 7:42a).

Both were unable to pay their debts. So the moneylender 'graciously' forgave both debts.

So Jesus asks,

> 'Which of them therefore will love him more?' (Luke 7:42b).

At this point Jesus begins to teach His lesson. To answer this question, Simon will need to recognize a number of the implications of the parable.

First, we are all debtors

Clearly Jesus has in mind the woman as the greater debtor and the Pharisee as the lesser. Some commit fewer sins than others. Some are more holy than others. Some lead more righteous lives. Prostitutes, pimps, gangsters, pushers, drunks, druggies, adulterers, embezzlers, and so on, may be more obvious, public, frequent, and defiant in their sin than Pharisees, the religiously devout, and the morally upright. But Jesus lumps them all together. Simon and the woman are both debtors.

Sometimes the Christian community is misunderstood, particularly when its prophetic ministry comes into conflict with its gospel ministry. The church is called to speak prophetically to the evils of our day, be they societal evils (such as injustice, bigotry, racism), or personal evils (such as hate, lying, immorality, or homosexuality). Obviously these two categories (societal and personal) have considerable overlap. Regrettably, our prophetic ministry is at times misinterpreted as self-righteousness, as if we were saying that we are better than others. With this parable we place ourselves on the same side of the line as all other sinners. We are all debtors. 'All have sinned and fallen short of the glory of God' (Rom. 3:23). Jesus is saying to the religious community, 'you are debtors. You are no different than the rest. You may or may not have fewer debts. That is not the crucial distinction.' We certainly are to seek to have fewer debts. But the fact remains that we are all debtors. This is our primary identity before God and we share it with all other sinners – we are debtors.

Second, we cannot pay our debts or escape their penalty
Jesus says of both, the one with great debts and the one with modest debts, 'They were unable to repay.' Our debts, be they large or small, are beyond our capacity to pay. We cannot pay them. We have no hope of paying them now or ever. They hang over our heads, we cannot remove them, and we will suffer the penalty for unpaid debts. In terms of another parable, the penalty means unending bondage and torment (Matt. 18:25, 30, 34, 35).

Simon, the woman, and we must not think for a moment that we can rescue ourselves. We cannot earn enough merits to pay down our debts. We cannot earn time off for good behavior. Even if we were to pursue good works with the zeal of a monk, we could never earn enough credits to escape the penalty! As the Apostle Paul writes,

By the works of the law shall no flesh be justified (Gal. 2:16).

In what relation do we stand to God? Our sins are a burden of debt that we cannot pay and whose penalty we cannot escape.

Third, God Himself pays our debts
Jesus says that the moneylender, the character who represents God, 'graciously forgave them both.' The word choice is intentional. Plummer says that in the word 'graciously' (*echarisato*) 'we have the Pauline doctrine of free grace and salvation for all' (212).

Why are our debts forgiven? Because God chooses to be gracious and forgive our debts. We couldn't earn forgiveness. We couldn't merit forgiveness. Simon and we all must understand this. We are all sinners, we are all debtors, we are all incapable of removing our debts, and our only hope of escape is God's gracious forgiveness. By 'gracious' we mean that God's forgiveness is unobligated, uncoerced, and unmerited. God made a free and sovereign determination to save us. Consequently, again, we stand on level ground as sinners, the worst and best of us. In Christ's atonement God provided a way to cancel our debts and free us from condemnation. The Apostle Paul writes,

> *And when you were dead in your transgressions and the uncircumcision of your flesh, He made you alive together with Him, having forgiven us all our transgressions, having canceled out the certificate of debt consisting of decrees against us and which was hostile to us; and He has taken it out of the way, having nailed it to the cross* (Col. 2:13, 14).

We were as dead men, crushed by the weight of our sin. But God in Christ has 'forgiven us all our transgressions,' and note what Scripture says next: 'having canceled out the certificate of debt' that was 'hostile' to us. He 'nailed (our debts) to the cross!'

All this must be understood before the primary lesson of the parable can be learned: We are all debtors, we cannot pay our debts, God Himself has paid them. Jesus now applies the primary lesson. We return to Jesus' question.

The Lesson

'Which of them therefore will love him more?' (Luke 7:42b).

Which of the two, Jesus asks, 'will love him more?' This is the point that was meant to be illustrated by the parable. Simon, you and the woman are fellow debtors, you both have been graciously forgiven. Why would I *not* receive her service? I would no more refuse her than I would refuse to come into your home. If she is more extravagant in her service, or more sacrificial, it is because she is more profoundly aware of the magnitude of the debt of which she has been forgiven. Of this you seem little aware. *The scope of one's love depends on one's perception of the scope of one's forgiveness.*

> *Simon answered and said, 'I suppose the one whom he forgave more.' And He said to him, 'You have judged correctly'* (Luke 7:43).

'Simon's reply is somewhat begrudging,' says Morris (148). 'I suppose,' he says lamely. 'It did not need a great deal of insight to recognize which would love the benefactor more,' Morris continues (148). Marshall says that probably 'Simon realizes that he has been caught in a trap; the answer reluctantly anticipates what follows, namely the criticism of Simon's own lack of gratitude to Jesus' (311). Jesus now interprets the behavior of the woman:

> *And turning toward the woman, He said to Simon, 'Do you see this woman?'* (Luke 7:44a).

'Do you see this woman?' Morris calls this 'an interesting point' (148). Simon could not see what the woman had become. He was blind to her transformation. He could only see what she had been. Jesus then contrasts the woman's behavior with that of Simon:

> *'I entered your house; you gave Me no water for My feet, but she has wet My feet with her tears, and wiped them with her*

hair. You gave Me no kiss; but she, since the time I came in, has not ceased to kiss My feet. You did not anoint My head with oil, but she anointed My feet with perfume' (Luke 7:44b-46).

Marshall points out that Simon has not done anything wrong. He had not acted 'discourteously.' He had acted correctly as a host but had not done anything special. He 'was not necessarily omitting an essential duty' (311, 312). But while he had felt no need to serve Jesus, she was unable to restrain herself. In each case she went beyond even normal hospitality. Simon didn't provide water to wash His feet, she provided tears; he 'gave no kiss,' which typically would have been a kiss on the cheek, but she continually kissed Jesus' feet; he didn't anoint His head with the relatively inexpensive oil, while she anointed Jesus' feet with expensive perfume. Everything that she did was exceptional, while he failed to do even those things which would have been ordinary. Within the framework of the occasion she did everything she could to express grateful love. Now Jesus drives home the point:

'For this reason I say to you, her sins, which are many, have been forgiven, for she loved much; but he who is forgiven little, loves little' (Luke 7:47).

'For this reason,' that is, in light of her conduct, here is what we conclude. 'Her sins, which are many,' He continues. Jesus doesn't whitewash her faults. He says that her sins were 'many.' She was an evil woman. She had much that needed to be forgiven. Yet her sins 'have been forgiven.' Forgiveness is available for the greatest of sinners. 'For she loved much' does not mean that she was forgiven because she loved, as though her love had merited or earned forgiveness. Rather, as Morris explains, 'Her love is proof that she had already been forgiven' (148). Her faith had saved her (v. 50). Calvin says, 'Christ's argument is not based on cause but on effect' (II, 86). She loved much *because* she was forgiven much. Marshall says, 'for' should be understood to mean 'as is evidenced by the fact that' (313), and renders the whole sentence as follows:

'Because of this conduct I tell you (that) her many sins have been forgiven, as evidenced by the fact that she loved much' (313).

Zerwick adds, 'Great love shows great forgiveness but does not cause it' (203). Calvin concurs: 'Her love is not said to be the cause of her forgiveness but a subsequent sign of it' (II, 87).

In the end, the issue is not a greater or lesser gratitude. Who in his right mind thinks he has little of which he needs to be forgiven? The real question is whether or not one realizes 'the magnitude of (one's) personal debt to the Savior.' Marshall continues,

Hence the saying ultimately asks those who have little love for Jesus whether they have realized the magnitude of their sin and their need of forgiveness (313).

Those who are forgiven little or think they need little forgiveness ('i.e. who thinks that he has committed little which could need forgiveness' – Plummer, 214), love little and don't understand themselves. Simon, of course, could love much if he were more aware of his self-righteousness, judgmentalism, and lovelessness. But his dim awareness of sin blunts his response of love. Little need means little love means little forgiveness. Self-righteousness and self-sufficiency shut him off from forgiveness. The Apostle Paul considered himself the 'chief of sinners' (2 Tim. 1:15). An awareness of the magnitude of our debt, that is, an awareness of the magnitude of our sin, is the key to a loving, grateful response to Christ. This doesn't necessarily mean that we scream the law and condemnation at sinners, but it does mean that by one means or another we all must grasp the distance between the holiness of God and our corruption.

The great saints have known this. St. Francis of Assisi said,

There is nowhere a more wretched and a more miserable sinner than I (quoted in Barclay, 94)

The greatest of sins, says Barclay, is to be conscious of no sin. Our great hymn writers have also understood this. John Newton referred to himself as a 'wretch;' Isaac Watts referred to himself as a 'worm.' They wondered at the 'amazing grace,' 'amazing pity,' and 'amazing love' which could save them. If we 'love little,' it is probably because we have never understood the scale of our debt to God and the graciousness of the forgiveness He offers.

The Declaration

Jesus now confirms what He has done on behalf of this woman. He does so through this declaration.

First, He declares her sins forgiven

> *And He said to her, 'Your sins have been forgiven'* (Luke 7:48).

Jesus asserts that which is God's prerogative – 'Your sins have been forgiven.' Why does He do this? To confirm her experience. Plummer says, 'Jesus now confirms her assurance and publicly declares her forgiveness' (214). This provokes a discussion:

> *And those who were reclining at the table with Him began to say to themselves, 'Who is this man who even forgives sins?'* (Luke 7:49)

They raise the key question, 'Who is this man?'

Second, Jesus declares she has been saved by faith
Jesus ignores their concerns. He declares further,

> *And He said to the woman, 'Your faith has saved you; go in peace'* (Luke 7:50).

'Your faith has saved you.' 'This is important,' says Morris, 'as showing that the love spoken of earlier was the consequence, not the cause, of her salvation' (149). She has believed in Jesus, in who He is and what He could do for her, and in Him she has found salvation.

Third, He declares she has peace with God
'Peace' is the present imperative, 'indicates the permanency of this state of peace – peace with God, and peace in the heart because all her sins are forgiven,' says Geldenhuys (237).

Who, then, is this Man? Who can say these things? Simon concluded on the basis of his encounter with the sinful woman that He could not be a prophet. Truth is, He is more than a prophet. He exercises divine authority. He is the Savior of the World (1 John 4:14). He is a Friend of sinners. What He offers to her, He offers to us as well – forgiveness, salvation, peace. We have the whole gospel in this parable.

Simon and the woman represent two kinds of persons against whom we are to measure ourselves. The woman represents the repentant sinner who grieves over her sin and rejoices in forgiveness and salvation. Simon represents one for whom the gospel is beyond comprehension. He does not understand the woman, or Jesus, or himself. He does not love much because he is not aware of the need to be forgiven much, because he cannot see his sin. Do we understand the magnitude of the debt that we owe? Do we understand that our sins are 'many?' Do we believe the warnings and promises of God, and so are ready to turn from those sins? When we do believe and turn, we, like the sinful woman, will be overwhelmed with gratitude. Jesus describes in this parable the basic outlook of His disciples. We love much, and seek to express that love in sacrificial service.

STUDY QUESTIONS

1. What did Jesus' opponents mean when they accused Him of being a 'friend of sinners?' (Luke 7:34).

2. What about the social setting of 7:36, 37 is surprising?

3. How are we to interpret the sinful woman's emotions and actions?

4. How does Simon respond to the woman's actions? (Luke 7:39).

5. Given the context, what is the Parable of the Two Debtors meant to explain?

6. The major points discussed in Question 5 above are subservient to a larger, more central lesson about love. What is it? (Luke 7:42b-43) How does Jesus drive home this lesson? (Luke 7:44-47).

7. What gifts of God does Jesus declare are given to the sinner/woman? (7:48-50) Does He still say that to us today?

~ 19 ~

'THE LOST SHEEP AND LOST COIN'

Luke 15:1-10

Love for the Lost

¹*Now all the tax-gatherers and the sinners were coming near Him to listen to Him.* ²*And both the Pharisees and the scribes began to grumble, saying, 'This man receives sinners and eats with them.'*

³*And He told them this parable, saying,* ⁴*'What man among you, if he has a hundred sheep and has lost one of them, does not leave the ninety-nine in the open pasture, and go after the one which is lost, until he finds it?* ⁵*And when he has found it, he lays it on his shoulders, rejoicing.* ⁶*And when he comes home, he calls together his friends and his neighbors, saying to them, "Rejoice with me, for I have found my sheep which was lost!"* ⁷*I tell you that in the same way, there will be more joy in heaven over one sinner who repents, than over ninety-nine righteous persons who need no repentance.*

⁸*Or what woman, if she has ten silver coins and loses one coin, does not light a lamp and sweep the house and search carefully until she finds it?* ⁹*And when she has found it, she calls together her friends and neighbors, saying, "Rejoice with me, for I have found the coin which I had lost!"* ¹⁰*In the same way, I tell you, there is joy in the presence of the angels of God over one sinner who repents.'*

As was the case with the previous parable, The Parable of the Two Debtors, the following three parables are set in the context of criticism for Jesus' association with sinners. But whereas Jesus used that occasion (Luke 7:36-50) to teach about loving gratitude and grateful service, here He has a different focus. Luke's parables in his 15th chapter (Lost Sheep, Lost Coin, Lost Son) have much to say to us about one particular subject to which they give their primary attention: *the love of God for each lost soul.* All the various circumstances of these parables (the ratios of lost to found, laying the sheep across the shoulders, gathering of friends and neighbors, the diligent searching of the woman) 'were simply intended to illustrate one great leading truth – the deep self-sacrificing love of Christ towards sinners, and the pleasure with which He saves them,' says J. C. Ryle (*Luke*, 179). While each parable has its distinctive nuances, they all focus on the central point that God loves sinners, pursues them at great length, and so should we.

Setting

> *Now all the tax-gatherers and the sinners were coming near Him to listen to Him* (Luke 15:1).

Context must always be considered when interpreting Scripture. In the preceding verses in Luke's gospel, Jesus explained the difficult way of the disciple. He must *hate* his family members, Jesus said, or he 'cannot be my disciple' (14:26). He must 'carry his own cross and come after me' (14:27). He must 'calculate the cost' (14:28). Jesus said,

> 'So therefore, no one of you can be My disciple who does not give up all his own possessions' (Luke 14:33).

Finally, He said,

> 'He who has ears to hear, let him hear' (Luke 14:35b).

Surprisingly, the next verse (15:1) tells us that the 'tax-gatherers and sinners,' that is, the worst and most degraded and most despised of sinners, 'were coming near Him to listen to Him.' According to Marshall, 'The use of *akouein* (to hear) gives a verbal link with 14:35: such were the kind of people who did have ears to listen to Jesus' (599). In spite of the severity of Jesus' demands, this unlikely and unsavory audience has assembled to hear from Him the way of salvation. 'Let us mark the accessibleness and affability of our Lord's demeanor in this expression,' Ryle urges. 'He was one of whom people were not afraid' (177).

This accessibility of Jesus was atypical of His day. Tax-gatherers 'were ostracized by many and regarded as outcasts by the religious,' says Morris. 'Sinners' were 'the immoral or those who followed occupations that the religious regarded as incompatible with the Law' (237). Together, they were 'outcasts from the Jewish religious and national life,' notes Geldenhuys (402).

Normally religious people wouldn't associate with sinners, 'even to teach (them) the Law (cf. Acts 10:28),' Morris explains (237). The Pharisees had said, 'Let not a man associate with the wicked, not even to bring him to the law' (Marshall, 599). Socializing with them implied guilt by association. It implied condoning their sinfulness or treating their evil as a thing indifferent. Consequently, the religious establishment objected:

And both the Pharisees and the scribes began to grumble, saying, 'This man receives sinners and eats with them' (Luke 15:2).

'As the one class drew near, so the other stood off and found fault,' says Lenski, noting the irony (794). They 'began to grumble,' or as Plummer renders it, 'murmured among themselves (cf. Exod. 16:2, 7, 8; Josh. 9:18b; Num. 14:2)' (368). Their complaint was twofold. He 'receives sinners,' he 'allows them access, gives them a welcome' (Plummer 368). Moreover, He 'eats with them.' According to Morris, '...eating with these people was regarded as worse than mere association: it *implied welcome* and *recognition*' (237).

Pharisees were willing to work with sinners who were penitent and ready to be taught. But they were not willing to seek them out. 'Sinners might indeed, after their conversion, come to them, but they did not first go to them to use their influence with them spiritually,' says Geldenhuys (403). Their attitude, we note, makes gospel outreach impossible.

J. C. Ryle is right to point out that 'the thing which they found fault with was the very thing He came on earth to do, and a thing of which he was not ashamed' (178). Saving sinners is the reason behind both the *cradle* and the *cross*. 'Christ Jesus came into the world to save sinners,' writes the Apostle Paul, 'among whom I am even the foremost of all' (1 Tim. 1:15). He came 'to save His people from their sins' (Matt. 1:21). He came 'to seek and to save that which was lost' (Luke 19:10). Jesus was willing to seek out sinners. He was willing to search for them, to rub shoulders with them, to interact with them, to persist in pursuing them, that they might be saved.

Consequently, Jesus teaches this parable to defend His practice:

And He told them this parable, saying (Luke 15:3).

The parables of Luke 15:3ff. are meant to justify, or explain, aggressive outreach to the lost. Through these parables Jesus is saying (in Ryles' words), 'If you would know my feeling towards sinners, mark the conduct of a shepherd seeking a lost sheep, a woman seeking a lost piece of money, and a kind father receiving a prodigal son' (II, 178). The point of these parables, says Plummer, is 'the particular love of God for each individual soul' (368). 'God so loved the world,' says the familiar verse (John 3:16). The 'characteristic feature' of both parables, T. W. Manson concurs, is 'the divine love that goes out to seek the sinner before he repents' (in Geldenhuys, 404). Jesus teaches us about this love to serve a further point: if this is God's outlook on the lost, it must be His disciples' as well.

The Lost Sheep

'What man among you, if he has a hundred sheep and has lost one of them, does not leave the ninety-nine in the open pasture, and go after the one which is lost, until he finds it?' (Luke 15:4).

'What man?' Jesus asks. He can appeal to what was common practice among them. If you love one sheep, though you have ninety-nine besides, what do you do? You search for the one until you find it. The point: 'Jesus tells the Pharisees and the scribes that they do the same thing that he is doing, they in the case of only a lost sheep, he in the case of a lost soul,' says Lenski (795).

We may elaborate on the five ways that Jesus emphasizes the love of God for the lost.

1. Jesus uses the metaphor of the sheep. It is a commonplace of Scripture to liken fallen humanity to sheep. 'All of us like sheep have gone astray,' said the prophet Isaiah (53:6). Because we are like sheep we need the Lord to be our Shepherd (Ps. 23), even our 'Good Shepherd' (John 10:1-18). It is not a flattering picture. Sheep are among the most defenseless, easily confused, and pitiful of all animals. If separated from the flock, they cannot *fight*: they have no claws, no sharp teeth, no means of defense; they cannot *flee* (as might a deer): they are slow in relation to their predators; they cannot *find their way* home (as a dog might), lacking the instincts and sensory receptors by which to navigate their way. If knocked over, they are not even able to right themselves. As one commentator summarized regarding a sheep, 'It is destitute both of the instinct necessary to find its way, and of every weapon of self-defense. It is prey to any beast which may meet it.' Note that in the terms of the parable we are all sheep – defenseless, easily confused, pitiful.

Unbelievers are like *lost* sheep, yet more pitiful than believers, who at least are sheep safely within the fold. But unbelievers are lost sheep. They wander from one thing to the next. They are short-sighted, unable to look beyond the immediate. They are vulnerable, wandering further and further from the fold, constantly exposed to dangers from which they cannot defend themselves.

The point of the metaphor, it seems to me, is one of simple compassion. How can one not look with pity upon such a helpless beast? In fact, you do look with pity on it, Jesus is saying, and that's why you all do what is described in the parable. You search. How then could you not look with compassion on lost souls? One is reminded of God's question to Jonah when he was pouting over God's sparing of Nineveh. Jonah grieved the destruction of a plant, the shade of which he had enjoyed. The incongruity of sorrow for the plant with contempt for the city begged comment:

> Then the Lord said, 'You had compassion on the plant for which you did not work, and which you did not cause to grow, which came up overnight and perished overnight. And should I not have compassion on Nineveh, the great city in which there are more than 120,000 persons who do not know the difference between their right and left hand, as well as many animals?' (Jonah 4:10, 11).

How can you be filled only with contempt or indignation? Where is your pity? Where is your compassion? These 'sinners' are lost sheep. They are weak, foolish, short-sighted, vulnerable. Go after them! Save them! Pursue them! Persist! God does. That is what God does for our lost souls. He seeks us. He seeks to rescue and deliver us from destruction.

2. *Jesus employs a found/lost ratio of 100 to 1.* According to Jeremias, 'A hundred sheep would be a herd of fairly normal size for a small farmer' (in Marshall, 601). The shepherd discovers that he has lost one of his sheep. So he 'go[es] after the one which is lost.' He does this though he suffers a relatively minor loss. He still has ninety-nine that are safe. One penny out of 100 is not much. Even the loss of $1 million out of a total investment of $100 million would be a minor, though significant, loss. 'The point is, not that he possesses so much, but that the loss in comparison to what remains

is so small,' says Plummer (368). He hasn't lost half of the herd. He has not even lost ten or fifteen sheep. Yet one lost sheep is significant. Jesus demonstrates that God values just one lost soul out of a hundred. The shepherd's pursuit of one lost sheep represents the love of God for lost sinners. Eager pursuit describes His outlook. Though His kingdom is 99% full, yet He does not cease to seek the few lost ones remaining. 'The safe possession of the ninety-nine is not substitute for the loss of one,' notes Morris (238). Similarly, Christ's disciples can never rest while there are lost ones around us. We so value one soul that we persist in pursuing its salvation until it is found. If surrounded by 10,000 times 10,000 lost souls, how much greater must be our willingness to befriend, love, rescue, provide for the lost that they might be found!

3. *Jesus speaks of a persistent search by the shepherd/owner.* Matthew's version leaves the result of the search in doubt ('if it turns out that he finds it,' Matt. 18:13). Here in Luke Jesus makes its success certain. He searches 'until he finds it.' This would involve some hardship and danger. The ninety-nine are left safely behind. But the shepherd heads out into the wilderness, braving the heat and cold, dangerous cliffs and gorges for the sake of the lost one. He so values even one sheep that he searches persistently, unceasingly, until he finds it. He considers 'no trouble, sacrifice and suffering too great to find the lost sheep and bring it back,' says Geldenhuys (402). This is what the incarnation reveals; this is what the cross expresses; the seeking grace of God, prompted by His great pity, by His mercy on the lost. Do you feel distant from God? Do you feel alienated? If so, then know that you created the distance. You've withdrawn. You've wandered off. With God in Christ there is still an open heart, an open invitation, and open arms.

4. *Jesus speaks of the shepherd's great joy in finding the lost sheep.*

'And when he has found it, he lays it on his shoulders, rejoicing' (Luke 15:5).

Marshall points out that carrying the sheep 'represents normal rural practice' (601). We mustn't read too much into it. Still, as Marshall himself explains, 'the action illustrates the care of the shepherd' (601). 'The owner does not drive it back, nor lead it back, nor have it carried: he carries it himself,' says Plummer (368). He carries the sheep 'rejoicing.' The tired shepherd is so overjoyed that he forgets his weary limbs and happily carries the beast home. This sheep, even one of a hundred, is no mere possession. It is an object of his love. He has great affection for it. So he gathers his friends:

'And when he comes home, he calls together his friends and his neighbors, saying to them, "Rejoice with me, for I have found my sheep which was lost!"' (Luke 15:6).

'It is a mark of great joy that it seeks sympathy,' says Plummer (368). One who rejoices seeks others to share in that joy.

5. *Jesus speaks of a joyful response in heaven.* Verse 7 gives us the main point of the parable:

'I tell you that in the same way, there will be more joy in heaven over one sinner who repents, than over ninety-nine righteous persons who need no repentance.'

Heaven is neither unaware nor indifferent when a sinner repents. Heaven rejoices. Heaven celebrates. I remember as a boy my surprise and pleasure when important people such as my parents and their friends cheered me when I accomplished something noteworthy in athletics or the classroom. Imagine a whole state or a nation or allied nations together celebrating something you had done. This heavenly celebration exceeds any earthly response. This is the ultimate audience. God and His angels are rejoicing (v. 10). Why? Because this is a victory over which He delights. The rescue of even one soul sets heaven to celebrating! The commentators are not sure whether verse 7 is intended in an ironic sense (as 'people who *think* they are righteous and have no need to repent') or straightforward (God is pleased with the righteous but more celebrative at the repentance of the unrighteous). The latter sense fits the parable better. The ninety-nine are safely in the fold. Lenski offers a helpful analogy from Luther:

> Luther understands this rightly when he speaks of the great and sudden joy of a mother, to find her sick child restored, a joy that is greater than for all her other children who are sound and well (803).

Whereas the rabbis had spoken of God's joy over the *downfall* of the godless, Jesus speaks of God's joy at the *salvation* of the godless. Notice the certainty with which Jesus speaks about heaven. He is able to speak emphatically and with certainty about what goes on in heaven. There is a special joy at the repentance of a lost sinner.

The parable of the Lost Sheep teaches us to pity, value, and pursue lost sinners. If God loves the lost, so must we. If heaven celebrates the rescue of the lost, we can do no less.

The Lost Coin

The second of these twin parables teaches the same lesson of God's love for the lost sinner, except this time the lost item is a coin.

> *'Or what woman, if she has ten silver coins and loses one coin, does not light a lamp and sweep the house and search carefully until she finds it?'* (Luke 15:8).

Palestinian houses were dark, light coming in by only one circular window about 18 inches across. The floor consisted of beaten earth covered with dried reeds and rushes. Barclay says, 'To look for a coin on a floor like that was very much like looking for a needle in a haystack' (209). Yet this is what she does, 'carefully,' and 'until she finds it.' As with the last parable, the emphasis is on 'the thoroughness with which the search is carried out,' says Geldenhuys (402). She 'lights a lamp,' 'sweep(s) the house,' and 'search(es) carefully.' Once she finds the coin she responds as the shepherd does:

'And when she has found it, she calls together her friends and neighbors, saying, "Rejoice with me, for I have found the coin which I had lost!"' (Luke 15:9).

And the conclusion is the same,

'In the same way, I tell you, there is joy in the presence of the angels of God over one sinner who repents' (Luke 15:10).

In other words, this parable teaches the same lessons but is nuanced to make certain points more emphatic. These nuanced lessons arise out of the difference between searching for a living being such as a *sheep*, versus searching for an inanimate object, a *coin*, which we may outline as follows.

1. *The hopelessness of the lost.* Jesus likens a lost sinner to a lost coin. A coin cannot assist in its own recovery. A sheep might wander home. Sheep can bleat. It might be heard. A coin can do nothing. The task of finding a coin is entirely up to the Searcher. Emphasis is being given to the activity of the searching woman that is not given to the searching shepherd. The lesson being made more emphatic is that of the hopelessness and helplessness of the lost. Unbelievers are like lost coins, as once were we. Most of the world's religions portray fallen humanity as seekers, even honest searchers after the truth. Man yearns for God, they say. Religion is the history of man's pursuit of God, they say. Jesus likens us to lifeless coins. 'I'm trying to find God,' an earnest person might say. Not really, the parable answers. A coin cannot find itself. A lost sinner cannot find his way back to God by establishing new priorities, or by moral reformation, or by turning over a new leaf, or by walking a new path. He cannot do it. He is incapable.

Like all sinners, apart from God's gracious initiative and intervention as the Searcher, we are like the coin. We need to know this about ourselves and others. We haven't the *eyes* with which to see spiritual truth, we haven't the *ears* with which to hear spiritual truth, we haven't the *heart* with which to receive spiritual truth, and we haven't the *mouth* with which to cry out for help. The biblical picture of lost humanity is that of death: 'you were dead in your transgressions and sins' (Eph. 2:1-3). We have all the spiritual responsive capacities of a coin or a corpse. 'While we were yet helpless, Christ died for the ungodly,' writes the Apostle Paul (Rom. 5:6). Without Christ we have 'no hope' and are 'without God in the world' (Eph. 2:12).

Ezekiel's vision of the valley of dry bones is one to which we return again and again to understand our lostness. Our spiritual condition is like that of dead, dry bones. Ezekiel is commanded to preach to them,

Again He said to me, 'Prophesy over these bones, and say to them, "O dry bones, hear the word of the LORD"' (Ezek. 37:4).

This would appear to be the ultimate exercise in futility. Dead bones cannot respond: they have no eyes, no ears, no hearts. Yet God promises,

'Thus says the LORD God to these bones, "Behold, I will cause breath to enter you that you may come to life. And I will put sinews on you, make flesh grow back on you, cover you with skin, and put breath in you that you may come alive; and you will know that I am the LORD"' (Ezek. 37:5, 6).

Let the lostness of the coin sink in. We are not to think that we sinners can correct our course and find our way whenever we please. The Christian religion is not a religion of moral reformation through personal effort. Christianity is a religion of grace. I cannot find myself. I cannot change myself. I cannot reform myself. I cannot pick myself up by the spiritual bootstraps. This was the mistake of Pelagius, the nemesis of St. Augustine (354-430). 'You could change if you would,' he said. 'Through moral effort you can believe and obey God,' he insisted. Augustine correctly responded, 'no you can't – not without the grace of God.' Grace must enable. Grace must give us the eyes with which to see, the ears with which to hear, the tongue with which to cry out, the heart with which to receive. We 'cannot' understand the things of God (1 Cor. 2:14). We 'cannot please God' (Rom. 8:8). 'No one can come to Me,' Jesus says, 'unless the Father who sent Me draws him' (John 6:44). We are not just lost, but *dead*, like a thing inanimate, like a field of dry bones, like a lost coin.

2. *The unilateral nature of the search.* The dead coin, over against the living sheep, throws all of the focus onto the action of the searcher while reducing the capacities of the lost one to that of the inanimate. We listeners are no longer distracted by the pitiful condition of the sheep. The coin does not evoke our sympathy. All our attention is on the woman as she 'light(s) a lamp' and 'sweep(s) the house' and 'search[es] carefully' (v. 8). She is relentless and comprehensive in her search. When she finds it, it is no thanks to the coin. It is entirely due to her diligence in searching.

What are we to understand? That if we are to be found, it will be as a result of a sovereign and gracious search of God. Further, we are to understand the great lengths to which God goes to find us. While we have remained oblivious and impervious, He has been on pursuit. He has brought circumstances to bear upon us – perhaps an affliction, or a broken heart, or the loss of a loved one. Perhaps he has brought blessing and obedience, His kindness being meant to lead us to repentance (Rom. 2:4). He has brought people and opportunities into our lives. We have been placed in just the right place at just the right time to hear what we needed to hear.

Like the woman in the parable, He too lights a lamp, and sweeps the house and searches carefully. He persists until He finds us. If I am a believer today it is because God went on the hunt. It is 'by His doing' that I am 'in Christ Jesus' (1 Cor. 1:30). I did not choose Him, He chose me (John 15:16). I did not love Him, He loved me (1 John 4:10). I did not decide to believe Him, He gave me faith (Eph. 2:8, 9). As with the Apostle Paul, He caused the scales to fall from my eyes (Acts 9:18). 'I once was lost but now am found, was blind but now I see.' The Apostle Paul writes,

> *...but God has chosen the foolish things of the world to shame*
> *the wise, and God has chosen the weak things of the world to*
> *shame the things which are strong, and the base things of the*
> *world and the despised, God has chosen, the things that are not,*
> *that He might nullify the things that are, that no man should*
> *boast before God* (1 Cor. 1:27-29).

Believers believe *not* because they are 'wise,' 'strong,' or somehow noteworthy. Quite the contrary. They are 'foolish,' 'weak,' 'base,' 'despised,' and unexceptional. We cannot boast in being 'found.' We are found only because of the relentless, comprehensive, gracious search of the Searcher.

The implication of this diligent searching of God would not be lost on the scribes and Pharisees who are listening. Jesus is explaining why He socializes with tax collectors and sinners. His answer, that He is like the searching woman, implies that we too are to be like the searching woman. The focus on the woman as the searcher makes the role of the Christian community as God's agents on earth in searching for the lost coins of the world more emphatic. The lost will not be found unless we go and find them. God uses a lamp. We are that lamp. God uses a broom. We are that broom. He searches 'carefully.' We are His hands and feet in that careful search. If the Parable of the Lost Sheep evoked our sense of *sympathy* for the lost one, this parable evokes our sense of *responsibility*. Don't expect the lost coin to crawl out from under the straw covering the floor. Don't expect it to call out for help. Don't expect it to wave its arms or send up a flare. Lost sheep may want to be rescued. Lost coins are oblivious to all.

We can explain our responsibility for the lost as that of *praying*, *giving*, and *going* on their behalf. We pray for the lost, we give to support others who go with the gospel to the lost, and we go ourselves with the gospel to the lost. We pray, give, and go for those who are lost at home, and we pray, give and go for those who are lost overseas. This is not a secondary matter to us. We take the broom of the law and the light of the gospel, and we 'search carefully.' Like Jesus, we go that we might 'seek and save' the lost (Luke 19:10). We preach, teach, and live the gospel as Christ's ambassadors, pleading, entreating, begging to 'be reconciled to God' (2 Cor. 5:20).

3. *The joy is greater.* This is brought out by the ten-fold reduction of the ratio of lost to found from 1 of 100 to 1 out of 10. The loss suffered by the woman was much greater than that of the shepherd. He lost but one of a hundred sheep. She lost one of only ten coins. Left unrecovered, the loss of the coin would be considerably more severe. Consequently, its recovery proportionately brings more relief and rejoicing. Perhaps this is why the expression in verse 10 is slightly different, being more personalized. The joy over the coin is not just 'in heaven,' as with the lost sheep, but 'in the presence of the angels of God' (Luke 15:10). If so, then what kind of priority ought joining this search for the lost be for us? We cannot stand aloof from the lost. We cannot despise the 'tax collectors and sinners.' We cannot ignore them or be indifferent to their plight.

When do we rejoice? When a thing of great importance, or one that we greatly value, occurs. We cheer for the touchdown and home run. We celebrate victory on the battlefield. We delight in a beautiful musical or artistic presentation. We rejoice at births, birthdays, weddings, and anniversaries. If we are looking at things as we should, we rejoice in gathering with the saints each Sunday to worship God and to hear His word. These are the things that we consider important or of great worth. Jesus is saying that if we value lost souls, we will find their repentance an occasion of great rejoicing, as do the angels of God. We will long to see the immoral man or woman, the dishonest crook, the harsh or cruel leader, the abuser of drugs and alcohol, the pusher, the gangster, the pornographer, the thug, the criminal, as well as the 'religious' but nominal believer, the religious but fraudulent, the religious but counterfeit and hypocritical, repent. And when they do, we will rejoice.

This all requires the outlook taught in the parables of the lost sheep and lost coin. I must:

- Perceive the worth of each lost soul
- Know the love of God for each lost soul
- Diligently engage in loving and befriending and reaching out to lost souls
- Rejoice when lost souls are brought to repentance and faith in Christ

The disciples of Christ are not to be like scribes and Pharisees who have contempt for the lost and despise them. The Christian life is patterned after that of Jesus, who 'receives sinners and eats with them,' who 'seeks and saves' the lost (Luke 19:10).

Study Questions

1. Leading into Chapter 15, Luke records Jesus saying,

   'So therefore, no one of you can be My disciple who does not give up all his own possessions ... He who has ears to hear, let him hear' (Luke 14:33, 35b).

   What is surprising about the audience of 15:1?

2. What is the objection of 15:2? What would the outlook of the scribes and Pharisees make impossible?

3. Considered from the context, what would appear to be the point in telling the parables of 15:3ff.?

4. To what does Jesus liken lost humanity in 15:5? What is meant by the metaphor? How are we meant to respond to the metaphor?

5. Only one sheep in one hundred is lost. What is meant by the 99 to 1 ratio? What are we to notice about the search?

6. What would Jesus have us understand about God on the basis of the response of the shepherd to the recovery of his lost sheep in 15:5, 6?

7. Draw the conclusion: if heaven rejoices over one lost sinner who was pursued and brought to repentance, then

what about our outlook on (a) lost sinners; (b) the pursuit of lost sinners; (c) the repentance of lost sinners?

8. Consider this summary of Luther's view of verses 6, 7:

'Luther understands this rightly when he speaks of the great and sudden joy of a mother, to find her sick child restored, a joy that is greater than for all her other children who are sound and well' (Lenski, 803).

9. The Parable of the Lost Coin contains many of the same lessons as the Lost Sheep. How does its emphasis differ?

10. Summarize what you've learned from the parables: why does Jesus socialize with sinners?

~ 20 ~

'THE PRODIGAL SON'

Luke 15:11-32

Love for the Lost (cont'd)

[11]*And He said, 'A certain man had two sons;* [12]*and the younger of them said to his father, "Father, give me the share of the estate that falls to me." And he divided his wealth between them.* [13]*And not many days later, the younger son gathered everything together and went on a journey into a distant country, and there he squandered his estate with loose living.* [14]*Now when he had spent everything, a severe famine occurred in that country, and he began to be in need.* [15]*And he went and attached himself to one of the citizens of that country, and he sent him into his fields to feed swine.* [16]*And he was longing to fill his stomach with the pods that the swine were eating, and no one was giving anything to him.* [17]*But when he came to his senses, he said, "How many of my father's hired men have more than enough bread, but I am dying here with hunger!"* [18]*"I will get up and go to my father, and will say to him, 'Father, I have sinned against heaven, and in your sight;* [19]*I am no longer worthy to be called your son; make me as one of your hired men.'"* [20]*And he got up and came to his father. But while he was still a long way off, his father saw him, and felt compassion for him, and ran and embraced him, and kissed him.* [21]*And the son said to him, "Father, I have sinned against heaven and in your sight; I am no longer worthy to be called your son."* [22]*But the father said to his slaves, "Quickly bring out the best robe*

and put it on him, and put a ring on his hand and sandals on his feet; [23]and bring the fattened calf, kill it, and let us eat and be merry; [24]for this son of mine was dead, and has come to life again; he was lost, and has been found." And they began to be merry. [25]Now his older son was in the field, and when he came and approached the house, he heard music and dancing. [26]And he summoned one of the servants and began inquiring what these things might be. [27]And he said to him, "Your brother has come, and your father has killed the fattened calf, because he has received him back safe and sound." [28]But he became angry, and was not willing to go in; and his father came out and began entreating him. [29]But he answered and said to his father, "Look! For so many years I have been serving you, and I have never neglected a command of yours; and yet you have never given me a kid, that I might be merry with my friends; [30]but when this son of yours came, who has devoured your wealth with harlots, you killed the fattened calf for him." [31]And he said to him, "My child, you have always been with me, and all that is mine is yours. [32]But we had to be merry and rejoice, for this brother of yours was dead and has begun to live, and was lost and has been found."'

The Parable of the Prodigal Son is among the most beloved of all the parables. Ryle calls it 'the most full and instructive' of the parables (*Luke*, II, 185). It has been called an *Evangelium in Evangelio*, a 'Gospel within the Gospel!' Barclay calls it 'the greatest short story in the world' (*Luke*, 211). Warfield regards it as 'a gem of story-telling, which must be pronounced nothing less than artistically perfect' (*Savior of the World*, 3-4).

It is the third of three parables that Jesus taught to explain His attitude toward 'tax-gatherers and sinners' (15:1-3). 'The central figure is the father,' Marshall points out, 'just as in the previous parables the shepherd and housewife stand at the center' (604). But rather than searching like the shepherd and housewife, the father waits. Helmut Thieliche describes it as the parable of 'the waiting Father' (Marshall, 604). Because he waits, the effect is to shift attention from the father to the actions of the Lost Son. Traditionally, the lost son has been called the 'Prodigal,' meaning 'one who is recklessly wasteful.' While the first two parables emphasize the *divine* side of salvation (the seeking love of God), this one 'sheds a clear light also on the *human* side,' says Geldenhuys (406, my emphasis). We follow the 'Prodigal' son as he demands his inheritance, leaves his father for a 'distant country,' surrenders his wealth, reaches the lowest point of degradation, comes to his senses, repents, and returns. Only then does the father come back into our view as he eagerly receives, forgives and restores the Prodigal. Then the scene shifts yet again, this time to the elder brother, another kind of sinner, as he angrily objects to the celebration for his returning brother.

The Parable of the Prodigal Son 'completes the trilogy of these parables of grace,' says Plummer (371). Marshall maintains that the point of the parable (like those preceding it) is to 'illustrate the pardoning love of God that cares for the outcasts' (604). This is the 'one great fact' with which it is concerned, says Morris (239). Marshall explains: 'The parable is ultimately concerned to justify the attitude of God to sinners' (604). In doing so it also 'justifies the attitude of Jesus Himself, since he is able to defend himself and his attitude to sinners by appeal to the attitude of God' (604). It also makes the point, says Morris, 'that those who reject repentant sinners are out of line with the Father's will' (240).

The younger son corresponds to the tax collectors and sinners, the older son to the scribes and Pharisees. The parable has something to say to both kinds of sinners, the 'tax collectors and sinners' (the younger brother), and the 'scribes and Pharisees' (the elder brother), as it teaches us about the love of the Father.

The Lost Son

> And He said, 'A certain man had two sons; and the younger of them said to his father, "Father, give me the share of the estate that falls to me." And he divided his wealth between them' (Luke 15:11, 12).

The younger son may have been about seventeen years old, since marriage normally occurred in the first century Middle East at about 18-20, and he appears to be unmarried.

Normally, one's inheritance was distributed at the time of the death of the parent, as is the case today. Jewish law allowed a son to request his portion of the inheritance prematurely, but in so doing he forfeited his right to 'any further claims on the father's estate,' says Marshall (607; cf. vv. 19, 31). Jesus says the father 'divided his wealth between them.' Once he gave to the younger son his portion of the inheritance, he assigned what remained to the elder son.

> 'And not many days later, the younger son gathered everything together and went on a journey into a distant country, and there he squandered his estate with loose living' (Luke 15:13).

The younger son, the lost son, the prodigal, provides a vivid picture of the lost sinner.

First, he flees from the father
He 'gathered everything' (*sunago*), a word which 'has the sense "to turn into cash,"' says Marshall (607). It also indicates the finality of his leaving. He left nothing behind, nothing for which to ever return. *Everything* was taken. He means to leave and never come back. Apparently he finds no particular pleasure in fellowship with his father. He finds life in the father's house restrictive, confining, suffocating. His desire is to leave him and go to a 'far country' (KJV), where he can indulge 'loose living.' He journeys to a distant land, traveling 'as far away as possible from the watchful eye of his father,' says Geldenhuys (406).

The lost son, like the lost sheep and lost coin, is a picture of the lost soul. The sinner in revolt runs from God. He aims to get as far away from God and reminders of God as he can. Of course, it is an illogical flight. Ultimately one cannot escape the omnipotent and omniscient and omnipresent God. But that doesn't mean that he doesn't try. He flees God, the people of God, the church, the word of God, accountability, responsibility, conscience. Off to a 'far country' he goes, where he makes new friends, picks up new habits, and speaks a new language. There, where no one knows him, he can do whatever he wants to do. He has a new life, without restriction, without comment, without disapproval, and without need to answer to anyone.

Second, he sows the flesh
The younger son 'squandered' (*diaskorpizō*) or wasted his money on 'loose living' (*asōtōs*), i.e. 'recklessly' or 'on dissolute pleasures,' says Marshall (608). The J. B. Phillips New Testament renders it, 'He squandered his wealth in the wildest extravagance.' The term indicates 'unrestrained sensuality and spendthrift extravagance' (Zahn in Geldenhuys, 411). No doubt he had 'fun.' He was living it up. He 'partied.' He enjoyed himself. Jesus classifies this as a waste. It is not just sinful. It is wasteful, a squandering of resources on unworthy and foolish ends.

Yet this is what the lost soul wants to do. All those things that he couldn't do at home because of all the restrictions that God, and the people of God, and a Christian home laid upon him, he now does with abandon. He holds nothing back. He has the money. He has the time. He finds the desired environment and companions. He gratifies his every lust. Every itch is scratched. Every appetite is satisfied. He drinks to drunkenness, he purchases the services of prostitutes, he deprives himself of nothing. He 'sows the flesh,' thinking that this is really living, this is what real life is all about.

Yet, third, he reaps what he sows
The Apostle Paul writes:

> *Do not be deceived, God is not mocked; for whatever a man sows, this he will also reap. For the one who sows to his own flesh shall from the flesh reap corruption, but the one who sows to the Spirit shall from the Spirit reap eternal life* (Gal. 6:7, 8).

His life apart from his father, apart from responsibility and accountability, his life in sin, turns out to be not so wonderful after all. It looked like fun. It looked exciting. But it took its toll. 'Sin is a hard master,' says J. C. Ryle (*Luke*, 182). Jesus says,

> 'Now when he had spent everything, a severe famine occurred
> in that country, and he began to be in need' (Luke 15:14).

The phrase, 'when he had spent' (*diapanaō*, to spend), 'may
have the connotation of wasteful spending,' says Marshall
(608). Morris says, 'Two disasters struck him simultaneously'
(241). He spent all of his money. Then a famine hit the land,
and 'the realities of life hit him,' as Marshall puts it (608).
For a time he was able to live in an unreal world, supported
by daddy's money. But when the money ran out, his dream
world, his fantasy, was shattered. He had no job. He had no
savings. He had no family. He had had a good time. But he
was now utterly unprepared for the contingencies of life.
Money was tight. Food was scarce. There was no help. He
'began to be in need.'

> 'And he went and attached himself to one of the citizens of
> that country, and he sent him into his fields to feed swine'
> (Luke 15:15).

He gets a job on the farm of a rich Gentile (Jews were not
permitted to keep pigs – see Luke 8:32ff.). Marshall explains
that 'Feeding (pigs) was an unclean occupation (Lev. 11:7),
and thoroughly degrading for a Jew ... feeding swine was thus
about as low as a Jew could go (609). Only one in 'desperate
straits' would even consider such a job, (Morris, 241). The
younger son has fallen into 'the cruelest and most hateful
forms of bondages and spiritual famine,' says Geldenhuys
(407). 'To a Jew,' says Warfield, 'degradation could not be
more poignantly depicted.' Warfield then reconsiders his
judgment: 'Yes it could: There was one stage worse and that
stage was reached' (25).

> 'And he was longing to fill his stomach with the pods that the
> swine were eating, and no one was giving anything to him'
> (Luke 15:16).

'To wish to share their food was the nadir of degradation,'
says Marshall (609). 'Pods' are carob pods, which Marshall

and the commentators identify as 'the fruit of a Palestinian tree, used for fodder and eaten only by very poor people' (609). He longs to eat even these. 'The lost son not only herded the swine; he herded with them,' observes Warfield. He ate 'from the swine's own store' (25). There is 'no one' to help. The point? 'Our Lord means to paint degradation in its depths,' says Warfield (25).

The Prodigal represents the lost sinner suffering the consequences of his rebellion. 'The way of the transgressor is hard,' say the Proverbs (13:15). 'By what a man is overcome, by this he is enslaved,' says the Apostle Peter (2 Pet. 2:19). His wealth, his energy, and probably his health have all been consumed. Rather than enjoying the dignity and abundance of service in the father's household, he is in bondage to poverty among swine. What begins as a thrill becomes a master. He provides an eloquent rebuttal of the 'sin has no consequences' message emitted constantly by the modern entertainment industry. The party drinker becomes a drunk, the drug user becomes an addict, the promiscuous playboy (or girl) becomes diseased or pregnant, a single parent or an aborter of babies. The *party* becomes a *prison*. Jesus' point is that the sinners with whom He socializes and whom He seeks (the people of vv. 1, 2) admittedly are 'bad past expression and past belief' (Warfield, 25). Jesus does not water down in the least their degradation. 'No depths are left beneath the depths which He portrays here for us,' Warfield continues (24). The Prodigal represents what sin does when it does its worst, and, at the same time, represents those whom Jesus seeks to save.

Yet the Lost Son is not so bad that he cannot be rescued. At the bottom he looks up. At the point of utter deprivation, degradation and futility, he begins to turn around. Jesus describes his recovery.

> 'But when he came to his senses, he said, "How many of my father's hired men have more than enough bread, but I am dying here with hunger!"' (Luke 15:17).

First, he 'came to his senses'

One day he wakes up. Why he wakes up at a given moment is not revealed. The prior two parables taught us that the lost are rescued due to the searching initiative of God. This parable must be read in the light of the previous two parables, where all the initiative is God's. He comes to his senses, we can conclude, because of God's gracious intervention. How does God do this? We're not told. But we do see the Prodigal's (God-ordained) circumstances bringing pressure to bear on him. 'Whatever friends the young man had had in the days of his wealth had melted away,' says Marshall (609). Pigs were fed, but he was not. Perhaps he came to realize that 'pigs were more valuable than he,' as Morris puts it (241). He 'came to his senses,' an expression which may reflect a Semitic expression meaning 'to repent' (Plummer, 374). Hardship has a way of doing this. 'Want rekindles what his revelry had extinguished,' notes Plummer (374). He awakens to his poverty and degradation. He reflects that his father's hired hands had 'more than enough,' which means even 'to have an abundance of,' says Marshall (609). He ponders life among swine and compares it with life with father, *and the lights go on*. 'What am I doing?' he asks. Look at what I have become!

There is a sense in which each one of us must come to see this. Sin is enticing. It is seductive. But sin has consequences. It promises what it cannot deliver. It promises freedom and fun, and what it delivers is bondage and pain. As it is often said, when we break God's laws, those laws break us. Finally lost souls must come to see this. Sin must come to be seen as evil, as darkness, as slavery, as degrading, as noxious and, finally, it must be repudiated. The lost son illustrates what the repentance mentioned in the previous two parables looks like (Luke 15:7, 10). It begins with an abhorrence of the degradation of sin.

Second, he returns to his father

He determines to leave his life of sin and return to his father.

'I will get up and go to my father' (Luke 15:18a).

Marshall notes that 'the youth is determined to act swiftly and decisively' (609). He wants out. He wants to go home. He sees the foolishness of his decisions and the wickedness of his behavior, and so is determined to leave his chosen way of life and return home. He is keenly aware of his distance from home. He is separated from his father, even alienated from him. He has lived apart from him for a season. But he can bear it no more. He must return to his father.

So it is with lost souls. Prodigals flee from God and His searching eye. They are glad to be rid of Him, and apart from His people and His church. But one day they wake up and realize that life without God is not working. A deep discontent settles in. Like the adopted children who yearn to know their natural parents, the desire grows to know the One who brought them into the world and gave them life. How did I get here? Why am I here? What is my Maker's outlook on me? How does He feel toward me? The desire to know God grows in a prodigal's heart, perhaps dimly, but surely. Who is He? What is His disposition towards me? Does my Maker not mean for me to know Him? So the heart turns towards God.

Third, he confesses his sin
Turning to his father involves departing the 'far country' and the life he lived there, and acknowledging the error of his ways. We can speak of *returning* to father and *repenting* of sin separately in order to analyze them, but in practice they are one act. He leaves the far country, that way of life, that circle of friends. He renounces it all, turns his back on it, and heads for home. As he does so, he confesses his sin.

'Father, I have sinned against heaven, and in your sight;' (Luke 15:18b).

Leon Morris regards the Prodigal's confession a classic.

He expressed sorrow not only for what he had lost but for what he had done: he had sinned. He recognized that his sin was first against God ... (he) had also sinned against his father and he saw this (242).

He has gone from the self-sufficient pride of one who flees home to a willingness to take the lowest place back in his father's household. He confesses without conditions and without qualifications. He makes no excuses. He offers no explanations. He had sinned. Period.

The problem with most confessions is that they primarily express regret for the consequences of sin rather than regret for the sin itself. 'I'm sorry that you got hurt;' 'I'm sorry that I have caused so much trouble;' 'I'm sorry that I wrecked the car;' etc. The prodigal, by comparison, acknowledges guilt and is willing to accept the consequences:

> 'I am no longer worthy to be called your son; make me as one of your hired men' (Luke 15:19).

He realizes and admits that he 'is morally unfit to be regarded as a son,' says Marshall (609). After the earlier settlement of the inheritance upon his departure to the 'distant country,' he has no further claims on his father. The most that he can hope for is to be given the position of a servant. Even that, given his rejection of his father, would be a gracious gift. What makes this confession so profound (and exemplary for us) is the full embracing of both the guilt and consequences of sin. He has squandered his share of the estate. So he makes no claim on what remains. He has deeply offended and hurt his father. So he makes no claim on the privileges of sonship. When we are gripped by the spirit of repentance, we will confess our sins without excuses, without qualification or explanations, and with a full accepting of consequences. He doesn't say to his father, 'I was wrong, but you were wrong for putting so much pressure on me. You should have given me a little more freedom and then I wouldn't have rebelled.' He doesn't say, 'You favored my elder brother. Resentment built up. I couldn't stand it any longer and had to get out.'

He doesn't say, 'Elder brother was always picking on me. He pushed me out of the house.' When a lost soul returns to God there is no attempt to shift blame to anyone else. No, he owns the guilt as his own. He shares it with no one else. A true spirit of repentance will grasp the extent of the punishment that we deserve and plead not for what is fair or just, but only for mercy. This is the pilgrimage of the prodigal, the journey of the lost soul back to God.

The Eager Father

I pondered what to label the outlook of the father. He could accurately be called 'the gracious father,' or 'the forgiving father,' or 'the merciful father.' But each of these characterizations misses the eager, expectant, hopeful outlook of the father in the parable. Jesus says,

> 'And he got up and came to his father. But while he was still a long way off, his father saw him, and felt compassion for him, and ran and embraced him, and kissed him' (Luke 15:20).

Because it was 'while he was still a long way off' that the father saw him, many have speculated that the father must have been looking for his son, trusting, eager, hopeful that one day he might return. 'The father has long been watching for this,' says Plummer (375). This may or may not be implied. What is emphatic is that the father 'felt compassion for him' before he ever had a word of remorse from the Prodigal. His outlook is one of sympathy. He is ready to forgive and receive his son back. This should surprise us to some extent. We could easily imagine the father looking away or turning his back. We can easily imagine the father erupting with fury once his son arrives, shouting, 'Do you realize what heartache you have caused us? Your mother has been worried sick. You have disgraced the family. Where is your inheritance? Do you mean that you have wasted it all?' And so on. No, compassion greets him, and it greets the lost sinner. God is angry with sin 'every day,' say the Psalms (Ps. 7:11). But his primary outlook on sinners is not anger but compassion. God is patient with us! As the Apostle Peter says,

The Lord is not slow about His promise, as some count slowness, but is patient toward you, not wishing for any to perish but for all to come to repentance (2 Pet. 3:9).

Morris comments,

> The Father's feeling precedes any confession of repentance by the son and corresponds to the seeking and searching in the two preceding parables (610).

The son has left the far country. But the verbal initiative in restoration is taken by the father. He is so eager for his son's return that he can't stand still. He doesn't wait for his son to arrive. He runs to him, an unusual move for an older middle-eastern father. And 'he kissed him.' The kissing of the son may be an additional sign of forgiveness (as in 2 Sam. 14:33).

God is not merely *willing* to forgive us. He certainly is not *reluctant* to forgive us, or *begrudging*. God is *eager* to forgive. This is the outlook that we sinners face. True, God requires repentance. We must leave the far country. We must confess and forsake our sin. But He looks upon us with compassion, eager for repentance, forgiveness, and restoration.

> *'And the son said to him, "Father, I have sinned against heaven and in your sight; I am no longer worthy to be called your son"'* (Luke 15:21).

Notice that before the son is able to complete his pre-planned repentance (vv. 18, 19), his father interrupts him. He is not given the opportunity to say, 'Make me as one of your hired hands,' as he had planned (v. 19). This underscores how eager the father is to forgive and restore.

As for the son receiving a reduced status as a slave, the father will hear none of it.

> *'But the father said to his slaves, "Quickly bring out the best robe and put it on him, and put a ring on his hand and sandals on his feet;"'* (Luke 15:22).

The father calls his 'slaves' (*doulos*), here referring to household servants. He orders that the son is to be dressed in the best robe and sandals, and to be given a ring. These are items 'appropriate to a son,' says Marshall (610). The robe is an indication of status (as in Gen. 41:42). The ring is 'a symbol of authority,' Marshall says (610). The sandals are 'a sign that a person was a freeman, not a slave.' In addition, 'they were worn in the house by the master, and not by guests,' and so indicate 'authority and possession as well as freedom,' says Morris (611). Together, 'He is doing him honour,' summarizes Plummer (376).

> 'and bring the fattened calf, kill it, and let us eat and be merry;'
> (Luke 15:23).

The 'fattened calf' was one fed and fattened for a special occasion. The return of the son was an occasion to feast and rejoice.

> '...'for this son of mine was dead, and has come to life again; he was lost, and has been found.' And they began to be merry'
> (Luke 15:24).

The father uses extreme language to express his outlook on the Prodigal. He was 'dead' and now has 'come to life.' Like the sheep and the coin, he was 'lost' and now is 'found.' We are right to think that the Prodigal had announced his intention never to return to home. Even the father had come to regard him as dead. Yet he had returned, as from the dead, as one long lost and at last found.

Are you one who has been in a 'far country?' Have you been in rebellion against God? Have you been immersed in the mire of moral degradation? Are you wondering what God's outlook might be? No matter how low you may have sunk, He is eager to forgive! He requires repentance. But He is anxious, ready, and eager to forgive and restore you to His family. 'Come home!' he says. Leave it all behind. Repudiate the past there. Leave the far country. Rise up from your moral filth. Come home. The Father will receive you warmly, compassionately and generously.

The Resentful Son

> 'Now his older son was in the field, and when he came and approached the house, he heard music and dancing' (Luke 15:25).

The scene shifts in verse 25 to the dutiful elder brother. There is nothing wrong with being a dutiful elder brother. Indeed, being a dutiful elder brother is a good thing. I like the elder brother. He's been out in the field working away faithfully, while the irresponsible brother has been living it up with his buddies. He hears the 'music and dancing.' One scholar (Jeremias) suggests that singing and clapping and dancing by the men of the farm is indicated. Morris says it 'would have been performed by entertainers, not the banqueters' (243). Either way, it's clear that a party's being thrown and he's not yet been included in the celebration.

> 'And he summoned one of the servants and began inquiring what these things might be. And he said to him, "Your brother has come, and your father has killed the fattened calf, because he has received him back safe and sound"' (Luke 15:26, 27).

Once informed of the nature of the occasion, the return of his prodigal brother, the older son angrily objects to the feast and refuses to participate.

> 'But he became angry, and was not willing to go in; and his father came out and began entreating him' (Luke 15:28).

We can understand why the elder brother feels this way. His prodigal brother has been living scandalously. His return, as he sees it, is an occasion not for celebration but for shame. Where the Prodigal has been and what he's been doing will become the gossip of the town once more. 'We've been trying to move on,' he might be thinking. 'For months all people could talk about was his departure and journey to the 'far country.' Just when everything had finally quieted down he returns to stir it all up again, bringing further disgrace to the family.' Pack up the band. Dismiss the partiers. Pull down the shades. Hide the boy in a closet.

The father 'came out' to the elder brother. Here is the seeking love of the previous two parables. 'The father does not wait for the elder brother to come into the house to him; he goes out to him,' Warfield observes (*Savior of the World*, 21). The father 'began entreating' the older boy (*parekalei*), rendered by Morris as 'he spoke kindly to him' (244). He speaks 'soothing words,' says Warfield (21). But the older brother obstinately refuses to go in. His father's pleas make no impact upon him. He chooses to remain outside.

> *'But he answered and said to his father, "Look! For so many years I have been serving you, and I have never neglected a command of yours; and yet you have never given me a kid, that I might be merry with my friends;"'* (Luke 15:29).

The father, the Prodigal son, and the household celebrate, while the elder brother remains outside, self-righteous, superior, and resentful. What does he resent? Having to serve his father? Missing out on the opportunity his brother had to indulge the flesh? The graciousness of his father? Whichever it is, there is profound darkness in the elder brother's heart, Warfield explains, as he compares him with the Pharisees and scribes:

> Their moving principle was not, as they fancied, a zeal for righteousness which would not have sin condoned, but just a mean-spirited jealousy which was incapable of the natural response of the human spirit in the presence of a great blessing. They are like some crusty elder brother, says our Lord, who, when the long-lost wanderer comes contritely home, is filled with bitter jealousy of the joyful reception he receives rather than with the generous delight that moves all human hearts at the recovery of the lost. (20)

Again we say we should see the elder brother as a *different kind of sinner*. Warfield continues:

> The effect (of the Parable), you see, is to place the Pharisaic objectors themselves in the category of sinners, side by side with the outcasts they had despised; to probe their hard hearts until they recognized their lost estate also; and so to bring them as prodigals back in repentance to the Father's house. (21)

The elder brother represents not the vile, degraded sinner, but the civilized, cultured, religious sinner. His sins are not the gross public kind, like his brother's, but the hidden, internal heart kind. But he too, without repentance, remains outside of the father's house. He represents, according to Ryle, 'a type of all narrow-minded self-righteous people in every age of the church' (*Luke*, II, 185). Jesus' point, Warfield summarizes, is that,

> the Father in heaven has no righteous children on earth; that His grace is needed for all, and most of all for those who dream they have no need of it ... our Lord breaks down the artificial distinction by which they had separated themselves from their sinful brethren, and in doing so breaks down also the barriers which held their sympathies back and opens the way to full appreciation by them of the joy He would have them feel in the recovery of the lost. (22)

Let us now look in detail at the sins of the elder brother.

First, he resents his life of service
'Look!' he says. 'For so many years I have been serving you...' What is he saying? Is he complaining? Is serving in his father's fields a burden or a privilege? Was there something that he would rather have been doing? Morris points out that 'his use of the verb *douleuō* 'to serve as a slave' (cf. NEB, 'I have slaved for you all these years') gives him away. 'He did not really understand what being a son means' (244). The NIV renders it, 'I've been slaving for you.'

This is the outlook of religious sinners. They view the service of God as sacrifice, as a burden, as self-deprivation, as drudgery. It is a duty, not a delight. They have only given in order to get. They want recognition, reward. If they are required to give up so much, they want a pay-off.

Service, *rightly* understood, is a privilege. When we properly serve God we do so out of gratitude, not for reward. Rewards there are in this life, and rewards there shall be in eternity, but they don't provide the motive for service. Grace does. It should have been enough for the elder brother to have lived in his father's presence and to have enjoyed his provisions of food, clothing, shelter, and love. It should be enough for us that God is our Father, that our sins are forgiven, that we have been promised eternity in heaven with God, and that He loves and provides for us in this life.

I've noticed over the years that among those who are truly godly, whether ministers, missionaries, Sunday School teachers, elders, deacons, or members, there is a tendency to completely depreciate any mention of sacrifice or cost in the service of God. Ask them what they have given up, they'll say 'nothing.' They have received so much that their sacrifice is as nothing. They just want to contribute. They just want to serve. They are ready to *give* and *work* and *go* and *do* in any way that they can, and count it their highest privilege.

The problem with the elder brother is that he views service as a *quid pro quo*. 'I've been slaving,' he says, 'yet you have never given me a kid,' that is, a young goat (i.e. one with particularly tender meat). He has worked in order to be paid. He sees work not as grateful service for father but as contract labor. He thinks he has *earned his inheritance through hard labor whereas his prodigal brother has not.* He does not see his reward as a gift. The elder brother is 'lost' after the fashion of religious sinners. Religious sinners are legalists. They imagine that they can merit the forgiveness of sin. They earn their reward, they think. They fail to understand that they could never do enough to earn a place in heaven with God. They cannot earn their inheritance. They cannot earn a place in the Father's household. They can never be good enough, or work hard enough. The elder brother, and the Pharisees and scribes with him, betray a fundamental misunderstanding of the ways of God with humanity.

Second, he resents his life of obedience

The elder brother continues in verse 29, 'and I have never neglected a command of yours.' Yes, and the point would be what? You've not been rewarded? There's been no 'kid' for you? That being the case, would your point be that your obedience has served no good purpose? There has been no 'pay off,' and so your obedience has been wasted? You've missed out because of your obedience? Missed out on what? The older brother is not only self-righteous (have you really *never* neglected a command?), but envious of his brother's wild lifestyle.

Note what his outlook isn't. He isn't saying, as I think he should, that obedience is its own reward. He is not grateful, as we should be, for the 'good' and 'righteous' and 'holy' and 'spiritual' law of God (Rom. 7:14ff.). The Psalmist delights in the law of God and meditates on it day and night (Ps. 1:2). He finds it more desirable than gold and sweeter than honey (Ps. 19:10). He says,

> O how I love Thy law! It is my meditation all the day (Ps. 119:97).

The Psalmist understands that the law of God promotes human dignity (6th Commandment), encourages strong marriages (7th Commandment), protects property (8th Commandment), guards the truth (9th Commandment), and provides rest (4th Commandment), among many other things. 'His commandments are not burdensome,' says the Apostle John (1 John 5:3). Christ's yoke is easy, His burden is light (Matt. 11:30). This is not the outlook of the older brother. No, he secretly envies the indulgence of the prodigal brother. He got to go to wild parties. He got to get drunk. He got to be promiscuous. He got to experiment with exotic drugs. 'I not only missed out on all that,' the elder brother is saying, 'but now he gets the fattened calf and I don't!'

Question: Are the evils indulged by the 'tax gatherers and sinners' to be envied or despised? Should we look upon their sins with desire? Or should we regard their evils with disgust, rejoicing over having been spared their consequences? The prodigal brother, let us not forget, ends up living with swine. The way of sin is hard (Prov. 13:15). The older brother has been spared the scars of sin. Obedience has been its own reward. Obedience has pleased his father and protected him from the ravages of sin.

But for the elder brother, obedience has been a burden that he bore for the sake of reward. He obeyed so as to earn his inheritance. This is the classic mistake of the religious sinners. They are trying to earn God's favor. In order to do so they are willing to give up some things that they'd rather be doing. Absent the reward, they can become resentful. When the wicked prosper, they become angry and are tempted to abandon the faith (e.g. Ps. 73). The real need of religious sinners is that they need new hearts. They need to be born again (John 3:1ff.). They need to become new creatures in Christ, so that in Christ the old carnal desires will pass away and all things will become new (2 Cor. 5:17). Then they will no longer envy evil, but despise it; they will no longer find darkness intriguing, but hate it; they will no longer find righteousness burdensome and boring, but will love it.

Third, he resents his father's grace

> '...but when this son of yours came, who has devoured your wealth with harlots, you killed the fattened calf for him' (Luke 15:30).

He goes on to complain that he has been under-rewarded for his service. 'You have never given me a kid,' he complains (v. 29). Not even a 'kid,' that is, 'a much cheaper meal than a fattened calf,' as Marshall points out (612).

Notice he refers to his brother as 'this son of yours' – 'He cannot bring himself to speak of his "brother,"' says Marshall (612). He is seething with resentment. He complains that his brother has consumed the family wealth, devouring the portion of the estate that had been given to him. The Prodigal had no doubt made a devastating impact on the family financial position. Moreover, he had done so for morally degrading reasons – with 'harlots,' or prostitutes. Consequently the father was wrong to celebrate his return, he says. 'He regards his father as utterly weak in his treatment of the prodigal,' says Plummer (378). The elder brother puts his opinion above that of this father, presuming to know better, to know more, to be wiser, fairer and more just than he.

At this point the older brother knows nothing about the attitude of his prodigal brother. Is his brother repentant? Is he a changed man? Is he returning as a servant, not a son? None of this seems to matter. We can assume that the father's entreaties would have included a description of the changed heart of the Prodigal. But for the elder brother, there is little room for grace, mercy, or forgiveness. As far as he is concerned, his younger brother is guilty, he committed terrible sins, and he is forever disqualified from restoration. He certainly should not be given a celebration upon his return. There can be no mercy for him.

The Psalmist asks,

> If Thou, LORD, shouldst mark iniquities, O LORD, who could stand? (Ps. 130:3).

Those who truly know God understand that we all have our own sins. This doesn't mean that we accept each other's *sins*, but it does mean that we accept each other's *repentance*. Remember, Jesus is describing sinners who repent (15:7, 10, 17). The distinction between sin *condoned* and sin *renounced* is crucial. We shouldn't say, 'Oh well, we all have our hang-ups,' and then affirm each other in our gossip, pride, hypocrisy, promiscuity, or drunkenness. No, what we should accept from each other is our repentance. 'I too am a sinner,' I say, 'though mine may be of a different stripe.' Warfield says, 'When all are in equal need of salvation, where is there room for censorious complaint of the goodness of God?' (23).

The elder brother seems to know nothing of this. His inability to celebrate betrays an inability to forgive. An inability to show mercy probably reveals a heart that has not received mercy.

He is harsh, and even censorious of his father's kindness.

The elder brother presents an ugly but accurate picture of the self-righteous but graceless Pharisaism to which religious people are vulnerable. At the heart of this problem is an inability to grasp the implications of God's grace. Am I, as a moral and religious person, superior to those who are morally degraded and irreligious? If I think so, I will come to despise or view with contempt those who do not measure up to my standard. We have seen this time and time again, especially in marriage. A typical scenario, if we might cite an example, is one in which a devout woman is married to a less devout man. He may be a good man but less spiritually minded, and perhaps prone to excesses in alcohol and tobacco. Or he may be obsessed with sports, or recreational activities like hunting or fishing or golf. Or he may have been buried in his work and non-communicative, insensitive to his wife's needs, and aloof from the church. She can grow first to feel superior to him, then to look down upon his worldliness, and finally to despise, even hate him. The irony is rich. The 'religious' one who complains so bitterly of the carnality of the worldly one, is filled with bitterness, contempt and hate, and is devoid of compassion, kindness, mercy and grace. The heart sins of the religious ones are far worse than the 'worldly' sins of the carnal ones. Jesus reserves His harshest words not for the tax-gatherers and sinners, but for scribes and Pharisees (e.g. Matt. 23). The elder brother must come to see himself and his brother as merely *different kinds of sinners*.

The Entreating Father
How does the father respond to his insufferably self-righteous elder son? Does he smack him, denouncing his poisonous envy and resentment? No. The father is tender with the elder brother:

'And he said to him, "My child, you have always been with me, and all that is mine is yours"' (Luke 15:31).

'The father responds with mild entreaties, addressing him tenderly as "child," proffering unbroken intercourse with him, endowing him with all his possessions – in a word, pleading with him as only a loving father can,' says Warfield (21). 'There is plenty of wealth to go around,' he is saying.

'My child,' he says, using the diminutive as a term of affection. 'You have always been with me, and I recognize that and am grateful for it. I long for your presence with me to continue. All that is mine is yours,' he assures him. This saying 'must be interpreted to mean that legally the son will inherit the farm, since it has already been promised to him,' says Marshall (613). It's yours and it has been and is at your disposal. You need only to ask for it. Nevertheless, the father continues, this was an occasion to celebrate and 'we had to rejoice.'

'But we had to be merry and rejoice, for this brother of yours was dead and has begun to live, and was lost and has been found' (Luke 15:32).

Why is it 'we had to be merry and rejoice?' Because a fellow lost sinner has been reclaimed. Heaven celebrates this and as fellow sinners so must we. Jesus is explaining why He socializes with sinners, why He seeks their conversion, and why we ought to rejoice when they do convert. Celebration is a natural and necessary response to the recovery of the lost.

The parable ends with the elder brother still outside, excluded by his own self-righteousness and pride. The parable leaves an unresolved question – will the elder brother go in to the celebration? Will he continue to think in terms of what is legally his and what he has earned and remain outside, or will he embrace the grace of God in Christ? 'In leaving these points unresolved He throws out a challenge to all His hearers, be they like the elder or like the younger,' says Morris (245). The same grace that saves the morally polluted but repentant Prodigal also saves the proud, self-righteous and legalistic Pharisee. *To reject the grace of God for the Prodigal, as the elder son has, is also to reject the grace of God for himself.*

He must come to understand, as must we all, that we, like the Prodigal, are sinners, and that we, like the Prodigal, need God's grace. Jesus suffered on the cross for sinners, for us all, for 'all have sinned and fall short of the glory of God,' for 'all we like sheep have gone astray' (Rom. 3:23; Isa. 53:6). Only when we grasp this do the doors of heaven open up for us.

Likewise, only when we grasp this will we, like our heavenly Father, love, seek, and receive the lost prodigals of the world. For the disciples of Christ, the polluted and morally repugnant prodigals are merely sinners of a different sort. When the religious community sees itself in continuity with the prodigals, its collective heart will open to the lost, and its energies will be directed to their rescue.

STUDY QUESTIONS

1. This is the third of three successive parables about seeking the lost (Luke 15:1-10). What is the nuance of this parable over against the Lost Sheep and Lost Coin?

2. What is the central lesson that the three parables have in common?

3. Describe the stages in the Prodigal's descent into sin (we can see three or more) (vv. 13-16). How do these stages parallel the descent of the lost soul?

4. How does Jesus describe the Prodigal's repentance? (15:17-19).

5. How would you characterize the outlook of the father? His response?

6. What can we say to those who have gone off to the 'far country' away from God?

7. We come now to the elder brother. What can one say that is good about him?

8. Why might the elder brother justly become angry (and we in similar circumstances?) (v. 28).

9. How does the father respond to the elder brother's anger? (v. 28) Where have we seen this side of God before?

10. How does the elder brother view himself? (v. 29). His service?

11. How does the elder brother view his obedience? His life? (v. 29) How should he be thinking?

12. How does the elder brother view his father's gift of the party and the fattened calf? (v. 30).

13. Where is the elder brother when the parable ends? (v. 32) What does this mean?

~ 21 ~

'THE GOOD SAMARITAN'

Luke 10:25-37

Love for Neighbor

^{25}*And behold, a certain lawyer stood up and put Him to the test, saying, 'Teacher, what shall I do to inherit eternal life?'* ^{26}*And He said to him, 'What is written in the Law? How does it read to you?'* ^{27}*And he answered and said, 'You shall love the Lord your God with all your heart, and with all your soul, and with all your strength, and with all your mind; and your neighbor as yourself.'* ^{28}*And He said to him, 'You have answered correctly; do this, and you will live.'* ^{29}*But wishing to justify himself, he said to Jesus, 'And who is my neighbor?'* ^{30}*Jesus replied and said, 'A certain man was going down from Jerusalem to Jericho; and he fell among robbers, and they stripped him and beat him, and went off leaving him half dead.* ^{31}*And by chance a certain priest was going down on that road, and when he saw him, he passed by on the other side.* ^{32}*And likewise a Levite also, when he came to the place and saw him, passed by on the other side.* ^{33}*But a certain Samaritan, who was on a journey, came upon him; and when he saw him, he felt compassion,* ^{34}*and came to him, and bandaged up his wounds, pouring oil and wine on them; and he put him on his own beast, and brought him to an inn, and took care of him.* ^{35}*And on the next day he took out two denarii and gave them to the innkeeper and said, "Take care of him; and whatever more you spend, when I return, I will* repay you.' ³⁶Which of these three do you think proved to be a neighbor to the man who fell into the robbers' hands?' ³⁷And he said, 'The one who showed mercy toward him.' And Jesus said to him, 'Go and do the same.'

After the 'Prodigal Son,' this parable is probably the best known, most frequently cited, and most widely appreciated of all of Jesus' parables. It is universally regarded for its capacity to portray the essence of the Christian life – sacrificial love for neighbor – with a memorable, easy to understand story-illustration. How are Christians to live? Look to the Parable of the Good Samaritan, countless Christians have said, and there you shall find its ideal.

But we must notice that the parable answers two questions. The second question of the 'certain lawyer,' 'Who is my neighbor?' (v. 29), leads us to see the parable as a description of the Christian way of life, a life of love to those in need, whoever and wherever they are. But the prior question of the lawyer, 'What shall I do to inherit eternal life?' (v. 25), though often ignored by interpreters of the parable, is still in view as Jesus delivers His parable. Wilcock speaks of the 'hidden depths' of the parable. Its 'barbed point,' says Wilcock, is the impossibility of law-keeping as a way of salvation. If we must love our neighbor after the manner of the Good Samaritan, we cannot fulfill its requirements. 'Keeping the law is a way *of* life, it is not a way *to* life,' says Wilcock (122, 123). He continues, 'It is only when by God's grace we have become the right sort of people – his people, by the new birth – that we begin to do the right sort of things' (127).

We will look at the whole passage, verses 25-29 as well as 30-37, so that we might understand the full intent of Jesus' parable.

The way to life

The Parable of the Good Samaritan did not originate in a vacuum, but arose out of Jesus' discussion with 'a certain lawyer' (v. 25) who asked Jesus the question of questions:

'Teacher, what shall I do to inherit eternal life?' (Luke 10:25b).

We ought to commend the lawyer for raising the right issue. He is not so caught up in the pursuit of fame, fortune, and fun that he fails to ponder eternity. Life is more than the here and now. He knows that this temporary life is not all that there is. Our time in this world is short and eternity is long. His question is the right one to ask, and we too should be asking it. Jesus gave a surprising answer:

> And He said to him, 'What is written in the Law? How does it read to you?' (Luke 10:26).

It is surprising to us that Jesus directs him to the Law of God. 'Law,' here, may mean no more than 'Bible.' But given the lawyer's answer (he cites the commandments in v. 27), and Jesus' commendation of the answer (v. 28), it seems the law as moral code is meant. Moreover, Jesus seems typically to have directed spiritual inquirers to the commandments. When approached by the 'Rich Young Ruler,' and others similarly in pursuit of 'eternal life,' Jesus said, 'You know the commandments,' and then quoted the fifth through the ninth (Mark 10:17-22; Matt. 19:16-22; Luke 18:18-23; cf. Matt. 22:34-40; Mark 12:28-31). In each case Jesus employs the law not as an end in itself, but as a means to an end. He directs or leads them to the law that they might understand their failure to keep the law, and might look to other, gracious means of salvation. In the case of the Rich Young Ruler, Jesus required that he sell all his treasure, and give it to the poor, and follow Him (Mark 10:21). By this means he showed the Rich Young Ruler that, contrary to his claim to have 'kept all (the commandments) from my youth' (Mark 10:20), he did not love God foremost, the *first* of the great commandments, but had idols of wealth and comfort in his heart to which he gave preference. With this 'certain lawyer' Jesus will tell the Parable of the Good Samaritan to illustrate his inability to keep the *second* of the great commandments, love of neighbor. The lawyer responds:

> And he answered and said, 'You shall love the Lord your God with all your heart, and with all your soul, and with all

your strength, and with all your mind; and your neighbor as yourself' (Luke 10:27).

He answered 'correctly,' Jesus says. Jesus affirms his response with a citation from Leviticus 18:5:

And He said to him, 'You have answered correctly; do this, and you will live' (Luke 10:28).

'Do this' (i.e. keep the commands to love God and love your neighbor) 'and you will live.' This is the promise of the law. Keep it and you will have life eternal. 'Practice what you preach,' Marshall paraphrases (447). But understand that the law also condemns all sin and every sin. If you live by the law you will die by the law. The Apostle Paul, quoting Deuteronomy 27:26, says,

For as many as are of the works of the Law are under a curse; for it is written, 'Cursed is everyone who does not abide by all things written in the book of the law, to perform them' (Gal. 3:10).

It is our inability to 'abide' by 'all things' in the law that kills us. 'Stumble at one point,' says James, and 'we become guilty of all' (James 2:10). At this point the lawyer should be thinking, 'Neither I nor anyone else can keep the two great commandments.' If 'life' comes through the keeping of the commandments, then I am doomed because I cannot keep them. I break them daily in 'thought, word, and deed,' as the old prayer of confession says. The problem is that he and we can't keep it, and so the law only condemns him and us. As the Apostle Paul says, the commandment 'which was to result in life, proved to result in death for me.'

and this commandment, which was to result in life, proved to result in death for me; for sin, taking opportunity through the commandment, deceived me, and through it killed me (Rom. 7:10, 11).

The lawyer doesn't understand this. He is hoping that he can 'inherit eternal life' through perfect, or at least adequate, obedience. He will be able, he thinks, by good works and love, to earn or merit his salvation. So he asks the question,

> But wishing to justify himself, he said to Jesus, 'And who is my neighbor?' (Luke 10:29).

Luke says that the lawyer was 'wishing to justify himself' in asking the question, 'Who is my neighbor?' 'Justify' here probably means 'explain,' 'excuse' or 'rationalize,' as when we say of the excuses of a glutton, 'he's just trying to justify his behavior.' The lawyer wants to define 'neighbor' narrowly enough so as to excuse lovelessness and claim fulfillment of the command. He wants to have 'eternal life.' But he knows that his only hope to qualify by the law is if 'neighbor' is defined merely as his family members or close associates or the members of his tribe or race. Only then, he knows, may it be possible to demonstrate obedience and earn 'life.'

In addition, no student of the New Testament can see the word 'justify' (*dikaiôsai*) and not associate it with the doctrine of justification in the rest of the New Testament. It is hard to believe that Luke, traveling companion of the Apostle Paul, would use it without some intended reference to its theological meaning as a 'just' or 'righteous' standing before God. While sometimes Luke uses 'to justify' in the broader sense of 'to excuse' or 'rationalize' (cf. 7:29; 7:35), he also uses it of those who *excuse themselves so as to appear righteous before God* (as in 10:29; 16:15). For example, we saw that the Parable of the Pharisee and the Publican began with these words:

> And He also told this parable to certain ones who trusted in themselves that they were righteous, and viewed others with contempt: (Luke 18:9).

And it ends with these:

> 'I tell you, this man went down to his house justified rather than the other; for everyone who exalts himself shall be humbled, but he who humbles himself shall be exalted' (Luke 18:14).

To be 'justified' in Luke 18 is the opposite of trusting in one's own righteousness. It is to look only to the mercy of God for forgiveness. It is the opposite of the outlook of those who trust 'in themselves,' that they are 'righteous.'

This is the same term (*dikaioô*) that is repeatedly used by the Apostle Paul to explain justification by faith alone. He says, for example,

> *for not the hearers of the Law are just before God, but the doers of the Law will be justified* (Rom. 2:13).

And again,

> *because by the works of the Law no flesh will be justified in His sight; for through the Law comes the knowledge of sin* (Rom. 3:20).

And positively he says,

> *being justified as a gift by His grace through the redemption which is in Christ Jesus;* (Rom. 3:24; cf. 3:26)

And again,

> *For we maintain that a man is justified by faith apart from works of the Law* (Rom. 3:28; cf 3:30).

And once more the Apostle Paul says of Abraham,

> *But to the one who does not work, but believes in Him who justifies the ungodly, his faith is reckoned as righteousness* (Rom. 4:5; cf. 4:2; 5:1, 9; 8:30; 8:33; Gal. 2:16; 3:8, 11, 24; etc.).

The term 'to justify' in Luke 10:29 carries a measure of this theological weight. It may primarily have psychological meaning (as in 'to excuse'). But there likely is in it at least a nod towards its rich theological implication. After all, in the end the lawyer wishes to justify himself, or be considered righteous before God, *so as to qualify for the eternal life he is seeking in verse 25 of Luke 10.*

The first point of the parable, then, is to drive home the truth that the 'certain lawyer,' and we along with him, cannot fulfill the commands of God. If my neighbor is defined by Jesus in the parable as whomever I might encounter, even my dreaded enemy, and if love is defined by the sacrificial, costly actions of the Good Samaritan, then this is a command I cannot keep. I cannot, do not, and will not love my neighbor as I do myself. I have not done so for one day, or even one moment of one day. I care for myself, serve myself, provide for myself far beyond that which I will ever do for others. I love my children. I love my wife. But even if I could restrict the definition of 'neighbor' to them, I still could not say that I love them as this parable requires that I love them. The parable proves that I am lost, I am doomed, and I cannot through law-keeping save myself. As Ryle summarizes, 'Passages like this should teach us our need of Christ's blood and righteousness' (I, 373).

Another way of stating this lesson is to understand that Jesus alone is the Good Samaritan. He alone loves neighbors and enemies as the parable requires. He alone fulfills gospel law and Mosaic Law. If I am to be justified or righteous before God, I must be 'found in Him, not having a righteousness of my own derived from the Law, but that which is through faith in Christ, the righteousness which comes from God on the basis of faith' (Phil. 3:9).

The way of life

In addition to illuminating how we are to be saved (or more precisely, how we cannot be saved), the parable is also told in order to describe the Christian way of life. 'Go and do the same,' Jesus says (v. 37). The parable clearly defines 'neighbor' and 'love' so as to exclude the possibility that there can be a non-neighbor whom we may ignore. There is no needy person whom I may encounter that I may bypass because he is not my neighbor. Everyone is my neighbor. The requirement to love transcends the categories of race, religion, nationality, or ethnicity. It is boundless, extending to every member of the human race of whose needs I am aware.

Jesus replied and said, 'A certain man was going down from Jerusalem to Jericho; and he fell among robbers, and they stripped him and beat him, and went off leaving him half dead' (Luke 10:30).

Jesus tells a story about a man traveling from 'Jerusalem to Jericho,' a journey of about seventeen miles through desolate and notoriously dangerous country. The traveler descends some 3,300 feet into a region where brigands could safely hide and often preyed upon vulnerable travelers. The traveler is set upon by bandits, who 'beat him,' rob him (we should understand), strip him of his clothes (which were valuable), and leave him 'half-dead.'

'And by chance a certain priest was going down on that road, and when he saw him, he passed by on the other side' (Luke 10:31).

Jesus identifies the first passerby as a 'priest.' His significance is that he is a very religious man, even a religious leader. The priest 'would be returning from a period of duty in the temple to his home in the country,' says Marshall, 'for Jericho was one of the principle country residences for priests' (448). The problem for the priest is that the man lying alongside the road may be dead. If so, touching him would involve ritual defilement and was forbidden to priests (Lev. 21:1ff.; Num. 19:11). But he can't know if he is dead without examining him more closely. So he is caught in conflict between the command to love his neighbor (Lev. 19:18) and the command to avoid ritual defilement (Lev. 21:1ff.); between the claims of charity and ceremony. For the priest, ritual defilement wins. He passes by. 'Other factors may have weighed with him, such as the possibility that the robbers might return, the nature of his business, and so on. We do not know,' Morris adds (189). Apparently other such contingencies are unimportant to Jesus. A wounded man should trump all other considerations. Whatever else he had to do, it was not more important than caring for this injured man. People come first. 'What we do know,' Morris continues, is 'that the priest left the man where he was in his suffering and his need' (189).

'And likewise a Levite also, when he came to the place and saw him, passed by on the other side' (Luke 10:32).

The pattern is repeated when a 'Levite' came by. Levites were inferior to priests in status, but also had responsibilities in the worship of the temple, and were 'a privileged group in Jewish society,' notes Marshall (448). He would have had similar qualifications (i.e. being very religious) and similar reservations (maintaining ceremonial purity). He too avoids involvement. Both religious Jews fail the requirements of love.

The stage is set. Two religious leaders have failed to perform the duties of love. Now a third man comes along.

'But a certain Samaritan, who was on a journey, came upon him; and when he saw him, he felt compassion' (Luke 10:33).

The introduction of a 'Samaritan' would have been unanticipated by Jesus' Jewish hearers. The word 'Samaritan' is placed in the emphatic first position in the sentence to underscore the surprise. If the third traveler had been a Jew, it would have given the parable 'an anti-clerical twist,' as Morris points out (189). But the point of the parable is not how bad the clergy are, but the unexpected 'compassion' of the Samaritan. Jews and Samaritans viewed each other with contempt. To devout Jews, Samaritans were half-breeds and idolaters. Considerable bitterness existed in both directions. For a Jew, a Samaritan would have been 'the last person who might have been expected to help,' notes Morris (190). Yet he 'felt compassion,' Jesus says. This translates into action:

'...and came to him, and bandaged up his wounds, pouring oil and wine on them; and he put him on his own beast, and brought him to an inn, and took care of him' (Luke 10:34).

Oil and wine were widely recognized as 'household remedies,' says Plummer (288). The Samaritan pours wine on the wounds, a procedure which was known to help, even if the antiseptic qualities of the alcohol in the wine were not understood. Similarly, olive oil would have 'eased the pain,' says Morris (190).

He 'put him on his beast,' indicating that the wounded traveler was too weak to walk or even to get up on the beast himself. It also means that the Samaritan himself would have had to walk. He took him to an 'inn,' and 'took care of him,' that is, got everything set up and in order for his care. He also provided for his continuing care:

'And on the next day he took out two denarii and gave them to the innkeeper and said, "Take care of him; and whatever more you spend, when I return, I will repay you"' (Luke 10:35).

'Two denarii' may have paid for as much as two month's board or, according to other scholars, closer to 3-4 weeks (Morris, 190). Either way, the provision is generous and the stay is extended. Beyond that, he promises when he returns, or 'on my return journey,' as Marshall renders it (450), to pay any other expenses incurred by the innkeeper beyond those for which he has already provided.

Jesus has now defined both 'neighbor' and 'love' in the telling of the parable, So He asks,

'Which of these three do you think proved to be a neighbor to the man who fell into the robbers' hands?' (Luke 10:36).

The lawyer asked, 'Who is my neighbor?' Jesus asks in return, 'Who proved to be a neighbor?'

By altering the question, Jesus transforms the concept of neighbor. Whereas his contemporaries thought of one's neighbors as those who belonged to one's group, and connected the duties of neighborliness to those living close at hand, Jesus defines neighbor not by proximity but by neighborliness, and requires its duties be fulfilled toward anyone who crosses one's path. 'One cannot define one's neighbor; one can only be a neighbor' (H. Greeven in Marshall, 450). Plummer put it this way: 'no one who is striving to love his neighbor

---

as himself can be in doubt as to who is his neighbor' (285). The question is not 'Who is my neighbor?' but 'To whom am I a neighbor?' or, in Plummer's words, 'Whose claims on my neighborly help do I recognize?' (288). J. C. Ryle sees an expansive application of Jesus' words: 'We should regard the whole world as our parish, and the whole race of mankind as our neighbors' (I, 377). Jesus demonstrates that the priest and Levite, who pride themselves on careful obedience to the law, in fact failed to keep the crucial command to love one's neighbor.

One can hardly overstate how significant the impact this second lesson of the parable ought to be upon our lives. When I am honest I have to admit that I want to pass by on the other side. I'm busy. I've got things to do. I don't want to get tangled up in other people's problems. But Jesus says we've got to do it. Draw out its implications further. If we must serve strangers in this way, how much more so those with whom we are acquainted? What about those with whom we are closely associated? The Scripture teaches a covenantal priority: we are to 'do good to all men, and especially to those who are of the household of faith' (Gal. 6:10). We are responsible to care for our families and then our church family, before all else (1 Tim. 5:4-8). But this is not to the exclusion of others. We have a responsibility to love *all those with whom we come in contact, and all those whose needs of which we are made aware.* Love, in this case, must be understood as concrete sacrificial acts requiring the expenditure of our time, energy, and treasure.

Will others take advantage of us? Yes, they will. We have to run that risk. We are not obligated to be naïve. But we are required to love. This means that we judge our response by its impact – does it help or hurt? Sometimes our generosity enables sinful and destructive behavior. Love in those circumstances requires the disciplined withholding of aid. We are not meant to contribute to a person's delinquency in the name of love. Love, sometimes, must be tough. So we mustn't interpret the parable simplistically. But with these qualifications we are required to love our neighbors, our enemies, strangers, foreigners, immigrants, and idolaters.

The Jew, to the Samaritan, represented all of these groups, and yet he loves him just the same. So must we.

One of the primary 'barbs' of the parable is aimed at the religious community. The churchgoers, represented by the priest and Levite, were outdone by the pagan Samaritan. The parable teaches that religion without love is worthless. I may have been saved in a great crisis experience. I may have walked an aisle, signed a card, or prayed a prayer. I may have been in church all my life. But if I don't love, I am nothing (1 Cor. 13:1-3). If I don't do good works, my faith is dead and no faith at all (James 2:14-26). To love like this I need a new heart. Love is the fruit of the Holy Spirit's presence within us (Gal. 5:22, 23). Only as the love of Christ is 'poured out within our hearts through the Holy Spirit' will I love as I ought (Rom. 5:5).

Whom would God have me love today? Whom would He have me serve? Answer: Anyone with whom I come in contact. Why should I? Not in order to be saved, but *because* I am saved. The Good Samaritan points me to both the way *to* life (not through the law but by faith in Christ) and a way *of* life (the life of love for all). It presents a picture of the whole Christian life. All who cross my path are my neighbors, and all my neighbors are to be recipients of the love that *The Good Samaritan Himself* has placed in my heart.

STUDY QUESTIONS

1. What question(s) is the Parable of the Good Samaritan designed to answer?

2. What is surprising (and for some, has proven misleading) about Jesus' answer to the first question in verse 26? Why does Jesus answer as He does?

3. Think about the lawyer's answer in verse 27 and Jesus' response in verse 28. Read Galatians 3:10 and James 2:10. How should the lawyer have responded to Jesus' promise 'do this, and you will live?'

4. What is the motive behind the lawyer's question, 'Who is my neighbor?' (Luke 10:29)

5. Read verses 30-32. Why do the priest and Levite not help?

6. Who extends the care to the beaten man in verses 33-35? What is the significance of this?

7. How has Jesus defined both 'love' and 'neighbor?'

8. What does the parable teach us about the way *to* life? The way *of* life?

~ 22 ~

'THE UNMERCIFUL SERVANT'

Matthew 18:21-35

Forgiving Others

²¹*Then Peter came and said to Him, 'Lord, how often shall my brother sin against me and I forgive him? Up to seven times?'* ²²*Jesus said to him, 'I do not say to you, up to seven times, but up to seventy times seven.* ²³*For this reason the kingdom of heaven may be compared to a certain king who wished to settle accounts with his slaves.* ²⁴*And when he had begun to settle them, there was brought to him one who owed him ten thousand talents.* ²⁵*But since he did not have the means to repay, his lord commanded him to be sold, along with his wife and children and all that he had, and repayment to be made.* ²⁶*The slave therefore falling down, prostrated himself before him, saying, "Have patience with me, and I will repay you everything."* ²⁷*And the lord of that slave felt compassion and released him and forgave him the debt.* ²⁸*But that slave went out and found one of his fellow slaves who owed him a hundred denarii; and he seized him and began to choke him, saying, "Pay back what you owe."* ²⁹*So his fellow slave fell down and began to entreat him, saying, "Have patience with me and I will repay you."* ³⁰*He was unwilling however, but went and threw him in prison until he should pay back what was owed.* ³¹*So when his fellow slaves saw what had happened, they were deeply grieved and came and reported to their lord all that had happened.* ³²*Then*

summoning him, his lord said to him, "You wicked slave, I forgave you all that debt because you entreated me. ³³Should you not also have had mercy on your fellow slave, even as I had mercy on you?" ³⁴And his lord, moved with anger, handed him over to the torturers until he should repay all that was owed him. ³⁵So shall My heavenly Father also do to you, if each of you does not forgive his brother from your heart.'

Expect to be hurt, mistreated, and abused in this world. Expect even in the church to have legitimate grievances, to be wronged, misunderstood, sinned against. I told myself years ago that if I ever had the privilege of speaking to seminary students, I would warn them of the amount of conflict they might encounter in the church. I was not warned, and was shocked by reality. This is the nature of life in the world and in the church. This is the way things are. Our world is fallen. Our church is made up of redeemed sinners, but sinners nonetheless.

Have you embraced reasonable expectations about life? Peter seems to have. As is so often the case, Peter takes the lead in raising questions:

'Lord, how often shall my brother sin against me and I forgive him? Up to seven times?' (Matt. 18:21).

Peter expects to be wronged. He knows that this will happen. He correctly anticipates that even his Christian 'brother,' a fellow disciple, will sin against him, and do so repeatedly.

So it happens. He is wronged. Now what? What is he to do? The rabbis recommended that forgiveness for a repeated offense be extended not more than three times. The fourth time one should refuse forgiveness, they reasoned. Peter, as France points out, is being generous when he suggests seven times. He has learned from Jesus about forgiveness, but surely, he reasons, there must be a limit. Jesus' answer, says France, 'does away with all limits and calculations' (277).

Jesus said to him, 'I do not say to you, up to seven times, but up to seventy times seven' (Matt. 18:22).

No, Peter, not seven times, 'but' (*alla*), on the contrary, or 'far from that,' seventy times seven! If we are 'calculating numbers of offenses,' as Morris puts it, 'we are walking down the wrong path' (471). 'Seventy times seven' is an allusion to Lamech's blustering threat of 'unlimited vindictiveness' notes France (277). Lamech said,

> 'If Cain is avenged sevenfold, then Lamech seventy-sevenfold' (Gen. 4:24).

There is a question as to whether the Hebrew of Genesis 4:24 and the Greek of Matthew 18:22 means seventy times seven or seventy-seven, the latter, according to the experts, being the more natural rendering. Either way the meaning is clear. Jesus is requiring 'unlimited forgiveness' of His disciples (France, 277). He does not mean that the seventy-eighth offense (or the 491st) need not be forgiven. For the disciples of Christ, says Morris, 'forgiveness is to be unlimited' (472). In Luke's account, Jesus says,

> 'And if he sins against you seven times a day, and returns to you seven times, saying, "I repent," forgive him' (Luke 17:4).

Sound unreasonable? Jesus tells a parable to explain why this must be. In doing so he explains the *context* of forgiveness (our own forgiveness), the *principle* that follows (graciousness towards others), and the *threat* that remains.

Our Forgiveness
Jesus begins by describing the context within which we forgive others. He does so in two ways.

First, Jesus describes the debt of our sins

> 'For this reason the kingdom of heaven may be compared to a certain king who wished to settle accounts with his slaves. And when he had begun to settle them, there was brought to him one who owed him ten thousand talents' (Matt. 18:23, 24).

This king wishes to 'settle accounts.' Morris sees a note of finality, a 'settled decision' to have a 'day of reckoning' (472). 'There was brought' may indicate a certain unwillingness, as one might well understand, on the part of the one who owed 'ten thousand talents' (Morris, 472). 'Talent' was the largest unit of currency. 'Ten thousand' is the highest Greek numeral. A billion dollars would convey the meaning in today's English. It is a 'vast sum,' says Morris (473). The debt is not only vast, as in the Parable of the Two Debtors (Luke 7:36-50); it is astronomical beyond comprehension. There, it was 500 denarii at most, or two years' wages. Here Jesus is underscoring with exclamation points that the debt is impossibly large and utterly unpayable. There is considerable speculation on the part of the commentators that the debtor envisioned would be a tax-collector, who had bid for the right to collect from a region far beyond that region's capacity to pay. By way of comparison, the whole region of Perea and Galilee produced only 200-600 talents of tax payments per year. He owes 10,000!

> 'But since he did not have the means to repay, his lord commanded him to be sold, along with his wife and children and all that he had, and repayment to be made' (Matt. 18:25).

Of course, he has no means to repay. Selling the man, his wife and children into slavery would not begin to pay the debt (slaves were often sold for 1 talent or even less). The emphasis is on 'the servant's desperate plight,' says Calvin (406). 'It is impossible that the sale of one so worthless should amount to the payment of so great a debt,' says Matthew Henry.

Jesus' aim in describing this impossible debt is that we should ponder the magnitude of our debt. God is likened to this king. Our situation is likened to that of this individual slave. Every day we sin, and not once or twice, but repeatedly and constantly. Not even for a moment do we love God with all our heart. Not even for a moment do we love our neighbors as ourselves. Consequently, we are constantly in violation of the two most important of the commandments (Matt. 22:37-39). There are constant passive sins such as pride, self-righteousness, hypocrisy, lust, hatred, covetousness, jealousy, envy, and more. As for active transgressions, let's use the numbers presented by Evangelism Explosion. Imagine you sin just three times a day in your thoughts, words, and deeds. Such a record would establish one as a saint of some sort, but let's go with it. Three sins a day equals how many per year? Let's round it off to one thousand. One thousand each year. Now let's imagine that you live to the modest age of seventy years old. How many sins is that in a lifetime? Seventy thousand! This to a God who says that if you keep the whole law and yet stumble at *one* point, you are guilty of all (James 2:10). This to a God who says 'the soul that sins will die;' who says, 'the wages of sin is death' (Ezek. 18:4; Rom. 6:23). Our sins number more 'than the hairs of our head' (Ps. 40:12). They have piled up as high as the heavens (Rev. 18:5; Ezra 9:6).

We cannot purchase our forgiveness (Ps. 49:6, 7). God cannot be bribed. We have this astronomical debt and we can't get rid of it. Left to ourselves, our situation is 'helpless' (Rom. 5:6) and hopeless (Eph. 2:12). As Augustus Toplady (1740–1788) in his beloved hymn, 'Rock of Ages,' wrote:

Not the labor of my hands
Can fulfill Thy law's demands;
Could my zeal no respite know,
Could my tears forever flow,
All for sin could not atone;
Thou must save, and Thou alone.

'Labor,' 'zeal,' 'fears' are all futile. Similarly, Horatius Bonar (1808–1889) wrote of the futility of our working 'hands,' our 'toiling flesh;' 'prayers,' 'sighs,' and 'tears' and all our feeling and doing in his 'Not What My Hands Have Done.'

Not what my hands have done can save my guilty soul;
Not what my toiling flesh has borne can make my spirit
   whole.
Not what I feel or do can give me peace with God;
Not all my prayers and sighs and tears can bear my awful
   load.

319

We are powerless. We cannot pay down this debt. Not in a million years. Our only hope is the sheer mercy of God.

Second, Jesus describes the freeness of our forgiveness

> 'The slave therefore falling down, prostrated himself before him, saying, "Have patience with me, and I will repay you everything"' (Matt. 18:26).

Seeing that he has no hope, he pleads for mercy, lying prostrate before the king, pleading. 'The imperfect tense indicates that he kept pleading; his was no half-hearted plea,' says Morris (474). This is all that he could do. He cast himself at the feet of the king and begged.

> 'And the lord of that slave felt compassion and released him and forgave him the debt' (Matt. 18:27).

He 'felt compassion' or 'pity' (RSV), as in Matthew 9:36. It indicates that he was 'deeply moved in his pity,' says Morris (474). He gives the slave far more than he requested, forgiving the entire debt, without hesitation or additions. 'It was an act of pure grace,' says Morris (475).

This is what God has done for believers in Christ. We brought to Him an unpayable debt of guilt. We were doomed, destined for an eternity of bondage. But out of His sheer goodness and grace in Christ, He forgave the entire debt. Not one obligation remains. Not a single sin remains unatoned. The guilt is gone. We are forgiven. He has 'released us from our sins by His blood' (Rev. 1:5). We paid nothing. We contributed nothing. Of His own free grace and mercy He has done it all.

Forgiving Others

This is the context in which we encounter the offenses of others. God has shown mercy to us. It is of such magnitude that we cannot but show mercy to others. As Jesus says elsewhere,

'Be merciful, just as your Father is merciful' (Luke 6:36).

Yet this is not what we encounter from the forgiven slave.

> *'But that slave went out and found one of his fellow slaves who owed him a hundred denarii; and he seized him and began to choke him, saying, "Pay back what you owe"'* (Matt. 18:28).

A denarius is only a few cents, a day's wage of a laborer. There are 6,000 denarii to a talent. The second debt is merely 1/600,000 of the first debt. France speaks of the 'ludicrous impropriety of the forgiven sinner's standing on his own rights' (277). The debt wasn't insignificant, but comparatively, it was 'a mere trifle,' says Morris (475), 'an infinitesimal fraction,' says Barclay (213). He 'began to choke him' is literally 'took him by the throat.' The point is that the man was 'greedy and grasping' (Morris, 475), and almost unbelievably oblivious to the implications of his own forgiveness.

> *'So his fellow slave fell down and began to entreat him, saying, "Have patience with me and I will repay you"'* (Matt. 18:29).

He had to have heard the echo of his own plea (v. 26). Still, he is unmoved.

> *'He was unwilling however, but went and threw him in prison until he should pay back what was owed'* (Matt. 18:30).

He was 'unwilling.' 'His will is set against clemency' (Morris, 475). He 'threw him into prison.' The verb 'threw' 'indicates vigorous actions,' says Morris (475). It indicates a ruthlessness in his dealing with his debtor.

This was more than the other slaves who observed all this could take.

> *'So when his fellow slaves saw what had happened, they were deeply grieved and came and reported to their lord all that had happened'* (Matt. 18:31).

The king calls this exactly what it is: wicked!

> 'Then summoning him, his lord said to him, "You wicked slave, I forgave you all that debt because you entreated me"' (Matt. 18:32).

The word order in Greek is, 'All that debt I forgave you,' with the emphasis on 'all.' 'All that immense amount,' is the sense of his words (Morris, 476).

> 'Should you not also have had mercy on your fellow slave, even as I had mercy on you?' (Matt. 18:33).

'Should' implies moral obligation. What the slave ought to have done is what was ethically required. Those who receive mercy are obligated to extend mercy. 'Should you not?' or 'Is it not necessary' (*edei*)? Showing mercy is obligatory on the part of those who have received it.

> 'And his lord, moved with anger, handed him over to the torturers until he should repay all that was owed him' (Matt. 18:34).

The king is moved with anger, with righteous indignation. The 'torturers' are not 'jailers' as in RSV and NIV. France calls this 'an unjustifiable euphemism' (277). Their job was to 'put pressure on the defaulter and his family to produce the money' (France, 278).

The Threat

This brings us to the point of the parable. Our Father is likened to the king, and our plight is that of the unforgiving servant if we cannot forgive others their offenses against us.

> 'So shall My heavenly Father also do to you, if each of you does not forgive his brother from your heart' (Matt. 18:35).

'So shall My heavenly Father also do to you,' says Jesus. 'The severity we discern in the punishment of the man in the parable is all that unforgiving sinners can look for from the hand of God,' says Morris (477). Moreover, the forgiveness of offenders required by Jesus cannot be faked. It must be 'from the heart,' which according to France 'excludes all casuistry and legalism' (278). Does this seem harsh? Carson comments, 'Jesus sees no incongruity in the actions of a heavenly Father who forgives so bountifully and punishes so ruthlessly, and neither should we' (407).

This teaching of Jesus is a tremendous challenge to us. But it is also a central plank of the Christian life. Most of us are slow to forgive and even slower to forget. We harbor resentments and refuse to let them go, and in some cases, with deliberation and forethought refuse to forgive. We may even boast that we'll never forgive so and so for what he did. Yet Jesus says,

> 'For if you forgive men for their transgressions, your heavenly Father will also forgive you. But if you do not forgive men, then your Father will not forgive your transgressions' (Matt. 6:14, 15).

How can it be that when our vast debts have been forgiven we refuse to forgive the trifling debts of others? There are certain factors of which we ought to be open and honest:

1. *Many of us enjoy martyrdom.* We relish the role of the aggrieved, of crying 'poor me.' We delight in having others pity us as we relate the wrongs we've suffered. We are slow to give up this role; we milk it for all it is worth.

2. *Many of us enjoy anger and hatred.* We nurse our grievances, rehearsing the crimes committed against us again and again, each time stirring up further our bitterness and resentment.

Who could enjoy such things? Those who otherwise would live passionless, boring, dull lives. Bitterness gives them something to talk about.

3. *Many of us make non-repentance an excuse for ongoing spite.* It's true that I cannot forgive those who will not repent. Forgiveness can only be granted when it is received. The

unrepentant do not admit the need for forgiveness and therefore do not accept it. But I can adopt a forgiving attitude. How do I do this? Calvin says, 'I set aside any feeling of revenge and do not cease to love him and even repay him with benefits instead of injuries.' In other words, I cleanse my soul of hatred, and love the offending person from the heart. The point, says Calvin, is that God 'only wishes our minds to be purged of hatred' (I, 234).

4. *Sometimes we fear being taken advantage of.* 'What if they only pretend to repent?', we ask. Won't I become a doormat? a laughingstock? 'Christ is not depriving believers of discretion,' says Calvin. Yet it is necessary for us to take risks. Jesus intends that we should be 'fair and humane' and receive back the penitent, Calvin continues, 'when they show signs of being sincerely displeased with themselves,' when they show 'a probable sign of conversion' (I, 235).

5. *Finally, we think too little of the magnitude of the debts that God has forgiven us.* In the end, whatever else may be contributing to our refusal to forgive, this must be the case. We could not refuse to forgive the relative trifles of others if we thought frequently of the free pardon that we have received. It would be obvious to us that to do so would trivialize the gospel, and especially our experience of it. Forgiving the debts of others is the least that we can do, given the scale of our own debt of sin and the scope of God's bounty towards us.

STUDY QUESTIONS

1. Note the setting. Who does Peter expect will sin against him? Is this a reasonable expectation? (v. 21).

2. Is Peter being generous or restrictive in his proposal to forgive 'up to seven times?' (v. 21).

3. What does Jesus mean by 'seventy-times seven?' (v. 22).

   'And if he sins against you seven times a day, and returns to you seven times, saying, 'I repent,' forgive him' (Luke 17:4).

4. The parable is meant to instruct the disciples about the limits of forgiveness. What does Jesus emphasize at the outset? (vv. 23-25).

5. How does the slave escape his debts? (vv. 26, 27).

6. Explain the incongruity of verses 28-30. What does this mean for your relationships?

7. Jesus uses the reaction of the 'fellow slaves' and the words of the king to make his point (vv. 31-33). What is it?

8. What can those who will not forgive expect from God? (vv. 34, 35).

9. Why, in spite of our vast debts, do we sometimes refuse to forgive?

~ 23 ~

'THE UNJUST JUDGE'

Luke 18:1-8

Persistent Prayer

¹Now He was telling them a parable to show that at all times they ought to pray and not to lose heart, ²saying, 'There was in a certain city a judge who did not fear God, and did not respect man. ³And there was a widow in that city, and she kept coming to him, saying, "Give me legal protection from my opponent." ⁴And for a while he was unwilling; but afterward he said to himself, "Even though I do not fear God nor respect man, ⁵yet because this widow bothers me, I will give her legal protection, lest by continually coming she wear me out."' ⁶And the Lord said, 'Hear what the unrighteous judge said; ⁷now shall not God bring about justice for His elect, who cry to Him day and night, and will He delay long over them? ⁸I tell you that He will bring about justice for them speedily. However, when the Son of Man comes, will He find faith on the earth?'

Prayer is difficult for us in the modern world. Our civilization is largely secular and materialistic in its outlook. It screams at us daily that all that is real, and certainly all that matters, is what we can see, handle, taste, and touch. Reality consists of the physical world around us. The material world is the only world that counts. Only with great difficulty can professing Christians rise above the

327

spirit of our age, its *zeitgeist*, and affirm with the Apostles that 'the things which are seen are temporal, but the things which are not seen are eternal' (2 Cor. 4:18). Instead we are sorely tempted to pour all of our time and energy into our houses, automobiles, clothes, food, and various recreations and entertainments by which we amuse ourselves. We lay up treasures on earth rather than heaven because, frankly, we can see and enjoy earthly treasures, but can scarcely believe that heavenly treasures exist (Matt. 6:19-21). Little thought is given to the soul and the eternal. We live like practical atheists Monday to Saturday, even if we are in church on Sunday.

This pervasive modern outlook of our day is called 'materialism.' Its prevalence explains why prayer is so difficult for us. Prayer is the consummate spiritual activity. To devote hours each week to prayer seems a waste of time. 'What are you doing?' someone might ask a person engaged in prayer. 'You're just sitting.' You are talking to yourself, it seems. Better to get up and do something concrete, something real. Prayer is difficult to sustain in the modern, secular, materialistic world.

Yet, Jesus assumes that His disciples will be devoted to prayer (cf. Rom. 12:12). They will maintain at least a daily prayer discipline, praying, as He seems to envision at the outset of the day, 'Give us this day our daily bread' (Matt. 6:11; cf. Luke 11:3). The Lord's Prayer is a daily prayer. Daily praise, daily confession of sin, daily thanksgiving, and daily supplications for all things necessary are all a part of the regular prayer life of the believer (cf. Phil. 4:6, 7).

Moreover, Jesus taught the disciples to persist in prayer. 'Keep on asking, keep on seeking, keep on knocking,' He taught us (Matt. 7:7-11; Luke 11:9-13).[1] Persist, like the persistent friend with his reluctant neighbor (Luke 11:5-8).

The Parable of the Unjust Judge is a companion of the Parable of the Persistent Friend (Luke 11:5-13), teaching

---

1. See *When Grace Comes Alive* (Christian Focus, 2003), p. 205ff. for the implications of the verb tenses; see also the next chapter.

much the same lessons. But because it follows Jesus' teaching in Luke 17 about the Second Coming, it has more particularly in mind the problem of unanswered prayer. The parable targets the prayers of the elect in the present age, the 'long interval' before Christ's return, as Morris calls it (262), or 'the long weary interval between the first and second advents,' as J. C. Ryle describes it (252), when the pleas of Christ's disciples seem to go unheard. That age, our age, is one of persecution and rejection. Yet God seems to hesitate in answering His people's prayers. These long delays between requests and answers are characteristic of our age, and give rise to problems which the parable is designed to answer.

The Introduction
'This parable has its key hanging at the door,' as Matthew Henry points out.

> *Now He was telling them a parable to show that at all times they ought to pray and not to lose heart,* (Luke 18:1).

The 'them' of verse 1 is the disciples. The purpose of the parable is given at the outset: 'at all times they ought to pray and not to lose heart.' 'At all times' means regularly, not continuously. Jesus is urging them to keep up 'the habit of prayer' and 'a prayerful frame of mind' (Ryle, II, 256). Maintain your regular prayer routines whether things are going well or poorly. 'The fear is that men will give up before they are answered,' says Marshall (671). They may 'lose heart' (*egkakeō*) or 'become weary' or 'despair,' he adds. 'It is far more easy to begin a habit of prayer than it is to keep it up,' Ryle observes (II, 253). A day goes by without prayer and we become discouraged. A week, and we are tired. A month, and we despair. Calvin comments similarly, 'We know how uncommon and difficult a virtue is persistence in prayer' (II, 125). There may be times when we may be called upon to pray for years towards a given end. The parable is designed to buttress our commitment to consistency, frequency, discipline, and perseverance in prayer.

The Parable

'There was in a certain city a judge who did not fear God, and did not respect man' (Luke 18:2).

In small towns prominent men were often appointed to act as judges and settle disputes. This one is a corrupt judge. He neither fears God nor respects man. He is 'controlled only by his own ideas and inclinations,' says Morris (263). He defies both 'Divine commands and public opinion,' says Plummer (411). What does he respond to? The implication is: bribes. He does what suits him, what is in his own interest, what profits him. He doesn't care what anyone thinks, or even what God says.

'And there was a widow in that city, and she kept coming to him, saying, "Give me legal protection from my opponent"' (Luke 18:3).

The widow is the proverbial needy and helpless person. Repeatedly she came to him to take her case (v. 5). But he refused, 'no doubt,' says Marshall, 'out of deference to a wealthy opponent and his bribes' (669). She had no money with which to buy his favor. Furthermore, she had no protector. 'She was armed with nothing but the fact that right was evidently on her side ... and her own persistence,' says Morris (263). 'Give me legal protection,' she cries, or literally 'avenge me' (KJV). But in this context the request means 'to procure justice for someone,' says Marshall (672). It means to 'defend' or 'vindicate' (Zerwick, 253). 'Right the wrong of which I am the victim,' she was saying. She sought not punishment for her opponent in law but payment of what was due (Marshall, 672; Plummer, 412).

'And for a while he was unwilling;' (Luke 18:4a).

Initially he refused, whether because of bribes, fear of her powerful opponent, disdain for a weak woman, or just laziness. He was 'unwilling.' There was no money in it for him. Indeed she would cost him time and money. The fact that God is the defender of the widow and orphan doesn't faze him at all. 'I do not fear God nor respect man,' he declares. But her persistence forced him to reconsider.

> '...but afterward he said to himself, "Even though I do not fear God nor respect man, yet because this widow bothers me, I will give her legal protection, lest by continually coming she wear me out"' (Luke 18:4b, 5).

He's annoyed by her. She 'bothers me,' he says. He is afraid that she'll keep bothering him. Otherwise, he says, she will 'wear me out' (*hupōriazo*), literally 'strike (me) under the eye,' a metaphor drawn from boxing. It is even possible that the reference is to the blackening of the judge's face, that is, the shaming of him for refusing to hear her case, a view favored by Marshall (673). But since he's already said that he doesn't fear man, or the opinions of others, this seems less likely. More typically it is understood as meaning 'wear out' (Zerwick, 253, NIV, NASB), or 'beat me down' (ESV), or 'weary me' (KJV). He gives in, promising 'legal protection' or 'justice' (NIV), because of the widow's annoying persistence.

The Lesson

> And the Lord said, 'Hear what the unrighteous judge said;' (Luke 18:6).

Pay attention to what the 'unjust judge' (KJV) said, says Jesus. We are to 'hear what the unrighteous judge said,' not because there is virtue in it, but the opposite. 'Jesus is not, of course, likening God to an unrighteous judge. The parable is of the 'How much more ...' variety,' explains Morris (262). Jesus 'intends a contrast, not a comparison,' agrees Wilcock (164). Geldenhuys even calls it a 'parable of contrast' (446). The point is, if even a corrupt man like him will eventually hear the cries of the needy, *how much more* will our righteous God.

*'...now shall not God bring about justice for His elect, who
cry to Him day and night, and will He delay long over them?'*
(Luke 18:7).

Yes, God does 'delay.' But the delay is not 'long.' God's
'elect' cry to him 'day and night,' that is, with 'unwearied
persistence,' says Morris (263). The woman was a stranger
to the judge. But the elect are 'His elect.' They are *His* own
people. He loves them and cares for them. Yet they are in the
position of having to 'cry' out to Him 'day and night.' They
are suffering, hurting, afflicted. In pain they cry; as victims
of injustice, they cry; oppressed and helpless, they cry. With
nowhere else to turn they cry out to God 'day and night,'
persistently, continually. Unremitting is their suffering,
relentless are their pleas.

Jesus promises God will provide 'justice' or 'vindication'
(*ekdikēsin*) for His chosen. There is considerable discussion
of verse seven's relation to time. Morris argues that 'the
use of the term implies that eschatological vindication is in
view, and not a purely this–worldly answer to prayer' (674).
'Eschatological vindication' would mean vindication at the
end of time, at the time of Christ's return. The final clause of
verse 7 in the NASB reads, 'will He delay long over them?' The
old RV rendered it, 'and He is longsuffering over them.' The
RSV and ESV (like the NASB) render it as a question – 'will he
long delay?' 'Will he keep putting them off?' the NIV translates
it. One commentator lists eight possible interpretations of
this clause. Marshall understands the sense to be,

> 'The elect cry to God night and day, but he puts their
> patience to the test by not answering them immediately'
> (675).

Whatever the precise nuance, the main point seems clear:
there is a delay, but it is not long. Its length is determined by
God's gracious purposes and according to His timing. 'The
general sense is clear enough,' as Plummer explains, 'that,
however long the answer to prayer may *seem* to be delayed,
constant faithful prayer always *is* answered' (414).

'I tell you that He will bring about justice for them speedily'
(Luke 18:8a).

Jesus answers His own question. God will vindicate His people 'speedily' (NASB, ESV, KJV), meaning either 'soon' or more likely 'suddenly' or 'quickly' (NIV). Yes, there will be a delay. Yes, the prayers will go on day and night. Yet suddenly God will defeat their enemies and secure their case. Time, of course, must be considered in relation to a God for whom a day is as a thousand years (2 Pet. 3:8).

What, then, should we learn from this parable?

First, pray
Don't trifle with prayer. Don't just say a quick prayer when you wake up and another when you go to sleep. Don't say a quick 'grace' at meals and think you are devoted to prayer. To pray as Jesus commends means that we will have a prayer routine. Our prayers will be regular and disciplined. Our prayers will be comprehensive and consistent. Provide time for prayer in your daily schedule. Set aside a chunk of time each day to pray. Use the acrostic: A–adoration; C–confession; T–thanksgiving; S–supplication, to guide you. Pray for victory over the enemies of the gospel who mock and ridicule Jesus' message and His cross. Pray for victory over the tormentors of Christ's disciples who scorn and ostracize, persecute, and, in many places in the world (e.g. Africa, the Middle East, and Asia), do much worse. It can be difficult to be a Christian in schools and colleges and workplaces. Pray for vindication. Pray for victory over your own flesh and worldliness, which drag you down and degrade and threaten your own soul. Pray 'day and night.' Pray persistently. Is there a delay? Does no answer come? Expect this. But pray on. Keep on praying. Like the watchman of Isaiah's day, 'give Him no rest' until righteousness is established (Isa. 62:7).

Second, pray confidently
The widow gets what she seeks. But note the points of contrast between her petitions to the unjust judge and ours to God.

1. *She was a stranger to the judge, whereas we are 'His elect' or 'chosen.'* We are God's own people as Christ's disciples. The judge had no affection for her, whereas God loves us.

2. *She was one and we are many.* She was a lone voice crying for help. We are many voices. We may seem few. We may seem outnumbered against the elite in the academy, the media, and among the entertainers. But we are many.

3. *She pled her own cause whereas we plead God's cause.* Our great end in all our prayers is that God's kingdom will come and His will will be done on earth and heaven. We are asking God to do that which He is already predisposed to do.

4. *Her judge was hostile and ours is inviting.* He says, 'Ask and you will receive.'

5. *Her judge was unjust and ours is righteous.*

6. *Her judge was provoked by her pleas and ours is pleased.*

7. *Her judge would hear her at certain times only, and our judge hears us at all times.*

And yet, she still got what she wanted. If she got what she was after from a dishonest, greedy, and unjust judge, how much more certain can we be that God will hear our cries and vindicate us, protect us, and provide for us? Our responsibility is to 'pray at all times' and not 'lose heart.' Persist. Pray without ceasing (1 Thess. 5:17).

Third, pray believing
This seems to be the implication of the final clause of verse 8.

> *'However, when the Son of Man comes, will He find faith on the earth?'* (Luke 18:8b).

Marshall finds an 'abrupt shift' in verse 8b. God will vindicate His people. But, will He find 'faith,' meaning 'faithfulness' (Marshall, 676), referring here to persistence in prayer, when he returns? 'The question as a whole presupposes a time of tribulation for the disciples in which they may be tempted to give up faith because their prayers are not answered,' says Marshall. That 'time of tribulation' is now. Trial and trouble are characteristic of the present age in which we live. Consequently, continues Marshall, 'it is meant as an exhortation to take seriously the lesson of the parable that God will certainly act to vindicate them' (677).

Will we heed Jesus' exhortation? Will we believe in prayer though answers are delayed? Will we be faithful to pray though God's response is, from our perspective, slow? The pressure to quit praying is enormous. The cultural *zeitgeist* is against us. Our secular, materialistic, naturalistic civilization offers discouragement and disincentives aplenty. Unpraying, practical atheism characterizes much of the church, providing few role models of persistent prayer. Yet the charge of Jesus, in our day and every day, is that 'at all times (we) ought to pray and not to lose heart.'

STUDY QUESTIONS

1. What is meant by 'materialism?' Why does its prevalence in the modern world make prayer difficult for modern people?

2. What is the context of this parable in Luke's Gospel? What is the focus of concern for the parable? (18:1).

3. What does the widow want from the judge (v. 3)? Why is she unlikely to get it (v. 2)?

4. Why does the judge finally give in to the widow? What is the lesson for us (vv. 4, 5)?

5. Is God like the unjust judge or unlike him (vv. 6, 7)?

6. What can we say about our prayer circumstances in this age (vv. 7, 8)?

7. What encouragement may one draw from the contrasts between God and the unjust judge?

8. What important ingredient in prayer is implied by the conclusion of verse 8?

~ 24 ~

'THE PERSISTENT FRIEND'

Luke 11:5-13

Persistent Prayer (cont'd)

⁵And He said to them, 'Suppose one of you shall have a friend, and shall go to him at midnight, and say to him, "Friend, lend me three loaves; ⁶for a friend of mine has come to me from a journey, and I have nothing to set before him"; ⁷and from inside he shall answer and say, "Do not bother me; the door has already been shut and my children and I are in bed; I cannot get up and give you anything." ⁸I tell you, even though he will not get up and give him anything because he is his friend, yet because of his persistence he will get up and give him as much as he needs. ⁹And I say to you, ask, and it shall be given to you; seek, and you shall find; knock, and it shall be opened to you. ¹⁰For everyone who asks, receives; and he who seeks, finds; and to him who knocks, it shall be opened. ¹¹Now suppose one of you fathers is asked by his son for a fish; he will not give him a snake instead of a fish, will he? ¹²Or if he is asked for an egg, he will not give him a scorpion, will he? ¹³If you then, being evil, know how to give good gifts to your children, how much more shall your heavenly Father give the Holy Spirit to those who ask Him?'

We made the case in a previous chapter (The Parable of the Pharisees and the Publican, Luke 18:9-14) that the quality of our prayer life says a great deal about the health of our Christian life. Prayer is a kind of spiritual thermometer. We pray as we believe. We live as we pray. The proud prayer of the Pharisee revealed his self-righteousness and self-sufficiency (his defective theology) and spilled over into his conduct toward others (his contempt for the less religious). The Publican understood his wickedness and so was considerate toward others and cried out to God for mercy. He was 'justified,' whereas the Pharisee was not.

All this could be learned on the basis of the *content* of their prayers. My children hate it when I exegete their table prayers, but you can see that there is precedent for doing so, and much to be learned. Our prayers reveal how we relate to God, that is, the nature of our relationship to God. If I think God is great, I'll praise His greatness. If I think God is holy, I'll confess my sins. If I think God is gracious, I'll claim His pardon. If I think God is good, I'll thank Him. If, on the other hand, I think God is the great unknown, I may merely mumble a request or two now and again when panic or despair overcomes lethargy and unbelief. Prayer is how we interact with God. The *content* of our prayers defines the nature of our relationship with God, and the *frequency* of our prayers determines if there is a relationship with God at all. I can hardly claim to know God (whom to know is eternal life – John 17:3) if I don't pray.

Is infrequency, or lack of persistence, in prayer a problem? As we saw in the preceding chapter (The Parable of the Unjust Judge, Luke 18:1-8), it is. Indeed, this is the second parable devoted to the problem. In our own observation we find that many are taught to pray when children, but give it up in their youth and early adulthood. Some pray in an emergency or special occasion, but once the trial passes lay it aside. Many fail to see the usefulness of it or begin to think that prayer is of little value. Their prayers are occasional at best. Too many subscribe to the Huck Finn theology of 'give it a shot and give up.' He describes his experience, which minus the humor, is too much like our own:

Then Miss Watson she took me in the closet and prayed, but nothing come of it. She told me to pray every day, and whatever I asked for I would get it. But it warn't so. I tried it. Once I got a fish-line, but no hooks. It warn't any good to me without hooks. I tried for the hooks three or four times, but somehow I couldn't make it work. By-and-by, one day, I asked Miss Watson to try for me, but she said I was a fool. She never told me why, and I couldn't make it out no way.

I set down, one time, back in the woods, and had a long think about it. I says to myself, if a body can get anything they pray for, why don't Deacon Winn get back the money he lost on pork? Why can't the widow get back her silver snuff-box that was stole? Why can't Miss Watson fat up? No, says I to myself, there ain't nothing in it. I went and told the widow about it, and she said the thing a body could get by praying for it was 'spiritual gifts.' This was too many for me ...

What we observe of impersistence in others, we see in ourselves as well. Our prayers are inconsistent, irregular, and infrequent. The need of persistence in believing prayer is the lesson that this parable, as well as the preceding, was given to teach. It builds on the lesson of the Unjust Judge, going beyond the fact of persistent to explain why persistence is so vital.

The Parable
'And he said to them,' Luke writes, as he leads into the Parable of the Persistent Friend. To whom? To His disciples, who had just asked, 'Lord, teach us to pray,' and to whom He had just taught the Lord's prayer in response (Luke 11:1-4). The parable is part of Jesus' continuing teaching about prayer. It is 'clearly meant to be an incentive to prayer,' says Marshall (462). This will become clear as we proceed.

> *And He said to them, 'Suppose one of you shall have a friend, and shall go to him at midnight, and say to him, "Friend, lend me three loaves;"'* (Luke 11:5).

Jesus begins the parable asking, 'Suppose,' or literally, 'which one of you,' a phrase the force of which is 'Can anyone of you imagine that ...?' explains Marshall (463). 'It establishes an incontrovertible fact of ordinary life as a basis for a spiritual lesson,' says Marshall (463, cf. 11:11). The situation described is one in which you are forced to go to your friend at midnight in order to borrow three loaves of bread, so that you can feed an unexpected guest. The loaves would be smaller than the typical loaf of bread today, more like the size of our dinner rolls or one of those fresh-baked small loaves that are sometimes served in fine restaurants. In larger villages there might be a bakery shop, but at that hour it would be closed. In smaller villages bread would have been baked in each home in the morning, and consumed by the end of each day. Not anticipating the arrival of the friend, the host has nothing to serve him. So he goes to his neighbor and explains his intrusion:

> '...for a friend of mine has come to me from a journey, and I have nothing to set before him'; (Luke 11:6).

A friend who has been traveling has come to him late at night, and he has nothing to give him. Remember, in these times reputable people did not stay in inns (inns were held in low regard, typically resembling houses of prostitution), and yet travel was often undertaken at night, to escape the heat of the day. The host could not turn his friend away. Hospitality was a 'sacred duty,' as Morris explains (195). 'It would be unthinkable not to provide him with hospitality,' adds Marshall (464). The relationship between the host and *guest* is one of friendship. So is the relationship between the host and his *neighbor*. The host's request of his neighbor arises out of necessity, and not from false or selfish motives. He's in a pinch, as we might say. He needs help.

> 'and from inside he shall answer and say, "Do not bother me; the door has already been shut and my children and I are in bed; I cannot get up and give you anything"' (Luke 11:7).

The neighbor, being asked to help, is clearly annoyed. He omits the customary address of 'friend' in his response.

'Do not bother me,' he says. Leave me alone. 'The door has already been shut,' probably bolted, and it may be difficult to manipulate. His house is likely to be simply one room in which the whole family typically huddled together to keep warm, including, perhaps, the barnyard animals (Barclay, 148). The children are asleep, and he doesn't want to awaken them. Another knock on the door and the chickens may be squawking, the sheep bleating, and the cows mooing. 'I cannot,' says Marshall, 'is tantamount to "I won't"' (465). 'It is the trouble that he minds, not the parting with the bread,' observes Plummer (299). The details of verses 5-7 are clearly meant to create the picture of an extremely unfavorable environment for getting one's request approved.

Yet the neighbor's reluctance is overcome. How? By persistence. Knock a few more times and he'll get you the loaves just to shut you up.

> '*I tell you, even though he will not get up and give him anything because he is his friend, yet because of his persistence he will get up and give him as much as he needs*' (Luke 11:8).

'Persistence' (NASB) is literally 'shamelessness,' his 'sheer impudence' (Marshall, 465) or 'importunity' (KJV), or 'shameless persistence' (Zerwick, 223).

The Lessons
First, we are to be persistent in prayer
What would Jesus have us learn from this parable? 'The point,' says Morris, 'is clear. We must not play at prayer, but must show persistence' (195). Jesus is encouraging His people to persist in prayer even though they may not receive an immediate answer. The host swallows his pride, humbles himself, and shamelessly keeps on knocking, and 'because of his persistence' he gets what he needs (11:8). Because of who God is, because He is kind, compassionate, and gracious, we need not nag. But we do need to persist. Jesus goes on to elaborate on the meaning of His lesson:

'And I say to you, ask, and it shall be given to you; seek, and you shall find; knock, and it shall be opened to you. For everyone who asks, receives; and he who seeks, finds; and to him who knocks, it shall be opened.' (Luke 11:9, 10).

The active verbs in verse 9 are present imperatives, denoting continual action. Their sense is, 'go on asking ... go on seeking ... go on knocking,' says Zerwick (223). Jesus is underscoring the need for persistence. He tells us six times using three different words to keep on praying, even as He promises six times in two verses that He will grant the requests of His disciples. But they must persist. It is not that God is unwilling and His arm must be twisted. He is eager to give. Indeed, this is the point of the contrast between God and the unwilling neighbor.

Why, then, is persistence so important? Why doesn't God just answer us immediately? Because persistence is a sign of sincerity, or earnestness. 'If we do not want what we are asking for enough to be persistent, we do not want it very much,' explains Morris. Again, 'It is not such tepid prayer that is answered' (195). My children ask me for a lot of different things. How do I determine at any given time if what they seek is only a fleeting desire, or if it is deep-rooted and permanent? Persistence. When my son Sam was a little boy he said he wanted to quit violin and play piano. I dismissed this as childish fickleness. But he persisted and urged the change with nine-year-old earnestness. When we saw his sincerity over time, we relented and arranged for lessons. Subsequent behavior proved his sincerity. He was self-motivated to practice and do well. Persistence landed his request.

There is a sense in which there is no such thing as unanswered prayer. Sometimes God overrules our requests and denies them because they are destructive or foolish. The answer on these occasions is 'no.' Normally He says 'yes' and grants our requests. But often our 'prayers' don't qualify as prayers, anymore than the 'hunter' who steps out his back door and fires randomly into the air can claim to have gone duck hunting. A real, that is, sincere hunt takes hours of preparation, travel, and patience. Anything less is self-deception, a mere trifling at hunting. One shouldn't claim to want to be a great golfer, or musician, or student, and then fail to put in the hours that are necessary. A monthly trip to the driving range, banging on the piano keys once a week, cracking a book now and again, do not a golfer/pianist/student make. Persistence is proof of sincerity, a sign of earnestness, an indication that one's requests represent not fleeting interests, not momentary impulses, but deeply held convictions and deeply felt desires.

This is how it is in prayer. Don't toy with prayer. Don't pray one day for *this*, then the next day for *that*. 'Be devoted to prayer,' says the Apostle Paul (Rom. 12:12). Don't play at it. Don't just pray when you feel like it, or when it happens to occur to you. You know what it is to be devoted to something. Focus your attention and energy on prayer. 'Pray without ceasing' (1 Thess. 5:17). Maintain your regular discipline of prayer. Don't quit your prayer routine. Keep at it. Don't cease. It was said of James, the author of the epistle, that his knees looked like camel's knees from all the time he spent on them praying. Persist! Do you want to know God? Pray. Do you really want to know God? Persist in prayer. Do you want to victory over sin? Persist in prayer. Do you want to see loved ones healed? Persist in prayer. Do you want to see loved ones saved? Persist in prayer.

Second, we are to be confident in prayer
This, of course, was a lesson from the previous parable. Yet it receives much fuller development here. Note that in the parable the host is going to his neighbor for things that are necessary. His requests are not self-indulgent. He is not seeking his own personal comfort or pleasure. He is going to a friend to get bread for a friend. His request is reasonable. Yet he must overcome the reluctance of his neighbor. The primary teaching point of the parable is the contrast between the neighbor's reluctance and God's willingness, even eagerness, to hear and grant our requests. Jesus elaborates on this in verses 11-13.

'Now suppose one of you fathers is asked by his son for a fish; he will not give him a snake instead of a fish, will he? Or if he is asked for an egg, he will not give him a scorpion, will he? If you then, being evil, know how to give good gifts to your children, how much more shall your heavenly Father give the Holy Spirit to those who ask Him?' (Luke 11:11-13).

Do parents know how to give good gifts to their children? Most parents will go to extreme lengths and make supreme sacrifices for the sake of their children. In a fit of childish self-centeredness, I once complained to my Mom that my Dad didn't really care about me. She then reminded me that he would do anything for me, citing the example of the multiple hours and days he spent driving all over Los Angeles to find an autographed Don Drysdale baseball glove. You do remember 'Big D,' don't you? Today countless American parents are killing themselves (not literally) to educate their children, paying enormous school and college tuition bills. If our evil neighbors and we, our evil selves, go to extreme lengths to give good gifts to our children, then how much more will God give us good gifts, especially the best and most necessary provision of all, His Holy Spirit? 'Your heavenly Father (shall) give the Holy Spirit to those who ask Him,' Jesus says. The Holy Spirit represents the power of holy living and the wisdom for right choices, and the guarantee of eternal life (see Eph. 1:15-23; Col. 1:9-12; Phil. 1:9-11). What more could any Christian want? Arguing from the greater to the lesser, with the Spirit God freely gives us *all* things (Rom. 8:32). If a neighbor friend with poor motives and a bad attitude eventually gives what we seek, how much more can we be certain that our heavenly Father, who is eager to hear and willing to answer, grants the requests of His people. The parable is first and foremost about God and His graciousness in hearing prayers and granting requests.

Pray. Pray consistently and confidently. Why? Because God is good. He gives good gifts to those who ask. Don't make the mistake of failing to ask. Many 'do not have' because they 'ask not,' James warns (James 4:2). No, persist in your prayers. Ask, seek, knock. Maintain your prayer

'THE PERSISTENT FRIEND'

routines. Be disciplined about your prayers. Be steadfast and consistent. As you are offering your prayers in Jesus' name, you can know that God will hear your prayers and grant your requests. 'This is the confidence which we have before Him,' writes the Apostle John.

> *...if we ask anything according to His will, He hears us. And if we know that He hears us in whatever we ask, we know that we have the requests which we have asked from Him* (1 John 5:14b-15; cf. Matt. 18:19).

STUDY QUESTIONS

1. Both this parable and the 'Parable of the Unjust Judge' (Luke 18:1-8) teach persistence in prayer. Why do we need to be persistent?

2. What is the point of all the details that Jesus relates in verses 5-7?

3. Yet the host does get what he requests. Why? (v. 8).

4. How does Jesus encourage us to persist in prayer in verses 9 and 10?

5. Persistence is valued as a sign of something else that God esteems. What can often be said of the outlook of those who persist in prayer?

6. How does Jesus encourage confidence in prayer in verses 11-13?

7. Why the surprising appearance of the Holy Spirit in verse 13?

345

~ 25 ~

'THE WICKED VINE-GROWERS'

Matthew 21:33-41

Bearing God's Fruit

³³'*Listen to another parable. There was a landowner who planted a vineyard and put a wall around it and dug a wine press in it, and built a tower, and rented it out to vine-growers, and went on a journey.* ³⁴*And when the harvest time approached, he sent his slaves to the vine-growers to receive his produce.* ³⁵*And the vine-growers took his slaves and beat one, and killed another, and stoned a third.* ³⁶*Again he sent another group of slaves larger than the first; and they did the same thing to them.* ³⁷*But afterward he sent his son to them, saying, "They will respect my son."* ³⁸*But when the vine-growers saw the son, they said among themselves, "This is the heir; come, let us kill him, and seize his inheritance."* ³⁹*And they took him, and threw him out of the vineyard, and killed him.* ⁴⁰*Therefore when the owner of the vineyard comes, what will he do to those vine-growers?'* ⁴¹*They said to Him, 'He will bring those wretches to a wretched end, and will rent out the vineyard to other vine-growers, who will pay him the proceeds at the proper seasons'* (cf. Mark 12:1-12; Luke 20:9-19).

Jesus followed the Parable of the Two Sons, a parable of kingdom entrance, with a second parable that was aimed at the religious leadership of Israel, the Parable of the Wicked Vine-Growers. He speaks in this parable of a man who plants a vineyard, builds a wall around it, digs a vat, puts in a wine press, builds a tower, rents it out to vine-growers, and leaves.

> 'Listen to another parable. There was a landowner who planted a vineyard and put a wall around it and dug a wine press in it, and built a tower, and rented it out to vine-growers, and went on a journey. And when the harvest time approached, he sent his slaves to the vine-growers to receive his produce' (Matt. 21:33-34).

The *social* background to the parable was the mostly-foreign absentee landlords of the upper Jordan, and the mostly Jewish dispossessed sharecroppers. A vineyard, as France explains, 'was a major and long-term investment, from which no return could be expected for at least four years' (308). There was considerable resentment by the sharecroppers toward the landlords. Part of the genius of the parable is that initially the natural sentiments of the listeners would be on the side of the sharecroppers.

The *biblical* background is Isaiah 5:1-7, where Israel is likened to a God-planted vineyard which fails to produce fruit, and God promises to break it down and 'lay it waste' (cf. Ps. 80:8ff.; Jer. 2:21; Ezek. 19:10ff.). The parable, then, has two points of contact: the social experience of Jesus' listeners and their awareness of biblical metaphors.

The meaning of the various elements in the parable is easily discerned. The *vineyard* is Israel, the *vine-growers*, or 'tenants' (NIV), are the religious leaders of Israel, the *owner* is God, the *fruit* is 'righteousness,' says Morris (539). The *slaves* whom He sends to receive the fruit are the prophets, the *son* (v. 37) is Jesus.

The chief priests and elders to whom He continues to speak (cf. v. 23) would probably be sympathizing with the growers through most of the parable. Only at the end would they realize the injustice of the attack on the owner, and how aptly the description fits them. The parable gives us God's view of His people, of their *privileges* (which they took for granted), their *responsibilities* (which they neglected), and their *consequences* (which they were soon to suffer). It is a parable that teaches us the importance of God's people bearing fruit for God's kingdom.

Privileges

'Listen to another parable. There was a landowner who planted a vineyard and put a wall around it and dug a wine press in it, and built a tower, and rented it out to vine-growers, and went on a journey' (Matt. 21:33).

The vineyard described in verse 33 is generously provisioned. The vineyard has a 'wall around it,' a 'wine press in it,' and a 'tower.' Morris describes each element. The wall 'would protect it from wild animals and the like.' The wine-press would consist of 'two basins cut out of rock, or if out of soil, lined with rocks and sealed with plaster; one would have been lower than the other, and they would have been connected by a channel' (540). The grapes would be trodden under foot in the upper basin, the juice then flowing into the lower where it would begin the process of fermentation. The tower 'would enable a watchman to survey the vineyard and the surrounding terrain so that he could take action against marauders, human and animal,' continues Morris (540). It is a well-equipped vineyard. Israel, Jesus is saying, is a privileged possession of God. Jesus is highlighting the privileges of the people of God, and the provision God has made for them. Israel was a well-protected, richly provisioned people. God said to them in days of old, 'You only have I chosen among all the families of the earth,' God said to them through His prophets (Amos 3:2). To them, said the Apostle Paul,

...belongs the adoption as sons and the glory and the covenants and the giving of the Law and the temple service and the promises, whose are the fathers, and from whom is the Christ according to the flesh, who is over all, God blessed forever. Amen (Rom. 9:4-5).

They alone were entrusted with 'the oracles of God' (Rom. 3:2).

Or, negatively, consider the Bible's description of the Gentiles, the reverse of which would be true of Israel:

> ...*remember that you were at that time separate from Christ, excluded from the commonwealth of Israel, and strangers to the covenants of promise, having no hope and without God in the world* (Eph. 2:12).

Of all the people in the world, the people of Israel were with God and had 'hope.' They were participants in the 'covenants of promise,' citizens of the 'commonwealth of Israel,' and united to the Messiah (Christ). 'He has not dealt thus with any nation,' the Psalmist says (Ps. 147:20).

My 'old school' 4th grade elementary school teacher once tried to make a similar point with me with regard to American citizenship, a lesson for which I remain grateful to this day. One morning as we rose to say the 'Pledge of Allegiance' one of my classmates asked, 'Do we have to?' There ensued a ten minute lecture from the teacher. 'Do you realize how rich you are?' she asked. 'People all over the world go hungry and you enjoy plenty; people all over the world lack shelter, and you enjoy a warm home; people all over the world lack clothing, and you are richly attired. Do you realize the liberties and freedoms that you enjoy as others live in constant dread?' On and on she went go. This is Jesus' point. We are privileged and well provisioned.

Jesus would ask similar questions of the church today. Do we realize our privileges and provisions? Do we realize how much God has given us? Do we know what we have? He has opened our blind eyes to the gospel, given us faith (Eph. 2:8, 9), united us to Christ (John 15:1-15), and saved our souls. He has justified, adopted, and shall glorify us (Rom. 8:32ff.). Salvation is the greatest and best gift, but it is only the beginning. Think of the privileges that we have in this country. We have our own Bibles. We have the privilege of worshiping freely, whenever we choose to do so. We have a place to meet.

Think of the special privileges which we have at our particular church. Think of our beautiful facilities. Think of our access to camp property and facilities. Think of the warmth of the fellowship that we enjoy. Think of the legacy of faithfulness to the word of God: ministers in our tradition who for centuries have been preaching the word of God without apology. We are the heirs of that legacy. But what have we done with it?

Responsibilities
Privileges beget responsibilities, as is always the case.

> 'And when the harvest time approached, he sent his slaves to the vine-growers to receive his produce. And the vine-growers took his slaves and beat one, and killed another, and stoned a third' (Matt. 21:34-35).

To whom much is given, much is required (Luke 12:48). Those with great gifts and great abilities and great opportunities are expected to bear much fruit and not squander their resources. It was important in ancient Palestine for owners to collect rents, even the nominal amounts for the first four, less productive years, in order to establish their rights as owners. Jewish law allowed tenants to establish a claim of ownership of land on which they had undisputed use for three years. When the owner in the parable 'rented it out' to the tenants (v. 33), they were 'responsible to pay him a fixed portion of the proceeds,' says France (308). When the owner came to 'receive the produce' from the vineyard, and thereby establish his rights as owner, the tenants resisted his agents. Their refusal was an attempt to deny his claim of ownership. They wished to keep the vineyard for themselves. They assaulted his servants. 'Evidently the tenants had already decided that they were going to make the vineyard their own,' says Morris (541). They refused to pay the rents that would have established the owner's possession of the land. They were hoping that because he was at a distance, he would consider dealing with the tenants too much trouble, and surrender his claim of the land. The tenants treated the slaves sent to collect the rents like robbers, trying to deprive them of what they considered already theirs.

The second delegation may have been sent after the second year's harvest. The owner again is attempting to assert his claim on the vineyard and collect the rent.

> *'Again he sent another group of slaves larger than the first; and they did the same thing to them'* (Matt. 21:36).

But the second group of slaves receives the same reception. 'Their rejection of the owner's claim is definite and vigorous,' explains Morris (541). So likewise Jesus would have His listeners understand Israel's leadership. The religious leaders were taking the fruit of God's kingdom and using it for their own ends, in the form of power and status. When God, through His prophets, began to demand of them the produce of the vineyard, they refused. They intended to keep the fruit for themselves. They had their own selfish aims and ambitions in mind. They were using the vineyard as a means of gaining power and prestige for themselves. It had become *their* vineyard.

Finally, the owner sends his son.

> *'But afterward he sent his son to them, saying, 'They will respect my son.' But when the vine-growers saw the son, they said among themselves, 'This is the heir; come, let us kill him, and seize his inheritance.' And they took him, and threw him out of the vineyard, and killed him'* (Matt. 21:37-39).

This is a prophecy of what the religious leadership *will* do to Jesus, the Son *of God*. This part of the story is 'unlikely' in real life, as Morris points out (541). The owner would likely have gone to the law and had the tenants ejected. The point of Jesus' story is not 'the way a businessman would act to protect his investment' but 'the way a compassionate and loving God acts toward sinners,' says Morris (541). We don't know exactly what the tenants' line of thinking would have been. They may have thought that the appearance of the heir meant that the owner was dead, and that the son had come to establish his claim upon the land. Or perhaps they thought that the title had been given to the son. Or perhaps that if they killed the son the father would give up his claim. Verse 39 says they 'cast him out of the vineyard.' If they had killed him in the vineyard, the land would have been regarded as unclean, and they would not have been able to sell its produce. So they threw him out and then killed him. If the owner were dead, the death of his heir would have secured their claim. They had never paid rent, which would have established the owner's claim. They had worked the land for several years. Besides, now the heir was dead. If the owner were alive, they would have reasoned that he would not dare to attempt to press his claim again.

Jesus' point is clear enough. The leaders of Israel (the vine-growers) were using Israel (God's vineyard) as their own. They were pursuing their own ends and purposes through God's nation. They were using it to enrich and empower themselves rather than to produce the fruit for which God designed it. So God sent prophets to warn them. But they would not listen, and instead mistreated and killed them. Finally, God sent His Son. This, by the way, is Jesus' first public claim to be the Son of God. So extreme does the religious leadership of Israel become in its plundering of God's vineyard, that they kill even His Son, thinking they could 'seize His inheritance,' making the vineyard their own.

The same happens today when the church is made to serve purposes other than those for which God created it. Some make the church the vehicle through which their *personal* goals are met. They may be seeking power, prestige, or fulfillment. Titles, honors, offices, and recognition are their goals, and the church is their means. Others have *social* designs on the church. They see it as the means through which they may advance the cause of equality for women or normalize homosexuality. Still others use the church as an instrument through which to advance a *political* agenda. The left pushes liberal or even revolutionary politics around the world through the church, and the right pushes back. These are among the uses to which people seek to put God's vineyard. They are, at best, tangential to God's design for the church, and at worst, contrary to it. Ministers and denominational bureaucrats are often the most abusive of all in this respect. They can begin to look at the church as their own fiefdom, referring to it as 'my church.' It's not. It is the church of God. Our Lord Jesus Christ is the head of the church. It exists for the purpose of bearing fruit for God's sake.

What God demands of His vineyard is His fruit. As we have seen in previous parables (e.g. The Sower, ch. 3), this means *qualitative* fruit, that is the fruit of righteousness, holiness and love (Eph. 5:9-11). And it means *quantitative* fruit, a transforming impact on all that is around it. The church is to be light and salt in society, transforming lives through conversions, and adding numbers to the church. While we wrongly might want it to produce the fruit that we have in mind, God is looking for His fruit. And He expects concerted effort on our part to see that this happens.

It is to these ends that we pray, we give, we worship, we maintain close fellowship, and we preserve our heritage of gospel preaching. Faithfulness in God's vineyard does not happen automatically. We all must put our shoulders to the plow in order to bear fruit.

Consequences

Finally, Jesus warns of God's judgment on Israel for its faithlessness.

> 'Therefore when the owner of the vineyard comes, what will he do to those vine-growers?' They said to Him, 'He will bring those wretches to a wretched end, and will rent out the vineyard to other vine-growers, who will pay him the proceeds at the proper seasons' (Matt. 21:40, 41).

We may note the following:

1. *God is patient with us.* One of the outstanding features of this parable is the longsuffering owner. When the growers beat and killed the first group of slaves (v. 35), one wonders, why doesn't the owner destroy them immediately? When they did the same to the second group (v. 36), one wonders,

why doesn't he destroy them now? Still he waits and tries one more time, and sends his son.

This sequence is a vivid illustration of the patience of God. How longsuffering He is! 'All the day long,' God said through Isaiah, 'I have spread out My hands all day long to a rebellious people' (Isa. 65:2; cf. Rom. 10:21). He gives 'time to repent' (Rev. 2:21). Peter says,

> The Lord is not slow about His promise, as some count slowness, but is patient toward you, not wishing for any to perish but for all to come to repentance (2 Pet. 3:9).

A young father was telling me just the other day how his very young children will at times run from him, though there is no possibility that they can ever get away. But when it is time for punishment, off they go. Children often provide good illustrations of aspects of fallen human nature. Their flight was not unlike Adam 'hiding' in the garden. Did he really think he could get away with it? Do children think that they can get away with it? For the moment they do. Why? Because sin is irrational.

This irrational characteristic of sin is what we see here. Do they really think that they will get away with killing the landowner's slaves and then his son? Does Israel think that it can stone God's prophets and get away with it? For the moment they do. Sin is utterly irrational and foolish. Yet God puts up with it. Think of all the foolish things that people fall for these days. Everywhere we see the most perverse glamorizations of sin, and yet multitudes succumb to it. Evil is sugar coated. It seems that one can get away with wrongdoing. Right at the top of the list of evil's deceptions is the idea that sin has no consequences. It's no big deal. Relax. Don't worry. There is no price to pay, they say. 'Stolen water is sweet,' the Proverbs agree (9:17). It is alluring. Daily we hear happiness is found in wealth, or promiscuity, or in a chemical substance. It is all a pack of lies, and yet people go, like the ox to the slaughter (Prov. 7:22). Still, God is patient with us. We reject His authority and ignore His blessings, and yet He is patient.

Israel's rebellion culminates in the rejection of God's Son. They conspire and kill even Him (v. 38-39). Their ingratitude, their foolishness, now reaches a crescendo. They won't listen even to the Son! Yet God patiently endures.

2. *But patience has its limits*. Even God's patience, as great as it is, eventually runs out. Jesus says,

> *They said to Him, 'He will bring those wretches to a wretched end, and will rent out the vineyard to other vine-growers, who will pay him the proceeds at the proper seasons'* (Matt. 21:41).

As in the Parable of the Two Sons (Matt. 21:31), Jesus leads the opposition to pronounce their own condemnation (cf. 2 Sam. 12:1-7). Jesus' listeners are exactly right in their answer. The owner will destroy the wicked tenants, and he will get new ones who will bring forth the expected fruit and pay the proper rents. Lest there be any doubt about Jesus' meaning, He says directly in verse 43,

> *'Therefore I say to you, the kingdom of God will be taken away from you, and be given to a nation producing the fruit of it'* (Matt. 21:43).

God eventually will destroy a disobedient and fruitless people, take away their right to the vineyard, and give it to others. The vine-growers failed in their calculations to reckon with the nature of the One with whom they were dealing. They misinterpreted His patience, and underestimated His persistence and power. Jesus' words are prophetic of AD 70 and the destruction of Israel, and of the creation of the international church, the new Israel, the 'other vine-growers' to whom He will 'rent out the vineyard.' It is also prophetic of the fate of self-serving, fruitless people in every age.

The church today must not repeat the mistakes of Israel. Yet, in the past, it has. Where is the great North African church that once gave to Christendom leaders such as Ambrose and Augustine? It is gone. It exists no more. Where is the great church of Western Europe, the church that gave to us Luther and Calvin and a host of others? It too is dying. Today the churches of Western Europe stand empty. Even Great Britain, the motherland of most American churches, is filled with empty, decaying churches. It can happen here too. There is a line that can be crossed, and woe to us if we cross it.

The church is God's vineyard. Jesus said, 'You will know them by their fruits' (Matt. 7:20). Authentic Christianity is fruitful. As God's vineyard, it is our responsibility to 'produce the fruit of it' (Matt. 21:43). Are we doing so? Is the *qualitative* fruit of holiness evident? Are the fruit of the Spirit (Gal. 5:22, 23)? Is the *quantitative* fruit of conversions and cultural transformation visible? Jesus taught these same lessons when He employed the metaphor of the Vine. He said,

> *'I am the vine, you are the branches; he who abides in Me, and I in him, he bears much fruit; for apart from Me you can do nothing'* (John 15:5).

As we abide in Christ *we will bear fruit*. Or better said, as we abide in Christ (i.e. remain in vital, living, dependent union with Him), *He bears fruit through us*. Fruit *will* grow. Here, too, He warns:

> *'If anyone does not abide in Me, he is thrown away as a branch, and dries up; and they gather them, and cast them into the fire, and they are burned'* (John 15:6).

Personally and collectively as a church, Jesus' expectation of His people is that they will bear the qualitative and quantitative fruit of God's kingdom. This is characteristic of the Christian life. It bears fruit, not for its own ends and ambitions, not for its own comforts or desires, but for the sake of God's kingdom and glory.

STUDY QUESTIONS

1. What are the social and the broader biblical contexts of this parable?

2. What is the meaning of each element in the parable: vineyard, vine-growers ('tenants' in NIV), owner, fruit, slaves, and the son? (v. 33).

3. Jesus provides a number of details about the vineyard. What is the point? (v. 33).

4. Verse 34 describes a very natural follow-up to verse 33. The owner wants to collect the produce of his vineyard. What does this represent?

5. What does the resistance of the tenants to the owner's delegations represent? (vv. 35-36). Can you think of examples of this today?

6. What does the tenants' rejection of the owner's son represent? (vv. 37-39).

7. What are the consequences for Israel and the church when they fail to produce God's fruit? (vv. 41, 43).

8. What are some of the lessons we learn about God, sin, and the church in this parable?

~ 26 ~

'THE BARREN FIG TREE'

Luke 13:6-9

The Necessity of Repentance

⁶And He began telling this parable: 'A certain man had a fig tree which had been planted in his vineyard; and he came looking for fruit on it, and did not find any. ⁷And he said to the vineyard-keeper, "Behold, for three years I have come looking for fruit on this fig tree without finding any. Cut it down! Why does it even use up the ground?" ⁸And he answered and said to him, "Let it alone, sir, for this year too, until I dig around it and put in fertilizer; ⁹and if it bears fruit next year, fine; but if not, cut it down."'

No understanding of the gospel can claim to be accurate that does not highlight both the gifts of God and His demands. He is 'compassionate and gracious,' yet 'He will by no means leave the guilty unpunished' (Exod. 34:6, 7). 'Behold then the kindness *and* severity of God,' the Apostle Paul says (Rom. 11:22). He is 'slow to anger.' He is patient. But He requires a receptive response from us. There *is* a day of reckoning. God gives us His good gifts. But He also requires *results*, or in the term employed in the parables, *fruit*.

The parable before us is given in the context of Jesus' teaching in verses 1-5 of Luke 13, where Jesus stressed the importance of repentance. The disciples asked Jesus about certain Galileans who were slaughtered by Pilate as they were in the temple offering sacrifices. Jesus answered saying,

> 'Do you suppose that these Galileans were greater sinners than all other Galileans, because they suffered this fate? I tell you, no, but unless you repent, you will all likewise perish' (Luke 13:2, 3).

The same conclusion was repeated after recounting a similar tragedy involving the collapse of the Tower of Siloam:

> 'I tell you, no, but unless you repent, you will all likewise perish' (Luke 13:5).

Even as the 'Parable of the Wicked Vine Growers' (Matt. 21:33-41) taught the necessity of bearing qualitative and quantitative fruit, so the 'Parable of the Barren Fig Tree' teaches specifically the necessity of the fruit of repentance. The parable is 'intended to enforce that word of warning immediately going before regarding repentance,' says Matthew Henry. The parable, agrees Plummer, 'is a continuation of the warning, "Except ye repent, ye shall all likewise perish"' (340). According to Morris the parable highlights 'both the need for repentance and the slowness of God to punish.' It also underscores 'the fact that opportunity does not last forever,' says Morris (222).

The Christian life is a life of faith, initiated by saving faith in the Christ of the gospel and sustained by a walk of faith. 'We walk by faith and not by sight,' says the Apostle Paul (2 Cor. 5:7). But it is also a life of repentance, initiated by a decisive act of repentance and continued by a life of repentance. Daily we are to pray, 'Forgive us our debts as we also have forgiven our debtors,' Jesus teaches us (Matt. 6:12). Luther's first thesis (of his 95) stated that

> When our Lord and Master, Jesus Christ, said 'Repent,' He called for the entire life of believers to be one of repentance.

The Expectation of Fruit

And He began telling this parable: 'A certain man had a fig tree which had been planted in his vineyard; and he came looking for fruit on it, and did not find any' (Luke 13:6).

There is a sense in which God has an investment in each one of us. He has given us gifts of knowledge and opportunity. We have been in His church, among His people, and under the sound of His gospel. But these privileges beget responsibilities. God expects a return on His investment. The parable begins by emphasizing the expectation that the people of God will bear fruit. The parable speaks of a man who plants a 'fig tree' in his 'vineyard.' Morris notes the 'fig tree' would be a mature or 'well-established' tree, since the planter expects fruit from it (222). 'Vineyard' is 'tantamount to "fruit garden,"' says Marshall, since fruit trees of all kinds were regularly planned in vineyards' (cf. Deut. 22:9; 1 Kings 4:25; 2 Kings 18:31; Micah 4:4) (555). That the fig tree is planted in a vineyard means that it is in fertile soil. The Old Testament frequently uses the fig tree as a metaphor for Israel (Hosea 9:10; Joel 1:7; Jer. 8:13; 24:1-8; Micah 7:1). The same is true of the vineyard (Isa. 5:1-7; Ps. 80:8; Jer. 12:10). Here the vineyard more specifically represents the kingdom of God. Fruit represents all those things that are indicative of a life of repentance: confession of sin, holy living, faithfulness, love. These are what the fig tree lacks. Israel had been 'cultivated and cherished over many centuries,' as Wilcock explains, but the result had been largely 'a barren religion' (138, 139). The owner 'came looking for fruit on it.' It was mature enough. It was planted in fertile soil. But he 'did not find any.' It was fruitless.

Think of the privileges enjoyed by Israel. They were the elect nation, separated by God from all the nations of the earth to be His own. To them He gave the law. With them He made His covenants. To them He gave the priesthood, sacrifices, and temple. They alone He brought out of slavery in Egypt and gave the land of Canaan. The Apostle Paul makes this point more than once. He asks,

> *Then what advantage has the Jew? Or what is the benefit of*
> *circumcision? Great in every respect. First of all, that they were*
> *entrusted with the oracles of God* (Rom. 3:1, 2).

As we saw in the previous chapter, the Apostle Paul says of
his fellow Israelites that to them

> *...belongs the adoption as sons and the glory and the covenants*
> *and the giving of the Law and the temple service and the*
> *promises, whose are the fathers, and from whom is the Christ*
> *according to the flesh, who is over all, God blessed forever.*
> *Amen* (Rom. 9:4, 5; cf. Eph. 2:12; Amos 3:2).

Their privileges were great. They possessed 'the adoption
as sons,' the 'glory,' the 'covenants,' the 'Law,' the 'temple
service,' the 'promises,' the 'fathers,' and from them came
'the Christ.' But God expected fruit from them. 'It might
reasonably be expected that there would be more faith, and
penitence, and holiness, and godliness in Israel than among
the heathen. This is what God looked for,' said Ryle (113).
While the parable in the first instance addresses the
fruitlessness of Israel, its secondary application has much to
say to the church as well. 'The primary application of this
parable must not shut out the secondary one,' Ryle reminds
us (117). 'In a secondary sense,' says Geldenhuys, 'the fig tree
symbolizes also every individual who remains unrepentant'
(373). The privileges of the church far exceed those of ancient
Israel. Messiah has come. The fullness of God's revelation
has come in Him. We have been privileged to receive that
revelation and hear it read in our churches and homes each
week. 'We live in a land of Bibles, and liberty, and Gospel
preaching,' Ryle reminds us again (113). Where is the fruit?
Where is the evidence? Young people who've been reared in
church and enjoyed the benefits of its gospel proclamation
since the day that you were born, where is the return on
God's investment in you? Long-time members of the church
who've spent decades in these pews, where is the fruit?
Where is the evidence of a life of repentance in our families,
our neighborhood, and in our workplaces?

What does God expect of us? Fruit. Specifically, the fruit of repentance and a life of repentance.

The Extension of Mercy

'And he said to the vineyard-keeper, "Behold, for three years I have come looking for fruit on this fig tree without finding any. Cut it down! Why does it even use up the ground?"' (Luke 13:7).

The owner discusses the situation with the 'vineyard-keeper,' or what we would probably call the 'gardener' (*ampelourgos*). The owner has been 'looking for fruit on this fig tree,' Jesus repeats. This is the theme of the parable. Where is the fruit? Fig trees normally bore fruit annually. This one had gone three years 'without [the owner] finding any.' 'It was unlikely that such a tree would bear again.' The situation 'sounds ominous,' says Morris (222; cf. Plummer, 340). 'Cut it down' (*ekkopto*), the owner says, using the same word as in Matthew 3:10 and 7:19 of fruitless trees that are cut down and thrown into the fire. The point is that 'unrepentant Israelites will be excluded from salvation,' says Marshall (555). 'Why does it even use up ('occupy,' 'keep barren,' 'cumber') the ground?' he asks. Why allow it to use up space in the garden and nutrients in the soil? Why not put that ground to fruitful use? 'Is there a hint that another vine will be planted in its place?' Marshall asks (555). Indeed there is. Time enough has passed. Soil enough has been wasted. Space in the garden has been squandered. Let justice be done; cut the fig tree down and plant another in its place. Jesus warned elsewhere,

'Therefore I say to you, the kingdom of God will be taken away from you, and be given to a nation producing the fruit of it' (Matt. 21:43).

But the vineyard-keeper urges mercy, and in so doing provides a picture of Jesus' own ministry.

> *'And he answered and said to him, "Let it alone, sir, for this year too, until I dig around it and put in fertilizer"'* (Luke 13:8).

The vineyard-keeper intercedes, urging the owner to give the fig tree one last opportunity. 'Leave it alone,' he says, 'for this year too.' He promises to give it special attention for yet another year. He will 'dig around it,' 'loosening the soil around the roots,' as Marshall explains, and 'put in fertilizer' or manure (*koprion*) (555). These activities represent additional gracious opportunities to bear fruit through repentance provided by Christ's incarnation and earthly ministry. Israel was ripe for judgment already, Jesus is saying. Yet one final and particularly unambiguous opportunity for repentance was given. No mere prophet was sent, but the Son of God Himself (cf. Matt. 21:38; Heb. 1:1-3). While the parable underscores the lesson of repentance, it also places emphasis on the patient mercy of God. Both for Israel and for us, Jesus represents God's final opportunity. Yet another year is to be given. Further time and attention is expended. Clear and costly revelation is given to us in Christ. God in Christ extends additional opportunities for us to repent. God delights to show mercy (Micah 7:18). He gives 'space to repent' (Rev. 2:21 KJV). Judgment is delayed because God is merciful. Additional opportunities are given because God is merciful. We must not imagine that God has become slack or that judgment has been canceled. We must not foolishly think that we've gotten away with evil and we will not be judged. No, reckoning is delayed because God is merciful. He is patient towards us, not being willing that any should perish but that all should come to repentance (2 Pet. 3:9).

Reckoning
But in the end, judgment delayed is not judgment canceled. A final opportunity will pass and then our day of reckoning will follow.

> *'and if it bears fruit next year, fine; but if not, cut it down'* (Luke 13:9).

This final opportunity leaves open two possibilities. Either the tree 'bears fruit next year' or it is to be 'cut down.' 'The day of grace will come to an end,' Marshall explains (556). This disaster is coming 'despite the intercession of the vine-dresser,' continues Marshall, who, as we have seen, is a figure of Christ (556). Jesus later acted out this parable the last week of His life in Jerusalem, cursing a fig tree that actually had no fruit (Matt. 21:18-20; Mark 11:12-14, 20-21).

The day of opportunity passed for Israel. The time came when it was too late. So it is for all of us. God is patient. He graciously provides many opportunities to repent and bear fruit. But in the end a day of reckoning comes. This can happen in this life, when God gives us over, or abandons us, to our sin (Rom. 1:24ff), or on the day of our death, when we find ourselves standing before our Maker, either in Christ, or alone without a mediator.

Ryle finds this parable to be 'peculiarly humbling and heart-searching' (112). It is both 'lit by grace and packed with warnings,' Barclay adds (179). Consequently it calls us to search our souls for the fruit of repentance. Is God getting a return on His investment in us? Have I turned from the pursuit of sin? Have I cultivated a loathing of evil and a hunger and thirst for righteousness? Have I developed a love for the word of God, the people of God, and the worship of God? Am I pursuing holiness? Do I have a zeal for good works? Am I characterized by love in my dealings with my neighbors? These are the fruits that are 'in keeping with repentance' (Luke 3:8).

Let's put it another way. For what am I living? For most people life is about pleasure, prestige (or fame), and power. They crave and pursue these things. They have bought the lie. Why am I a Christian? Because there is a holy God to whom I must be reconciled. Yet it is beyond my power to affect that reconciliation myself. Only in Christ can that reconciliation occur. And I am a Christian because there is more to life than the benefits of this world. All that the world offers is vanity and striving after the wind. True life is found in serving, pleasing, honoring, and glorifying God, and making Him known. This is the fruit that Jesus seeks.

STUDY QUESTIONS

1. What is the context of this parable? What are we to understand about the meaning of this parable in light of the context? (vv. 1-5).

2. What is meant by the various elements of the parable? The 'certain man' or owner of the vineyard, the fig tree, the vineyard, the fruit? (v. 6).

3. What does the owner expect to find but doesn't? (v. 6) What does he propose to do? Why? (v. 7).

4. Who was the original fruitless fig tree? Who might it be today?

5. Who intervenes in verse 8? Whom does he represent? What does he promise to do?

6. While the day of reckoning may be graciously delayed, can it be avoided? (v. 9) What are the two alternatives?

7. The commentators speak of the two sides of this parable, gracious on the one hand and threatening on the other. How is this so?

~ 27 ~

'STRAYING SHEEP'

Matthew 18:12-14

Pursuing Wayward Believers

[12] *'What do you think? If any man has a hundred sheep, and one of them has gone astray, does he not leave the ninety-nine on the mountains and go and search for the one that is straying?* [13]*And if it turns out that he finds it, truly I say to you, he rejoices over it more than over the ninety-nine which have not gone astray.* [14]*Thus it is not the will of your Father who is in heaven that one of these little ones perish' (cf. Luke 15:4-7).*

How is the church to respond when one of its members goes astray? Earlier in Matthew's eighteenth chapter, Jesus had been warning us against tripping up one of His 'little ones' (Matt. 18:6-10). What happens when one of His disciples indeed does stumble and fall into sin? What is to be our outlook? Do we forsake and abandon the lost one? Publicly flog him? Jesus gives the answer in The Parable of the Straying Sheep in Matthew 18:12-14, further elaborating in Matthew 18:15-20 (the *locus classicus* on church discipline), and 18:21-35 (The Parable of the Unmerciful Servant, ch. 22 of the present work).

A form of this parable is taught by Jesus in two different contexts in the gospels. The Parable of the Lost Sheep

(Luke 15:4-7, ch. 19 of the present work) is addressed to Jesus' opponents, who, as France points out, 'objected to his 'evangelistic' concern with undesirables' (273). We read there,

> *Now all the tax-gatherers and the sinners were coming near Him to listen to Him* (Luke 15:1).

Jesus' opponents objected to His associating with this crowd,

> *And both the Pharisees and the scribes began to grumble, saying, 'This man receives sinners and eats with them'* (Luke 15:2).

Jesus' response:

> *And He told them this parable* (Luke 15:3).

The parable he told on that occasion was what we have called the 'Lost Sheep.' It was designed to address the attitude with which Jesus' disciples are to look upon the *unconverted*.

In Matthew's gospel, we are calling it 'The Parable of the Straying Sheep' because in this case, it is concerned with backslidden disciples. France says 'it is addressed to disciples, to remind them that God's "pastoral" care is extended to all his "little ones"' (273). In Luke's Gospel the parable is addressed to the problem of associating with unbelievers, urging that they be pursued so as to be *converted*. In Matthew's Gospel it addresses the problem of straying disciples, urging that they be pursued so as to be *recovered*. Consequently, the parable has two applications for us. We'll look now at the meaning in Matthew's Gospel and then relate that to what we saw in Luke's.

Straying Disciples
Jesus says,

> *'What do you think? If any man has a hundred sheep, and one of them has gone astray, does he not leave the ninety-nine on the mountains and go and search for the one that is straying?'* (Matt. 18:12).

'What do you think?' Jesus asks. He invites us to 'think.' Ponder this, He says. Be wise. Use common sense. Then He tells the parable of the shepherd who has a hundred sheep. One goes 'astray.' What does he do? Does he say, 'It's just one. I've still got my ninety-nine. Oh well, tough luck. Better take care of what remains'? No, that's not what he says, not if he's a good shepherd. What does he do then?

First, he seeks the straying one
He leaves the ninety-nine 'on the mountains,' that is – not in a sheltered area where they might be safe. Rather, they are scattered about the hills and, therefore, are at some risk. Yet he'll 'go and search.' The present tense 'points to the continuous effort of seeking,' says Carson (465). He abandons his normal routine and concentrates all of his energy on the one lost one. Barclay points out, 'The Palestinian shepherds were experts at tracking down their sheep. They could follow the track of the lost sheep for miles; and they would brave the cliffs and the precipice to bring it back' (203). This is what the shepherd will do.

Second, he rejoices when the straying one is found

> *'And if it turns out that he finds it, truly I say to you, he rejoices over it more than over the ninety-nine which have not gone astray'* (Matt. 18:13).

Because he loves and cares for all his sheep, the recovery of just one out of a hundred is a cause of joy. The point of this is twofold.

1. *This is a picture of God the shepherd.* Jesus is providing us with a glimpse of God's love and forgiveness. He makes the application Himself in the next verse:

> *'Thus it is not the will of your Father who is in heaven that one of these little ones perish'* (Matt. 18:14).

'Thus,' He says. Here is the point. This parable is all about God. Though it is not explicitly stated, the implicit argument, or to put it another way, the assumed deduction, is that if ordinary people vigorously pursue mere sheep when they are lost, it follows that God will respond similarly with valued disciples, when they go astray, particularly given that we are 'worth much more than they,' as Jesus said of the birds (Matt. 6:26). The same line of reasoning was used in defense of healing on the Sabbath. Everyone who has a sheep fall into a pit on the Sabbath day lifts it out. If it is lawful to help an afflicted sheep, the deduction then follows: it must be lawful to heal an afflicted man on the Sabbath. 'Of how much more value then is a man than a sheep?' Jesus asks (Matt. 12:11, 12). 'What do you think?' Jesus asks here. Isn't this logical? Doesn't it make sense? If you seek after or pursue and then rejoice at the recovery of one lost sheep, then God certainly must pursue and rejoice over the recovery of lost disciples. It must follow as true.

Here is the situation that the parable envisions. One of God's disciples, His 'little ones' stumbles. He or she may be the weakest, most immature, most contemptible, most difficult of all believers. Yet God pursues the straying one. He is determined not to lose even one. He seeks him. He searches. This is a picture of God's mercy. He woos back those who go astray. He stands ready to forgive, to accept, to readmit them to the fold. He doesn't wash his hands of them. He doesn't turn away in disgust. He doesn't stand aloof requiring that the wretched one crawl back on hands and knees, all the while begging for pardon. He pursues, He seeks, He searches. And when the straying one is found, He rejoices! It's not that there is no joy over the non-straying. Yet 'there is a peculiar joy over bringing one that is lost safely into the fold,' explains Morris (466).

Why does He seek the lost? Because 'it is not the will of your Father ... that one of these little ones perish.' He would not have them 'perish' or be eternally destroyed (*apollumi*). God's 'will' here means His 'desire' or 'wish.' Some who were numbered among the fold but who were actually wolves in sheep's clothing do perish. But none of the elect

or true sheep could ever be lost (John 6:39; 10:27-29). Some
straying members of the visible flock may come to be
regarded as Gentiles and tax collectors (Matt. 18:17). Still,
the Father's desire is that they should not perish. For this
reason, He takes extreme measures to restore the straying
one. He pursues. He searches. When He finds a lost one He
rejoices.

Have I strayed? What is God's outlook towards me? Will
He accept me back? Will He forgive me? Indeed, before
I have had the first inclination to return to Him, He has been
in pursuit of me. How? His Holy Spirit has been prodding
my conscience. He has used the people I work with or family
members to say just the right thing to me to stir up regret
and remorse. My eyes have gradually been opening to the
reality of the world and its false promises, its counterfeits
and lies, its emptiness and futility. My memory has begun to
recall the benefits and blessing of life under the wings of the
Almighty (Ps. 91:1ff.). He has been wooing me back. He is
ready to receive me, if I am ready to come. Jesus is giving us
a profound glimpse of the love of God for His children, even
when they stray.

2. *This is a picture of the church as shepherd.* There are still
more deductions to make if we are to arrive at the main
point. 'The moral is clear,' says France. The disciple 'must
share God's concern for each "little one," and not despise any
(v. 10)' (273). It is all too easy to turn from straying members
with disgust and want nothing to do with them. Think of
what they do –

- They bring dishonor to Christ through their sin
- They bring disgrace to the church
- They may damage and even destroy their families
- They abandon friends and fellow believers and deprive them of fellowship, support, and encouragement.

Anger, disgust, contempt, and finally indifference come to
characterize our natural response to straying sheep. They've
torn apart their families, wounded and weakened the church,

and frankly, we want nothing to do with them. *We want them to go away and never come back.*

Understandable and human though this response may be, this is not the outlook that God wants us to have. It is understandable and right that we should hate the sin. But the old guideline must be maintained: hate the sin but love the sinner, even the believer/sinner. Since God pursues the wayward, so must we pursue. Since He seeks, we must seek. Since He searches, we must search.

Let us pause to offer further clarification before we proceed further. The eager, searching, pursuing outlook here described is not a denial of the necessity and propriety of church discipline (see also The Parable of the Wheat and the Tares, ch. 12). Jesus goes on in this same chapter of Matthew's Gospel, in the next three verses, to say,

> *'And if your brother sins, go and reprove him in private; if he listens to you, you have won your brother. But if he does not listen to you, take one or two more with you, so that by the mouth of two or three witnesses every fact may be confirmed. And if he refuses to listen to them, tell it to the church; and if he refuses to listen even to the church, let him be to you as a Gentile and a tax-gatherer'* (Matt. 18:15-17).

There are times when the unrepentant must be put out of the church. The pursuit of the straying is not a denial of the necessity and propriety of excluding and even shunning those who are under discipline. The Apostles of Jesus taught us to do that very thing:

> *Remove the wicked man from among yourselves* (1 Cor. 5:13b).

> *Now we command you, brethren, in the name of our Lord Jesus Christ, that you keep aloof from every brother who leads an unruly life and not according to the tradition which you received from us* (2 Thess. 3:6).

> *If anyone comes to you and does not bring this teaching, do not receive him into your house, and do not give him a greeting; for the one who gives him a greeting participates in his evil deeds* (2 John 10, 11).

At times, to 'remove' the unrepentant, to 'keep aloof,' to refuse even to 'give him a greeting' is necessary and proper. Jesus' parable of Matthew 18:12-14 does not contradict Jesus' principles of discipline of Matthew 18:15-17. Indeed, church discipline, properly administered, is one means by which the church seeks after those who have gone astray. Love prompts discipline. Discipline aims ultimately to jolt the wayward to repentance and restoration to the fold. Discipline is exercised as a means of pursuing and seeking wayward believers. The attitude which says 'go away and never come back' is the opposite of that found in church discipline properly exercised. Through its discipline the church refuses to walk way. It gets involved. It pursues the unrepentant.

And what if the straying one returns to the fold? What if the lost one is found? We receive him or her back. We stand ready to accept, to forgive, to restore. We (and this is the most difficult part) are ready, no, even more than that, we are *eager* to rejoice, to celebrate when the straying one returns.

I say that it is difficult to rejoice because sometimes we are so angry with wayward believers, for all the damage they've done, for all the pain they've inflicted, that we can hardly bear the sight of them. Yet clearly this attitude will not stand up under the light of Scripture. These words of Jesus will not permit us to indulge in this outlook. He rejoices at the recovery of lost ones and so must we if we are His children. Our contempt for the wayward reveals the need for a significant 'attitude adjustment,' as they say. Behind our contempt are pride, self-righteousness, and mercilessness. Here's what Scripture would ask us:

For who regards you as superior? And what do you have that you did not receive? But if you did receive it, why do you boast as if you had not received it? (1 Cor. 4:7).

Here's Scripture's warning to us:

Therefore let him who thinks he stands take heed lest he fall (1 Cor. 10:12).

If I have not strayed, it is not a cause for boasting, but for humble gratitude. We stand only because 'the Lord is able to make (us) stand' (Rom. 14:4). When formerly wayward but now repentant ones return, our response should be to receive them back and love them. Addressing a situation of this nature, the Apostle Paul told the Corinthians the following:

> *Sufficient for such a one is this punishment which was inflicted by the majority, so that on the contrary you should rather forgive and comfort him, lest somehow such a one be overwhelmed by excessive sorrow. Wherefore I urge you to reaffirm your love for him* (2 Cor. 2:6-8).

'Forgive and comfort,' he insists. 'Reaffirm your love for him.'

Lost Humanity

As we've seen (ch. 19 of this work), all the same sorts of things can be said about God's love from the parallel parable in Luke, The Parable of the Lost Sheep, not only about straying believers but about fallen humanity. Remember the context *there* was Jesus' attitude towards the unbelieving. What is Jesus' outlook on them? Even greater emphasis was given to the joy of retrieving the lost.

> *'And when he has found it, he lays it on his shoulders, rejoicing. And when he comes home, he calls together his friends and his neighbors, saying to them, "Rejoice with me, for I have found my sheep which was lost!"'* (Luke 15:5, 6).

There the concluding point was this:

> *'I tell you that in the same way, there will be more joy in heaven over one sinner who repents, than over ninety-nine righteous persons who need no repentance'* (Luke 15:7).

Matthew's and Luke's versions of this parable have different targets (straying disciples versus unbelievers) but the same lesson: God seeks the lost.

Whether you are an unbeliever who just happens to be reading these words, or a backslidden believer, you must ask:

What does God think of me? Would He ever pay attention to me? Would He listen if I called? Indeed, He would. Before you ever began to even glance in God's direction, He was already in pursuit of you. He began to open your mind to biblical ideas. He began to open your heart to Christian ideals. He began to send people into your life. He began to work through 'chance' events and circumstances. The unbeliever or the backslidden believer who thinks that he is so awful, so bad, so degraded that God would never have anything to do with him or her, has got it all wrong. You're not wrong about being bad. You *are* bad, and indeed, much worse than you realize. But you are wrong about how this affects God's outlook on you. He is not discouraged from the pursuit of you by your corruption. Francis Thompson referred to the Holy Spirit as 'the hound of heaven.' God has been on your trail for some time. He has been tracking you down. 'Christ Jesus came into the world to save sinners,' says the Apostle Paul, even the 'foremost of all' (1 Tim. 1:15). He pursues, seeks after, searches for the worst.

After listing terrible sinners: fornicators, homosexuals, drunkards, idolaters, thieves, revilers, adulterers, covetous, swindlers, effeminate, the Apostle Paul says,

And such were some of you; but you were washed, but you were sanctified, but you were justified in the name of the Lord Jesus Christ, and in the Spirit of our God (1 Cor. 6:11).

These are the kinds of persons God has been saving for 2,000 years. These are the folks that He has been recruiting for His organization. He searches for the worst, the most corrupt and degraded. He seeks and pursues them. If they stray, He pursues them again.

Moreover, God rejoices when the lost are found. On the basis of the authority of Jesus these parables give us a picture of the heart of God towards the worst of sinners and the worst of saints. What does God think of us? He pursues us, and if we come to Him, He is delighted! He celebrates! Where our sin abounds, God's grace abounds all the more (Rom. 5:20).

The door is open to us all, Jesus says.

'For the Son of Man has come to seek and to save that which was lost' (Luke 19:10).

Since God's door is open, our door is open to all as well. Churches can project an image that is unhelpful and untrue. We show up Sunday morning, freshly scrubbed and polished, and we should. Worship is important, and we dress up for important things. We're meeting with the King. But the impression may be that we are a church only for *good* people. Middle class good people. *Nice* people. This is not the case. We are a church for sinners. We have some sophisticated sinners, whose sins are much hidden, but who nonetheless have very dark hearts. We also have blunt, crude sinners, whose failings are obvious. We have white collar sinners, we have blue collar sinners, we have rich sinners, we have poor sinners, we have professionals who are sinners, we have service-industry people who are sinners. Our 'saints' are all inconsistent saints, compromised saints, even backslidden saints. Red and yellow, black and white, we are all sinners in His sight.

My point is – we welcome all. All lost or straying sheep are sought. We are *seeking* not *shunning* the lost. And we are *seeking even when shunning* the wayward. Sometimes Christian folks are seen as being angry at people who have different moral convictions than they do. Let me clarify again – God teaches us to be mad at sin, but not sinners. Sin is destructive – sin hurts people, destroys lives, and is offensive to God. But unbelievers and backslidden believers, though their trials are often self-inflicted, are to be prayed for and pursued. They are welcomed and we rejoice over them when they come.

That is our heart, let us pray that it will be our active response as well. Is there a lost soul that you are pursuing? Are there lost souls that we as a church are pursuing? We cannot be content to minister only to the faithful. 'Christ wanted to show that a good teacher (and we would add, a good church) must no less labor to recover the lost than to keep what he already has in his hand' (Calvin, II, 219). In our personal lives, and in our life together as a church, we must aggressively seek to recover straying members and retrieve lost humanity.

STUDY QUESTIONS

1. A number of weeks ago we studied a similar text, 'The Parable of the Lost Sheep.' It began like this:

   [1] Now all the tax-gatherers and the sinners were coming near Him to listen to Him. [2] And both the Pharisees and the scribes began to grumble, saying, 'This man receives sinners and eats with them.' [3] And He told them this parable, saying, (Luke 15:1-3).

   What issue was it designed to address?

2. This text, 'The Parable of the Straying Sheep,' addresses a different issue indicated by verses 7-11, where Jesus warns of 'stumbling blocks,' and especially verse 10:

   'See that you do not despise one of these little ones, for I say to you, that their angels in heaven continually behold the face of My Father who is in heaven' (Matt. 18:10).

   What issue is it designed to address?

3. What is the implication of Jesus' question, 'What do you think?' (vv. 12-14). Compare Matthew 12:11, 12.

4. What is the outlook of God upon wayward believers? Will He accept the wayward back into the fold?

5. If God's outlook is that of the searching shepherd, what must be the outlook of the church?

6. Why might it be considered absurd to use these verses as an argument against church discipline? On the other hand, what do these verses teach us about the nature of church discipline?

   [15] 'And if your brother sins, go and reprove him in private; if he listens to you, you have won your brother. [16] But if he does not listen to you, take one or two more with you, so that by the mouth of two or three witnesses every fact may be confirmed. [17] And if he refuses to listen to them, tell it to the church; and if he refuses to listen even to the church, let him be to you as a Gentile and a tax-gatherer' (Matt. 18:15-17).

7. How is the church to respond when a wayward member repents and returns?

8. Whether I am an unbeliever or a backslidden believer, what does God think of me? How ought the church to think of such?

V

FINISHING IN GOD'S KINGDOM

Our last classification of the parables is eschatological. Two of Jesus' parables give focused attention to the themes of final judgment and the consummation of all things. God's judgment is not a popular preaching theme. No one today goes out of his way to preach about it. But it did make up a considerable part of the content of Jesus' teaching ministry. We have seen this already in our study of the parables (e.g. The Wedding Feast, The Rich Fool, Rich Man and Lazarus, Wheat and Tares, Dragnet, Two Debtors, Unmerciful Servant). Here we will see the theme of judgment in a more concentrated form.

~ 28 ~

'THE TEN VIRGINS'

Matthew 25:1-13

Being Ready

[1]'Then the kingdom of heaven will be comparable to ten virgins, who took their lamps, and went out to meet the bridegroom. [2]And five of them were foolish, and five were prudent. [3]For when the foolish took their lamps, they took no oil with them, [4]but the prudent took oil in flasks along with their lamps. [5]Now while the bridegroom was delaying, they all got drowsy and began to sleep. [6]But at midnight there was a shout, "Behold, the bridegroom! Come out to meet him." [7]Then all those virgins rose, and trimmed their lamps. [8]And the foolish said to the prudent, "Give us some of your oil, for our lamps are going out." [9]But the prudent answered, saying, "No, there will not be enough for us and you too; go instead to the dealers and buy some for yourselves." [10]And while they were going away to make the purchase, the bridegroom came, and those who were ready went in with him to the wedding feast; and the door was shut. [11]And later the other virgins also came, saying, "Lord, lord, open up for us." [12]But he answered and said, "Truly I say to you, I do not know you." [13]Be on the alert then, for you do not know the day nor the hour.'

Matthew Henry says of the second coming of Christ that it 'is the center in which all the lines of our religion meet, and to which the whole of the divine life hath a constant reference and tendency.' Few of us tend to attribute to eschatology that level of importance. Many of us may have called ourselves 'panmillennialists,' convinced that figuring out the end times was not worth the effort. We have rested, only partly tongue-in-cheek, in the conviction that 'it will all pan out in the end.' Yet if the details are difficult and at times obscure, the big picture is clear and crucial. Because the return of Christ will be sudden and unexpected, because it will bring final judgment, the end of this age, and usher in eternity, and because it will strike so divisively and decisively, it casts its shadow back over the whole of the Christian life and the whole Christian era. It is at the 'center,' where 'all the lines of our religion meet,' says Henry, to which the whole Christian life has 'a constant reference and tendency.'

Eschatology at the same time is a theology of the Christian life. Why? Because the Christian life is to be lived with an immediate awareness of Christ's imminent return. If I believe that at any moment history could come to a screeching halt, and I could find myself standing before Christ the judge of the living and the dead, will it not affect the way I live now (John 5:25-29)? Of course it will. Consequently, we are to live in a constant state of careful preparedness. Jesus said,

> 'Therefore be on the alert, for you do not know which day your Lord is coming' (Matt. 24:42).

The Context
The Second Coming and the lesson of readiness have been the theme of Jesus' teaching, beginning with Matthew 24:36 and extending to the end of the chapter (Matt. 24:51).[1] The division between Matthew 24 and 25 is somewhat regrettable because it obscures the fact that both the theme and the larger discourse (the 'Olivette Discourse,' so known because it was

---

1. For our understanding of Matthew 24, see the booklet 'Things to Come,' available from the IPC Bookshop, P.O. Box 9266, Savannah, GA 31412, U.S.A., 912-236-3346; see also www.ipcsav.org.

delivered from the Mount of Olives – Matt. 24:3) in which it is placed continues unabated. Jesus delivers the parables in Matthew 25 in order to teach the same lessons he introduced in Matthew 24. Jesus is so eager that we should understand the lesson of readiness for His return that He repeats it over and over again in these two chapters. He has done so with:

- The comparison with the days of Noah (24:37-41)
- The illustration of the thief (24:42-44)
- The illustration of the good and evil stewards (24:45-51)

He will do so again in chapter 25 with:

- The Parable of the Ten Virgins (25:1-13)
- The Parable of the Talents (25:14-30)
- The separation of the sheep and goats (25:31-46)

The Parable

Our understanding is that the Parable of the Ten Virgins provides 'further reinforcement,' as France puts it, 'of the same call for constant readiness for a 'coming' which will be at a time no one can predict' (349). It contrasts the wise and the foolish from among those anticipating the groom's return (vv. 2, 8-9) (cf. 7:24-27; cf. 24:45). Consequently, it should be read as 'a warning addressed specifically to those inside the professing church who are not to assume that their future is unconditionally assured,' argues France (350). All ten bridesmaids are anticipating the banquet. All ten bridesmaids are expecting to be there. All may be identified as members of the visible church. The difference between them is that some are ready and some are not.

The Christian life, Jesus is saying, is a life to be lived in a state of preparedness. *Careful, constant readiness to meet Christ and face final judgment defines the outlook with which life is to be lived.*

Readiness, however, is not fretfulness. The disciples of Christ are (of all people) to enjoy the creator's *gifts*, e.g. food, drink, marriage, children, music, art (1 Cor. 7-10; 1 Tim. 4:1-5;

Col. 2:20-23), and so live lives characterized by peace, joy, and contentment, and rejoice in the Redeemer's *grace* (Phil. 4:1-13; 1 Pet. 1:8). Yet, in light of the high stakes involved, Christ's disciples are to be characterized by temperance, sobriety, and good sense (1 Thess. 5:6-8; Titus 2:1-10; 1 Pet. 1:13; 5:8). The Apostle Paul summarizes this outlook in this way,

> For the grace of God has appeared, bringing salvation to all men, instructing us to deny ungodliness and worldly desires and to live sensibly, righteously and godly in the present age, looking for the blessed hope and the appearing of the glory of our great God and Savior, Christ Jesus; (Titus 2:11-13).

The same grace in which we rejoice teaches us to 'deny ungodliness and worldly desires and to live sensibly, righteously, and godly in the present age,' even as we anticipate the 'blessed hope' of Christ's appearing.

With this overview of the context and theme in mind, let us now look at the parable itself.

> 'Then the kingdom of heaven will be comparable to ten virgins, who took their lamps, and went out to meet the bridegroom' (Matt. 25:1).

'Then' (*tote*) means 'at that time,' that is, at the time of the return of Christ. The 'kingdom of heaven' at that time will become like the situation described in this parable. Morris ties the temporal connection closer, understanding *tote* also to refer to the same teaching context. 'We are to understand that this parable was delivered on the same occasion as the teaching Matthew has recorded at the end of chapter 24, *and* that it refers to the time of the Lord's return' (620, my emphasis).

The 'virgins' are unmarried girls, who, of course, are assumed to be chaste. They may be bridesmaids, friends, or neighbors. Our ignorance of first century wedding practices leaves us unclear with respect to their particular role. France suggests that 'they are waiting to escort the bridegroom in festal procession, probably in the last state of the ceremonies as he brings his bride home for the wedding feast' (351). Morris adds further that 'these girls would have helped in the dressing of the bride and acted as her attendants' (620, note 4).

The ten virgins 'took their lamps,' said Jesus. The 'lamps' are probably 'torches,' that is, 'oil-soaked rags wrapped on a stick,' says France (351). Another word would have been used for a standing lamp (*luchnos*) or a lantern (*phanos*). A festive, torch-light procession is in view.

The metaphor of the 'bridegroom' or 'groom,' as we would call him, was frequently used in the Old Testament as a figure for God (Isa. 54:4-5; 62:5; Jer. 2:2; Ezek. 16:7-34; Hosea 1-3; etc.). Israel was His bride; the wedding feast should be seen as the Messianic banquet, as in 22:1-14. Both Jesus and John identified Jesus as the bridegroom (John 3:27-30; Matt. 9:15), as do the writers of the New Testament (Eph. 5:21ff.; Rev. 19:7-10). Jesus says that the ten virgins 'went out' to greet the bridegroom.

Normally, the bridegroom with his close friends would go to the bride's home for certain ceremonies. Once those relatively brief ceremonies were completed, the girls assisting the bride would participate in the torch-light processional back to the groom's home. The time for the procession had come, so the girls 'went out to meet the bridegroom' and escort him back. Everyone would carry his or her own torch. 'Those without a torch would be assumed to be party crashers or even brigands,' says Carson (513). Upon arrival, festivities would commence at the groom's house and might continue for several days.

'*And five of them were foolish, and five were prudent*' (Matt. 25:2).

Five of the bridesmaids were 'prudent' (*phronimos*), 'wise,' or 'sensible,' and five were 'foolish,' the opposite.

'*For when the foolish took their lamps, they took no oil with them*' (Matt. 25:3).

Here is why five of the girls were described as 'foolish.' 'For,' or 'because' they took no oil, or perhaps no extra oil, with them. The wisdom or foolishness of the girls is determined by their preparedness in the things pertaining to the groom's return. The failure to take the necessary oil is judged an act of foolishness (*mōros*). Morris cites Jeremias with approval: 'Their negligence ... must be judged as inexcusable, punishable carelessness' (621). They were not ready for the groom's delay.

> '...but the prudent took oil in flasks along with their lamps' (Matt. 25:4).

The prudent girls factored into their preparations the likelihood of the groom's delay. There was no way to know exactly when the groom might appear, or how much time the procession would take.

Jesus' point is, this is how we must live. We must live wisely. We must be prepared for contingencies. We must be ready for Christ's return whenever that might be. We don't know when He will be coming and so we must live as though it were always imminent (24:42, 44; 25:13).

But do note, all of the bridesmaids are anticipating the arrival of the groom. They are all representing, as we have noted, professing believers, even 'members of the church,' says Matthew Henry. Yet some are prepared and others are not. Some were careful and some weren't. The foolish ones didn't take the time and trouble to get ready. They were culpably negligent.

The parable poses to church members the question, am I ready to meet Christ? He could return in the next hour. Am I prepared? I could meet Him through death tomorrow. Am I ready? Have I prepared my soul? Have I repented of my sin? Have I placed all my hope of life in eternity in Christ? Have I surrendered to Jesus as Lord? Am I seeking to sanctify and prepare my soul for eternity through the word, prayer, sacraments, and the life of the church?

> 'Now while the bridegroom was delaying, they all got drowsy and began to sleep' (Matt. 25:5).

Here is the problem for the unprepared. 'The bridegroom was delaying.' The parable picks up the theme of delay (24:48), which will return in 25:19. Jesus knew that this would be a concern of the early Christians and all throughout the history of the church (cf. 2 Pet. 3:3-13). Jesus doesn't return immediately. The suffering church is eager for Him to come, but He delays. So the girls 'got drowsy and began to sleep.' Life goes on. Calvin identifies the sleep of the virgins to 'the distraction of this world's business' (III.1). There is no sin in sleep. The question is, while tackling life's tasks, have preparations been made? Are they ready should He come?

Finally the time comes, and the announcement is made.

> 'But at midnight there was a shout, "Behold, the bridegroom! Come out to meet him." Then all those virgins rose, and trimmed their lamps' (Matt. 25:6, 7).

The girls 'trimmed their lamps,' or literally, 'put their torches in order,' says France (351). They either applied oil to their torches for the first time or added additional oil to torches that had already been burning during the period of delay. France notes that, 'A well-soaked torch would burn for a quarter of an hour or so, but those with no oil were no sooner lit than they went out' (351). Whether they lacked sufficient oil or never had any oil, their lamps now are out. They plead to the prudent ones that they should share their oil.

> 'And the foolish said to the prudent, "Give us some of your oil, for our lamps are going out"' (Matt. 25:8).

But there was not enough oil.

> 'But the prudent answered, saying, "No, there will not be enough for us and you too; go instead to the dealers and buy some for yourselves"' (Matt. 25:9).

'No, there will not be enough for us and you too.' If the wise girls shared with the foolish, all the torches would go out and the procession would fail. If the parable were meant to teach a lesson on sacrificial sharing, Jesus might have described the prudent girls sharing with the foolish. But that would teach a different lesson than that which Jesus wanted to teach. The parable is not a lesson in sharing or 'a charter for selfish unconcern for others,' France says (351). Rather it is 'intended to remind us that no one can ultimately rely on another's preparedness' (351). Or, as Carson puts it, 'the foresight and preparedness of the wise virgins cannot benefit the foolish virgins when the eschatological crisis dawns' (vv. 8-9). 'Preparedness can neither be transferred nor shared' (514-515). They will have to make their own provision. 'Go to the dealers, and buy some for yourselves,' the wise tell the foolish. We can imagine the foolish girls frantically attempting to obtain the necessary provisions. 'Oh, no,' they will say to themselves. 'What have I done?' Likewise, we might find ourselves saying, 'I am not ready. I have wasted my life, the years that God gave me in order to prepare for the next world. I have failed to prepare. Now it is too late.'

'And while they were going away to make the purchase, the bridegroom came, and those who were ready went in with him to the wedding feast; and the door was shut' (Matt. 25:10).

The bridegroom returns 'while they were going' to get more oil. The wedding party progresses to the groom's house and goes in for the celebration. 'And the door was shut,' signaling the finality of exclusion. True, it 'hardly fits the atmosphere of a village wedding.' Yet Jesus is not attempting to teach or describe wedding etiquette as it ought to be or as it was. His point is that 'there is a 'too late' in God's time-table (cf. Heb. 3:7–4:13),' says France (351). 'It simply means that all must be excluded from entry to heaven who at the precise moment are not prepared,' adds Calvin (III.111).

'And later the other virgins also came, saying, "Lord, lord, open up for us"' (Matt. 25:11).

Later the foolish girls arrive, pitiful, anxious to get in. Since they were invited, there should be a place for them. They plead to be let in. 'Lord, Lord, open up to us,' they say.

'But he answered and said, "Truly I say to you, I do not know you"' (Matt. 25:12).

Jesus answers the girls with the awful words, 'I do not know you' (Matt. 25:12), words which recall the chilling judgment of 7:22-23. They are not meant literally. The groom knows the bridesmaids. Rather, his expression may be the equivalent of our expression, 'I don't know who you are,' used at times of catastrophic betrayal or moral failure. I've heard wives and husbands use it of their spouses, and parents of their children, upon receiving particularly egregious news of unfaithfulness or moral failure, 'Who are you?' That the girls should have had so little regard for the groom's wedding that they neglected to bring a thing so basic as oil was a colossal social failure. 'I don't know you. I thought I did. I thought you cared about me. I thought you loved my bride. I thought you considered our wedding important. But clearly you don't, and I must conclude that I have misjudged who you are and misjudged our relationship.' France calls it 'a decisive formula of rejection, rather than a mere statement of fact (which could hardly be true of half the bridal procession!)' (352).

The point is that this is what God will say to some professed believers. Jesus' answer, says Carson, 'must not be construed as callous rejection of their lifelong desire to enter the kingdom.' Instead, 'it is the rejection of those who, despite appearances, never made preparation for the coming of the kingdom' (514). Those so-called believers who on judgment day cry out 'Lord, Lord,' but who never cared enough to prepare, never took the time or trouble to ready their souls, never took the claims of Christ or the call of the gospel seriously, will not be allowed into God's eternal kingdom (Matt. 7:21-23). They will be excluded. 'I don't know who you are,' Jesus will say, with 'devastating impact' (Morris, 625).

The Lesson

'Be on the alert then, for you do not know the day nor the hour'
(Matt. 25:13).

The lesson is obvious. A true disciple must 'be on the alert.'
He or she must be ready, must be prepared for the 'ultimate
encounter,' as France puts it (352). This parable doesn't teach
us how to prepare. For that we have to wait for the next
parable. Instead, it urges a way of life, a constant readiness,
because we 'do not know the day or the hour.'

This verse summarizes the message of the whole section
stretching back to 24:36. Be ready. Be alert. Watch! (cf. 24:42, 43).
You do not know the day or hour (24:36, 44, 50).

Nominal, distracted, unprepared, disinterested Christianity is served notice. Such is not the religion of Christ. It is not
enough to be a member of the church, or even to faithfully
sit in a pew each Sunday. Thorough, careful preparations for
eternity must be made.

'I want to be ready,' a person might say. 'How can I prepare?
How can I be sure that I will get into the kingdom of God
and enjoy the marriage supper of the Lamb?' (Rev. 19:7-11)

The simple answers of the old gospel are still the best
answers.

1. *Repent* – admit the darkness of your heart, the depth
of your depravity, the corruption of your thoughts, words,
and deeds, and turn from your sin and forsake it with holy
revulsion.

2. *Believe* – believe all that the Bible says, and more
specifically, believe that Jesus is Who He says He is: the Son
of God and God the Son, the Savior of the world, whose death
is an atoning blood sacrifice that God accepts as payment for
my sin. Receive Him (John 1:12ff.). Surrender to Him. Follow
Him (Matt. 16:24-26).

3. *Continue* – this is perhaps the crucial point. Christianity
is not a one moment religion. The gospel is not fire insurance.
When I receive Christ as Savior, I receive Him as Lord,
for life. Continue them to seek to know God. Continue to

grow in your love of God. Continue to serve Christ and His kingdom. Continue to obey the commands of God. Continue to pursue holiness. Continue in fruitful service to Christ.

Don't stop. Don't quit. Don't backslide. Don't get distracted. Don't lose heart. In this way eschatology is a theology of Christian life. In this way the second coming is at the center of the Christian life and we make constant reference to it. Prepare your soul. Be constantly ready. Live careful, sober, urgent, sensible lives. Be always ready to face Christ. Be always ready for Christ's return. 'Be on the alert,' Jesus says, 'for you do not know the day or the hour.'

STUDY QUESTIONS

1. What is the context within which this parable is given?

2. Does one's view of the end (i.e. of eschatology) affect the way one lives?

3. What separates the wise from the foolish virgins? What unites them? (vv. 2-4).

4. What problem is posed by verse 5, realized in verses 6-8?

5. If verse 9 is not a lesson in sharing, what is it meant to teach?

6. If verse 10 is not a lesson in wedding etiquette, what is it meant to teach?

7. If verses 11-12 are not an example of human or divine forgetfulness, what are they meant to teach?

8. We don't have to guess at the application of this parable. Jesus tells us in verse 13. What is it?

~ 29 ~

'THE TALENTS'

Matthew 25:14-30

Using God's Gifts

¹⁴*'For it is just like a man about to go on a journey, who called his own slaves, and entrusted his possessions to them.* ¹⁵*And to one he gave five talents, to another, two, and to another, one, each according to his own ability; and he went on his journey.* ¹⁶*Immediately the one who had received the five talents went and traded with them, and gained five more talents.* ¹⁷*In the same manner the one who had received the two talents gained two more.* ¹⁸*But he who received the one talent went away and dug in the ground, and hid his master's money.* ¹⁹*Now after a long time the master of those slaves came and settled accounts with them.* ²⁰*And the one who had received the five talents came up and brought five more talents, saying, "Master, you entrusted five talents to me; see, I have gained five more talents."* ²¹*His master said to him, "Well done, good and faithful slave; you were faithful with a few things, I will put you in charge of many things, enter into the joy of your master."* ²²*The one also who had received the two talents came up and said, "Master, you entrusted to me two talents; see, I have gained two more talents."* ²³*His master said to him, "Well done, good and faithful slave; you were faithful with a few things, I will put you in charge of many things; enter into the joy of your master."* ²⁴*And*

the one also who had received the one talent came up and said, "Master, I knew you to be a hard man, reaping where you did not sow, and gathering where you scattered no seed. ²⁵And I was afraid, and went away and hid your talent in the ground; see, you have what is yours." ²⁶But his master answered and said to him, "You wicked, lazy slave, you knew that I reap where I did not sow, and gather where I scattered no seed. ²⁷Then you ought to have put my money in the bank, and on my arrival I would have received my money back with interest. ²⁸Therefore take away the talent from him, and give it to the one who has the ten talents." ²⁹For to everyone who has shall more be given, and he shall have an abundance; but from the one who does not have, even what he does have shall be taken away. ³⁰And cast out the worthless slave into the outer darkness; in that place there shall be weeping and gnashing of teeth.'

In the Parable of Talents, Jesus continues His exhortation to vigilance begun in Matthew 24:36, which may be summarized as 'be on the alert' (Matt. 24:42; 25:13). But as France points out, this parable takes the exhortation a step further than it had gone in the Parable of the Ten Virgins (25:1-13). It 'takes up the question which that of the bridesmaids left unanswered: what *is* "readiness?"' (352). It takes us a step further by 'showing what readiness means,' says Morris (627). The Parable of the Ten Virgins told us to be prepared for Christ's return. The Parable of the Talents tells us what it means to be prepared. Readiness, according to this parable, is faithfully responding to what we'll call 'gospel opportunities.' The commentators agree about this. The preparedness, readiness, or watchfulness commended by this parable is a matter of 'actual diligence in our present work and service,' says Matthew Henry. It 'is not a matter of passively 'waiting' but of responsible activity, producing results which the coming 'master' can see and approve,' says France. The period of delay (our era), France continues, 'is a period of opportunity to put to good use the 'talents' entrusted to his "slaves"' (352). Carson says watchfulness leads not to 'passivity but to doing one's duty, to growing, to husbanding and developing the resources God entrusts to us' (518). It 'consists in having already faithfully discharged our responsibilities as disciples, whether they have been small or great,' France adds (352-3).

Properly understood, this parable asks us to examine our response to our 'gospel opportunities:' have we acted upon the gospel word that we have heard, believing, obeying, and serving in response? Have we acted upon all our providential capacities, gifts, and opportunities as well, wisely employing them to the glory of God?

The Parable

> 'For it is just like a man about to go on a journey, who called his own slaves, and entrusted his possessions to them' (Matt. 25:14).

'For' (*gar*) 'indicates a close link with the theme of 24:36–25:13,' says France, 'and particularly with the exhortation of verse 13,' the concluding verse of the Parable of the Ten Virgins (353). 'Be on the alert,' Jesus had said, summarizing the point of that parable. 'For' means 'because.' 'It' is the kingdom of heaven. Here's *why* you should 'be on the alert,' as you were urged to be in the Parable of the Ten Virgins. The theme of readiness continues to be illustrated in the Parable of the Talents. The second parable can begin in this fairly abrupt manner because it shares both the introduction and theme with the previous one (v. 1).

'Be on the alert because ('for') the kingdom of God ('it') is like a man going on a journey,' Jesus says. He is like a rich man, a man of great wealth who owned a number of slaves. The journeying man is the Christ-figure of this parable. He is soon to go on a 'journey' to a 'far country,' as the King James Version puts it. Consequently he 'entrusted his possessions' to his servants. 'Slaves' (*doulos*) is best understood as 'servants,' according to Morris (627, n.23).

> 'And to one he gave five talents, to another, two, and to another, one, each according to his own ability; and he went on his journey' (Matt. 25:15).

The picture, then, is that of the present era. Jesus has gone to a 'far country,' leaving us, His servants, behind and in charge of His affairs. Each of us is given a measure of ability, and a measure of responsibility. Certain emphases emerge from the parable.

First, God distributes His gifts universally though unevenly
The master distributed his 'talents' to all of his servants, though he did so unevenly. A 'talent' was a monetary unit. It varied somewhat in value, but generally is regarded as equal to 6,000 denarii. A denarius was the standard wage for a day's work for a common laborer. 6,000 denarii is approximately 20 years' work for a laborer. The sums entrusted are 'vast,' Carson summarizes. Though a talent is not a capacity or skill, as in English usage, nevertheless the English meaning is useful because in the terms of the parable the monetary represent far more than money. It stands for the sum of all our God-given abilities, resources, and opportunities.

He gave five talents to one servant, two to another, and one to the last. The principle of distribution was 'according to his own ability.' The parable recognizes that both abilities and responsibilities are unequal. All that we have comes from God (Ps. 24:1; 1 Cor. 4:7; James 1:17). But what He gives, He gives unequally. Some have greater faculties, opportunities, and resources than others. Some have less. This is a fact of creation and providence. It is not good, it is not bad, it just is. We should not envy those who have more. We should not snub those who have less. It is the prerogative of the Giver to distribute His gifts as He is pleased to do so. Everyone gets something. Some have more, some have less.

'And he went on his journey.' The master leaves no instructions for the servants. He wants them to 'use their own initiative,' as Morris puts it (627). 'He wanted them to trade as best they could with the money he had left them' (627). But they must not lose sight of the fact that they are *his* talents. 'You are not your own,' the Apostle Paul reminds us, 'you have been bought with a price' (1 Cor. 6:19, 20).

Second, God requires that His gifts be used for His ends.

> *'Immediately the one who had received the five talents went and traded with them, and gained five more talents'* (Matt. 25:16).

The diligent servants got to work 'immediately.' The servant 'must be prompt, active, and efficient in promoting the interests of his Master,' says Plummer (346). The one with five talents 'traded,' or literally 'worked with them,' that is, 'put them to good use in some way,' says Morris (628). Carson says that *ergazomai* ('worked') means that he did more than invest the money in a lending agency, but rather 'set up some business and *worked* with the capital to make it grow' (516). Zerwick gives it the sense of 'do business' or 'work for profit' (II, 82). The same diligence was demonstrated by the second servant with his two talents.

> *'In the same manner the one who had received the two talents gained two more'* (Matt. 25:17).

But Jesus says of the third servant:

> *'But he who received the one talent went away and dug in the ground, and hid his master's money'* (Matt. 25:18).

The third servant played it safe. He avoided the risky work of buying, selling, and trading. He merely buried it for safekeeping.

> *'Now after a long time the master of those slaves came and settled accounts with them'* (Matt. 25:19).

The theme of delay, found also in the previous parable (25:5), as well as in the illustration of 24:45-51, is found here as well. It was only 'after a long time' that the master returned to 'settle accounts,' a 'standard commercial term,' says Carson (516), which 'makes it clear that they had been given the money specifically for trading,' says France (353).

The master settles accounts because the original and the multiplied talents are his talents. The servants were not to use the talents entrusted to them for their own purposes. They were not to spend his resources on themselves. The implication for us is that we are not to use our own opportunities, abilities, and capacities for our own glory. Our assets are God's assets, to be used to honor and praise Him. The criterion for evaluation or judgment shall be what we have done for the sake of God's kingdom with what we have been given.

Third, God commends and rewards the labors of the diligent

> 'And the one who had received the five talents came up and brought five more talents, saying, "Master, you entrusted five talents to me; see, I have gained five more talents." His master said to him, "Well done, good and faithful slave; you were faithful with a few things, I will put you in charge of many things, enter into the joy of your master"' (Matt. 25:20, 21).

The master both commends and rewards his faithful servants. 'Well done,' he says, 'good and faithful slave.' He 'approves both his character and his diligence,' notes Morris (629). He received an abundance of gospel provision and believed it. He obeyed and served the gospel message that he heard. He used all his gifts, spiritual and natural, to multiply his opportunities to the glory of God. He is both an excellent and trustworthy servant.

'You were faithful with a few things,' Jesus continues. Note that the master is a very rich man. He describes the vast sum entrusted to the first servant (100 years worth of wages) as 'a few things.' 'I will put you in charge of many things.' The reward for good service is expanded opportunity, what we would call a promotion. He is given 'a position that will give him more scope for the use of the abilities that he has shown he possesses,' says Morris (629).

'Enter in the joy of your master,' Jesus continues (v. 21). France notes that this 'is hardly commercial language.' Rather 'the application is again creeping into the telling of the story' (354). We should note how life with God is typified – it is a life of *joy* into which we enter. God's eternal kingdom provides not only 'glorious new responsibilities' but also 'holy delight,' observes Carson (516). Don't be deceived by the propaganda of the world and its promise of 'passing pleasures' (Heb. 11:25). Life with God will be joyful because we will be with the One for Whom we were made. As the fish was made for water, grass for the soil, and the bird for flight, so we were made to know and serve God. He is the environment for which we were designed. Only as we find Him do we find fulfillment and satisfaction (Ps. 16:11).

> 'The one also who had received the two talents came up and said, "Master, you entrusted to me two talents; see, I have gained two more talents." His master said to him, "Well done, good and faithful slave; you were faithful with a few things, I will put you in charge of many things; enter into the joy of your master"' (Matt. 25:22, 23).

The second servant receives exactly the same commendation. He too seized upon the gospel message, believed it, obeyed it, and served it. He too used his gifts, spiritual and natural, for the glory of God. That the sum of his abilities, resources, and opportunities was less than that of the first servant is of no consequence to the master, and that his gain was quantitatively less, was without relevance. What was important was that they both doubled the amount entrusted to them. The one entrusted with two talents is not expected to produce the five talents of the first servant. He is praised for producing two additional talents with praise that is equal with that received by the one who was entrusted with five and produced five. We observe that five is more than two. Should not the one who did the most receive the most praise? No, God's judgment and rewards are proportionate with the distribution of His gifts. Jesus said, 'To whom much is given, much is required' (Luke 12:48 paraphrase). Conversely, to whom little is given, little is required. Both stewards did, we might say, the best they could with what they had. One had more, one had less. But their efforts were equal, and their outcomes proportionate.

Fourth, God condemns and punishes those who waste their talents
The third servant failed to use his more limited gifts and opportunities.

> *'And the one also who had received the one talent came up and said, "Master, I knew you to be a hard man, reaping where you did not sow, and gathering where you scattered no seed"'* (Matt. 25:24).

Plenty, though less, was given to the third servant. But he did nothing with what he had. He heard the gospel and failed to respond. He refused to believe or rejected it. He would not fulfill the plan of the Master. Essentially, he blames the master for this failure. I squandered my opportunity, he says, because 'I knew you to be a hard man.' You are a hard, demanding man with high expectations. This frightened me. In other words, it is your fault. If you weren't so demanding, I would have done better. You both robbed me of my initiative and filled me with fear. By 'hard' the servant means 'grasping, exploiting the labor of others ... and putting the servant in an invidious position,' says Carson (517). 'Reaping where you did not sow,' according to Morris, 'means that the master had the habit of enjoying a crop on which he had expended no labor' (630). So also does the next phrase, 'gathering where you did not scatter.' The latter phrase refers to the process of separating the grain and the chaff. The third servant is complaining that the master collects profits from situations from which he has contributed no labor.

Yet in characterizing the master as a 'hard' man, the third servant undermined his excuse. He admitted that he knew that he must produce a profit, yet failed to do so. 'His *defense* was his *offense*,' says Matthew Henry. He accuses the master of oppression, compounding his guilt of sloth with his further sin of blameshifting.

> 'And I was afraid, and went away and hid your talent in the ground; see, you have what is yours' (Matt. 25:25).

Naturally enough, given the master's demanding requirements, 'I was afraid,' says the third servant. He was afraid that he would lose the money through poor investments. So he hid the one talent he had in the ground. 'You have what is yours,' he says. I haven't done anything bad. At least I didn't spend the talent on myself, he is saying. The problem with the third slave is that service for him meant merely avoiding doing wrong, rather than embracing the gospel with such faith that it results in active, faithful, fruitful service.

> 'But his master answered and said to him, "You wicked, lazy slave, you knew that I reap where I did not sow, and gather where I scattered no seed"' (Matt. 25:26).

'But' is adversative, or even adversarial. The master does not accept the third servant's explanation. Sure you didn't do anything wrong. But it is 'wicked' to squander talents. It's not just ill-advised. It's wicked, evil to waste one's ability and opportunities to serve God's kingdom. What you are, the master says, is 'lazy.' You preferred your own comfort and self-indulgence to strenuous service. You allowed your dislike of my profit-taking to combine with your disinclination to work, which resulted in your doing nothing. Then you blamed me!

> 'Then you ought to have put my money in the bank, and on my arrival I would have received my money back with interest' (Matt. 25:27).

'You ought' is 'a strong term' (*edei*) notes Morris, meaning 'it was necessary' (632). This was the least that he was obligated to do. This could have been done with minimal risk and minimal exertion.

Here are the consequences: he is deprived of all opportunities for service.

'Therefore take away the talent from him, and give it to the one who has the ten talents' (Matt. 25:28).

It is as though the master says, 'You might have served. Your life might have counted for something. Instead, you will lose all your opportunities for contributing.

The Lesson

'For to everyone who has shall more be given, and he shall have an abundance; but from the one who does not have, even what he does have shall be taken away' (Matt. 25:29).

Verse 29 repeats Matthew 13:12 and underscores this important principle of spiritual life. Fail to use your talents and you will forfeit them. 'For to fail to do good and use what God has entrusted to us to use is grievous sin,' says Carson (518). Use a talent, and it develops and grows. Believe, and your faith will grow. Obey, and you will grow in holiness. Serve, and you will be given increased opportunities and responsibilities. Use your mind for the glory of God, and your mental capacities will expand. Use your wealth for the glory of God, and your wealth will increase. Fail to use these resources for Christ's kingdom, and you will forfeit them. God does not expect great things from all of us. Some of us have limited resources. There is nothing wrong with that. What he does require is that we use what we have to serve Him, and if we do, He promises that He will increase our gifts and responsibilities.

'And cast out the worthless slave into the outer darkness; in that place there shall be weeping and gnashing of teeth' (Matt. 25:30).

This is the language with which Jesus typically described the fate of the wicked (8:12; 13:42, 50). He is 'worthless' or 'unprofitable.' He failed to believe. He failed to obey. He failed to serve. He squandered his gospel opportunities. He is consigned to a place in the 'outer darkness' where there shall be 'weeping and gnashing of teeth.' 'It stands for complete and final rejection and for unceasing sorrow and regret,' says Morris (632). And this is not for one who had committed a heinous act, but who had neglected to use the talent entrusted to him.

These final grim words force us to examine ourselves and our preparations for eternity. Are we using what we have for the betterment of our souls and the glory of God?

First, have we believed the gospel?
Most of us have heard the gospel of Jesus Christ over and over again. Have we believed? Have we acted upon what we have heard? Have we responded 'immediately,' as did the faithful servants, or are we waiting, like the wicked servant? This is the first and primary question of this parable. Do I know I am a sinner? Have I heard the call to repentance? Do I believe that Christ's death was no mere tragedy, but an atoning sacrifice that God receives as sufficient payment for my sin? Seize your gospel opportunities! Believe, repent, surrender to Jesus Christ as Savior and Lord.

Second, have we obeyed and served the gospel?
The gospel is far more than a call to salvation. It is also a call to holiness, to love, and to service. Most of us have heard this over and over again. Have we heeded this call? Or are we squandering the opportunity to serve, to make a difference, for our lives to count?

Third, have we used our various capacities to serve God and prepare for eternity?
Each of us has certain natural capacities. Added to these are spiritual gifts which are given to all who are in Christ (Rom. 12, 1 Cor. 12). We are unequally endowed, but we are all endowed. 'Since we have gifts that differ according to the grace given to us,' says the Apostle Paul, 'let each exercise them accordingly' (Rom. 12:6). Again he says,

> But to each one is given the manifestation of the Spirit for the common good (1 Cor. 12:7).

Christ's gifts are distributed 'to each one individually just as He wills' (1 Cor. 12:11). Some have great *mental abilities*, and can serve as theologians and teachers in the church, and apologists or defenders of the church. Some have wonderful *artistic talents*, and can serve as musicians, architects, decorators, and publicists for the church. Some have pleasant *personalities*, graced as they are with unusual charm, and can serve as magnets, attracting others to the ministry of the church, or as visitors of the sick, spreading cheer and joy wherever they go. Some have *organizational skills*, and can bring order and efficiency to the ministry of the church. Some have other *practical skills* (for lack of a better term), and can use their abilities as woodworkers, painters, planters, mechanics, typists, and so on. Some have exceptional *physical capacities*, and can perform difficult manual labor here at home, or endure the pain and deprivation of Third-World mission service.

Some of these capacities might be classified as 'natural.' Others might be 'spiritual.' Either way, the question is, is the Lord getting a return on His investment in you? Are you using His gifts to serve Him or just serve yourself? We mustn't be too narrow about these things or create the wrong impression. One engaged in a secular vocation who uses these gifts in his employment in order to support his family and the ministry of his church, even to build a business, is to a large extent using his God-given gifts to the glory of God, given right motives. We would seriously err if we were to say that one only serves Christ when one is using one's capacities directly in the work of the gospel. No, the real question is, are your faculties, be they mental, artistic, personality, organizational, practical or physical, primarily used for your own ends, your own pleasure, your own name and fame, or for the kingdom of Christ? Are they being used to raise a family for Christ? Are they being used to build a business for Christ? Are they being used to raise revenues for the Church of Christ? Are they being used to lead others to Christ? Are they being used to bring love to those of Christ's people who suffer?

I have some vivid pictures in mind when I think of limited capacities and maximum service. I think of Renee

Hutton, a young woman in our congregation, working at a local hospital, battling a brain tumor, hardly able to walk herself, limping into the room of other members who were hospitalized, in order to bring a bit of sunshine into their lives. She also, by the way, in spite of a hand crippled by cancer and multiple surgeries, cross-stitched little framed pictures for my first two children when they were born. Her capacities were severely restricted by the cancer. But she maximized what was left, squeezing every last drop of service out of her weakened body.

I think of Rose Payne, an older member of our church living with chronic pain, presenting an aggressive but tactful Christian witness to the medical professionals who provided treatment for her. She would find out where they went to church, tell them about her own, would further work the conversation, telling them of the Lord's kind care for her, inviting them to church if they had none, and urging them to rejoice in all things. Her mobility was restricted. She couldn't get up and go as she once did. But she used what she still had.

There are many others as well. But these two are examples of ones who had severe limitations on their ability to serve, who had few 'talents' in that respect. Yet, what a return in the Lord's investment! And He appeared to multiply at least one aspect of their giftedness, as both Renee and Rose seemed to grow more gracious and sweet-spirited as time passed and their conditions worsened. At the very same time, one could watch others not use their limited gifts, and grow more unpleasant and bitter in similar circumstances. Even what they had was taken away.

With what capacities has the Lord entrusted you? Don't say none, because it isn't true. Don't be like the steward entrusted with just one 'talent' who refused to use it because it was too small. We all have capacities. Are you using them to honor and serve the one who gave them to you?

Fourth, have we used our various opportunities to serve God and prepare for eternity?
In addition to faculties, God has given to us opportunities to put our faculties to use. Theoretically, one could have talent

but no opportunity to use one's talent. Instead, God has opened doors of opportunity for us through which we have been able to put our various capacities to full use. Behind all of these opportunities is a matter of *time*. An opportunity implies the time to make use of that opportunity. Time, in other words, is another of God's gifts which we have a responsibility to use for His glory. What are we doing with our time? We all have a finite amount of time. How are we using it? Are we spending it to seize our opportunities or wasting it upon frivolous and silly ends? Let's look now at our opportunities.

Some of these opportunities have been created by your *family.* I remember a conversation a few years ago with a fellow who didn't want to live in his hometown after graduation from college because he wanted to get his own job, not one based on his family connections. I understood what he meant but still asked, why would you not use the opportunities that God gives you through your family? What is wrong with that? Didn't God give to you your family? Didn't He give to your family the relationships that it has in the community? Why would you not use what He has given?

Some of these opportunities have been generated by *gifts.* Some doors have opened not because of *family* connections, not because of our own *abilities*, but seemingly for no reason at all. These opportunities have appeared out of nowhere, they have been what some have called 'happy providences.' A job is offered. An opportunity to serve appears. A position opens up. A need is made known.

We may now summarize what we've said about abilities, opportunities, and gifts. Because God is Lord of all our circumstances, we know that ultimately all of our opportunities come to us by His hand. If you have great mental gifts, are you using the opportunities that God has given you to develop your mind, or is it going to waste? Even if you only have an average mind, are you developing the mind that you have, or are you letting it rot in front of the television? I remember fellows in junior high school who had fantastic athletic ability who completely wasted it, either because they were lazy, or because they destroyed their gifts through drugs and alcohol. Are you burying your artistic 'talents' or using them as opportunities arise for doing so? We know of a world-class musician who never developed his natural genius because he refused to maximize his God-given opportunities to do so. Don't sit back passively and wait. As doors swing open, it takes courage and initiative to walk through them. The wicked steward is afraid of the risks of life. He says, 'I was afraid' (v. 25).

The Proverbs identify the wicked, lazy man as one who won't get out of bed because 'there is a lion in the square' (Prov. 26:13; cf. 22:13). He is afraid of life. He fears risk. Our society is making strenuous efforts to create a risk-free world. But it is impossible, and the effort can be oppressive. Just ask any boy whose mom tried to remove the possibility of accidents from his childhood. He grew up in a straightjacket, he'll tell you. We mustn't live recklessly. But there are legitimate risks that must be run. There are open doors through which we must walk. There are closed doors which we must open. There are even bolted doors which we must kick down.

I once heard Josh McDowell, the popular evangelist-apologist for the Christian faith, recall a conversation in which a young man said to him, 'I'd like to serve Christ on the mission field. I'm just waiting for God to open the door.' McDowell's response was incredulous. 'Open the door?' he asked. 'Open the door?' he repeated. 'There are 50,000 open doors right now! God doesn't need to open the door. You need to walk through one of the 50,000 that are already open.' The same would be true for many of us. We do not lack opportunities for service. We don't lack outlets for our gifts and abilities. We just need to open our eyes and begin to serve.

Fifth, have we used our material resources to serve God and prepare for eternity?
Is God receiving a return on the resources which He has entrusted to us?

We may begin with our *non-monetary assets,* such as homes and cars and things. Are they being used for the glory of God? Is your home a place for ministry? Are you having other believers into your home? Are you inviting unbelievers over? We have noted many times that the kitchen table is among the most effective weapon in our spiritual arsenal. Admittedly there are seasons in life when this is easier than others. If you are rearing young children or caring for an elderly relative, it can be difficult to use the home as a base for hospitality. You are already taken up full-time in the care of others. But those seasons are relatively short when measured against a lifetime. We are stewards of our homes and cars and things. Are we using them for the sake of Christ's kingdom?

Closely related to this question, we might ask as well, are we caring for the things we have? How much of our wealth is wasted because we are constantly replacing things that would have lasted longer if we had only cared properly for them? Furniture is broken, clothes are rotting, cars are rusting, all because of poor maintenance.

What have we done with our monetary assets? Our capacities and opportunities regularly generate a tangible, visible, liquid resource by which we may measure our commitment to stewardship – money! Stewardship is certainly more than giving, as we have seen. But it isn't less. What are we doing with our income? Are we wise stewards of what we earn?

First, *are we wise stewards of that portion of our income that 'belongs' to us?* We have a whole string of questions that we can ask in order to answer accurately.

1. *Are we avoiding debt?* Scripture is full of warnings about debt, most pointedly perhaps warning that 'the borrower becomes the lender's slave' (Prov. 22:7). Ongoing personal debt means basically one thing – we are living beyond our means. The burden of debt can be crushing, destroy marriages and families. Interest payments are money down a rat-hole. Assume as little debt as possible. Work to pay down the debt you have already assumed.

2. *Are we buying wisely?* Ours is a consumer society. Much of what we buy is junk, pure and simple. Our children's toy boxes are full of junk. Our homes are full of junk – stuff that is poorly made out of cheap materials and guaranteed not to last. When my children were young, they loved to play cowboys. I can't tell you how many toy six-shooters we went through. They were all made of junk. They were plastic, or a combination of metal and plastic, or cheap metal. They were definitely not boy-proof. I even called up toy companies and begged them to make a six-shooter that would last, telling them that I was willing to pay a premium for it, to no avail. Our trash can full of broken pistols represented today's consumer mentality. Get it now, get it cheap, and buy it again in a few years. Instead, insist on quality. Buy quality clothes, not stuff that will fall apart after a season or go out of style. Buy quality furniture, of the sort that can be passed down for two or three generations, not junk that breaks down after five years. Buy less, or if beyond one's financial reach, buy used, but buy better. In the long run, the family will save by waiting for quality and doing without until such can be found.

Second, *are we returning to God a due proportion of our income?* Again, we have several questions.

1. *Am I tithing my income?* A tithe, by definition, is a tenth. A tenth of all that we make is owed to God. We ought to give this joyfully. Paul writes,

> *Let each one do just as he has purposed in his heart; not grudgingly or under compulsion; for God loves a cheerful giver* (2 Cor. 9:7).

But even if we are not joyful as we contemplate giving, we should know that tithing is a duty. Abraham paid pre-Mosaic tithes to Melchizedek, a type of Christ, as a means of recognizing his supremacy (Gen. 14:20; cf. Heb. 7). Jacob followed the example of Abraham by paying tithes to God

(Gen. 28:22). Israel was commanded to pay tithes (Lev. 27:30; 2 Chron. 31:5). Jesus commended the paying of tithes saying,

> 'Woe to you, scribes and Pharisees, hypocrites! For you tithe mint and dill and cummin, and have neglected the weightier provisions of the law: justice and mercy and faithfulness; but these are the things you should have done without neglecting the others' (Matt. 23:23).

Notice that Jesus comments on their precise tithing, criticizing their warped priorities, tithing even their spices, while neglecting 'the weightier provisions of the law.' He says, 'these are the things *you should have done*,' speaking of their tithing, 'without neglecting the others,' speaking of 'justice, mercy, and faithfulness.' Tithing was not their error. Tithing *should be done.* Their error was tithing while neglecting the 'weightier provisions.' Malachi says if we fail to tithe, it is as though we are robbing God!

> Will a man rob God? Yet you are robbing Me! But you say, 'How have we robbed Thee?' In tithes and offerings (Mal. 3:8).

What are we do to? Malachi explains:

> 'Bring the whole tithe into the storehouse, so that there may be food in My house, and test Me now in this,' says the LORD of hosts, 'if I will not open for you the windows of heaven, and pour out for you a blessing until it overflows' (Mal. 3:10).

The picture here is that of the people of God bringing their whole tithe, the whole ten percent, into the 'storehouse,' which we would identify as the church. Old Testament tithes went to 'the elders at the gate' (Deut. 14:28, 29; cf. Deut. 22:15, 25:7). They were not and we are not to bring five percent to the elders, and then make our own decisions about the other five percent, designating some here, there, and everywhere. No, the whole tithe is brought to the church to be distributed by the leadership of the church.

2. *Am I giving sacrificially?* We generally think of sacrificial giving as 'offerings' over and above the tithe. But even if

you think that tithing is only an Old Testament obligation and not a New Testament one (and some do), we are still called to give sacrificially. It is difficult to believe that, given that the New Testament era is one of a better hope, a better covenant, enacted on better promises, we should give less (see Heb. 7:19, 22; 8:6). Jesus observed the widow bringing her 'mite' to the temple and He commended her saying,

> And calling His disciples to Him, He said to them, 'Truly I say to you, this poor widow put in more than all the contributors to the treasury; for they all put in out of their surplus, but she, out of her poverty, put in all she owned, all she had to live on' (Mark 12:43, 44).

Sacrificial giving, giving that hurts, giving that leads to self-deprivation and requires self-denial, is commended. She gave 'all she owned.' We may assume that Jesus still commends such giving. *Some* may still be called to do so, to give all they own. But *all* are called to give sacrificially, and *all* are called to tithe.

We have attempted to give a comprehensive view of readiness. How are we to prepare for Christ's return? What does it mean to 'Be on the alert?' (24:42; 25:13). Basically, it comes down to this: God has given us all that we have. Our political rights and privileges are His gifts. Our personal abilities (capacities), opportunities, and resources are His gifts to us. We have a responsibility to use, preserve, and protect these assets. We have a responsibility to multiply and extend these assets. And we have the responsibility to provide God with a return on His investment in us, even as we build His kingdom through our service. In these ways we remain prepared, in a state of readiness, as we anticipate the always imminent return of Christ.

Study Questions

1. If the Parable of the Ten Virgins is an exhortation to 'be on the alert' (Matt. 25:13; cf. Matt. 24:42), what is the concern of the Parable of the Talents that follows it? (v. 14).

2. In the terms of the parable, who do the journeying man and his slaves represent? The talents? (v. 15).

3. What does the parable teach us about the distribution of God's gifts? (v. 15).

4. What are we expected to do with God's gifts? (vv. 16-18).

5. For what does the Master commend his servants in verses 19-23?

6. Of what does the reward of the commended servants consist? (vv. 20-23). Why are the rewards and commendations of the first two servants the same though their outcomes were different?

7. What excuses does the wicked servant offer? (vv. 24-25).

8. What does the parable teach us about those who squander their gifts and opportunities? (vv. 26-27).

9. Final question – are you 'on the alert?' Is the Lord getting a return on His investment in you? What are some specific evidences of this?

~ 30 ~

EPILOGUE

The thirty story-parables of our study have not taught us everything that Jesus meant for us to know about living the Christian life. Important lessons were powerfully taught using more conventional didactic means, as in the Sermon on the Mount (Matt. 5–7). We've seen that proverbs and illustrations, in addition to story-parables, were an important element of Jesus' overall teaching method (see ch. 1). Nevertheless, the parables have taken us a long way down the path of understanding the nature of the life that Jesus would have us live.

A review and summary of what we have learned may be in order. What have the parables taught us?

Christ-Centered
First, we have seen that the Christian life is *centered on Christ*. There is a sense in which we can say, directly and indirectly, the parables are all about Jesus. The Christian life begins and ends in Christ (cf. ch. 2, Matt. 13:34, 35). He is the *Sower* who casts the gospel seed upon the soil of the human heart (ch. 3, Matt. 13:1-9, 18-23). He is the *Scribe* who dispenses the new and old treasures of God's word (ch. 15, Matt. 13:51-53). He

is the *Bridegroom* whose wedding feast we have been invited to attend (ch. 4, Matt. 22:1-14), and for whose arrival we must be ready (ch. 28, Matt. 25:1-13).

He is the *Hidden Treasure* and *Pearl of Great Price*, that is, One Who is of such great value that we joyfully relinquish all that we have to gain Him (ch. 9, Matt. 13:44-46). He is the example that we are to follow. He is the *Good Shepherd* who pursues the *Lost Sheep* (ch. 26, Matt. 18:12-14; ch. 19, Luke 15:1-7), and He is like the *persistent woman* who carefully searches for the *Lost Coin* (ch. 19, Luke 15:8-10). He is the *Good Samaritan* who sacrificially loves and cares for the needy and unlovely (ch. 21, Luke 10:25-37). He and His words are the *Rock* which cannot be shaken by the storms of life (ch. 16, Matt. 7:24-27). As the *Two Sons* taught us, entering God's kingdom is not about talking about God or practicing religion, but about doing the will of the Father by receiving Jesus (Matt. 21:28-32). Jesus is the initiator of the Christian life, the aim or goal of the Christian life, and the pattern for living the Christian life, the foundation upon which we are to build.

Divine Growth

Second, we have seen that the Christian life is *divinely empowered*. The *Growing Seed* of God's word grows 'by itself' in supernatural ways of which the preacher-sower 'does not know' (ch. 11, Mark 4:26-29). We plant and water, as the Apostle Paul explains, but it is 'God who causes the growth' (1 Cor. 3:6, 7). By the inherent power of His word and Spirit, He grows His people and His kingdom into Christ-likeness.

Opposition is to be expected along the way. The *Wheat and the Tares* grow up together (ch. 12, Matt. 13:24-30; 36-43). Perfection is not to be expected in this life, whether in our hearts or in the church. The *Dragnet* gathers both 'good' and 'bad' fish into God's kingdom (ch. 13, Matt. 13:47-50). Good and bad may be found in the pews, in the pulpit, and in our hearts.

The gospel starts small, like the *Mustard Seed* and *Leaven* in their contexts. Yet it grows irrepressibly into preeminence, becoming the largest of the garden plants, leavening the whole loaf (ch. 14, Matt. 13:31-33). Growth comes not through frantic activity, nor by clever words of worldly wisdom (1 Cor. 2:1-5), but by the proclamation of a simple gospel, which is the power of God unto salvation (Rom. 1:16), which is 'divinely powerful for the destruction of fortresses' (2 Cor. 10:4).

Faithful Response

The parables do not err by emphasizing the divine initiative in salvation at the expense of the human response, or the human response at the expense of the divine initiative (ch. 1, Matt. 13:10-17). The parables persistently call for us to *respond to God's gracious initiative*. We are urged to do so negatively, positively, and with contrasting examples. We are not to be like the *Rich Fool* who spent his life accumulating wealth and 'building bigger barns,' yet was unprepared on the night that his soul was required of him (ch. 6, Luke 12:13-21). We are to believe God's word and repent, like poor *Lazarus*, not live a life of luxurious self-indulgence like the *Rich Man*, who upon death 'lifted up his eyes, being in torment,' because he would not believe Moses and the prophets (ch. 7, Luke 16:19-31). We are to humble ourselves like the *Publican* who cried out, 'God, be merciful to me, the sinner,' and not pray like the proud *Pharisees* who 'trusted in themselves that they were religious,' who prayed proudly giving thanks that they were 'not like other people' (ch. 8, Luke 18:9-14).

The *Parable of the Sower* taught us to pay attention to our hearts. We enter God's kingdom through receiving God's word with an open heart: not superficially, in which case the word has 'no firm root' and 'affliction or persecution' causes it to 'fall away;' not with a divided heart, in which 'the worry of the world and the deceitfulness of riches choke the word,' but with understanding and fruit-producing depth (ch. 3, Matt. 13:1-9; 18-23). Yet like the *Laborers in the Vineyard* we are to know that salvation is all of God's free grace and not of our merit (ch. 10, Matt. 20:1-16). We must choose Christ. But we do so only because He first chose us (John 15:16). We must love Christ. But we do so only because He first loved us (1 John 4:19). We must believe Christ. But even our faith is a gift of His grace (Eph. 2:8, 9).

Fruitful

Finally, the parables teach that the Christian life *produces the fruit of love and humility*. Like the larger of the *Two Debtors* whose massive debt was forgiven, and the sinful woman who anointed Jesus with expensive perfume, wet his feet with her tears, and wiped them with her hair, we are to love God much because we have been forgiven much (ch. 18, Luke 7:36-50). Conversely, unlike the *Unmerciful Servant*, we are to forgive others their debts because of the unpayable debts of our own that God has forgiven (ch. 22, Matt. 18:21-35). Like the *Prodigal*, we are to admit our sin and unworthiness, and like the *Prodigal's father*, we are to love and forgive the lost sons who return home, even as we know that we have in the same way been loved by the Father (ch. 20, Luke 15:11-32). We are to be *Good Samaritans* who love even unlovely neighbors (ch. 21, Luke 10:25-37), *Sowers* and *Scribes* who, out of love for the lost, proclaim the richness of God's gospel (chs. 3 and 15, Matt. 13:1-9, 18-23, 51-53); *shepherds, housekeepers* and *fathers* who pursue, welcome, and restore lost sheep, lost coins, and prodigal sons (chs. 19 and 20, Luke 15:1-32).

We are to pursue God's kingdom with focus and intensity, as the *Unrighteous Steward* did in his crisis (ch. 17, Luke 16:1-13). Knowing how weak and foolish we are, we are to persist in seeking God's strength and wisdom in prayer, as did the woman before the *Unjust Judge*, and as did the *Persistent Friend* at the door of the reluctant neighbor (chs. 23 and 24, Luke 18:1-8; 11:5-13). We are to be a fruitful vineyard or a fruitful fig tree, not appropriating the church for our own ends as did the *Wicked Vine-Growers* and not proving ourselves to be barren and worthless, as did the *Barren Fig Tree*, but bearing the fruit of repentance and righteousness for the sake of God's kingdom (chs 25 and 26, Matt. 21:33-41; Luke 13:6-9). We are to maximize the *Talents* that God has given to us, providing Him with a spiritual return on His investment in us (ch. 29, Matt. 25:14-30).

No, the parables have not taught us everything that we need to know about life in God's kingdom. But with arresting stories and memorable characters Jesus has opened a window to eternity that, so long as these parables are studied, shall forever remain open.

What have we learned about the Christian life from the thirty story-parables that we have studied? A review and summary may help us to answer this question.

STUDY QUESTIONS

1. The Christian life is centered on Christ.

How is Jesus like each of the following?

    i.   *Sower* (Matt. 13:1-9; 18-23).

    ii.   *Scribe* (Matt. 13:51-52).

    iii. *Bridegroom* (Matt. 22:1-14; 25:1-13).

    iv. *Hidden Treasure and Pearl of Great Price* (Matt. 13:44-46)

    v.   *Good Shepherd* (Matt. 18:12-14; Luke 15:1-7).

    vi. *Persistent woman* (Luke 15:8-10).

    vii. *Good Samaritan* (Luke 10:25-37).

    viii. *Rock* (Matt. 7:24-27).

2. The Christian life is Divinely empowered.

The Christian life begins and grows like ...

    i.   *Growing Seed* (Mark 4:26-29).

    ii.   *Mustard Seed and Leaven* (Matt. 13:31-33).

    iii. *Wheat and Tares* (Matt. 13:24-30; 36-43).

    iv. *Dragnet* (Matt. 13:47-50).

3. The Christian life requires a faithful response.

God initiates, but we must respond. Negative, positive, and contrasting examples were given ...

    i.   *Two Sons* (Matt. 21:28-32).

    ii.   *Rich Fool* (Luke 12:13-21).

    iii. *Rich Man and Lazarus* (Luke 16:19-31).

    iv. *Pharisee and the Publican* (Luke 18:9-14).

    v.   *Soils* (Matt. 13:1-9; 18-23).

    vi.   *Laborers in the Vineyard* (Matt. 20:1-16).

4. **The Christian life produces the fruit of love and humility.**

Because we know we have been forgiven much and loved much ...

    i.   *The Two Debtors* (Luke 7:36-50.)

    ii.   *The Unmerciful Servant* (Matt. 18:21-35).

    iii. *Prodigal Son* (Luke 15:11-32).

    iv. *Unrighteous Steward* (Luke 16:1-13).

    v.   *Unjust Judge and Persistent Friend* (Luke 18:1-8; 11:5-13).

    vi.   *Wicked Vine-Growers and Barren Fig Tree* (Matt. 21:33-41; Luke 13:6-9.)

    vii. *Talents* (Matt. 25:14-30).

BIBLIOGRAPHY
OF
PRIMARY WORKS CITED

Works on the Parables

Boice, James M. *The Parables of Jesus*, Chicago, Illinois: Moody Press, 1983.

Capon, Robert F. *The Parables of Grace*, Grand Rapids, Michigan: Eerdmans Publishing Co., 1988.

Capon, Robert F. *The Parables of Judgment*, Grand Rapids, Michigan: Eerdmans Publishing Co., 1989.

Capon, Robert F. *The Parables of the Kingdom*, Grand Rapids, Michigan: Eerdmans Publishing Co., 1985.

Dodd, C. H. *The Parables of the Kingdom*, New York: Charles Scribner's Sons, 1961.

Hunter, A. M. *Interpreting the Parables*, London: SCM Press Ltd., 1960, 1976.

Jeremias, Joachim. *Rediscovering the Parables*, New York: Charles Scribner's Sons, 1966.

Kistemaker, Simon J. *The Parables: Understanding the Stories Jesus Told*, Grand Rapids: Baker Books, 1980, 2002, 2005.

Longenecker, Richard N. *The Challenge of Jesus' Parables*, Grand Rapids, Michigan: Eerdmans Publishing Co., 2000.

Phillips, Richard D. *Turning Your World Upside Down: Kingdom Priorities in the Parables of Jesus*, Phillipsburg, New Jersey: P&R Publishing, 2003.

Scott, Jack B. *Those Puzzling Parables,* Philadelphia, Pennsylvania: Great Commission Publications, 1987, 1990.

Trench, Archbishop Richard D. *Notes on the Parables of Our Lord,* London: Paul, Trench, Trübner & Co., Ltd., 1906.

Works on Multiple Gospels

Barclay, William. *The Daily Study Bible: Matthew, Mark, and Luke,* Edinburgh: The Saint Andrews Press, 1956 ff.

Calvin, John. *A Harmony of the Gospels, Matthew, Mark, and Luke, vol. 1-3,* Grand Rapids, Michigan: Eerdmans Publishing Company, 1555, 1972.

Henry, Matthew. *A Commentary on the Whole Bible – Vol.5.* Iowa Falls, Iowa: World Bible Publishers, 1721, n.d.

Ryle, J.C. *Expository Thoughts on the Gospels – Matthew, Mark and Luke (Vols. 1 & 2).* Cambridge, England: James Clarke & Co. Ltd., 1856, 1974.

Zerwick & Grosvenor, *A Grammatical Analysis of the Greek New Testament,* Vol. 1, Gospel-Acts. Rome: Biblical Institute Press, 1974.

The Gospel of Matthew

Carson, D. A. 'Matthew' In *The Expositor's Bible Commentary – Vol. 8.* ed. Frank E.Gæbelein, 1-599. Grand Rapids, Michigan: Zondervan, 1984.

Dickson, David. *A Brief Exposition of Jesus Christ According to Matthew.* Edinburgh: The Banner of Truth Trust, 1647, 1981.

France, R. T. *Tyndale New Testament Commentaries – Matthew.* Grand Rapids, Michigan: Eerdmans Publishing Co., 1985.

Hill, David. *The Gospel of Matthew.* New Century Bible. Grand Rapids, Michigan: Eerdmans; London: Marshall, Morgan and Scott, 1972.

Keener, Craig S. *A Commentary on the Gospel of Matthew.* Grand Rapids, Michigan; Cambridge, UK: Eerdmans, 1999.

Morris, Leon. *The Gospel According to Matthew.* Grand Rapids, Michigan: Eerdmans Publishing Co., 1992.

Plummer, Alfred. *An Exegetical Commentary on the Gospel According to St. Matthew*. Grand Rapids, Michigan: Eerdmans Publishing Company, 1909, 1953.

Tasker, R. V. G. *Tyndale New Testament Commentaries – The Gospel According to St. Matthew*. Grand Rapids, Michigan: Eerdmans Publishing Company, 1961.

The Gospel of Mark
Alexander, J. A. *A Commentary on the Gospel of Mark*, Edinburgh: The Banner of Truth Trust, 1858, 1960.

Cole, R. A. *The Gospel According to St. Mark*, Grand Rapids, Michigan: Eerdmans Publishing Company, 1961, 1975.

Cranfield, C. E. B. *The Cambridge Greek Testament Commentary: The Gospel According to St. Mark*, Great Britain: Cambridge University Press, 1959, 1974.

Lindsay, Thomas M., D.D., *Handbooks for Bible Classes and Private Students: The Gospel of St. Mark*, Edinburgh: T & T Clark, 1883.

Edwards, James R. *The Gospel According to Mark*, Grand Rapids, Michigan/Cambridge, U.K.: Eerdmans Publishing Company/Apollos, 2002.

English, Donald. *The Message of Mark: The Mystery of Faith*, England/Downers Grove, Illinois: Inter-Varsity Press, 1992.

Ferguson, Sinclair B. *Let's Study Mark*, Edinburgh: The Banner of Truth Trust, 1999.

France, R. T. *The New International Greek Testament Commentary: The Gospel of Mark*, Grand Rapids: Michigan/Cambridge, U.K., Eerdmans Publishing Company/Paternoster Press, 2002.

France, R. T. *The Gospel of Mark*, New York, New York: Doubleday, 1998.

Lane, William L. *Commentary on the Gospel of Mark*, Grand Rapids, Michigan: Eerdmans Publishing Company, 1974.

Plummer, Alfred. *The Cambridge Bible for Schools and Colleges: The Gospel According to St. Mark*. Cambridge: at the University Press, 1920.

The Gospel of Luke

Geldenhuys, Norval. *Commentary on the Gospel of Luke*. Grand Rapids, Michigan: Eerdmans, 1951.

Marshall, I. Howard. *The Gospel of Luke: A Commentary on the Greek Text*. Grand Rapids, Michigan: Eerdmans Publishing Co., 1978.

Plummer, Alfred. *The Gospel of Luke: International Critical Commentary*, Edinburgh: T&T Clark, 1898.

Wilcock, Michael. *Savior of the World: The Message of Luke's Gospel*. Downers Grove, Illinois: InterVarsity Press, 1979.

Subject Index

Page references in **bold** indicate where a subject is treated over an entire chapter.

Scripture Index

Page references in **bold** indicate passages discussed over an entire chapter.

Christian Focus Publications
publishes books for all ages

Our mission statement –

STAYING FAITHFUL

In dependence upon God we seek to help make His infallible Word, the Bible, relevant. Our aim is to ensure that the Lord Jesus Christ is presented as the only hope to obtain forgiveness of sin, live a useful life and look forward to heaven with Him.

REACHING OUT

Christ's last command requires us to reach out to our world with His gospel. We seek to help fulfill that by publishing books that point people towards Jesus and help them develop a Christ-like maturity. We aim to equip all levels of readers for life, work, ministry and mission.

Books in our adult range are published in three imprints.

Christian Focus contains popular works including biographies, commentaries, basic doctrine and Christian living. Our children's books are also published in this imprint.

Mentor focuses on books written at a level suitable for Bible College and seminary students, pastors, and other serious readers. The imprint includes commentaries, doctrinal studies, examination of current issues and church history.

Christian Heritage contains classic writings from the past.

Christian Focus Publications Ltd.,
Geanies House, Fearn, Ross-shire,
IV20 1TW, Scotland, United Kingdom
info@christianfocus.com

www.christianfocus.com